P9-DEH-631

WITHDRAWN

WITHDRAWN

TWENTIETH-CENTURY CULTURE

The Breaking Up

The Cultures of Mankind

Twentieth-Century Culture

Culture

The Breaking Up

Edited by Robert Phelps

WITHDRAWN

George Braziller · *New York*

Copyright © 1965, by Robert Phelps

Published simultaneously in Canada by Ambassador Books, Ltd., Toronto

All rights reserved
For information, address the publisher,
George Braziller, Inc.
One Park Avenue, New York 16

First Printing

Library of Congress Catalogue Card Number: 65-23182

Printed in the United States of America

901.9
P539t

ACKNOWLEDGMENTS

The editor and publisher have made every effort to determine and credit the holders of copyright of the selections in this book. Any errors or omissions may be rectified in future volumes. The editor and publisher wish to thank the following for permission to reprint the material included in this anthology:

Basic Books, Inc. — for a selection from "On the History of the Psychoanalytical Movement" by Sigmund Freud, tr. by Joan Riviere, from *The Collected Papers of Sigmund Freud,* Vol. I. Reprinted by permission of the publisher.

Editions Stock — for selections from *Professional Secrets* by Jean Cocteau, tr. by Rollo H. Myers. Reprinted by permission of the publisher.

Grove Press and Rosica Colin Ltd. — for *The Funambulists* by Jean Genet, tr. by Bernard Frechtman. English translation originally published in *Evergreen Review,* Vol. 8, No. 32, April-May, 1964, Copyright © 1964 by Evergreen Review, Inc. Reprinted by permission of the publisher and Rosica Colin Ltd.

Harcourt, Brace & World, Inc. — for "The Olive Garden" by Rainer Maria Rilke, tr. by Randall Jarrell in his *The Seven-League Crutches,* copyright, 1951, by Randall Jarrell; — and Faber & Faber Ltd. for "Marie Lloyd" from *Selected Essays* by T. S. Eliot, New Edition, copyright, 1932, 1936, 1950 by Harcourt, Brace & World, Inc.; copyright, © 1960, 1964, by T. S. Eliot, and for "East Coker" from *Four Quartets* by T. S. Eliot, copyright, 1943, by T. S. Eliot. (This poem was published in England in *Collected Poems 1909–1962* by T. S. Eliot.); — and Sidgwick & Jackson Ltd. for "The Story of the Siren" from *The Eternal Moment and Other Stories* by E. M. Forster, copyright, 1928, by Harcourt, Brace & World, Inc.; renewed, 1956, by E. M. Forster. (This story was published in England in *The Collected Short Stories of E. M. Forster.*) All selections reprinted by permission of the publishers.

Harper & Row, Publishers — for a selection from *Fear and Trembling* by Glenway Wescott, Copyright 1932, 1960 by Glenway Wescott; — and Hamish Hamilton Ltd. for selections from "Ecce Gubernator" from *The Unquiet Grave* by Palinurus (Cyril Connolly). Copyright 1945 by Cyril Connolly. Both selections reprinted by permission of the publishers.

Harvard University Press — for a selection from *Poetics of Music* by Igor Stravinsky, Copyright, 1947, by the President and Fellows of Harvard College. Reprinted by permission of the publisher.

15734

Houghton Mifflin Company — for a selection from *The Education of Henry Adams* by Henry Adams. Reprinted by permission of the publisher.

Alfred A. Knopf, Inc. — for a selection from *Monsieur Teste* by Paul Valéry, tr. by Jackson Mathews, copyright 1947 by Alfred A. Knopf, Inc.; — and Martin Secker and Warburg Ltd. for selections from "Theseus" from *Two Legends* by André Gide, tr. by John Russell. Copyright 1950 by Alfred A. Knopf, Inc. Reprinted with deletions by permission. Both selections reprinted by permission of the publishers.

The Macmillan Company and A. P. Watt & Son — for "Anima Hominis" from *Per Amica Silentia Lunae* by W. B. Yeats. Copyright 1918 by The Macmillan Company. Renewed 1946 by Bertha Georgie Yeats. (This essay was published in England in *Mythologies* by W. B. Yeats.) Reprinted by permission of the publishers.

The Museum of Modern Art — for a selection from *Picasso: Fifty Years of His Art* by Alfred H. Barr, Jr., copyright 1946 by The Museum of Modern Art, New York, and reprinted with its permission. The "Statement by Picasso: 1923" was made in Spanish to Marius de Zayas. Picasso approved de Zayas' manuscript before it was translated into English and published, originally, in *The Arts,* New York, May, 1923, under the title "Picasso Speaks." As to the "Statement of 1935," Christian Zervos put down these remarks of Picasso immediately after a conversation with him at Boisgeloup in 1935. Picasso went over the notes and approved them informally. They were first published under the title "Conversation avec Picasso" in *Cahiers d'Art,* 1935, Vol. 10, No. 10, pp. 173–8. The above translation is based on one by Myfanwy Evans. Reprinted by permission of the publisher.

New Directions — for a selection from *The Day of the Locust* by Nathanael West. Copyright 1939 by the Estate of Nathanael West; — and for "How to Read" from *The Literary Essays of Ezra Pound,* ed. and with an introduction by T. S. Eliot. All rights reserved. Both selections reprinted by permission of the publisher.

W. W. Norton & Co., Inc. and The Hogarth Press Ltd. — for "The Eighth Elegy" from *The Duino Elegies* by Rainer Maria Rilke, tr. by J. B. Leishman and Stephen Spender. Copyright 1939 by W. W. Norton & Co., Inc. Reprinted by permission of the publishers.

Laurence Pollinger Ltd. — for "Reflections on the Death of a Porcupine" from *Selected Essays of D. H. Lawrence.* Reprinted by permission of Laurence Pollinger Ltd. and the Estate of the late Mrs. Frieda Lawrence.

G. P. Putnam's Sons — for a selection from *Waiting for God* by Simone Weil. Copyright 1951 by Simone Weil. Reprinted by permission of the publisher.

Random House, Inc. — for a selection from *Prater Violet* by Christopher Isherwood. Copyright 1945 by Christopher Isherwood; — for "Composition as Explanation" from *Selected Writings of Gertrude Stein,* ed. by Carl Van Vechten. Copyright 1946 by Random House, Inc.; — and Faber and Faber Ltd. for "Letter to a Wound" from *The Collected Poetry of W. H. Auden.* Copyright 1934 and renewed 1961 by W. H. Auden. (This essay was published in England in *The Orators* by W. H. Auden.); — and Chatto and Windus Ltd. for a selection from "The Past Recaptured" from *Remembrance of Things Past* by Marcel Proust. Copyright 1932 and renewed 1959 by Random House, Inc. All selections reprinted by permission of the publishers.

Schocken Books, Inc. — for "The Great Wall of China" from *The Great Wall of China* by Franz Kafka, Copyright 1946, 1948 by Schocken Books, Inc., New York, tr. by Willa and Edwin Muir. Reprinted by permission of the publisher.

Charles Scribner's Sons — for a selection from *Death in the Afternoon* by Ernest Hemingway. Copyright 1932 Charles Scribner's Sons; renewal copyright 1960 Ernest Hemingway. Reprinted by permission of the publisher.

The Viking Press, Inc. — for a selection from *Portrait of the Artist as a Young Man* by James Joyce, copyright 1916 by B. W. Huebsch, Inc., 1944 by Nora Joyce, © by the Estate of James Joyce. All rights reserved; — for a selection from *Henderson the Rain King* by Saul Bellow. Copyright © 1958, 1959 by Saul Bellow; — for a selection from *Finnegans Wake* by James Joyce. Copyright 1939 by James Joyce; — and The Hogarth Press Ltd. for a selection from *Concluding* by Henry Green. Copyright 1948 by Henry Green. All selections reprinted by permission of the publishers.

Contents

Part I   Breaking Down

Part II . Breaking Up

Part III   Breaking Through

List of Illustrations

1. Pablo Picasso, *Family of Saltimbanques* (1905). National Gallery of Art, Washington, D.C. Chester Dale Collection.
2. Pablo Picasso, *"Ma Jolie"* (*Woman with a Zither or Guitar*) (1911–1912). The Museum of Modern Art, New York. Acquired through the Lillie P. Bliss Bequest. PHOTO: SOICHI SUNAMI.
3. Pablo Picasso, *Nessus and Dejanira* (1920). The Museum of Modern Art, New York. Acquired through the Lillie P. Bliss Bequest. PHOTO: SOICHI SUNAMI.
4. Pablo Picasso, *The Three Musicians* (1921). Philadelphia Museum of Art. A. E. Gallatin Collection.
5. Pablo Picasso, *Painter with a Model Knitting* (1927). Etching for Balzac: *Le Chef-d'œuvre inconnu,* Paris, Vollard, 1931. The Museum of Modern Art, New York. Gift of Henry Church. PHOTO: SOICHI SUNAMI.
6. Pablo Picasso, *The Studio* (1927–1928). The Museum of Modern Art, New York. Gift of Walter P. Chrysler, Jr. PHOTO: SOICHI SUNAMI.
7. Pablo Picasso, *Interior with Girl Drawing* (1935). Private Collection, New York.
8. Pablo Picasso, *Guernica* (mural) (1937). On extended loan to the Museum of Modern Art. New York, from the artist, M. Picasso. PHOTO: SOICHI SUNAMI.
9. Pablo Picasso, *She-Goat* (1950). Bronze (cast 1952). The Museum of Modern Art, New York. Mrs. Simon Guggenheim Fund. PHOTO: SOICHI SUNAMI.
10. Pablo Picasso, *The Old Painter's Studio* (March 14, 1954). The Museum of Modern Art, New York. Curt Valentin Bequest. PHOTO: SOICHI SUNAMI.

Numbers 1–10 follow page 60

11. Constantin Brancusi, *The New-Born* (1920, after a marble of 1915). Bronze. The Museum of Modern Art, New York. Acequired through the Lillie P. Bliss Bequest.
12. Alexander Calder, *Lobster Trap and Fish Tail* (1939). Mobile. The Museum of Modern Art, New York. Gift of the Advisory Committee. PHOTO: SOICHI SUNAMI.
13. Henri Matisse, *The Red Studio* (1911). The Museum of Modern Art, New

York. Mrs. Simon Guggenheim Fund. PHOTO: SOICHI SUNAMI.

14. Georges Braque, *Guitar* (1913–1914). The Museum of Modern Art, New York. Acquired through the Lillie P. Bliss Bequest. PHOTO: SOICHI SUNAMI.

15. Jean (Hans) Arp, *Collage with Squares Arranged According to the Law of Chance* (1916–1917). The Museum of Modern Art, New York. Purchase. PHOTO: SOICHI SUNAMI.

16. Yves Tanguy, *Slowly Toward the North* (1942). The Museum of Modern Art, New York. Gift of Philip C. Johnson. PHOTO: SOICHI SUNAMI.

17. Wassily Kandinsky, *Composition (4)* (1914). The Museum of Modern Art, New York. Mrs. Simon Guggenheim Fund. PHOTO: SOICHI SUNAMI.

18. Piet Mondrian, *Composition with Red, Yellow and Blue* (1935–1943). Collection of Mr. and Mrs. James H. Clark, Dallas.

19. Robert Motherwell, *Elegy to the Spanish Republic, 70* (1961). Courtesy, Marlborough-Gerson Gallery, New York.

20. Jackson Pollock, *Grayed Rainbow* (1953). The Art Institute of Chicago. Gift of the Society for Contemporary American Art.

21. Frank Lloyd Wright, *Project for Roger Lacy Hotel,* Dallas, Texas (1947). Reprinted by permission of the publisher, Horizon Press, from *An American Architecture* by Frank Lloyd Wright, ed. by Edgar Kaufmann. Copyright 1955.

22. Buckminster Fuller, *Geodesic Dome,* Honolulu, Hawaii.

23. Arnold Schoenberg, from *Drei Klavierstücke* (Op. 11). Copyright by Universal Editions. Used by permission.

24. Karlheinz Stockhausen, from *Etude II.* Copyright by Universal Editions. Used by permission.

25. Jean Cocteau himself, as Heurtebise in *Orpheus.* PHOTO: LIPNITSKI, PARIS.

26. Bertolt Brecht, scene from *Mother Courage* with Helene Weigel. Courtesy, Ullstein-Verlag.

27. Sergei Eisenstein, scene from *Potemkin.* Courtesy, The Museum of Modern Art Film Library, New York.

28. Martha Graham and Company in *Primitive Mysteries.* PHOTO: BARBARA MORGAN.

Numbers 11–28 follow page 204

29. David Smith, *The Letter* (1950). Munson-Williams-Proctor Institute, Utica, New York.

30. Alberto Giacometti, *Chariot* (1950). Bronze. The Museum of Modern Art, New York. Purchase. PHOTO: SOICHI SUNAMI.

31. Pierre Bonnard, *The Breakfast Room* (c. 1930–1931). The Museum of Modern Art, New York. PHOTO: SOICHI SUNAMI.

32. Henri Matisse, *Woman, Full Face, Beside an Aquarium* (1929). The Museum of Modern Art, New York. Purchase. PHOTO: SOICHI SUNAMI.

33. Amedeo Modigliani, *Yellow Sweater* (1919?). The Solomon R. Guggenheim Museum.

34. Joan Miró, *Composition* (1933). Collection of Mr. James J. Sweeney, Houston.

35. Paul Klee, *Lady Apart* (1940). The Museum of Modern Art, New York. A. Conger Goodyear Fund. PHOTO: SOICHI SUNAMI.

INTRODUCTION

As I write this, it is early 1965. Our twentieth century has more than one-third of its course to run — over 35 years, or time enough for a second Shakespeare to be born, come to the great city, and write his *Hamlet;* time for another Christ to have a vision and suffer his Passion in the streets of some obscure colonial town; time, too, for our Columbus to put the shoe of his space suit on another planet, and for our Kierkegaard to scribble truths in a private journal which no one else will see for generations.

In some sense, therefore, this is an impossible book. It is guesswork, at best, and if it were honest, there would be a sheaf of blank pages at the end. We cannot know what we shall be seen to have meant, because we are still in the act of meaning it. As Sartre reminds us, "every truth has *become* so," and this is especially pertinent when speculating about a whole century's place in history.

Of course, we can be fairly sure that certain great landmarks and weathervanes — Picasso or Stravinsky, Yeats or Proust — are not going to be replaced. But we must be equally unsure about others. Only my instinct (or perhaps I should say my personal necessity) tells me that Saul Bellow's *Henderson the Rain King* speaks as resonantly as I seem to hear it speaking; or that Georg Groddeck's vision of the human psyche will turn out to be as true to our experience as Freud's; or that Henry Green's novels reveal more about *la condition humaine* in 1950 than Malraux or Camus or Bertrand Russell.

So anyone using this anthology must be prepared to share not my dogmatisms, which I hope I have kept in check, but my instincts, which are all that I really have to work with in the present case. I do not believe I have been capricious, though I do not know how I can help seeming arbitrary. The omissions alone are staggering, and when I realize

that I have tried to represent twentieth century culture without including,
for instance, Heidegger, Whitehead, Jung, St.-Jean Perse, Faulkner, Co-
lette, John Dewey, Henry Miller, John Maynard Keynes, Malinowski,
Norbert Wiener, Arnold Toynbee, Martin Buber, Karen Horney, Paul
Tillich, Isaac Babel, Thomas Mann, Robert Frost, Stefan George,
Virginia Woolf — to name a random twenty — I am rightly abashed.

But choices had to be made. Rules had to be set, and limits observed;
limits not only of space and permissions, but of meaning and symmetry.
Omissions within pieces are indicated by three centered dots. I stand
by my choices and their implications, eagerly, but I should like to
add that the single piece of twentieth-century writing which I wanted
most of all to include, D. H. Lawrence's *Introduction to the Memoirs of
Maurice Magnus,* was entirely too long, and had to be left out. If I
mention it here, it is not only to ease my conscience, but to urge readers
who may someday come across it in another context to stop short and
take possession at once. It makes nourishing, exemplary ballast for anyone's lifetime quest.

"Culture," says the O.E.D., is "the intellectual side of civilization." But
if a survey such as this is to be anything more than brand names and
samples, it must refine the focus. Let us say, then, that culture is the
honey in the hive; not all, but some of the best and most original products
of our spirit which we have to pass on: the poems and stories, buildings
and music, paintings and personal examples which people may remember
in two hundred years as we now remember *King Lear* and *Moby Dick,*
Versailles and the Brandenburg concertos, the *Embarkation for Cytherea*
and the lives of Dr. Johnson, Voltaire, Cardinal Newman and Montaigne.

If I seem hereby to be sidestepping the vast area of our culture which
includes scientific discovery and material progress, this is not inadvertent,
nor unprincipled. For the ground rule I have made myself is that every
selection must speak for a particular man's personal experience. No matter
what its original occasion, a public lecture or a private letter, it must
amount to one human being talking to another. "One must know concrete
instances first," said William James. "One can see no farther into a generalization than just so far as one's previous acquaintance with particulars enables one to take it in."

If we are to wonder about our century and its groundswells, then the
least we must do is to begin with particulars, with private "I"s who speak
for what they have felt or beheld, believed or discovered in the substance of their own lives. This seems to me particularly important in
1965, when, if we presuppose anything that our fathers did not presuppose

before us, it is that every man is aware, in some unprecedented sense, of being alone. Movement, trends, groups, masses continue to flourish in our midst. We meet, march, join, and tell ourselves that we belong. But it is the loners who speak for what distinguishes our lives from those of prior centuries and the cultures of the past.

Imagine, then, that this book has convoked a Round Table, not of white knights, but of "concrete instances," first persons, poet-witnesses. Let each one speak for himself, and try to hear him out on his own terms. His deposition may take the form of an essay, a poem, a letter, a parable; perhaps he may even use some other medium than language. But in every case, imagine, above all, that he is not measuring a trend, or intoning an editorial, or reading something into the Congressional Record. Just imagine that he is speaking for himself, not in arrogance or self-absorption, but in humility and trust, unofficially, and in something like the same needful tone of voice in which Thoreau once said, "I desire to speak somewhere without bounds, like a man in a waking moment to men in their waking moments . . ."

What, then, is he saying? What is happening in these decades which has not happened before, and which makes our twentieth-century culture unlike the nineteenth century's?

Yes, certainly, we have the results of the Industrial Revolution — atomic power, IBM computers, frozen orange juice, mass communications. Yes, we have X rays and radar, government based on universal franchise, and an apparently still viable consumer economy. Yes, too, we have insurance policies and credit cards and literally millions of those fuming automobiles which, in his Futurist Manifesto of 1909, the Italian poet Marinetti hailed as "more beautiful than the Nike of Samothrace . . ."

But this is all on the *outside*. It is the inside stories which our culture will record, and by which we shall be judged as a century in noisy decline, or baffled transition, or secret rebirth. And of these stories, there are at least three which are plain by now, which are interrelated and even overlap, and which I shall try to abridge here, as unapocalyptically as possible.

1. Since 1900 — give or take a decade — individuals have been conscious of the passing of community, of losing the sense of unconditional belonging which every culture before us has taken for granted. It was something which happened slowly but persistently, on every social and economic level, and in every form of community from the family and the church congregation to the city and the nation. The forms themselves

did not vanish. Many appear to go on functioning as solidly as ever. But now they are under siege. They have to be force-fed and defended. They are no longer simply *given,* as cards dealt out in a game of poker. And more and more people, in their hearts, no longer feel with assurance that they belong to anyone, or anything, anywhere.

2. About this same time, in the earliest decades after 1900, we find a radical change transpiring in the arts, in the *use* for which they are created and consumed. Once upon a time, a poet thought of himself as an accessory to his community. He entertained, or decorated, or sang praises, and if he got in a lick or two about his own mysteries, that was curious perhaps, but incidental. Now and then a real misfit appeared — Villon or Blake or Christopher Smart — but he was either ignored or regarded as insane. The great majority of artists in every medium produced their work to please someone. It might be Queen Elizabeth, or it might be the thousands of families who subscribed to Dickens' *Household Words* magazine. But the purpose was to please.

Then for a brief time, in the nineteenth century, artists thought of themselves as pariahs, outcasts, abandoned by the community, and they either rejoiced or howled. But by 1910, and increasingly since, they have come to think of themselves as personal witnesses, bringers of revelation, self-ordained priests. The artist offers us not only his work, but the gospel according to his own committed living. When, in all the history of the arts, would another painter have said what Picasso said:

> I paint the way some people write their autobiography. The paintings, finished or not, are the pages of my journal, and as such they are valid. The future will choose the pages it prefers. It's not up to me to make the choice.

Or when would a painter have declared, like Braque, that "art is made to disturb"? To some degree all painters, all poets have done this, but they did so without thinking of it as their purpose. Keats revealed truth, so did Racine. But the *Ode on a Grecian Urn* and *Phèdre* cannot be compared with a novel by Jean Genet, which is a testament first, and a work of art second.

Early in our century, then, as community began to lapse, and as more and more people realized for themselves what Nietzsche had meant when he said "God is dead!" and what Dostoyevsky had suffered when he cried "This consciousness is a disease!" the arts were overwhelmed by this infra-artistic purpose. At first, throughout Europe and America, there was a mighty burst of house-cleaning, of throwing out and breaking up. If the arts were no longer mere frosting and *divertissement,* then all those old traditions and assumptions — that art is an *art,* for instance — must be called into question. "Make it new!" cried Ezra Pound, and a hundred "little magazines" sprang up like minutemen to fight for Imagism, Futurism, Vorticism, Dadaism, Surrealism and two generations of inspired clash about the act, itself, of creating. Yeats, Cocteau, Valéry, Gide, Stein, Proust, Joyce, Eliot — they are all as obsessed with the theory and meaning of art, as with the practice and mere making of it. And at the dead center of their brilliant generation stands the figure of D. H. Lawrence and his flagrant claim, which would have been almost meaningless to Dr. Johnson: "I always say, my motto is 'Art for my sake.' "

3. "Aloneness is man's real condition," said Auden, and whether they rejoice or despair, the most characteristic voices of the twentieth century will know and echo what he means. Poets have written about loneliness since Sappho. But loneliness and aloneness are different. To be lonely implies separation from another, from a lover, a neighbor, God. To be alone means separateness *tout court.* Once the umbilical cord has been cut, you are on your own. Love, neighborhood, God have to be sought for, worked for; and earning them is a daily, uninnocent, solo business which depends upon a daily, uninnocent solo will. Nothing is given — or not in the old way, not any more.

Even so, there are certain joys to be had, if we are to believe our poets. By the sole authority of their own examples, some of them have already shown us how the time on earth each of us is named for may not be just endured, or diverted, but actively embodied and possessed, so that however alone and unbelonging your "I," or mine, may be, it can still break through, break *in,* and find something like "the Kingdom of Heaven" waiting there. Gide's Thescus dies replete and fully used, as Gide himself did, after a thoroughly expended life; and Saul Bellow's quixotic Rain King comes home from his African quest with a quickened sense of himself. Forster, Kafka, Eliot, even Jean Genet, leave us wondering, and hopeful. And shrewd, theatrical, enigmatic Yeats, in the very month he was to die, was writing a letter in which he said: "Man can embody truth, but he cannot know it." Our mystery, then, may always be greater than the mere part we can put into words, into "culture," and call self-knowledge.

But that same year, 1939, another poet, as young and American and little-known as Yeats was old and Irish and famous, was writing a book in which he said just the opposite: "I believe," declared James Agee, "that the discovery and use of 'consciousness,' which has always been and is our deadliest enemy and deceiver, is also the source and guide of all hope and cure, and the only one."

Perhaps one useful way — pro-tem and not too pretentious — of looking at our own culture, is to think of it as turning on an axis whose poles are these two avowals of faith. Agee's, naturally, is presupposed in Yeats'. Indeed, it has been the rock assumption of our whole Western civilization, ever since Socrates first said the unexamined life was not worth living. For we *are* conscious, *are* self-conscious, if nothing else. Like Hamlet, we may find it a mixed blessing, or like Dostoyevsky, a corrosive sickness. But it is our mode, our nature, to which we must assent, and be loyal.

At the same — and isn't this what Yeats meant? — we must not be arrogant. Like diamonds and flowers and lions, we, too, in some degree *are lived,* are more than we can understand. We too, as Louise Bogan has put it, are "the fruit of powers beyond us, within us, which we must in some manner trust . . ."

The operative word is trust. What our century may be learning, in its prideful aloneness, may be our need simply to trust. After all, the privilege of finding oneself here, "an animal with imagination," is still just that, a privilege. What if more and more of us, again in our secret hearts, came to believe Yeats was right? Wouldn't it make some part of our life quite literally awesome? Wouldn't we then be able to share and rejoice in Picasso's airy dogmatism when he was once asked (by Jean Cocteau) about the propriety of miracles: "Miracles? There's nothing surprising about them. Why it's a miracle every morning that I don't melt in my bath!"

Robert Phelps

PART

I

Breaking Down

Mr. Holmes, they were the footprints
of a giant hound.
> —*A. Conan Doyle, 1902*

On montera mon cénotaphe
Aux côtes brulantes de Mozambique.
> —*T. S. Eliot, 1917*

1

HENRY ADAMS *and* T. S. ELIOT

The century began with a sigh. "We are lemonade," said Chekhov in Russia, and in America, a minor novelist named William Dean Howells wrote to a major one, Mark Twain: "Even you won't tell the black heart's truth. . ."

But in their own ways, Henry Adams and T. S. Eliot soon began to try. It is true that they represented only a small minority of Western society. But they also represented, in their very family names as well as their ideals, the same minority which had substantially shaped America in the eighteenth and seventeenth centuries, and before that, Reformation England.

Adams looked at the Paris Exposition in 1900; Eliot looked at the British music hall in 1922; and both painfully foresaw the same decline of community as it had been known for centuries, whether in church or the theater, in the small-town paper or the corner pub, where, in fact, a second cousin of Adams' Dynamo, in the form of a small, grayish, animated screen would soon be inhibiting even the community a man might establish by chatting with his neighbor.

The Dynamo and the Virgin

from *The Education of Henry Adams*

[1900]

HENRY ADAMS

Until the Great Exposition of 1900 closed its doors in November, Adams haunted it, aching to absorb knowledge, and helpless to find it. He would have liked to know how much of it could have been grasped by the best-informed man in the world. While he was thus meditating chaos, Langley came by, and showed it to him. At Langley's behest, the Exhibition dropped its superfluous rags and stripped itself to the skin, for Langley knew what to study, and why, and how; while Adams might as well have stood outside in the night, staring at the Milky Way. Yet Langley said nothing new, and taught nothing that one might not have learned from Lord Bacon, three hundred years before; but though one should have known the "Advancement of Science" as well as one knew the "Comedy of Errors," the literary knowledge counted for nothing until some teacher should show how to apply it. Bacon took a vast deal of trouble in teaching King James I and his subjects, American or other, towards the year 1620, that true science was the development or economy of forces; yet an elderly American in 1900 knew neither the formula nor the forces; or even so much as to say to himself that his historical business in the exposition concerned only the economies or developments of force since 1893, when he began the study at Chicago.

Nothing in education is so astonishing as the amount of ignorance it accumulates in the form of inert facts. Adams had looked at most of the accumulations of art in the storehouses called Art Museums; yet he did not know how to look at the art exhibits of 1900. He had studied Karl Marx and his doctrines of history with profound attention, yet he could not apply them at Paris. Langley, with the ease of a great master of experiment, threw out of the field every exhibit that did not reveal a new application of force, and naturally threw out, to begin with, almost the

24

whole art exhibit. Equally, he ignored almost the whole industrial exhibit. He led his pupil directly to the forces. His chief interest was in new motors to make his airship feasible, and he taught Adams the astonishing complexities of the new Daimler motor, and of the automobile, which, since 1893, had become a nightmare at a hundred kilometres an hour, almost as destructive as the electric tram which was only ten years older; and threatening to become as terrible as the locomotive steam-engine itself, which was almost exactly Adams's own age.

Then he showed his scholar the great hall of dynamos, and explained how little he knew about electricity or force of any kind, even of his own special sun, which spouted heat in inconceivable volume, but which, as far as he knew, might spout less or more, at any time, for all the certainty he felt in it. To him, the dynamo itself was but an ingenious channel for conveying somewhere the heat latent in a few tons of poor coal hidden in a dirty engine-house carefully kept out of sight; but to Adams the dynamo became a symbol of infinity. As he grew accustomed to the great gallery of machines, he began to feel the forty-foot dynamos as a moral force, much as the early Christians felt the Cross. The planet itself seemed less impressive, in its old-fashioned, deliberate, annual or daily revolution, than this huge wheel, revolving within arm's-length at some vertiginous speed, and barely murmuring — scarcely humming an audible warning to stand a hair's-breadth further for respect of power — while it would not wake the baby lying close against its frame. Before the end, one began to pray to it; inherited instinct taught the natural expression of man before silent and infinite force. Among the thousand symbols of ultimate energy, the dynamo was not so human as some, but it was the most expressive.

Yet the dynamo, next to the steam-engine, was the most familiar of exhibits. For Adams's objects its value lay chiefly in its occult mechanism. Between the dynamo in the gallery of machines and the engine-house outside, the break of continuity amounted to abysmal fracture for a historian's objects. No more relation could he discover between the steam and the electric current than between the Cross and the cathedral. The forces were interchangeable if not reversible, but he could see only an absolute *fiat* in electricity as in faith. Langley could not help him. Indeed, Langley seemed to be worried by the same trouble, for he constantly repeated that the new forces were anarchical, and specially that he was not responsible for the new rays, that were little short of parricidal in their wicked spirit towards science. His own rays, with which he had doubled the solar spectrum, were altogether harmless and beneficent; but Radium denied its God — or, what was to Langley the same thing, denied the truths of his Science. The force was wholly new.

A historian who asked only to learn enough to be as futile as Langley or Kelvin, made rapid progress under this teaching, and mixed himself up in the tangle of ideas until he achieved a sort of Paradise of ignorance vastly consoling to his fatigued senses. He wrapped himself in vibrations and rays which were new, and he would have hugged Marconi and Branly had he met them, as he hugged the dynamo; while he lost his arithmetic in trying to figure out the equation between the discoveries and the economies of force. The economies, like the discoveries, were absolute, supersensual, occult; incapable of expression in horse-power. What mathematical equivalent could he suggest as the value of a Branly coherer? Frozen air, or the electric furnace, had some scale of measurement, no doubt, if somebody could invent a thermometer adequate to the purpose; but X-rays had played no part whatever in man's consciousness, and the atom itself had figured only as a fiction of thought. In these seven years man had translated himself into a new universe which had no common scale of measurement with the old. He had entered a supersensual world, in which he could measure nothing except by chance collisions of movements imperceptible to his senses, perhaps even imperceptible to his instruments, but perceptible to each other, and so to some known ray at the end of the scale. Langley seemed prepared for anything, even for an indeterminable number of universes interfused — physics stark mad in metaphysics.

Historians undertake to arrange sequences, — called stories, or histories — assuming in silence a relation of cause and effect. These assumptions, hidden in the depths of dusty libraries, have been astounding, but commonly unconscious and childlike; so much so, that if any captious critic were to drag them to light, historians would probably reply, with one voice, that they had never supposed themselves required to know what they were talking about. Adams, for one, had toiled in vain to find out what he meant. He had even published a dozen volumes of American history for no other purpose than to satisfy himself whether, by the severest process of stating, with the least possible comment, such facts as seemed sure, in such order as seemed rigorously consequent, he could fix for a familiar moment a necessary sequence of human movement. The result had satisfied him as little as at Harvard College. Where he saw sequence, other men saw something quite different, and no one saw the same unit of measure. He cared little about his experiments and less about his statesmen, who seemed to him quite as ignorant as himself and, as a rule, no more honest; but he insisted on a relation of sequence, and if he could not reach it by one method, he would try as many methods as science knew. Satisfied that the sequence of men led to nothing and that the sequence of their society could lead no further, while the mere sequence of time was artificial, and the sequence of thought was chaos, he turned at last to the sequence of force; and thus it happened that, after ten years' pursuit, he found himself lying in the Gallery of Machines at the Great Exposition of 1900, his historical neck broken by the sudden irruption of forces totally new.

Since no one else showed much concern, an elderly person without other cares had no need to betray alarm. The year 1900 was not the first to upset schoolmasters. Copernicus and Galileo had broken many professorial necks about 1600; Columbus had stood the world on its head towards 1500; but the nearest approach to the revolution of 1900 was that of 310, when Constantine set up the Cross. The rays that Langley disowned, as well as those which he fathered, were occult, supersensual, irrational; they were a revelation of mysterious energy like that of the Cross; they were what, in terms of mediæval science, were called immediate modes of the divine substance.

The historian was thus reduced to his last resources. Clearly if he was bound to reduce all these forces to a common value, this common value could have no measure but that of their attraction on his own mind. He must treat them as they had been felt; as convertible, reversible, interchangeable attractions on thought. He made up his mind to venture it; he would risk translating rays into faith. Such a reversible process would vastly amuse a chemist, but the chemist could not deny that he, or some of his fellow physicists, could feel the force of both. When Adams was a boy in Boston, the best chemist in the place had probably never heard of Venus except by way of scandal, or of the Virgin except as idolatry; neither had he heard of dynamos or automobiles or radium; yet his mind was ready to feel the force of all, though the rays were unborn and the women were dead.

Here opened another totally new education, which promised to be by far the most hazardous of all. The knife-edge along which he must crawl, like Sir Lancelot in the twelfth century, divided two kingdoms of force which had nothing in common but attraction. They were as different as a magnet is from gravitation, supposing one knew what a magnet was, or gravitation, or love. The force of the Virgin was still felt at Lourdes, and seemed to be as potent as X-rays; but in America neither Venus nor Virgin ever had value as force — at most as sentiment. No American had ever been truly afraid of either.

This problem in dynamics gravely perplexed an American historian. The Woman had once been supreme; in France she still seemed potent, not merely as a sentiment, but as a force. Why was she unknown in America? For evidently America was ashamed of her, and she was ashamed of herself, otherwise they would not have strewn fig-leaves so profusely all over her. When she was a true force, she was ignorant of fig-leaves, but the monthly-magazine-made American female had not a feature that would have been recognized by Adam. The trait was notorious, and often humorous, but any one brought up among Puritans knew that sex was sin. In any previous age, sex was strength. Neither art nor beauty was needed. Every one, even among Puritans, knew that neither Diana of the Ephesians nor any of the Oriental goddesses was worshipped for her beauty. She was goddess because of her force; she was the animated dynamo; she was reproduction — the greatest and most mysterious of all energies; all she needed was to be fecund. Singularly enough, not one of Adams's many schools of education had ever drawn his attention to the opening lines of Lucretius, though they were perhaps the finest in all Latin literature, where the poet invoked Venus exactly as Dante invoked the Virgin: —

"Quae quoniam rerum naturam *sola* gubernas."

The Venus of Epicurean philosophy survived in the Virgin of the Schools: —

"Donna, sei tanto grande, e tanto vali,
   Che qual vuol grazia, e a te non ricorre,
   Sua disianza vuol volar senz' ali."

All this was to American thought as though it had never existed. The true American knew something of the facts, but nothing of the feelings; he read the letter, but he never felt the law. Before this historical chasm, a mind like that of Adams felt itself helpless; he turned from the Virgin to the Dynamo as though he were a Branly coherer. On one side, at the Louvre and at Chartres, as he knew by the record of work actually done and still before his eyes, was the highest energy ever known to man, the creator of four-fifths of his noblest art, exercising vastly more attraction over the human mind than all the steam-engines and dynamos ever dreamed of; and yet this energy was unknown to the American mind. An American Virgin would never dare command; an American Venus would never dare exist.

The question, which to any plain American of the nineteenth century seemed as remote as it did to Adams, drew him almost violently to study, once it was posed; and on this point Langleys were as useless as though they were Herbert Spencers or dynamos. The idea survived only as art.

There one turned as naturally as though the artist were himself a woman. Adams began to ponder, asking himself whether he knew of any American artist who had ever insisted on the power of sex, as every classic had always done; but he could think only of Walt Whitman; Bret Harte, as far as the magazines would let him venture; and one or two painters, for the flesh-tones. All the rest had used sex for sentiment, never for force; to them, Eve was a tender flower, and Herodias an unfeminine horror. American art, like the American language and American education, was as far as possible sexless. Society regarded this victory over sex as its greatest triumph, and the historian readily admitted it, since the moral issue, for the moment, did not concern one who was studying the relations of unmoral force. He cared nothing for the sex of the dynamo until he could measure its energy.

Vaguely seeking a clue, he wandered through the art exhibit, and, in his stroll, stopped almost every day before St. Gaudens's General Sherman, which had been given the central post of honor. St. Gaudens himself was in Paris, putting on the work his usual interminable last touches, and listening to the usual contradictory suggestions of brother sculptors. Of all the American artists who gave to American art whatever life it breathed in the seventies, St. Gaudens was perhaps the most sympathetic, but certainly the most inarticulate. General Grant or Don Cameron had scarcely less instinct of rhetoric than he. All the others — the Hunts, Richardson, John La Farge, Stanford White — were exuberant; only St. Gaudens could never discuss or dilate on an emotion, or suggest artistic arguments for giving to his work the forms that he felt. He never laid down the law, or affected the despot, or became brutalized like Whistler by the brutalities of his world. He required no incense; he was no egoist; his simplicity of thought was excessive; he could not imitate, or give any form but his own to the creations of his hand. No one felt more strongly than he the strength of other men, but the idea that they could affect him never stirred an image in his mind.

This summer his health was poor and his spirits were low. For such a temper, Adams was not the best companion, since his own gaiety was not *folle;* but he risked going now and then to the studio on Mont Parnasse to draw him out for a stroll in the Bois de Boulogne, or dinner as pleased his moods, and in return St. Gaudens sometimes let Adams go about in his company.

Once St. Gaudens took him down to Amiens, with a party of Frenchmen, to see the cathedral. Not until they found themselves actually studying the sculpture of the western portal, did it dawn on Adams's mind that, for his purposes, St. Gaudens on that spot had more interest to him than the cathedral itself. Great men before great monuments express great truths, provided they are not taken too solemnly. Adams never tired of quoting the supreme phrase of his idol Gibbon, before the Gothic cathedrals: "I darted a contemptuous look on the stately monuments of superstition." Even in the footnotes of his history, Gibbon had never inserted a bit of humor more human than this, and one would have paid largely for a photograph of the fat little historian, on the background of Notre Dame of Amiens, trying to persuade his readers — perhaps himself — that he was darting a contemptuous look on the stately monument, for which he felt in fact the respect which every man of his vast study and active mind always feels before objects worthy of it; but besides the humor, one felt also the relation. Gibbon ignored the Virgin, because in 1789 religious monuments were out of fashion. In 1900 his remark sounded fresh and simple as the green fields to ears that had heard a hundred years of other remarks, mostly no more fresh and certainly less simple. Without malice, one might find it more instructive than a whole lecture of Ruskin. One sees what one brings, and at that moment Gibbon brought the French Revolution. Ruskin brought reaction against the Revolution. St. Gaudens had passed beyond all. He liked the stately monuments much more than he liked Gibbon or Ruskin; he loved their dignity; their unity; their scale; their lines; their lights and shadows; their decorative sculpture; but he was even less conscious than they of the force that created it all — the Virgin, the Woman — by whose genius "the stately monuments of superstition" were built, through which she was expressed. He would have seen more meaning in Isis with the cow's horns, at Edfoo, who expressed the same thought. The art remained, but the energy was lost even upon the artist.

Yet in mind and person St. Gaudens was a survival of the 1500's; he bore the stamp of the Renaissance, and should have carried an image of the Virgin round his neck, or stuck in his hat, like Louis XI. In mere time he was a lost soul that had strayed by chance into the twentieth century, and forgotten where it came from. He writhed and cursed at his ignorance, much as Adams did at his own, but in the opposite sense. St. Gaudens was a child of Benvenuto Cellini, smothered in an American cradle. Adams was a quintessence of Boston, devoured by curiosity to think like Benvenuto. St. Gaudens's art was starved from birth, and Adams's instinct was blighted from babyhood. Each had but half of a nature, and when they came together before the Virgin of Amiens they ought both to have felt in her the force that made them one; but it was not so. To Adams she became more than ever a channel of force; to St. Gaudens she remained as before a channel of taste.

For a symbol of power, St. Gaudens instinctively preferred the horse, as was plain in his horse and Victory of the Sherman monument. Doubtless Sherman also felt it so. The attitude was so American that, for at least forty years, Adams had never realized that any other could be in sound taste. How many years had he taken to admit a notion of what Michael Angelo and Rubens were driving at? He could not say; but he knew that only since 1895 had he begun to feel the Virgin or Venus as force, and not everywhere even so. At Chartres — perhaps at Lourdes — possibly at Cnidos if one could still find there the divinely naked Aphrodite of Praxiteles — but otherwise one must look for force to the goddesses of Indian mythology. The idea died out long ago in the German and English stock. St. Gaudens at Amiens was hardly less sensitive to the force of the female energy than Matthew Arnold at the Grande Chartreuse. Neither of them felt goddesses as power — only as reflected emotion, human expression, beauty, purity, taste, scarcely even as sympathy. They felt a railway train as power; yet they, and all other artists, constantly complained that the power embodied in a railway train could never be embodied in art. All the steam in the world could not, like the Virgin, build Chartres.

Yet in mechanics, whatever the mechanicians might think, both energies acted as interchangeable forces on man, and by action on man all known force may be measured. Indeed, few men of science measured force in any other way. After once admitting that a straight line was the shortest distance between two points, no serious mathematician cared to deny anything that suited his convenience, and rejected no symbol, unproved or unproveable, that helped him to accomplish work. The symbol was force, as a compass needle or a triangle was force, as the mechanist might prove by losing it, and nothing could be gained by ignoring their value. Symbol or energy, the Virgin had acted as the greatest force the Western world ever felt, and had drawn man's activities to herself more strongly than any other power, natural or supernatural, had ever done; the historian's business was to follow the track of the energy; to find where it came from and where it went to; its complex source and shifting channels; its values, equivalents, conversions. It could scarcely be more complex than radium; it could hardly be deflected, diverted, polarized, absorbed more perplexingly than other radiant matter. Adams knew nothing about any of them, but as a mathematical problem of influence on human progress, though all were occult, all reacted on his mind, and he rather inclined to think the Virgin easiest to handle.

The pursuit turned out to be long and tortuous, leading at last into the vast forests of scholastic science. From Zeno to Descartes, hand in hand with Thomas Aquinas, Montaigne, and Pascal, one stumbled as stupidly as though one were still a German student of 1860. Only with the instinct of despair could one force one's self into this old thicket of ignorance after having been repulsed at a score of entrances more promising and more popular. Thus far, no path had led anywhere, unless perhaps to an exceedingly modest living. Forty-five years of study had proved to be quite futile for the pursuit of power; one controlled no more force in 1900 than in 1850, although the amount of force controlled by society had enormously increased. The secret of education still hid itself somewhere behind ignorance, and one fumbled over it as feebly as ever. In such labyrinths, the staff is a force almost more necessary than the legs; the pen becomes a sort of blind-man's dog, to keep him from falling into the gutters. The pen works for itself, and acts like a hand, modelling the plastic material over and over again to the form that suits it best. The form is never arbitrary, but is a sort of growth like crystallization, as any artist knows too well; for often the pencil or pen runs into side-paths and shapelessness, loses its relations, stops or is bogged. Then it has to return on its trail, and recover, if it can, its line of force. The result of a year's work depends more on what is struck out than on what is left in; on the sequence of the main lines of thought, than on their play or variety. Compelled once more to lean heavily on this support, Adams covered more thousands of pages with figures as formal as though they were algebra, laboriously striking out, altering, burning, experimenting, until the year had expired, the Exposition had long been closed, and winter drawing to its end, before he sailed from Cherbourg, on January 19, 1901, for home.

Marie Lloyd

[1922]

T. S. ELIOT

It requires some effort to understand why one person, among many who do a thing with accomplished skill, should be greater than the others; and it is not always easy to distinguish superiority from great popularity, when the two go together. Although I have always admired the genius of Marie Lloyd I do not think that I always appreciated its uniqueness; I certainly did not realize that her death would strike me as the important event that it was. Marie Lloyd was the greatest music-hall artist of her time in England: she was also the most popular. And popularity in her case was not merely evidence of her accomplishment; it was something more than success. It is evidence of the extent to which she represented and expressed that part of the English nation which has perhaps the greatest vitality and interest.

Among all of that small number of music-hall performers, whose names are familiar to what is called the lower class, Marie Lloyd had far the strongest hold on popular affection. The attitude of audiences toward Marie Lloyd was different from their attitude toward any other of their favourites of that day, and this difference represents the difference in her art. Marie Lloyd's audiences were invariably sympathetic, and it was through this sympathy that she controlled them. Among living music-hall artists none can better control an audience than Nellie Wallace. I have seen Nellie Wallace interrupted by jeering or hostile comment from a boxful of Eastenders; I have seen her, hardly pausing in her act, make some quick retort that silenced her tormenters for the rest of the evening. But I have never known Marie Lloyd to be confronted by this kind of hostility; in any case, the feeling of the vast majority of the audience was so manifestly on her side, that no objector would have dared to lift his voice. And the difference is this: that whereas other comedians amuse their audiences as much and sometimes more than Marie Lloyd, no other comedian succeeded so well in giving expression to the life of that audience, in raising it to a kind of art. It was, I think, this capacity for expressing the soul of the people that made Marie Lloyd unique, and that made her audiences, even when they joined in the chorus, not so much hilarious as happy.

In the details of acting Marie Lloyd was perhaps the most perfect, in her own style, of British actresses. There are no cinema records of her; she never descended to this form of money-making; it is to be regretted, however, that there is no film of her to preserve for the recollection of her admirers the perfect expressiveness of her smallest gestures. But it is less in the accomplishment of her act than in what she made it, that she differed from other comedians. There was nothing about her of the grotesque; none of her comic appeal was due to exaggeration; it was all a matter of selection and concentration. The most remarkable of the survivors of the music-hall stage, to my mind, are Nellie Wallace and Little Tich; [1] but each of these is a kind of grotesque; their acts are an orgy of parody of the human race. For this reason, the appreciation of these artists requires less knowledge of the environment. To appreciate, for instance, the last turn in which Marie Lloyd appeared, one ought to know what objects a middle-aged woman of the charwoman class would carry in her bag; exactly how she would go through her bag in search of something; and exactly the tone of voice in which she would enumerate the objects she found in it. This was only part of the acting in Marie Lloyd's last song, "One of the Ruins that Cromwell Knocked Abaht a Bit."

Marie Lloyd's art will, I hope, be discussed by more competent critics of the theatre than I. My own chief point is that I consider her superiority over other performers to be in a way a moral superiority; it was her understanding of the people and sympathy with them, and the people's recognition of the fact that she embodied the virtues which they genuinely most respected in private life, that raised her to the position she occupied at her death. And her death is itself a significant moment in English history. I have called her the expressive figure of the lower classes. There is no such expressive figure for any other class. The middle classes have no such idol: the middle classes are morally corrupt. That is to say, their own life fails to find a Marie Lloyd to express it; nor have they any independent virtues which might give them as a conscious class any dignity. The middle classes, in England as elsewhere, under democracy, are morally dependent upon the aristocracy, and the aristocracy are subordinate to the middle class, which is gradually absorbing and destroying them. The lower class still exists; but perhaps it will not exist for long. In the music-hall comedians they find the expression and dignity of their own lives; and this is not found in the most elaborate and expensive revue. In England, at any rate, the revue expresses almost nothing. With the decay of the music-hall, with the encroachment of the cheap and rapid-breeding cinema, the lower classes will tend to drop into the same state of proto-plasm as the bourgeoisie. The working man who went to the music-hall and saw Marie Lloyd and joined in the chorus was himself performing part of the act; he was engaged in that collaboration of the audience with the artist which is necessary in all art and most obviously in dramatic art. He will now go to the cinema, where his mind is lulled by continuous senseless music and continuous action too rapid for the brain to act upon, and will receive, without giving, in that same listless apathy with which the middle and upper classes regard any entertainment of the nature of art. He will also have lost some of his interest in life. Perhaps this will be the only solution. In an interesting essay in the volume of *Essays on the Depopulation of Melanesia,* the psychologist W. H. R. Rivers adduced evidence which has led him to believe that the natives of that unfortunate archipelago are dying out principally for the reason that the "Civiliza-tion" forced upon them has deprived them of all interest in life. They are

dying from pure boredom. When every theatre has been replaced by
100 cinemas, when every musical instrument has been replaced by 100
gramophones, when every horse has been replaced by 100 cheap motor-
cars, when electrical ingenuity has made it possible for every child to
hear its bedtime stories from a loud speaker, when applied science has
done everything possible with the materials on this earth to make life as
interesting as possible, it will not be surprising if the population of the
entire civilized world rapidly follows the fate of the Melanesians.

2

D. H. LAWRENCE *and* ERNEST HEMINGWAY

If the Judeo-Christian tradition, and its immanent source of values, did not hold, then what was an individual man to do? Two of the century's most original personalities, as well as two of its most widely read writers, decided for themselves.

Lawrence watched himself kill a porcupine. Hemingway watched someone else kill a bull. Each improvised an honorable, workable morality on the spot.

Reflections on the Death of a Porcupine

[1924]

D. H. LAWRENCE

There are many bare places on the little pine trees, towards the top, where the porcupines have gnawed the bark away and left the white flesh showing. And some trees are dying from the top.

Everyone says, porcupines should be killed; the Indians, Mexicans, Americans all say the same.

At full moon a month ago, when I went down the long clearing in the brilliant moonlight, through the poor dry herbage a big porcupine began to waddle away from me, towards the trees and the darkness. The animal had raised all its hairs and bristles, so that by the light of the moon it seemed to have a tall, swaying, moonlit aureole arching its back as it went. That seemed curiously fearsome, as if the animal were emitting itself demon-like on the air.

It waddled very slowly, with its white spiky spoon-tail steering flat, behind the round bear-like mound of its back. It had a lumbering, beetle's, squalid motion, unpleasant. I followed it into the darkness of the timber, and there, squat like a great tick, it began scrapily to creep up a pine-trunk. It was very like a great aureoled tick, a bug, struggling up.

I stood near and watched, disliking the presence of the creature. It is a duty to kill the things. But the dislike of killing him was greater than the dislike of him. So I watched him climb.

And he watched me. When he had got nearly the height of a man, all his long hairs swaying with a bristling gleam like an aureole, he hesitated, and slithered down. Evidently he had decided, either that I was harmless, or else that it was risky to go up any further, when I could knock him off so easily with a pole. So he slithered podgily down again, and waddled away with the same bestial, stupid motion of that white-spiky repulsive spoon-tail. He was as big as a middle-sized pig: or more like a bear.

I let him go. He was repugnant. He made a certain squalor in the moonlight of the Rocky Mountains. As all savagery has a touch of squalor, that makes one a little sick at the stomach. And anyhow, it seemed almost more squalid to pick up a pine bough and push him over, hit him and kill him.

A few days later, on a hot, motionless morning when the pine trees put out their bristles in stealthy, hard assertion; and I was not in a good temper, because Black-eyed Susan, the cow, had disappeared into the timber, and I had had to ride hunting her, so it was nearly nine o'clock before she was milked: Madame came in suddenly out of the sunlight, saying: "I got such a shock! There are two strange dogs, and one of them has got the most awful beard, all round his nose."

She was frightened, like a child, at something unnatural.

"Beard! Porcupine quills, probably! He's been after a porcupine."

"Ah!" she cried in relief. "Very likely! Very likely!" — then with a change of tone: "Poor thing, will they hurt him?"

"They will. I wonder when he came."

"I heard dogs bark in the night."

"Did you? Why didn't you say so? I should have known Susan was hiding — "

The ranch is lonely, there is no sound in the night, save the innumerable noises of the night, that you can't put your finger on; cosmic noises in the far deeps of the sky, and of the earth.

I went out. And in the full blaze of sunlight in the field, stood two dogs, a black-and-white, and a big, bushy, rather handsome sandy-red dog, of the collie type. And sure enough, this latter did look queer and a bit horrifying, his whole muzzle set round with white spines, like some ghastly growth; like an unnatural beard.

The black-and-white dog made off as I went through the fence. But the red dog whimpered and hesitated, and moved on hot bricks. He was fat and in good condition. I thought he might belong to some shepherds herding sheep in the forest ranges, among the mountains.

He waited while I went up to him, wagging his tail and whimpering, and ducking his head, and dancing. He daren't rub his nose with his paws any more: it hurt too much. I patted his head and looked at his nose, and he whimpered loudly.

He must have had thirty quills, or more, sticking out of his nose, all the way round: the white, ugly ends of the quills protruding an inch, sometimes more, sometimes less, from his already swollen, blood-puffed muzzle.

The porcupines here have quills only two or three inches long. But they are devilish; and a dog will die if he does not get them pulled out. Because they work further and further in, and will sometimes emerge through the skin away in some unexpected place.

Then the fun began. I got him in the yard: and he drank up the whole half-gallon of the chickens' sour milk. Then I started pulling out the quills. He was a big, bushy, handsome dog, but his nerve was gone, and every time I got a quill out, he gave a yelp. Some long quills were fairly easy. But the shorter ones, near his lips, were deep in, and hard to get hold of, and hard to pull out when you did get hold of them. And with every one that came out, came a little spurt of blood and another yelp and writhe.

The dog wanted the quills out: but his nerve was gone. Every time he saw my hand coming to his nose, he jerked his head away. I quieted him, and stealthily managed to jerk out another quill, with the blood all over my fingers. But with every one that came out, he grew more tiresome. I tried and tried and tried to get hold of another quill, and he jerked and jerked, and writhed and whimpered, and ran under the porch floor.

It was a curiously unpleasant, nerve-trying job. The day was blazing hot. The dog came out and I struggled with him again for an hour or more. Then we blindfolded him. But either he smelled my hand approaching his nose, or some weird instinct told him. He jerked his head, this way, that way, up, down, sideways, roundwise, as one's fingers came slowly, slowly, to seize a quill.

The quills on his lips and chin were deep in, only about a quarter of an inch of white stub protruding from the swollen, blood-oozed, festering black skin. It was very difficult to jerk them out.

We let him lie for an interval, hidden in the quiet cool place under the porch floor. After half an hour, he crept out again. We got a rope round his nose, behind the bristles, and one held while the other got the stubs with the pliers. But it was too trying. If a quill came out, the dog's yelp startled every nerve. And he was frightened of the pain, it was impossible to hold his head still any longer.

After struggling for two hours, and extracting some twenty quills, I gave up. It was impossible to quiet the creature, and I had had enough. His nose on the top was clear: a punctured, puffy, blood-darkened mess; and his lips were clear. But just on his round little chin, where the few white hairs are, was still a bunch of white quills, eight or nine, deep in.

We let him go, and he dived under the porch, and there he lay invisible: save for the end of his bushy, foxy tail, which moved when we came near.

Towards noon he emerged, ate up the chicken-food, and stood with that doggish look of dejection, and fear and friendliness, and greediness, wagging his tail.

But I had had enough.

"Go home!" I said. "Go home! Go home to your master, and let him finish for you."

He would not go. So I led him across the blazing hot clearing, in the way I thought he should go. He followed a hundred yards, then stood motionless in the blazing sun. He was not going to leave the place.

And I! I simply did not want him.

So I picked up a stone. He dropped his tail, and swerved towards the house. I knew what he was going to do. He was going to dive under the porch, and there stick, haunting the place.

I dropped my stone, and found a good stick under the cedar tree. Already in the heat was that sting-like biting of electricity, the thunder gathering in the sheer sunshine, without a cloud, and making one's whole body feel dislocated.

I could not bear to have that dog around any more. Going quietly to him, I suddenly gave him one hard hit with the stick, crying: "Go home!" He turned quickly, and the end of the stick caught him on his sore nose. With a fierce yelp, he went off like a wolf, downhill, like a flash, gone. And I stood in the field full of pangs of regret, at having hit him, unintentionally, on his sore nose.

But he was gone.

And then the present moon came, and again the night was clear. But in the interval there had been heavy thunder-rains, the ditch was running with bright water across the field, and the night, so fair, had not the terrific, mirror-like brilliancy, touched with terror, so startling bright, of the moon in the last days of June.

We were alone on the ranch. Madame went out into the clear night, just before retiring. The stream ran in a cord of silver across the field, in the straight line where I had taken the irrigation ditch. The pine tree in front of the house threw a black shadow. The mountain slope came down to the fence, wild and alert.

"Come!" said she excitedly. "There is a big porcupine drinking at the ditch. I thought at first it was a bear."

When I got out he had gone. But among the grasses and the coming wild sunflowers, under the moon, I saw his greyish halo, like a pallid living bush, moving over the field, in the distance, in the moonlit *clair-obscur.*

We got through the fence, and following, soon caught him up. There he lumbered, with his white spoon-tail spiked with bristles, steering behind almost as if he were moving backwards, and this was his head. His long, long hairs above the quills quivering with a dim grey gleam, like a bush.

And again I disliked him.

"Should one kill him?"

She hesitated. Then with a sort of disgust:

"Yes!"

I went back to the house, and got the little twenty-two rifle. Now never in my life had I shot at any live thing: I never wanted to. I always felt guns very repugnant: sinister, mean. With difficulty I had fired once or twice at a target: but resented doing even so much. Other people could shoot if they wanted to. Myself, individually, it was repugnant to me even to try.

But something slowly hardens in a man's soul. And I knew now, it had hardened in mine. I found the gun, and with rather trembling hands, got it loaded. Then I pulled back the trigger and followed the porcupine. It was still lumbering through the grass. Coming near, I aimed.

The trigger stuck. I pressed the little catch with a safety-pin I found in my pocket, and released the trigger. Then we followed the porcupine. He was still lumbering towards the trees. I went sideways on, stood quite near to him, and fired, in the clear-dark of the moonlight.

And as usual I aimed too high. He turned, went scuttling back whence he had come.

I got another shell in place, and followed. This time I fired full into the mound of his round back, below the glistening grey halo. He seemed to stumble on his hidden nose, and struggled a few strides, ducking his head like a hedgehog.

"He's not dead yet! Oh, fire again!" cried Madame.

I fired, but the gun was empty.

So I ran quickly, for a cedar pole. The porcupine was lying still, with subsiding halo. He stirred faintly. So I turned him and hit him hard over the nose; or where, in the dark, his nose should have been. And it was done. He was dead.

And in the moonlight, I looked down on the first creature I had ever shot.

"Does it seem mean?" I asked aloud, doubtful.

Again Madame hesitated. Then: "No!" she said resentfully.

And I felt she was right. Things like the porcupine, one must be able to shoot them, if they get in one's way.

One must be able to shoot. I, myself, must be able to shoot, and kill.

For me, this is a *volte-face*. I have always preferred to walk round my porcupine, rather than kill it.

Now, I know it's no good walking round. One must kill.

I buried him in the adobe hole. But some animal dug down and ate him; for two days later there lay the spines and bones spread out, with the long skeletons of the porcupine-hands.

The only nice thing about him — or her, for I believe it was a female, by the dugs on her belly — were the feet. They were like longish, alert black hands, paw-hands. That is why a porcupine's tracks in the snow look almost as if a child had gone by, leaving naked little human footprints, like a little boy.

So, he is gone: or she is gone. But there is another one, bigger and blacker-looking, among the west timber. That too is to be shot. It is part of the business of ranching: even when it's only a little half-abandoned ranch like this one.

Wherever man establishes himself, upon the earth, he has to fight for his place, against the lower orders of life. Food, the basis of existence, has to be fought for even by the most idyllic of farmers. You plant, and you protect your growing crop with a gun. Food, food, how strangely it relates man with the animal and vegetable world! How important it is! And how fierce is the fight that goes on around it.

The same when one skins a rabbit, and takes out the inside, one realizes what an enormous part of the animal, comparatively, is intestinal, what a big part of him is just for food-apparatus; for *living on* other organisms.

And when one watches the horses in the big field, their noses to the ground, bite-bite-biting at the grass, and stepping absorbedly on, and bite-bite-biting without ever lifting their noses, cropping off the grass, the young shoots of alfalfa, the dandelions, with a blind, relentless, unwearied persistence, one's whole life pauses. One suddenly realizes again how all creatures devour, and *must* devour the lower forms of life.

So Susan, swinging across the field, snatches off the tops of the little wild sunflowers as if she were mowing. And down they go, down her black throat. And when she stands in her cowy oblivion chewing her cud, with her lower jaw swinging peacefully, and I am milking her, suddenly the camomiley smell of her breath, as she glances round with glaring, smoke-blue eyes, makes me realize it is the sunflowers that are her ball of cud. Sunflowers! And they will go to making her glistening black hide, and the thick cream on her milk.

And the chickens, when they see a great black beetle, that the Mexicans call a *toro*, floating past, they are after it in a rush. And if it settles, instantly the brown hen stabs it with her beak. It is a great beetle two or three inches long: but in a second it is in the crop of the chicken. Gone!

And Timsy, the cat, as she spies on the chipmunks, crouches in another sort of oblivion, soft, and still. The chipmunks come to drink the milk from the chickens' bowl. Two of them met at the bowl. They were little squirrely things with stripes down their backs. They sat up in front of one another, lifting their inquisitive little noses and humping their backs. Then each put its two little hands on the other's shoulders, they reared up, gazing into each other's faces; and finally they put their two little noses together, in a sort of kiss.

But Miss Timsy can't stand this. In a soft, white-and-yellow leap she is after them. They skip with the darting jerk of chipmunks, to the wood-heap, and with one soft, high-leaping sideways bound Timsy goes through the air. Her snow-flake of a paw comes down on one of the chipmunks. She looks at it for a second. It squirms. Swiftly and triumphantly she puts her two flowery little white paws on it, legs straight out in front of her, back arched, gazing concentratedly yet whimsically. Chipmunk does not stir. She takes it softly in her mouth, where it dangles softly, like a lady's tippet. And with a proud, prancing motion the Timsy sets off towards the house, her white little feet hardly touching the ground.

But she gets shooed away. We refuse to loan her the sitting-room any more, for her gladiatorial displays. If the chippy must be "butchered to make a Timsy holiday," it shall be outside. Disappointed, but still high-stepping, the Timsy sets off towards the clay oven by the shed.

There she lays the chippy gently down, and soft as a little white cloud lays one small paw on its striped back. Chippy does not move. Soft as thistle-down she raises her paw a tiny, tiny bit, to release him.

And all of a sudden, with an elastic jerk, he darts from under the white release of her paw. And instantly, she is up in the air and down she comes on him, with the forward-thrusting bolts of her white paws. Both creatures are motionless.

Then she takes him softly in her mouth again, and looks round, to see if she can slip into the house. She cannot. So she trots towards the wood-pile.

It is a game, and it is pretty. Chippy escapes into the wood-pile, and she softly, softly reconnoitres among the faggots.

Of all the animals, there is no denying it, the Timsy is the most pretty, the most fine. It is not her mere *corpus* that is beautiful; it is her bloom of aliveness. Her "infinite variety"; the soft, snow-flakey lightness of her, and at the same time her lean, heavy ferocity. I had never realized the latter, till I was lying in bed one day moving my toe, unconsciously, under the bedclothes. Suddenly a terrific blow struck my foot. The Timsy had sprung out of nowhere, with a hurling, steely force, thud upon the bed-clothes where the toe was moving. It was as if someone had aimed a sudden blow, vindictive and unerring.

"Timsy!"

She looked at me with the vacant, feline glare of her hunting eyes. It is not even ferocity. It is the dilation of the strange, vacant arrogance of power. The power is in her.

And so it is. Life moves in circles of power and of vividness, and each circle of life only maintains its orbit upon the subjection of some lower circle. If the lower cycles of life are not *mastered,* there can be no higher cycle.

In nature, one creature devours another, and this is an essential part of all existence and of all being. It is not something to lament over, nor something to try to reform. The Buddhist who refuses to take life is really ridiculous, since if he eats only two grains of rice per day, it is two grains of life. We did not make creation, *we* are not the authors of the universe. And if we see that the whole of creation is established upon the fact that one life devours another life, one cycle of existence can only come into existence through the subjugating of another cycle of existence, then what is the good of trying to pretend that it is not so? The only thing to do is to realize what is higher, and what is lower, in the cycles of existence.

It is nonsense to declare that there *is* no higher and lower. We know full well that the dandelion belongs to a higher cycle of existence than the hartstongue fern, that the ant's is a higher form of existence than the dandelion's, that the thrush is higher than the ant, that Timsy, the cat, is higher than the thrush, and that I, a man, am higher than Timsy.

What do we mean by higher? Strictly, we mean more alive. More vividly alive. The ant is more vividly alive than the pine tree. We know it, there is no trying to refute it. It is all very well saying that they are both alive in two different ways, and therefore they are incomparable, incommensurable. This is also true.

But one truth does not displace another. Even apparently contradictory truths do not displace one another. Logic is far too coarse to make the subtle distinctions life demands.

Truly, it is futile to compare an ant with a great pine tree, in the absolute. Yet as far as *existence* is concerned, they are not only placed in comparison to one another, they are occasionally pitted against one another. And if it comes to a contest, the little ant will devour the life of the huge tree. If it comes to a contest.

And, in the cycles of *existence,* this is the test. From the lowest form of existence, to the highest, the test question is: *Can thy neighbour finally overcome thee?*

If he can, then he belongs to a higher cycle of existence.

This is the truth behind the survival of the fittest. Every cycle of existence is established upon the overcoming of the lower cycles of existence. The real question is, wherein does *fitness* lie? Fitness for what? Fit merely to survive? That which is only fit to survive will survive only to supply food or contribute in some way to the existence of a higher form of life, which is able to do more than survive, which can really *vive,* live.

Life is more vivid in the dandelion than in the green fern, or than in a palm tree.

Life is more vivid in a snake than in a butterfly.

Life is more vivid in a wren than in an alligator.

Life is more vivid in a cat than in an ostrich.

Life is more vivid in the Mexican who drives the wagon, than in the two horses in the wagon.

Life is more vivid in me, than in the Mexican who drives the wagon for me.

We are speaking in terms of *existence:* that is, in terms of species, race, or type.

The dandelion can take hold of the land, the palm tree is driven into a corner, with the fern.

The snake can devour the fiercest insect.

The fierce bird can destroy the greatest reptile.

The great cat can destroy the greatest bird.

The man can destroy the horse, or any animal.

One race of man can subjugate and rule another race.

All this in terms of *existence.* As far as existence goes, that life-species is the highest which can devour, or destroy, or subjugate every other life-species against which it is pitted in contest.

This is a law. There is no escaping this law. Anyone, or any race, trying to escape it, will fall a victim: will fall into subjugation.

But let us insist and insist again, we are talking now of existence, of species, of types, of races, of nations, not of single individuals, nor of *beings*. The dandelion in full flower, a little sun bristling with sun-rays on the green earth, is a nonpareil, a nonsuch. Foolish, foolish, foolish to compare it to anything else on earth. It is itself incomparable and unique.

But that is the fourth dimension, of *being*. It is in the fourth dimension, nowhere else.

Because, in the time-space dimension, any man may tread on the yellow sun-mirror, and it is gone. Any cow may swallow it. Any bunch of ants may annihilate it.

This brings us to the inexorable law of life.

1. Any creature that attains to its own fullness of being, its own *living* self, becomes unique, a nonpareil. It has its place in the fourth dimension, the heaven of existence, and there it is perfect, it is beyond comparison.

2. At the same time, every creature exists in time and space. And in time and space it exists relatively to all other existence, and can never be absolved. Its existence impinges on other existences, and is itself impinged upon. And in the struggle for existence, if an effort on the part of any one type or species or order of life can finally destroy the other species, then the destroyer is of a more vital cycle of existence than the one destroyed. (When speaking of existence we always speak in types, species, not individuals. Species exist. But even an individual dandelion has *being*.)

3. The force which we call *vitality*, and which is the determining factor in the struggle for existence, is, however, derived also from the fourth dimension. That is to say, the ultimate source of all vitality is in that other dimension, or region, where the dandelion blooms, and which men have called heaven, and which now they call the fourth dimension: which is only a way of saying that it is not to be reckoned in terms of space and time.

4. The primary way, in our existence, to get vitality, is to absorb it from living creatures lower than ourselves. It is thus transformed into a new and higher creation. (There are many ways of absorbing: devouring food is one way, love is often another. The best way is a pure relationship, which includes the *being* on each side, and which allows the transfer to take place in a living flow, enhancing the life in both beings.)

5. No creature is fully itself till it is, like the dandelion, opened in the bloom of pure relationship to the sun, the entire living cosmos.

So we still find ourselves in the tangle of existence and being, a tangle which man has never been able to get out of, except by sacrificing the one to the other.

Sacrifice is useless.

The clue to all existence is being. But you can't have being without existence, any more than you can have the dandelion flower without the leaves and the long tap root.

Being is *not* ideal, as Plato would have it: nor spiritual. It is a transcendent form of existence, and as much material as existence is. Only the matter suddenly enters the fourth dimension.

All existence is dual, and surging towards a consummation into being. In the seed of the dandelion, as it floats with its little umbrella of hairs, sits the Holy Ghost in tiny compass. The Holy Ghost is that which holds the light and the dark, the day and the night, the wet and the sunny, united in one little clue. There it sits, in the seed of the dandelion.

The seed falls to earth. The Holy Ghost rouses, saying: *"Come!"* And out of the sky come the rays of the sun, and out of earth comes dampness and dark and the death-stuff. They are called in, like those bidden to a feast. The sun sits down at the hearth, inside the seed; and the dark, damp death-returner sits on the opposite side, with the host between. And the host says to them: *"Come! Be merry together!"* So the sun looks with desirous curiosity on the dark face of the earth, and the dark damp one looks with wonder on the bright face of the other, who comes from the sun. And the host says: *"Here you are at home! Lift me up, between you, that I may cease to be a Ghost. For it longs me to look out, it longs me to dance with the dancers."*

So the sun in the seed, and the earthy one in the seed take hands, and laugh, and begin to dance. And their dancing is like a fire kindled, a bonfire with leaping flame. And the treading of their feet is like the running of little streams, down into the earth. So from the dance of the sun-in-the-seed with the earthy death-returner, green little flames of leaves shoot up, and hard little trickles of roots strike down. And the host laughs, and says: *"I am being lifted up! Dance harder! Oh wrestle, you two, like wonderful wrestlers, neither of which can win."* So sun-in-the-seed and the death-returner, who is earthy, dance faster and faster and the leaves rising greener begin to dance in a ring above-ground, fiercely overwhelming any outsider, in a whirl of swords and lions' teeth. And the earthy one wrestles, wrestles with the sun-in-the-seed, so the long roots reach down like arms of a fighter gripping the power of earth, and strangle all intruders, strangling any intruder mercilessly. Till the two fall in one strange embrace, and from the centre the long flower-stem lifts like a phallus, budded with a bud. And out of the bud the voice of the Holy Ghost is heard crying: *"I am lifted up! Lo! I am lifted up! I am here!"* So the bud opens, and there is the flower poised in the very middle of the universe, with a ring of green swords below, to guard it, and the octopus, arms deep in earth, drinking and threatening. So the Holy Ghost, being a dandelion flower, looks round, and says: *"Lo! I am yellow! I believe the sun has lent me his body! Lo! I am sappy with golden, bitter blood! I believe death out of the damp black earth has lent me his blood! I am incarnate! I like my incarnation! But this is not all. I will keep this in-carnation. It is good! But oh! if I can win to another incarnation, who knows how wonderful it will be! This one will have to give place. This one can help to create the next."*

So the Holy Ghost leaves the clue of himself behind, in the seed, and wanders forth in the comparative chaos of our universe, seeking another incarnation.

And this will go on forever. Man, as yet, is less than half grown. Even his flower-stem has not appeared yet. He is all leaves and roots, without any clue put forth. No sign of bud anywhere.

Either he will have to start budding, or he will be forsaken of the Holy Ghost: abandoned as a failure in creation, as the ichthyosaurus was abandoned. Being abandoned means losing his vitality. The sun and the earth-dark will cease rushing together in him. Already it is ceasing. To men, the sun is becoming stale, and the earth sterile. But the sun itself will never become stale, nor the earth barren. It is only that the *clue* is missing inside men. They are like flowerless, seedless fat cabbages, nothing inside.

Vitality depends upon the clue of the Holy Ghost inside a creature, a man, a nation, a race. When the clue goes, the vitality goes. And the Holy Ghost seeks forever a new incarnation, and subordinates the old to the new. You will know that any creature or race is still alive with the Holy Ghost, when it can subordinate the lower creatures or races, and assimilate them into a new incarnation.

No man, or creature, or race can have vivid vitality unless it be moving towards a blossoming: and the most powerful is that which moves to-wards the as-yet-unknown blossom.

Blossoming means the establishing of a pure, *new* relationship with all the cosmos. This is the state of heaven. And it is the state of a flower, a cobra, a jenny-wren in spring, a man when he knows himself royal and crowned with the sun, with his feet gripping the core of the earth.

This too is the fourth dimension: this state, this mysterious other reality of things in a perfected relationship. It is into this perfected relationship that every straight line curves, as if to some core, passing out of the time-space dimension.

But any man, creature, or race moving towards blossoming will have to draw immense supplies of vitality from men, or creatures below, passionate strength. And he will have to accomplish a perfected relation with all things.

There will be conquest, always. But the aim of conquest is a perfect relation of conquerors with conquered, for a new blossoming. Freedom is illusory. Sacrifice is illusory. Almightyness is illusory. Freedom, sacrifice, almightyness, these are all human side-tracks, cul-de-sacs, bunk. All that is real is the overwhelmingness of a new inspirational command, a new relationship with all things.

Heaven is always there. No achieved consummation is lost. Procreation goes on forever, to support the achieved revelation. But the torch of revelation itself is handed on. And this is all important.

Everything living wants to procreate more living things.

But more important than this is the fact that every revelation is a torch held out, to kindle new revelations. As the dandelion holds out the sun to me, saying: *"Can you take it!"*

Every gleam of heaven that is shown — like a dandelion flower, or a green beetle — quivers with strange passion to kindle a new gleam, never yet beheld. This is not self-sacrifice: it is self-contribution: in which the highest happiness lies.

The torch of existence is handed on, in the womb of procreation.

And the torch of revelation is handed on, by every living thing, from the protococcus to a brave man or a beautiful woman, handed to whosoever can take it. He who can take it, has power beyond all the rest.

The cycle of procreation exists purely for the keeping alight of the torch of perfection, in any species: the torch being the dandelion in blossom, the tree in full leaf, the peacock in all his plumage, the cobra in all his colour, the frog at full leap, woman in all the mystery of her fathomless desirableness, man in the fullness of his power: every creature become its pure self.

One cycle of perfection urges to kindle another cycle, as yet unknown.

And with the kindling from the torch of revelation comes the inrush of vitality, and the need to consume and *consummate* the lower cycles of existence, into a new thing. This consuming and this consummating means conquest, and fearless mastery. Freedom lies in the honourable yielding towards the new flame, and the honourable mastery of that which shall be new, over that which must yield. As I must master my horses, which are in a lower cycle of existence. And they, they are relieved and *happy* to serve. If I turn them loose into the mountain ranges, to run wild till they die, the thrill of real happiness is gone out of their lives.

Every lower order seeks in some measure to serve a higher order: and rebels against being conquered.

It is always conquest, and it always will be conquest. If the conquered be an old, declining race, they will have handed on their torch to the conqueror: who will burn his fingers badly, if he is too flippant. And if the conquered be a barbaric race, they will consume the fire of the conqueror, and leave him flameless, unless he watch it. But it is always conquest, conquered and conqueror, forever. The kingdom of heaven is the kingdom of conquerors, who can serve the conquest forever, after their own conquest is made.

In heaven, in the perfected relation, is peace: in the fourth dimension. But there is getting there. And that, forever, is the process of conquest.

When the rose blossomed, then the great Conquest was made by the vegetable kingdom. But even this conqueror of conquerors, the rose, had to lend himself towards the caterpillar and the butterfly of a later conquest. A conqueror, but tributary to the later conquest.

There is no such thing as equality. In the kingdom of heaven, in the fourth dimension, each soul that achieves a perfect relationship with the cosmos, from its own centre, is perfect, and incomparable. It has no superior. It is a conqueror, and incomparable.

But every man, in the struggle of conquest towards his own consummation, must master the inferior cycles of life, and never relinquish his mastery. Also, if there be men beyond him, moving on to a newer consummation than his own, he must yield to their greater demand, and serve their greater mystery, and so be faithful to the kingdom of heaven which is within him, which is gained by conquest and by loyal service.

Any man who achieves his own being will, like the dandelion or the butterfly, pass into that other dimension which we call the fourth, and the old people called heaven. It is the state of perfected relationship. And here a man will have his peace forever: whether he serve or command, in the process of living.

But even this entails his faithful allegiance to the kingdom of heaven, which must be forever and forever extended, as creation conquers chaos. So that my perfection will but serve a perfection which still lies ahead, unrevealed and unconceived, and beyond my own.

We have tried to build walls round the kingdom of heaven: but it's no good. It's only the cabbage rotting inside.

Our last wall is the golden wall of money. This is a fatal wall. It cuts us off from life, from vitality, from the alive sun and the alive earth, as *nothing* can. Nothing, not even the most fanatical dogmas of an iron-bound religion, can insulate us from the inrush of life and inspiration, as money can.

We are losing vitality: losing it rapidly. Unless we seize the torch of inspiration, and drop our money-bags, the moneyless will be kindled by the flame of flames, and they will consume us like old rags.

We are losing vitality, owing to money and money-standards. The torch in the hands of the moneyless will set our house on fire, and burn us to death, like sheep in a flaming corral.

from *Death in the Afternoon*
[1932]

ERNEST HEMINGWAY

At the first bullfight I ever went to I expected to be horrified and perhaps sickened by what I had been told would happen to the horses. Everything I had read about the bull ring insisted on that point; most people who wrote of it condemned bullfighting outright as a stupid brutal business, but even those that spoke well of it as an exhibition of skill and as a spectacle deplored the use of the horses and were apologetic about the whole thing. The killing of the horses in the ring was considered indefensible. I suppose, from a modern moral point of view, that is, a Christian point of view, the whole bullfight is indefensible; there is certainly much cruelty, there is always danger, either sought or unlooked for, and there is always death, and I should not try to defend it now, only to tell honestly the things I have found true about it. To do this I must be altogether frank, or try to be, and if those who read this decide with disgust that it is written by some one who lacks their, the readers', fineness of feeling I can only plead that this may be true. But whoever reads this can only truly make such a judgment when he, or she, has seen the things that are spoken of and knows truly what their reactions to them would be.

Once I remember Gertrude Stein talking of bullfights spoke of her admiration for Joselito and showed me some pictures of him in the ring and of herself and Alice Toklas sitting in the first row of the wooden barrerras at the bull ring at Valencia with Joselito and his brother **Gallo** below, and I had just come from the Near East, where the Greeks broke the legs of their baggage and transport animals and drove and shoved them off the quay into the shallow water when they abandoned the city of Smyrna, and I remember saying that I did not like the bullfights because of the poor horses. I was trying to write then and I found the greatest difficulty, aside from knowing truly what you really felt, rather than what you were supposed to feel, and had been taught to feel, was to put down what really happened in action; what the actual things were which produced the emotion that you experienced. In writing for a newspaper you told what happened and, with one trick and another, you communicated the emotion aided by the element of timeliness which gives a certain emotion to any account of something that has happened on that day; but the real thing, the sequence of motion and fact which made the emotion and which would be as valid in a year or in ten years or, with luck and if you stated it purely enough, always, was beyond me and I was working very hard to try to get it. The only place where you could see life and death, *i.e.,* violent death now that the wars were over, was in the bull ring and I wanted very much to go to Spain where I could study it. I was trying to learn to write, commencing with the simplest things, and one of the simplest things of all and the most fundamental is violent death. It has none of the complications of death by disease, or so-called natural death, or the death of a friend or some one you have loved or have hated, but it is death nevertheless, one of the subjects that a man may write of. I had read many books in which, when the author tried to convey it, he only produced a blur, and I decided that this was because either the author had never seen it clearly or at the moment of it, he had physically or mentally shut his eyes, as one might do if he saw a child that he could not possibly reach or aid, about to be struck by a train. In such a case I suppose he would probably be justified in shutting his eyes as the mere fact of the child being about to be struck by the train was all that he could convey, the actual striking would be an anti-climax, so that the moment before striking might be as far as he could represent. But in the case of an execution by a firing squad, or a hanging, this is not true, and if these very simple things were to be made permanent, as, say, Goya tried to make them in *Los Desastros de la Guerra,* it could not be done with any shutting of the eyes. I had seen certain things, certain simple things of this sort that I remembered, but through taking part in them, or, in other cases, having to write of them immediately after and consequently noticing the things I needed for instant recording, I had never been able to study them as a man might, for instance, study the death of his father or the hanging of some one, say, that he did not know and would not have to write of immediately after for the first edition of an afternoon newspaper.

So I went to Spain to see bullfights and to try to write about them for myself. I thought they would be simple and barbarous and cruel and that I would not like them, but that I would see certain definite action which would give me the feeling of life and death that I was working for. I found the definite action; but the bullfight was so far from simple and I liked it so much that it was much too complicated for my then equipment for writing to deal with and, aside from four very short sketches, I was not able to write anything about it for five years — and I wish I would have waited ten. However, if I had waited long enough I probably never would have written anything at all since there is a tendency when you really begin to learn something about a thing not to want to write about it but rather to keep on learning about it always and at no time, unless you are very egotistical, which, of course, accounts for many books, will you be able to say: now I know all about this and will write about it. Certainly I do not say that now; every year I know there is more to learn, but I know some things which may be interesting now, and I may be away from the bullfights for a long time and I might as well write what I know about them now. Also it might be good to have a book about bullfighting in English and a serious book on such an unmoral subject may have some value.

So far, about morals, I know only that what is moral is what you feel good after and what is immoral is what you feel bad after and judged by these moral standards, which I do not defend, the bullfight is very moral to me because I feel very fine while it is going on and have a feeling of life and death and mortality and immortality, and after it is over I feel very sad but very fine. Also, I do not mind the horses; not in principle, but in fact I do not mind them. I was very surprised at this since I cannot see a horse down in the street without having it make me feel a necessity for helping the horse, and I have spread sacking, unbuckled harness and dodged shod hoofs many times and will again if they have horses on city streets in wet and icy weather, but in the bull ring I do not feel any horror or disgust whatever at what happens to the horses. I have taken many people, both men and women, to bullfights and have seen their reactions to the death and goring of horses in the ring and their reactions are quite unpredictable. Women that I felt sure would enjoy the bull-fights with the exception of the goring of the horses were quite unaffected by it; I mean really unaffected, that is, something that they disapproved of and that they expected would horrify and disgust them did not disgust them or horrify them at all. Other people, both men and women, were so affected that they were made physically ill. I will go into the way some of these people acted in detail later but let me say now that there was no difference, or line of difference, so that these people could be divided by any standard of civilization or experience into those that were affected and those that were not affected.

From observation I would say that people may possibly be divided into two general groups; those who, to use one of the terms of the jargon of psychology, identify themselves with, that is, place themselves in the position of, animals, and those who identify themselves with human beings. I believe, after experience and observation, that those people who identify themselves with animals, that is, the almost professional lovers of dogs, and other beasts, are capable of greater cruelty to human beings than those who do not identify themselves readily with animals. It seems as though there were a fundamental cleavage between people on this basis although people who do not identify themselves with animals may, while not loving animals in general, be capable of great affection for an individual animal, a dog, a cat, or a horse for instance. But they will base this affection on some quality of, or some association with, this individual animal rather than on the fact that it is an animal and hence worthy of love. For myself, I have felt profound affection for three different cats, four dogs, that I remember, and only two horses; that is horses that I have owned, ridden or driven. As for horses that I have followed, watched race and bet on I have had profound admiration and, when I had bet money on them, almost affection for a number of these animals; the ones that I remember best being Man of War, Exterminator, I believe I honestly had affection for him, Epinard, Kzar, Heros XII, Master Bob, and a half-bred horse, a steeplechaser like the last two, named Uncas. I had great, great admiration for all of those animals, but how much of my affection was due to the sums staked I do not know. Uncas, when he won a classic steeplechase race at Auteuil at odds of better than ten to one, carrying my money on him, I felt profound affection for. But if you should ask me what eventually happened to this animal that I was so fond of that Evan Shipman and I were nearly moved to tears when speaking of the noble beast, I would have to answer that I do not know.[1] I do know that I do not love dogs as dogs, horses as horses, or cats as cats.

The question of why the death of the horse in the bull ring is not moving, not moving to some people that is, is complicated; but the fundamental reason may be that the death of the horse tends to be comic while that of the bull is tragic. In the tragedy of the bullfight the horse is the comic character. This may be shocking, but it is true. Therefore the worse the horses are, provided they are high enough off the ground and solid enough so that the picador can perform his mission with the spiked pole, or vara, the more they are a comic element. You should be horrified and disgusted at these parodies of horses and what happens to them, but there is no way to be sure that you will be unless you make up your mind to be, no matter what your feelings. They are so unlike horses; in some ways they are like birds, any of the awkward birds such as the adjutants or the wide-billed storks, and when, lifted by the thrust of the bull's neck and shoulder muscles their legs hang, big hoofs dangling, neck drooping, the worn-out body lifted on the horn, they are not comic; but I swear they are not tragic. The tragedy is all centred in the bull and in the man. The tragic climax of the horse's career has occurred off stage at an earlier time; when he was bought by the horse contractor for use in the bull ring. The end in the ring, somehow, seems not unfitting to the structure of the animal and when the canvases are stretched over the horses, the long legs, and necks, the strange-shaped heads and the canvas covering the body to make a sort of wing, they are more like birds than ever. They look a little as a dead pelican does. A live pelican is an interesting, amusing, and sympathetic bird, though if you handle him he will give you lice; but a dead pelican looks very silly.

This is not being written as an apology for bullfights, but to try to present the bullfight integrally, and to do this a number of things must be admitted which an apologist, making a case, would slide over or avoid. The comic that happens to these horses is not their death then; death is not comic, and gives a temporary dignity to the most comic characters, although this dignity passes once death has occurred; but the strange and burlesque visceral accidents which occur. There is certainly nothing comic by our standards in seeing an animal emptied of its visceral content, but if this animal instead of doing something tragic, that is, dignified, gallops in a stiff old-maidish fashion around a ring trailing the opposite of clouds of glory it is as comic when what it is trailing is real as when the Fratellinis give a burlesque of it in which the viscera are represented by rolls of bandages, sausages and other things. If one is comic the other is; the humor comes from the same principle. I have seen it, people running, horse emptying, one dignity after another being destroyed in the spattering, and trailing of its innermost values, in a complete burlesque of tragedy. I have seen these, call them disembowellings, that is the worst word, when, due to their timing, they were very funny. This is the sort of thing you should not admit, but it is because such things have not been admitted that the bullfight has never been explained.

These visceral accidents, as I write this, are no longer a part of the

Spanish bullfight, as under the government of Primo de Rivera it was decided to protect the abdomens of the horses with a sort of quilted mattress designed in the terms of the decree "to avoid those horrible sights which so disgust foreigners and tourists." These protectors avoid these sights and greatly decrease the number of horses killed in the bull ring, but they in no way decrease the pain suffered by the horses; they take away much of the bravery from the bull, this to be dealt with in a later chapter, and they are the first step toward the suppression of the bullfight. The bullfight is a Spanish institution; it has not existed because of the foreigners and tourists, but always in spite of them and any step to modify it to secure their approval, which it will never have, is a step towards its complete suppression.

This that has been written about one person's reaction to the horses in the bull ring is not put in because of a desire of the author to write about himself and his own reactions, considering them as important and taking delight in them because they are his, but rather to establish the fact that the reactions were instant and unexpected. I did not become indifferent to the fate of the horses through the callousness of seeing a thing many times so that the emotions are no longer touched. It was not a matter of the emotions becoming insulated through familiarity. However I feel about the horses emotionally, I felt the first time I saw a bullfight. It might be argued that I had become callous through having observed war, or through journalism, but this would not explain other people who had never seen war, nor, literally, physical horror of any sort, nor ever even worked on, say, a morning newspaper, having exactly the same reactions.

I believe that the tragedy of the bullfight is so well ordered and so strongly disciplined by ritual that a person feeling the whole tragedy cannot separate the minor comic-tragedy of the horse so as to feel it emotionally. If they sense the meaning and end of the whole thing even when they know nothing about it; feel that this thing they do not understand is going on, the business of the horses is nothing more than an incident. If they get no feeling of the whole tragedy naturally they will react emotionally to the most picturesque incident. Naturally, too, if they are humanitarians or animalarians (what a word!) they will get no feeling of the tragedy but only a reaction on humanitarian or animalarian grounds, and the most obviously abused thing is the horse. If they sincerely identify themselves with animals they will suffer terribly, more so perhaps than the horse; since a man who has been wounded knows that the pain of a wound does not commence until about half an hour after it has been received and there is no proportional relation in pain to the horrible aspect of the wound; the pain of an abdominal wound does not come at the time but later with the gas pains and the beginnings of peritonitis; a pulled ligament or a broken bone, though, hurts at once and terribly; but these things are not known or they are ignored by the person who has identified himself with the animal and he will suffer genuinely and terribly, seeing only this aspect of the bullfight, while, when a horse pulls up lame in a steeplechase, he will not suffer at all and consider it merely regrettable.

The aficionado, or lover of the bullfight, may be said, broadly, then, to be one who has this sense of the tragedy and ritual of the fight so that the minor aspects are not important except as they relate to the whole. Either you have this or you have not, just as, without implying any comparison, you have or have not an ear for music. Without an ear for music the principle impression of an auditor at a symphony concert might be of the motions of the players of the double bass, just as the spectator at the bullfight might remember only the obvious grotesqueness of a picador. The movements of a player of the double bass are grotesque and the sounds produced are many times, if heard by themselves, meaningless. If the auditor at a symphony concert were a humanitarian as he might be at the bullfight he would probably find as much scope for his good work in ameliorating the wages and living conditions of the players of the double bass in symphony orchestras as in doing something about the poor horses. However, being, let us suppose, a man of culture and knowing that symphony orchestras are wholly good and to be accepted in their entirety he probably has no reactions at all except pleasure and approval. He does not think of the double bass as separated from the whole of the orchestra or as being played by a human being.

As in all arts the enjoyment increases with the knowledge of the art, but people will know the first time they go, if they go open-mindedly and only feel those things they actually feel and not the things they think they should feel, whether they will care for the bullfights or not. They may not care for them at all, no matter whether the fight should be good or bad, and all explanation will be meaningless beside the obvious moral wrongness of the bullfight, just as people could refuse to drink wine which they might enjoy because they did not believe it right to do so.

The comparison with wine drinking is not so far-fetched as it might seem. Wine is one of the most civilized things in the world and one of the natural things of the world that has been brought to the greatest perfection, and it offers a greater range for enjoyment and appreciation than, possibly, any other purely sensory thing which may be purchased. One can learn about wines and pursue the education of one's palate with great enjoyment all of a lifetime, the palate becoming more educated and capable of appreciation and you having constantly increasing enjoyment and appreciation of wine even though the kidneys may weaken, the big toe become painful, the finger joints stiffen, until finally, just when you love it the most you are finally forbidden wine entirely. Just as the eye which is only a good healthy instrument to start with becomes, even though it is no longer so strong and is weakened and worn by excesses, capable of transmitting constantly greater enjoyment to the brain because of the knowledge or ability to see that it has acquired. Our bodies all wear out in some way and we die, and I would rather have a palate that will give me the pleasure of enjoying completely a Chateaux Margaux or a Haut Brion, even though excesses indulged in in the acquiring of it has brought a liver that will not allow me to drink Richebourg, Corton, or Chambertin, than to have the corrugated iron internals of my boyhood when all red wines were bitter except port and drinking was the process of getting down enough of anything to make you feel reckless. The thing, of course, is to avoid having to give up wine entirely just as, with the eye, it is to avoid going blind. But there seems to be much luck in all these things and no man can avoid death by honest effort nor say what use any part of his body will bear until he tries it.

This seems to have gotten away from bullfighting, but the point was that a person with increasing knowledge and sensory education may derive infinite enjoyment from wine, as a man's enjoyment of the bullfight might grow to become one of his greatest minor passions, yet a person drinking, not tasting or savoring but *drinking,* wine for the first time will know, although he may not care to taste or be able to taste, whether he likes the effect or not and whether or not it is good for him. In wine, most people at the start prefer sweet vintages, Sauternes, Graves, Barsac, and sparkling wines, such as not too dry champagne and sparkling Burgundy because of their picturesque quality while later they would trade all these for a light but full and fine example of the Grand crus of Medoc though it may be in a plain bottle without label, dust, or cobwebs, with nothing picturesque, but only its honesty and delicacy and the light body of it on your tongue, cool in your mouth and warm when you have drunk it. So in bullfighting, at the start it is the picturesqueness of the paseo, the color, the scene, the picturesqueness of farols and molinetes, the bullfighter putting his hand on the muzzle of the bull, stroking the horns, and all such useless and romantic things that the spectators like. They are glad to see the horses protected if it saves them from awkward sights and they applaud all such moves. Finally, when they have learned to appreciate values through experience what they seek is honesty and true, not tricked, emotion and always classicism and the purity of execution of all the suertes, and, as in the change in taste for wines, they want no sweetening but prefer to see the horses with no protection worn so that all wounds may be seen and death given rather than suffering caused by something designed to allow the horses to suffer while their suffering is spared the spectator. But, as with wine, you will know when you first try it whether you like it as a thing or not from the effect it will have on you. There are forms of it to appeal to all tastes and if you do not like it, none of it, nor, as a whole, while not caring for details, then it is not for you. It would be pleasant of course for those who do like it if those who do not would not feel that they had to go to war against it or give money to try to suppress it, since it offends them or does not please them, but that is too much to expect and anything capable of arousing passion in its favor will surely raise as much passion against it.

The chances are that the first bullfight any spectator attends may not be a good one artistically; for that to happen there must be good bull-fighters and good bulls; artist bullfighters and poor bulls do not make interesting fights, for the bullfighter who has ability to do extraordinary things with the bull which are capable of producing the intensest degree of emotion in the spectator will not attempt them with a bull which he cannot depend on to charge; so, if the bulls are bad, that is only vicious rather than brave, undependable in their charges, reserved and unpredictable in their attacks, it is best that they be fought by bullfighters with knowledge of their profession, integrity, and years of experience rather than artistic ability. Such bullfighters will give a competent performance with a difficult animal, and because of the extra danger from the bull and the skill and courage they must use to overcome this danger, to prepare for the killing and kill with any degree of dignity, the bullfight is interesting, even to a person who has never seen one before. However, if such a bullfighter, skilful, knowing, brave and competent but without either genius or great inspiration happens to receive in the ring a truly brave bull, one which charges in a straight line, which responds to all the cites of the bullfighter, which grows braver under punishment, and has that technical quality that the Spanish call "nobility" and the bullfighter has only bravery and honest ability in the preparation for killing and killing of bulls and nothing of the wrist magic and æsthetic vision that, given a bull that will charge in a straight line, has produced the sculptural art of modern bullfighting; then he fails completely, he gives an undistinguished, honest performance and he goes on lower down in the commercial ranking of bullfighting while men in the crowd who earn, perhaps, less than a thousand pesetas a year will say, and mean it truly, "I would

have given a hundred pesetas to have seen Cagancho with that bull."
Cagancho is a gypsy, subject to fits of cowardice, altogether without integrity, who violates all the rules, written and unwritten, for the conduct
of a matador but who, when he receives a bull that he has confidence in,
and he has confidence in them very rarely, can do things which all bullfighters do in a way they have never been done before and sometimes
standing absolutely straight with his feet still, planted as though he were
a tree, with the arrogance and grace that gypsies have and of which all
other arrogance and grace seems an imitation, moves the cape spread full
as the pulling jib of a yacht before the bull's muzzle so slowly that the
art of bullfighting, which is only kept from being one of the major arts
because it is impermanent, in the arrogant slowness of his veronicas becomes, for the seeming minutes that they endure, permanent. That is the
worst sort of flowery writing, but it is necessary to try to give the feeling,
and to some one who has never seen it a simple statement of the method
does not convey the feeling. Any one who has seen bullfights can skip
such flowerishness and read the facts which are much more difficult to
isolate and state. The fact is that the gypsy, Cagancho, can sometimes,
through the marvellous wrists that he has, perform the usual movements
of bullfighting so slowly that they become, to old-time bullfighting, as
the slow motion picture is to the ordinary motion picture. It is as though
a diver could control his speed in the air and prolong the vision of a swan
dive, which is a jerk in actual life, although in photographs it seems a
long glide, to make it a long glide like the dives and leaps we sometimes
take in dreams. Other bullfighters who have or have had this ability with
their wrists are Juan Belmonte and, occasionally with the cape, Enrique
Torres and Felix Rodriguez.

The spectator going to a bullfight for the first time cannot expect to
see the combination of the ideal bull and the ideal fighter for that bull
which may occur not more than twenty times in all Spain in a season and
it would be wrong for him to see that the first time. He would be so
confused, visually, by the many things he was seeing that he could not
take it all in with his eyes, and something which he might never see again
in his life would mean no more to him than a regular performance. If
there is any chance of his liking the bullfights the best bullfight for him
to see first is an average one, two brave bulls out of six, the four undistinguished ones to give relief to the performance of the two excellent
ones, three bullfighters, not too highly paid, so that whatever extraordinary things they do will look difficult rather than easy, a seat not
too near the ring so that he will see the entire spectacle rather than, if he
is too close, have it constantly broken up into bull and horse, man and

bull, bull and man—and a hot sunny day. The sun is very important. The theory, practice and spectacle of bullfighting have all been built on the assumption of the presence of the sun and when it does not shine over a third of the bullfight is missing. The Spanish say, "El sol es el mejor torero." The sun is the best bullfighter, and without the sun the best bullfighter is not there. He is like a man without a shadow.

1. Pablo Picasso, *Family of Saltimbanques* (1905).

I paint the way some people write their autobiography. The paintings, finished or not, are the pages of my journal, and as such they are valid. The future will choose the pages it prefers. It's not up to me to make the choice.   PABLO PICASSO

(from Françoise Gilot, *Life with Picasso*, p. 123)

2. Pablo Picasso, *"Ma Jolie"*
(Woman with a Zither or Guitar)
(1911–1912).

3. Pablo Picasso,
Nessus and Dejanira (1920).

4. Pablo Picasso, *The Three Musicians* (1921).

5. Pablo Picasso, *Painter with a Model Knitting* (1927). (Etching for Balzac: *Le Chef-d'œuvre inconnu.*)

6. Pablo Picasso, *The Studio* (1927–1928).

7. Pablo Picasso, *Interior with Girl Drawing* (1935).

8. Pablo Picasso, *Guernica* (1937).

9. Pablo Picasso, *She-Goat* (1950).

10. Pablo Picasso, *The Old Painter's Studio* (1954).

3

W. H. AUDEN
and CHRISTOPHER ISHERWOOD

*"We are all sick," wrote Cocteau, "and we only know how to
read books which deal with our illness." Who would have said
this elsewhere than in a secret journal before the twentieth
century?*

*Sickness, in fact, has been one of our favorite metaphors.
For his great allegory of* The Magic Mountain, *Thomas Mann
used a sanatorium and an entire cast of tubercular patients.
One of Eliot's most beautiful lyrics speaks of "the wounded
surgeon" who must operate to save us all. In "Letter to a
Wound," originally part of an ambitious, diagnostic poem
called* The Orators, *Auden writes ironically, clinically. In the
last few pages of* Prater Violet, *Isherwood writes gravely, inti-
mately. Their subject is the same.*

Letter to a Wound

[1934]

W. H. AUDEN

The maid has just cleared away tea and I shall not be disturbed until
supper. I shall be quite alone in this room, free to think of you if I
choose and believe me, my dear, I do choose. For a long time now I have
been aware that you are taking up more of my life every day, but I am
always being surprised to find how far this has gone. Why, it was only
yesterday, I took down all those photographs from my mantelpiece—
Gabriel, Olive, Mrs. Marshall, Molim, and the others. How could I have

left them there like that so long, memorials to my days of boasting? As it is, I've still far too many letters. (Vow. To have a grand clearance this week—hotel bills—bus tickets from Damascus, presentation pocket-mirrors, foreign envelopes, etc.)

Looking back now to that time before I lost my "health" (Was that really only last February?) I can't recognise myself. The discontinuity seems absolute. But of course the change was really gradual. Over and over again in the early days when I was in the middle of writing a newsy letter to M, or doing tricks in the garden to startle R. and C., you showed your resentment by a sudden bout of pain. I had outbursts, wept even, at what seemed to me then your insane jealousy, your bad manners, your passion for sporting things. What a little idiot I was not to trust your more exquisite judgment, which declined absolutely to let me go on behaving like a child. People would have tried to explain it all. You would not insult me with pity. I think I've learned my lesson now. Thank you, my dear. I'll try my hardest not to let you down again.

Do you realise we have been together now for 'almost a year? Eighteen months ago, if anyone had foretold this to me I should have asked him to leave the house. Haven't I ever told you about my first interview with the surgeon? He kept me waiting three-quarters of an hour. It was raining outside. Cars passed or drew up squeaking by the curb. I sat in my overcoat, restlessly turning over the pages of back numbers of illustrated papers, accounts of the Battle of Jutland, jokes about special constables and conscientious objectors. A lady came down with a little girl. They put on their hats, speaking in whispers, tight-lipped. Mr. Gangle would see me. A nurse was just coming out as I entered, carrying a white-enamelled bowl containing a pair of scissors, some instruments, soiled swabs of cotton wool. Mr. Gangle was washing his hands. The examination on the hard leather couch under the brilliant light was soon over. Washing again as I dressed he said nothing. Then reaching for a towel turned, "I'm afraid," he said. . . .

Outside I saw nothing, walked, not daring to think. I've lost everything, I've failed. I wish I was dead. And now, here we are, together, intimate, mature.

Later. At dinner Mrs. T. announced that she'd accepted an invitation for me to a whist-drive at the Stewarts' on Wednesday. "It's so good for you to get out in the evenings sometimes. You're as bad as Mr. Bedder." She babbled on, secretly disappointed, I think, that I did not make more protest. Certainly six months ago she couldn't have brought it off, which makes me think what a great change has come over us recently. In what I might call our honeymoon stage, when we had both realised what we meant to each other (how slow I was, wasn't I?) and that this would always be so, I was obsessed (You too a little? No?) by what seemed my extraordinary fortune. I pitied everybody. Little do you know, I said to myself, looking at my neighbour on the bus, what has happened to the little man in the black hat sitting next to you. I was always smiling. I mortally offended Mrs. Hunter, I remember, when she was describing her son's career at Cambridge. She thought I was laughing at her. In restaurants I found myself drawing pictures of you on the bottom of the table mats. "Who'll ever guess what that is?" Once, when a whore accosted me, I bowed, "I deeply regret it, Madam, but I have a friend." Once I carved on a seat in the park "We have sat here. You'd better not."

Now I see that all that sort of thing is juvenile and silly, merely a reaction against insecurity and shame. You as usual of course were the first to realise this, making yourself felt whenever I had been particularly rude or insincere.

Thanks to you, I have come to see a profound significance in relations I never dreamt of considering before, an old lady's affection for a small boy, the Waterhouses and their retriever, the curious bond between Offal and Snig, the partners in the hardware shop on the front. Even the close-ups on the films no longer disgust nor amuse me. On the contrary they sometimes make me cry; knowing you has made me understand.

It's getting late and I have to be up betimes in the morning. You are so quiet these days that I get quite nervous, remove the dressing. No I am safe, you are still there. The wireless says that the frost is coming. When it does, we know what to expect, don't we? But I am calm. I can wait. The surgeon was dead right. Nothing will ever part us. Good-night and **God** bless you, my dear.

Better burn this.

from *Prater Violet*

[1945]

CHRISTOPHER ISHERWOOD

At the party which followed, Bergmann was terrific. He clowned he told stories, he sang songs, he imitated German actors, he showed Anita how to dance the *Schuhplattler*. His eyes shone with that last reserve of energy which one puts out in moments of extreme exhaustion, with the aid of a few drinks. And I felt so happy in his success. The way you feel when your father is a success with your friends.

It must have been close on four o'clock when we said good night. Eliot offered us a ride in his car. Bergmann said he preferred to walk. "I'm coming with you," I told him. I knew that I wouldn't be able to sleep. I was wound up like a watch. In Knightsbridge, I could probably find a taxi to take me home.

It was that hour of the night when the street lamps seem to shine with an unnatural, remote brilliance, like planets on which there is no life. The King's Road was wet-black, and deserted as the moon. It did not belong to the King, or to any human being. The little houses had shut their doors against all strangers and were still, waiting for dawn, bad news and the milk. There was nobody about. Not even a policeman. Not even a cat.

It was that hour of the night at which man's ego almost sleeps. The sense of identity, of possession, of name and address and telephone number grows very faint. It was the hour at which man shivers, pulls up his coat collar, and thinks, "I am a traveler. I have no home."

A traveler, a wanderer. I was aware of Bergmann, my fellow-traveler, pacing beside me: a separate, secret consciousness, locked away within itself, distant as Betelgeuse, yet for a short while, sharing my wanderings. Head thrust forward, hat perched on the thick bush of hair, muffler huddled around the throat under the gray stubble, hands clasped behind the back. Like me, he had his journey to go.

What was he thinking about? *Prater Violet,* his wife, his daughter, myself, Hitler, a poem he would write, his boyhood, or tomorrow morning? How did it feel to be inside that stocky body, to look out of those dark, ancient eyes? How did it feel to be Friedrich Bergmann?

There is one question which we seldom ask each other directly: it is too brutal. And yet it is the only question worth asking our fellow-travelers. What makes you go on living? Why don't you kill yourself? Why is all this bearable? What makes you bear it?

Could I answer that question about myself? No. Yes. Perhaps . . . I supposed, vaguely, that it was a kind of balance, a complex of tensions. You did whatever was next on the list. A meal to be eaten. Chapter eleven to be written. The telephone rings. You go off somewhere in a taxi. There is one's job. There are amusements. There are people. There are books. There are things to be bought in shops. There is always something new. There has to be. Otherwise, the balance would be upset, the tension would break.

It seemed to me that I had always done whatever people recommended. You were born; it was like entering a restaurant. The waiter came forward with a lot of suggestions. You said, "What do you advise?" And you ate it, and supposed you liked it, because it was expensive, or out of season, or had been a favorite of King Edward the Seventh. The waiter had recommended teddy bears, football, cigarettes, motor bikes, whisky, Bach, poker, the culture of Classical Greece. Above all, he had recommended Love: a very strange dish.

Love. At the very word, the taste, the smell of it, something inside me began to throb. Ah yes, Love . . . Love, at the moment, was J.

Love had been J. for the last month — ever since we met at that party. Ever since the letter which had arrived next morning, opening the way to the unhoped-for, the unthinkable, the after-all-quite-thinkable and, as it now seemed, absolutely inevitable success of which my friends were mildly envious. Next week, or as soon as my work for Bulldog was finished, we should go away together. To the South of France, perhaps. And it would be wonderful. We would swim. We would lie in the sun. We would take photographs. We would sit in the café. We would hold hands, at night, looking out over the sea from the balcony of our room. I would be so grateful, so flattered, and I would be damned careful not to show it. I would be anxious. I would be jealous. I would unpack my box of tricks, and exhibit them, once again. And, in the end (the end you never thought about), I would get sick of the tricks, or J. would get sick of them. And very politely, tenderly, nostalgically, flatteringly, we would part. We would part, agreeing to be the greatest friends always. We would part, immune, in future, from that particular toxin, that special twinge of jealous desire, when one of us met the other, with somebody else, at another party.

I was glad I had never told Bergmann about J. He would have taken possession of that, as he did of everything else. But it was still mine, and it would always be. Even when J. and I were only trophies, hung up in the museums of each other's vanity.

After J., there would be K. and L. and M., right down the alphabet. It's no use being sentimentally cynical about this, or cynically sentimental. Because J. isn't really what I want. J. has only the value of being now. J. will pass, the need will remain. The need to get back into the dark, into the bed, into the warm naked embrace, where J. is no more J. than K., L., or M. Where there is nothing but the nearness, and the painful hopelessness of clasping the naked body in your arms. The pain of hunger beneath everything. And the end of all love-making, the dreamless sleep after the orgasm, which is like death.

Death, the desired, the feared. The longed-for sleep. The terror of the coming of sleep. Death. War. The vast sleeping city, doomed for the bombs. The roar of oncoming engines. The gunfire. The screams. The houses shattered. Death universal. My own death. Death of the seen and known and tasted and tangible world. Death with its army of fears. Not the acknowledged fears, the fears that are advertised. More dreadful than those: the private fears of childhood. Fear of the height of the high dive, fear of the farmer's dog and the vicar's pony, fear of cupboards, fear of the dark passage, fear of splitting your finger nail with a chisel. And behind them, most unspeakably terrible of all, the arch-fear: the fear of being afraid.

It can never be escaped — never, never. Not if you run away to the ends of the earth (we had turned into Sloane Street), not if you yell for Mummy, or keep a stiff upper lip, or take to drink or to dope. That fear sits throned in my heart. I carry it about with me, always.

But if it is mine, if it is really within me . . . Then . . . Why, then . . . And, at this moment, but how infinitely faint, how distant, like the high far glimpse of a goat track through the mountains between clouds, I see something else: the way that leads to safety. To where there is no fear, no loneliness, no need of J., K., L., or M. For a second, I glimpse it. For an instant, it is even quite clear. Then the clouds shut down, and a breath off the glacier, icy with the inhuman coldness of the peaks, touches my cheek. "No," I think, "I could never do it. Rather the fear I know, the loneliness I know . . . For to take that other way would mean that I should lose myself. I should no longer be a person. I should no longer be Christopher Isherwood. No, no. That's more terrible than the bombs. More terrible than having no lover. That I can never face."

Perhaps I might have turned to Bergmann and asked, "Who are you? Who am I? What are we doing here?" But actors cannot ask such questions during the performance. We had written each other's parts, Christopher's Friedrich, Friedrich's Christopher, and we had to go on playing them, as long as we were together. The dialogue was crude, the costumes and make-up were more absurd, more of a caricature, than anything in *Prater Violet:* Mother's Boy, the comic Foreigner with the funny accent. Well, that didn't matter. (We had reached Bergmann's door, now.) For, beneath our disguises, and despite all the kind-unkind things we might ever say or think about each other, we knew. Beneath outer consciousness, two other beings, anonymous, impersonal, without labels, had met and recognized each other, and had clasped hands. He was my father. I was his son. And I loved him very much.

Bergmann held out his hand.

"Good night, my child," he said.

He went into the house.

4

RAINER MARIA RILKE *and* HENRY GREEN

Lonesome and faltering adults tend to dream of pure Ur-states of being, and one whole stratum of twentieth-century literature is about the innocence and invulnerability of some form of child — from Peter Pan to the elusive heroine of Nightwood.

Rilke's poem is not about children, but about the entire "creature world" of flowers and animals where a child, too, "sometimes gets quietly lost," but from which the rest of us are exiled by our given nature. And in Henry Green's Concluding, *a bevy of girls whose names even begin with the same letter, dance down the hall in perfect community, while the sorry, self-conscious, unresolute adults watch them from another world. The scene is a boarding school, the evening of the Annual Founder's Day Ball, at some future time of total socialization. Miss Baker and Miss Edge are head mistresses; Mr. Rock is an illustrious but superannuated scientist whom the State has pastured out in a cottage on the school grounds; Elizabeth is his granddaughter, who lives with him and is in love with Sebastian, one of the young instructors.*

The Eighth Elegy

[1922]

Dedicated to Rudolf Kassner

RAINER MARIA RILKE

With all its eyes the creature-world beholds
the open. But our eyes, as though reversed,
encircle it on every side, like traps
set round its unobstructed path to freedom.
What *is* outside, we know from the brute's face
alone; for while a child's quite small we take it
and turn it round and force it to look backwards
at conformation, not that openness
so deep within the brute's face. Free from death.
We only see death; the free animal
has its decease perpetually behind it
and God in front, and when it moves, it moves
into eternity, like running springs.
We've never, no, not for a single day,
pure space before us, such as that which flowers
endlessly open into: always world,
and never nowhere without no: that pure,
unsuperintended element one breathes,
endlessly knows, and never craves. A child
sometimes gets quietly lost there, to be always
jogged back again. Or someone dies and *is* it.
For, nearing death, one perceives death no longer,
and stares ahead — perhaps with large brute gaze.
Lovers — were not the other present, always
spoiling the view! — draw near to it and wonder. . . .
Behind the other, as though through oversight,
the thing's revealed . . . But no one gets beyond
the other, and so world returns once more.

Always facing Creation, we perceive there
only a mirroring of the free and open,
dimmed by our breath. Or that a dumb brute's calmly
raising its head to look us through and through.
That's what Destiny means: being opposite,
and nothing else, and always opposite.

Did consciousness such as we have exist
in the sure animal that moves towards us
upon a different course, the brute would drag us
round in its wake. But its own being for it
is infinite, inapprehensible,
unintrospective, pure, like its outward gaze.
Where we see Future, it sees Everything,
itself in Everything, for ever healed.

And yet, within the wakefully-warm beast
there lies the weight and care of a great sadness.
For that which often overwhelms us clings
to him as well, — a kind of memory
that what we're pressing after now was once
nearer and truer and attached to us
with infinite tenderness. Here all is distance,
there it was breath. Compared with that first home
the second seems ambiguous and draughty.
Oh bliss of *tiny* creatures that *remain*
for ever in the womb that brought them forth!

Joy of the gnat, that can still leap *within*,
even on its wedding-day: for womb is all.
Look at the half-assurance of the bird,
through origin almost aware of both,
like one of those Etruscan souls, escaped
from a dead man enclosed within a space
on which his resting figure forms a lid.
And how dismayed is any womb-born thing
that has to fly! As though it were afraid
of its own self, it zigzags through the air
like crack through cup. The way the track of a bat
goes rending through the evening's porcelain.

And we, spectators always, everywhere,
looking at, never out of, everything!
It fills us. We arrange it. It decays.
We re-arrange it, and decay ourselves.

Who's turned us round like this, so that we always,
do what we may, retain the attitude
of someone who's departing? Just as he,
on the last hill, that shows him all his valley
for the last time, will turn and stop and linger,
we live our lives, for ever taking leave.

Translated by J. B. Leishman and Stephen Spender

from *Concluding*

[1948]

HENRY GREEN

When the music began a third time, eighteen children waiting in the corridor lifted heads from their confabulations but did not immediately move off towards the Hall because of two previous disappointments. Then the valse continued, on and on, and they could see couples circle into view, their short reflections upon the floor continually on the move behind swinging skirts over polished wax, backwards and forwards, in and out again as each pair swung round under chandeliers. And at the sight these others walked on the lighted scene, held white arms up to veined shoulders, in one another's arms moved off, turning to the beat with half shut eyes, entranced, in a soft ritual beneath azalea and rhododendron; one hundred and fifty pairs in white and while, — equally oblivious, inside their long black dresses, Miss Baker and Miss Edge lovingly swayed in one another's bony grip, on the room's exact centre, to and fro, Edge's eyes tight closed, both in a culmination of the past twelve months, at spinsterish rest in movement, barely violable, alone.

Above, locked safe into a sick bay, curtains close drawn against the moon, Merode's infant breathing told she was asleep.

Still farther off, in the retiring room, unaware that the dance had opened, the staff sat to make scant conversation. They were embarrassed; and, out of sympathy, perhaps, for the lovesick Winstanley, had chosen to pretend, by ignoring him, that Birt, who seemed most ill at ease, was not present in fat flesh amongst them.

All over the Institute hardly a word more was now spoken, not one down the Hall where Inglefield had taken up her stand to drive the deafening music. Then, suddenly at a doorway, there loomed unheralded the figures of Elizabeth and the old man. Both were dressed as black as those two Principals.

His great white head nodded to rapt, dancing students.

"The first will have to be with me, then," he announced to the granddaughter loud under music, for Inglefield had turned the power full on and because, as he looked around, he had seen no sign of Sebastian. Then Moira whirled past, hair spread as if by drowning over Marion's round, boneless shoulder. He let his arms, which he had held out to Elizabeth, drop back as he followed the child with carefully expressionless, lensed eyes. And Liz gave a gasp of disenchantment as she bent to raise the old hands from his sides; after which they launched out together onto the turning, dazzled floor. But not for them, as with the others, in a smooth glide. Because Mr Rock went back to the days before his own youth, was a high stepper.

He stepped high, which is to say he woodenly, uproariously lifted knees as if to stamp while he held the granddaughter at arm's length, but did not cover much ground. Still the one man on that floor, they made a twice noticeable pair because they were alone in paying heed to where they went, in his case to avoid a fall when he might break a hip, certainly fatal for a man his age, and she for the boy who remained, at the moment, her one hope of continuing to live.

"They are here," Baker, who kept an eye half open, murmured to Miss Edge. The news came to this lady as though from a distance.

"Let all enjoy themselves. They must," she mumbled in return.

There was just one note might have jarred at the outset, though it passed unnoticed. Mrs Blain had, as was natural, been amongst the first starters. She'd grabbed hold of an orderly, and was saying while she blindly danced,

"Oh, we're champion."

"You do waltz beautifully," her girl replied.

"Soft soap," the cook answered. "But I've one matter on my mind. Why my Mary's not here to enjoy things. I can't make out the reason she never phoned." Mrs Blain panted, because puffed.

"Perhaps she couldn't," the child lazily suggested.

"Oh, aren't we all dancing?" Mrs Blain enthused. "Just look at us," she said, from closed eyes. "I do wish she could be here, though. She might've given me a ring. Mind now, will you look how you go? This night's for all to enjoy, isn't it, bumpin' into people? Yes, I'd've liked to get a word. Illness in the family can be a terrible upset."

"I hardly think it is," this vague girl told her, after they had danced some more.

"There, you're only dizzy, a bit. What do you know?" Mrs Blain demanded.

"I don't fancy she's home," the child softly insisted.

"Then where is she?" Mrs Blain cried out, and opened green eyes rather wild. It seemed they danced like a whirling funnel.

"She's gone, you'll discover."

"Nowhere to be come upon?" the cook wailed, and pushed that spiralling orderly away at arm's length until, she felt, the girl revolved about her like a wisp of kitchen paper. "Lost?" she yelled, but it was drowned by music. "What's this? So that was it, then? Oh, you wicked things."

"Not to do with me, Mrs Blain," the orderly gently protested, given over to her shivering, glazed senses.

"Wicked deceivers," the woman said, in a calmer voice. "I'll have my enquiries to make on that, all right."

"We think it's pretty rotten of her to want to spoil this heaven evening."

"Well then," the cook said, quietened at once, and folded the child to an enormous bosom. Upon which both gave their two selves over, entire. As they saw themselves from shut eyes, they endlessly danced on, like horns of paper, across warm, rustling fields of autumn fallen leaves.

Quite soon, girls began to cut in. While Inglefield kept the instrument hard at it, the original partners began to break up, to step back over the wax mirror floor out of one another's arms, moving sideways by such as would not be parted yet, each to tap a second favourite on a bare, quiet shoulder. Then the girl so chosen would give a little start, open those great shut eyes, much greater than jewels as she circled and, circling yet, would dip into these fresh limbs which moved already in the dance, disengaging thus to leave her first choice to slip sideways in turn past established, whirling partners until she found another who was loved and yet alone.

Less satisfactory was the crush of fortune hunting children, with more fabulous gems for eyes, round Baker and Miss Edge, both of whom affected to ignore their riches as, oblivious yet well aware, they danced out together the dull year that was done. One after the other they would be tapped on a hard, black garmented back. But, as was traditional on

these occasions, they lingered in one another's orbit, until at last Edge had
had enough. When that moment came she simply opened eyes, from
which long years had filched the brilliants, said "Why Moira," in simu-
lated wonder, and so chose this child who, of all the suitors, was the first
she saw in her hurried tiredness.

"Oh, ma'am," the girl said, delighted, while they drifted off on music,
Moira leading.

"Isn't it wonderful?" the child asked, when she proudly noted the
Principal had once more closed her eyes.

"I could go on for ever," she murmured further, when there was no
response.

Then, as was usual at these Dances, but which came, as it always did,
in all parts of the room at one and the same time because it occurred to
almost everyone at once, there was mooted the project of a gift to their
Principals.

"Why don't we get up a sub for Edgey and Bakers?"

"I think we ought to do something for both. They're sweet."

"This is too marvellous. We must manage a present in return."

"Ma'am," said Moira to the dreaming guv'nor like a black ostrich
feather in her arms. "You're wonderful. So good."

The music was a torrent, to spread out, to be lost in the great space
of this mansion, to die when it reached the staff room to a double beat,
the water wheel turned by a rustling rush of leaf thick water. It was so
dispersed and Winstanley, seated alongside Sebastian, could, for the
conversation of her fellow teachers, hear no breath, neither the whispering
in the joists from a distant slither of three hundred pairs of shoes, nor the
cold hum of violins in sharp, moonstruck window glass. She did not know
until Sebastian, who could not tell why, other than that he was restless,
got up to open a door, when at once she realised the house had come to
life, and recognised the reason. — He would never listen for me, she
accused Elizabeth.

It came to all the staff along the outside passage, first as a sort of jest,
a whispered doublemeaning almost, then as a dance master's tap in time
with music. After which, at any rate for the women, a far rustling of
violins once recognized called as air, beaten through stretched feathers,
might have spoken to the old man's goose, that long migratory flight
unseen. So they rose, as Ted had never yet, and, with a burst of nasal
conversation, made haste toward their obligations in the excitement of a
year's end; not without a sense of dread in every breast which, in
Sebastian's case was even more, — for him it was the violin conjured,
sibilant, thin storm of unease about a halting heart.

While they hurried closer the whole edifice began to turn, even wooden pins which held the panelling noiselessly revolved to the greater, ever greater sound. Thus they almost ran to their appointment, so giddy they were fit to tumble down; but once in the room, paired off quietly, decently as best they might.

Sebastian stood against a wall, Winstanley could only take on Marchbanks, and Dakers was left with the last woman he would have picked.

"He's here," Miss Rock said to her grandfather, but he did not catch on.

"Care? Of course I care," he replied, in the deepest voice. Yet she took her hand out of his, was slipping from his arms.

She detached herself, and not unnoticed, made her way to where the young man waited. As for Mr Rock, when he saw himself abandoned, he moved clumsily over to the dais. Moira steered past with Miss Edge, whose eyes were tight closed. The child's lips sent "Later," at him, and he read them. Then, when he reached the sort of throne he had picked out, he climbed up and sat himself heavily where none but the Principals had a right to be seated. He was proud.

It was such a grand sight Mr Rock was almost glad he had attended.

Miss Winstanley noticed Elizabeth make for Sebastian, and it turned her sick as she circled about Marchbanks.

"How are you, dear?" she asked the older woman, thinking of herself.

Miss Marchbanks danced with great concentration, and the little smile of a martyr.

"Thank you, my shoulders are broad enough," she replied.

"There is something presumptuous in all this," Winstanley said of the evening with what was, for her, an unusually sad voice. She was watching Elizabeth give herself over, dance as one with Sebastian, deep in his arms. They moved as though their limbs had mutual, secret knowledge, were long acquainted cheek to cheek; the front of their thighs kissed through clothes; an unconscious couple which fired burning arrows through gasping music at her.

"Our dear girls must have a marvellous time," Marchbanks volunteered, with conviction. "But if you spoke of Mr Rock, the uninvited guest, then you knew of this fresh honour, that he is to be elected? I expect he feels sure of himself now."

The repetition of the beat, and her lazy misery about Sebastian, began to make Winstanley drowse.

"How goes your head?" she asked again.

There was a silence between them. Then Marchbanks murmured,

"I'm so used to my heads I don't notice."

"There's anaesthesia in a valse."

"But I do wonder time and again, dear," Miss Marchbanks dreamily answered. "Do we not meet this modern music the same way, in the old days, as they used to go to fairs? You will have read of it. People plunging into the hurly-burly to forget their miserable condition, their worries."

"Ah, they weren't fools, then, they seldom are," Winstanley said at random, and shut her eyes tight. Through a blinding headache Miss Marchbanks guided the younger woman, who still had hope.

"Darling," Elizabeth said to her young man, out of shut eyes also, "I spoke to him. He'll do it."

"Oh Liz," he answered, looking over his shoulder. "But you should neither of you have come."

She smiled the little smile of satisfaction.

"Aren't you glad we came?" she asked.

He did not answer. Still from her closed eyes she thought how the hand she had on his shoulder must seem to him like his heart's white flower.

"I'd have imagined you'd be glad," she said, still satisfied.

Moira had long been succeeded in Miss Edge's arms by other partners, but Mr Rock had forgotten the girl in his wait for the Principal to be vacant. He sat on alone, a monument, determined to buttonhole Edge the first moment he might. But she was too popular. Even when he saw Moira come crabwise through the serious, frantic dancers, he did not imagine she was after him. As he concentrated on the guv'nor, he did not notice the child again until she stood below his chair, to make the usual offer of herself, to present, as she always instinctively did, the endless prize of her fair person.

"Are you ready?" she asked.

"Hullo," he said. "I've danced enough."

"Mr Rock, d'you mean to say you've forgotten?" she protested. "I was to show you," she lied. "Now, don't you remember?"

He did not wish to appear confused in a crowd, or by this music.

"Where do we go, then? Lead away," he said, blithe, and got up with difficulty.

"Over here," she told him, took the little finger of his right hand.

Once they were outside, the passages seemed quite deserted, although there was one girl yawned alone in the pantry.

"Not many down yet, Moira," she greeted, unlocking a door which opened onto a steep flight of stairs that led to the depths. There was no hand rail, only a length of rope looped to some rusted stanchions. Mr Rock's courage failed.

"Have I to negotiate these?" he pleaded aghast, unwilling to admit his disabilities. "I don't think I can manage."

Meantime, the other girl bolted the door through which they had entered.

"Oh, but you must," Moira said, calm but firm.

"You might tell them to hurry my relief," the first child suggested.

"It's my eyes," Mr Rock confessed, and put a foot forward as though about to enter an ocean.

"Come on," Moira begged, started to descend in front, still holding his finger. "We don't want to get caught, do we?"

When he thought over the episode a day later, Mr Rock felt this last remark, with its suggestion of conspiracy, had been the prime factor, squalid as it was to have to admit it, which induced him to embark on the first venture.

"Wait," he said, abandoning himself to the descent.

As soon as he was fairly engaged on these stone steps, the other child locked the door above, and, with it, shut away a last murmur of the dance. So they haltingly crept down into blinding silence, lighted by dirty bulbs festooned with cobwebs.

"Where are you taking me?" he demanded, and awkwardly pulled the rope.

"Wait. You'll find out," she answered.

— Age made a man very dependent, he thought, for this was like the pretty child that led the blind. Indeed his eyes were adequate, even if thick lenses distorted edges of vision, but it was his feet were blind, which fumbled air. Then, with a great feeling of relief, he had arrived; he stood on a level cellar passage, but nevertheless, still groped forward, with the forefingers of his free hand brushing a wall, and picked up more cobwebs. — He was on the way to wet wine and dry coke, he thought, for this was the region of bins and boilers, and also, presumably, of somewhat else.

Moira, in order not to dirty her frock, led the old man as if they had to pass through a tall bed of white and black nettles. She walked sideways, delicately, held his other hand high which seemed to protest in the traditional manner of the sightless.

"Isn't it awful?" she exclaimed.

"Now look, my dear," Mr Rock said, "All this is very flattering, I don't doubt, but we have to get back upstairs, some time. Surely we've done enough."

Then he saw the bare corridor turn to an upended empty crate and a green baize door.

"Stay two minutes," she said, going round one and through the other, to leave him alone.

"What foolishness is this?" he pettishly demanded aloud of his solitude, hard of hearing, yet with an idea he could catch whispers, even more the other side. Then she was back, and had closed the door. She looked sad, listened a moment. But she climbed onto the crate, so that the rajah's hoard of her eyes was on a level with the old man's spectacles.

"We're too soon," she said. "You mustn't look before they're ready. Come here," she demanded. He went up. She laid a cheek against him, and, before he knew what she was at, had rolled her face over until soft lips brushed his that were dry as an old bone.

"Stop it," he muttered, and stepped violently away until his back became covered with powdered whitewash. He rubbed a hand over his mouth, left a cobweb on the corner.

"You're mad, Moira. You did this for a bet," he said frightened.

"Yes," she lied. It was only part of the routine; also she had wanted to make up to him, of course, for the fruitless journey.

He hurriedly started off towards the stairs. Her eyes, as they turned to watch, hung out more diamonds.

"Come on at once, my poor girl," he ordered, and did not look for her. Mopping at his face with a handkerchief, as Dakers had at breakfast, he set the pace out of it. He trod high again, as though afraid of a wire that might trip him. She followed obediently, in immodest silence.

When Inglefield allowed the instrument its first interval, the usual twenty minutes, and that Banqueting Hall spun down to a flower hung cavern of still white couples, Elizabeth had the sense not to make at once for moonlight with Sebastian, but joined a sideways drift which had begun to the buffet next door. In front of the willow pattern, hand-basin of lemonade, however, they became quite a centre of interest. For word had gone round that at last they were engaged; the students, one and all, were in a giving mood; and the idea, which seemed to each gently panting chest to be unique, the possessor's very own, took shape, flowed spontaneously into a project of the wedding gift. But not so loud that it could be expressed, not yet at least, not all at once.

"Careful with the lemonade," they said to her. "It's poison. I ought to know, I made it."

"Isn't your grandfather wonderful? I'm so proud he came."

"Sweet for us that Edgey asked you."

"Do try one of these."

Elizabeth simpered at the girls about, accepted all they offered with small cries.

"What of your Daise," a student began. "Will she like company?"

Liz took this up.

"What does one, I mean it isn't possible, is it? Animals you know. There's no way, can there be? But you see all I'm trying to say is, you may never tell, and not only with pigs when everything's told, you can't be sure of human beings, either?"

Sebastian hurried to the rescue.

"Surely this much could be assumed," he said, unaffected and serious, in his lecturer's voice. "That where waste occurs, and, mark you, waste as such, in normal times, is not so bad a thing, it can represent no more than the effect of a high standard of life, then, in those conditions, isn't it better that what waste may naturally exist should be diverted to a guise in which those who cause the self same waste may employ it to replace what has been wasted? I'm afraid I've got a bit involved, you know. In other words, if you are in a position to be able to afford not to eat potatoes in their jackets, why not feed the peelings to pigs?"

"But that's what happens, surely, Mr. Birt," one of them objected.

"Daisy doesn't have all," he said. "The rest goes to pig farms, I agree, but here we touch on what might be termed the ethics of political economy. I wouldn't exactly recommend your using this in exam papers, but I do put it forward that, if there is waste, then you should keep your own pigs. Clean up so to speak, behind."

"Then what are they going to eat on pig farms?"

"But, surely, that is the affair of the State?" he asked. "A mass feeding of swine should not be haphazard. The surplus of a hundred thousand State factories must be made up into balanced pig foods."

"And what if the pigs don't like?"

"They will. That is the purpose of the State," he said.

"But how can you tell, which is my whole point, don't you see?" Elizabeth rushed in. "You never know with animals, or anyone."

"Yet, Liz," he explained patiently, "the one goes thin, the other complains aloud, and both go thin."

"Oh it's not only food, I wouldn't be so silly, there's lots of things people are as silent as animals over. In what way is any single person sure how a certain matter will turn out?" She told him this with such intensity that he grew cautious. "Whether they will like it, or no?" she explained, about their sharing the cottage with Gapa.

"I'm not sure I follow," he said, as well he might.

"Wouldn't you say that was like a man, all over?" she exclaimed, favouring the girls about with a delighted smile. "Why it's quite simple." Then she sheered off again. "If you had to cook for someone, you'd soon learn," she said. "There need be no question of waste in the least. What does count is what's available. Don't you see how? Suppose I know my grandfather likes prawns and I can only get shrimps. As a matter of fact," she elaborated to the students, "he adores a prawn tea," pretending that she invariably arranged his meals every day. "But very likely I can only manage the other. What's the difference? Why, shrimps give him a pain." Then she had an urge to be open with them. "As a matter of fact," she went on, "I had a breakdown at work, you may have heard, and I haven't seemed able to do a great lot lately. Oh, Gapa's been marvellous, hasn't he, Seb? He's cooked for all of us," she said, to underline the special, though as yet unpublicised, relationship between her and the young man. "Of course, it's not a mere matter of food and cooking. There's everything comes into this. Someone wanted to know whether Daisy would like all the other pigs on either side. Well, what about us? Who can say if we shall like? D'you see what's back of my mind?"

She gave Sebastian a piercing glance. Some of the students had already had enough, were discussing other topics.

"My point was, dear, you would feel better if what you had to support was nourished on your left overs," Sebastian said.

"That's not so," she cried. "How about children?"

"When they're nursed, it exactly bears out my point."

"I don't think we need go into biological details here," she said. "Anyway, after six months or so they're weaned, surely? No, but when children are growing up. You don't give them your leavings then."

"We were on the subject of pigs," he insisted.

"You will, sometimes, be so dense, well pigheaded," she archly complained. "Oh my dears, what must you think of us?" she asked the girls who, for the most part, had long ceased to pay attention. "You know Gapa's notion, about what he might decide to do," she said with a loaded look at everyone, which even Sebastian did not seem to understand. "The last one, of course. What he suggested to Miss Edge just now? Well, could anything be better?" She referred to Mr Rock's unexpected offer to give talks on pigs. "To hold you know what," she ended, to make it doubly plain she meant their cottage.

"Isn't it splendid Mr Rock's to teach about Daisy," one of the students took her up, innocent as the day, obviously under the impression that she was opening a fresh topic.

"Why whoever told you that, then?" Elizabeth asked, delighted at what she took to be confirmation.

"Oh everyone knows. Don't they, girls?"

"Sebastian, did you hear? Isn't it marvellous?" Miss Rock crowed. "You see? It means Miss Edge must have thought of our plan first." In such a way the granddaughter both claimed the idea for her very own and assumed Edge's acquiescence, thus wilfully ignoring the heights, or depths, of gossip prevalent amongst these children.

Miss Edge, when the gramophone stopped a second time, once more found herself the centre of a slightly panting group plying her with invitations. She shooed them off towards the buffet, and stalked to the dais that she might rest herself. She had not gone far before she perceived Mr Rock up there again, alone, as though lionised. She paused. But, after all, it would be too absurd if the man's presence hindered one of the Principals taking her rightful place. So she glided over despite him.

With an acute struggle against his old joints, he rose to this approach.

"My congratulations, ma'am," he said. "A memorable sight we have tonight."

"My dear Mr Rock. Sweet indeed to bother."

"I trust your exertions will permit, later, your partnering an old man."

"My dear Sir, how could I forget? I shall hold you to it."

In no time they were seated side by side, Miss Edge delicately inclined towards the sage. Her eyes roved over the Hall of her girls, in stiff pairs as if bereft at this interruption of music. He, for his part, looked on the old fashioned dancing pumps he wore, while he leaned in her direction to minimise the deafness.

"Takes me quite back to my young days," he persisted.

"And mine, if you please," she countered.

In this he lied, however. It was true the more distant past now made a sharper picture; the time at school, hard work, then six months chasing girls and finally the signal triumph; but he was concentrated now on his granddaughter, on how best to approach Miss Edge.

"I do know a little about these things. It is your powers of organisation, if I may say so, which I especially applaud," he said.

"You understand our Tamashas are traditional," the lady condescended. "They run themselves. All Baker and I must do, is to watch that there are no departures."

— Departures? Escapes? Was this a reference to poor Mary, he wondered?

"Ah, the sudden, the unexpected," he tested her.

The sudden, she asked herself? Could he be aiming at that unfortunate child? The whole trouble really was, too many knew about Merode and Mary.

"The odious deviations from what is usual," she corrected, dashing him a glance. "One of the things we should provide here is memories, which is why I strive for the repetitive. It is a minor function, of course, in a great Place like this, but we must send them out so they can look back on the small pleasures shared. I dare say there are several reunion parties to celebrate Founder's Day in many a State Recreation Room this self same moment. You know, it is not long since that Baker and I were privileged by the State to create the Institute out of a void. Believe me, Mr Rock, it was a vacuum indeed when we first came. But already our old girls would be distressed to hear of change in any shape."

"It is a sadness in old age," he agreed. "One's contemporaries die. One can no longer share one's youth."

"Ah, you have lived the lonely life," she said.

— Now what could she mean? He wondered. He waited.

"But there have been compensations, surely?" she continued. "Of course, noone can speak for another, life has at least taught me that, I hope. Yet to remain on in this beautiful Place, as a reward for great work well done, must be a remarkable privilege I cannot help feeling."

"One has a pride in achievement," he answered, to show that he, at any rate, need not be modest. "Still, old age is a lonely condition, as you'll find in due course, Miss Edge."

— What could the wily old man be hinting, she impatiently asked under her breath?

"Yet you do have company," she insisted.

He reminded himself to be careful. Doubtless she intended a sly reference to his habit of speech with certain students when they strolled down to the cottage.

"Not the life shared, memories in common," he brought out, conscious of his deep, pathetic tones.

"But your granddaughter?"

"She's only here when ill."

"I have noticed, Mr Rock, how much improved she seems in herself."

— Now, what was she after? Was this to be the clean sweep, to rid herself of Elizabeth and him at the single, Machiavellian stroke.

"I wish I could think so, ma'am," he said, with anxious care.

"Just look at Moira," Miss Edge then changed the subject without warning. The old man wildly raised his head, in guilt. "Really she stares out of those great eyes of hers as though she were going to be ill."

He said not a word. Did these two blockheaded Principals never have any idea of the strains and stresses, he wondered? And what was all this about sickness? He kept his face a blank for the child's sake.

"Yes, I'm sure she's ever so much better."

"Moira, ma'am?"

"No, your granddaughter Elizabeth, naturally. Tell me, what are your plans for her?" This was to come out into the open with a vengeance, he thought.

"It is in the hands of the doctor, of course," he replied, with a sidelong glance.

"Sick notes seem quite to govern all our decisions these days," Miss Edge agreed, to abandon the subject. She fell silent, the better to watch her girls at rest.

This silence made the old man increasingly nervous.

Then, with no further word exchanged, the Principal made a sign to Inglefield, who at once restarted the gramophone.

The crowd of girls in white poured back. Even before they were in one another's arms they twirled in doorways.

This music was heavy, stupendous for Mr Rock.

"May I have my honour now, ma'am?" he enquired.

"How kind," she answered. "But I wonder if I might rest a little."

"I never knew you had trouble with your eyes, ma'am," he said. "How blind," was what he had heard.

"Kind," Miss Edge shouted, with a brilliant, fixed smile at her circling throng of children. — It will be such a tiresome bore if I have to try to make him hear above this perfectly heavenly valse, she thought.

"You did not catch what I said. Only Tired, want to Rest a minute," she explained in a great voice.

— Why must Moira watch him like it, as if he had done her injury, he asked himself? The foolish little intriguer. She was perilous. Because Edge who had noticed already, might end by getting it into her narrow skull.

Then, at that precise moment, Elizabeth came just below, dancing, as he thought, in a manner which could not be permissible in any era, so as to flaunt the fact of Sebastian no doubt. He assumed an idiot look of pride, in the way he could the swill man's cry, and turned towards Miss Edge to note her reaction. He saw she had not bothered to see them, which was a relief, though at the same time he resented the culpable blindness.
— Perhaps she is really having trouble with her eyes, as I with my ears, he wondered.

Edge may have sensed he watched, because she swung her head round
with a dry smile.

"The dears," she said. "They must and shall enjoy themselves."

Now the music was in full flood he could not be sure of what he heard.
When he thought he caught what had been said, he was often wrong;
and the few times he was confident he had the sense, he still knew he
hardly ever did have it when, as now, under a difficulty. So he assumed
she was speaking of Liz.

"Thanks to you, the time of her life," he assured Miss Edge.

— Why cannot the sad man realise I will not be bothered tonight with
individuals, she asked herself?

"There must not be a child who does not take a happy memory of this
away in her, for the rest of her days," she answered.

"And so they ought," he agreed stoutly, leaving the Principal in ignorance as to whether he had heard.

Another silence fell between them. But there was a deal he had to tell
her yet. He was determined to have it out. Accordingly he tried to bring
the conversation back somewhere near the more immediate topics.

"Is this correct, what I hear about pigsties, like mushrooms after rain,
over the magnificent grounds?" he asked.

"Why, whoever gave you that idea, Mr Rock?"

"A flat idea? I don't quite follow, ma'am."

— Really, the man was intolerable. It was indeed time for him to go
where he could be properly looked after with his deafness and everything,
she thought.

"I never question a decision of my Superiors," she reproved. "No, I
asked how you had learned?" She yelled this at an ear. He took it in.

"Amazing the way things get about a community such as ours, ma'am,"
he replied. She wondered at his effrontery, that he should claim kinship
with their Work. "No," he went on, "of course I have given a hand with
the swill in the past, and now, I suppose, you will want all of it for yourselves? But to tell you the truth, ma'am, time has lain a bit heavy on my
hands. In fact I don't know that I've been pulling my weight. It is a
privilege to lead my existence," he said with an irony just sufficiently
controlled to escape her notice. "What I had wondered, since you don't
seem to be too keen that I should give them a few plain talks on pigs, was
whether I could not, after all, work up a little course of lectures on what
I may have done. Something along the lines of the joy, and reward, of
achievement," he ended in great bitterness, effectively disguised behind a
mandarin smile.

— Of all bores, Miss Edge moaned to herself, the persistent ones are worst. He could not have appreciated, then, what she had told him on this very subject in the Sanctum.

"Well," she said genially. "Well! That will need thinking over. But how lucky for the Girls."

"No trouble at all," he lied at random.

"Shall we leave it till tomorrow, Mr Rock?" she suggested. "I hardly feel, just at the crux of our little Jollification, that we can give your project the attention it deserves."

"Whatever you say, ma'am," he agreed. — At least Elizabeth could hardly now make out that he had not explored every avenue, he told himself.

Soon after, he got up and left Miss Edge. The lady was so obviously lost in happy contemplation of her charges. And he felt he had done enough. Honour was satisfied, he thought.

Perhaps forty minutes later, Edge was joined on the dais by her colleague who declared she could dance no longer, and sat herself heavily down, to fan a cheek with a lace bordered black and white handkerchief.

"It is excellent, dear, quite excellent," she cried.

"I think so, Baker," Miss Edge answered, in an exalted mood again.

"What a good notion of yours, Mabel, to ask the Rocks," Baker, full of enthusiasm, gaily cried above the music. "It will give those two so much pleasure later, when they get home," she added.

"I did no such thing," her colleague said, but did not seem to pay attention.

"The old man really cuts quite a distinguished figure," Baker insisted, to all appearances not having taken in Edge's negligent reply, perhaps because of this great spring tide of music.

"Nevertheless," Edge enquired, "what was it led you to ask them, Hermione?"

"I?" Miss Baker demanded. "I never invited anyone, dear."

Edge leaned over her colleague in one swift movement, as though to peer up Baker's nostrils.

"Then you mean they are here unasked?" she hissed. "Oh no, Hermione, not that, for it would be too much."

"I didn't," Baker promised. They looked wildly at one another. "Now careful, Mabel," she went on. "We don't wish to make ourselves conspicuous."

"But this is preposterous persecution. It could even be wicked."

"Mabel don't, I beg of you. Just when we were so enjoying ourselves.

If you could only catch sight of your expression, dear. We shall have everyone look our way in a minute."

"Hermione, they shall leave at once," Miss Edge proposed.

"To brazen themselves like this," Baker hastily agreed. "Why, it's wrong."

In time, however, both ladies gained sufficient control to be able to look straight out over the Hall with a glare above the dancers. But when Elizabeth came by once more, still in Sebastian's arms, hair still disarranged, still dancing as though glued to him, they both deflected their vision through the degrees necessary to take in this orgiastic behaviour, which they had not previously bothered to notice. They then followed the couple with palsied indignation, rooted to valse trembling chairs.

"You saw?" Miss Edge brought out at last.

"Yes, and alas I still do, Mabel."

"Well, whatever else we may decide, dear, their little display of animalism must be stopped at once."

"Whatever you think," Miss Baker agreed. But seemed hesitant.

"Yes, Hermione, and why on earth not?"

"Is it always wise to bring matters of this kind out in the open? The thought just flashed through my mind, that's all."

"Hermione, I wish I could follow your reasoning."

"It's just I can't quite make out that any of the children appear to have caught on, particularly. You see?" Miss Baker asked.

"Should we wait for the girls to copy this themselves?"

"It does seem a most ambiguous style to dance, I must admit, Mabel."

"In a moment, when the first flush of this glorious music has worn off, I'm very much afraid the cat will be out of the bag, Hermione."

"Where has Mr Rock got to, then? I don't see him," Miss Baker said, to draw a red herring across the trail. She was a cautious woman.

"Oh, drinking, undoubtedly drinking outside," Miss Edge proclaimed.

"But there's no more than lemonade, dear."

"He had a flask, Hermione. I saw the bulge myself, in his pocket."

"You appal me."

"Ah, if it were only that."

"Oh surely, Mabel?"

"I insist he is far too close to some of the girls."

"Be that as it may," Miss Baker sternly said, pulling herself together, "I do beg you to take this fresh affront in a Christian spirit."

"Why should I?" her colleague demanded. "When he flaunts our authority?"

"You know how deaf Mr Rock is. Perhaps he misheard some time this week. Thought you had invited him?"

"Oh no, no, that simply will not wash. You must realise all he misunderstands is just what he does not wish to hear. Besides I have not said two words to the man in months."

"Of course there may have been . . . but I don't think . . . wait, I'm trying to remember," Miss Baker said. "He might have thought, when I mentioned, when we met by the Lake," she delicately hinted, to scale down Mr Rock's offence. "But of course I'm in no two minds. A member of the staff has no business whatever dancing with the misguided woman. If we don't pull together on occasions of this sort, what good are we, after all? And to go about it in that disgraceful way is too bad of Sebastian. As to her, I cannot believe she can be responsible for her actions. Oh no, don't think I don't agree with you, dear."

"Then, Hermione, I am going straight onto the floor. I shall simply tap him on the shoulder, gesture him Off. I shall not say a word," Miss Edge announced, and made as though to get down from her chair.

"But Mabel, is this wise?" Miss Baker asked, in a sort of shriek to pierce the double basses which, at the moment, held the recorded melody.

"There is more to our duties than a kind of still-born native caution," Edge complained, but stayed seated.

"Yes, dear," her colleague comforted, satisfied that she had, at least, held off immediate action.

"If we see another woman ridiculed before our very eyes, are we to sit by without a word?" Miss Edge demanded. "There is a double obligation on us, surely. To call Elizabeth Rock to order, for she is leading him along to make a fool of her, to compromise herself with him, Baker; and, second, to show our girls we shall not turn a blind eye upon wrongdoing, which this disgraceful behaviour most surely is."

"You are right, Mabel, of course. But how will Mr Rock react?"

"He should be eternally grateful. You cannot tell me he wants his girl compromised with Sebastian Birt."

"No, Mabel. But you know the way he is. He might take our reproof for an affront."

"And if he did?"

"My dear, he is such friends with Mr Swaythling. This can hardly be a moment to invite publicity, the attention of the Supervisor, just when we are face to face with the enigma of Mary, not to mention Merode."

"Yes, but there must be some justice in our affairs, Baker. If we are to harbour the informer in our midst, let us have nothing to hide, at least."

"Leave sleeping dogs lie, Edge."

"And what have we done? My conscience is clear. Can you point to any single circumstance under which we could possibly be said to have countenanced the girl's disappearance?"

"Of course, this whole thing's absurd," her colleague answered. "At the same time, I didn't quite care for Mrs Manley's attitude. After she had seen Merode she rather made capital out of Mary's being such a favourite of ours."

"I trust, whenever we make friends with one of the Students, that will not be considered sufficient justification for the child concerned to make off at dead of night, and in her pyjamas."

Miss Baker laughed elegantly at this sally.

Just then Sebastian bumped Elizabeth, through carelessness, into another couple and she opened hers to find herself gazing into the Principals' four eyes.

"Look out Seb," she said. "They're glaring like a couple of old black herons down in the meadow, over the daisies."

After this, they danced with more circumspection.

"It is a matter of elementary justice, Baker," Edge insisted, but in so much calmer a voice, now Elizabeth was no longer dancing cheek to cheek, that her colleague could be satisfied the danger of an open breach was past. "If one sees wrong done, one cannot sit idly by, dear."

"Of deportment, or behaviour? Even on a special occasion?" Miss Baker asked.

"But really, sometimes you astound me," Edge said, mildly warming to the subject. "That sort of thing is like an infection, surely? I refer of course to the way those two have been dancing. If you find scarlet fever in a community, you isolate it. There is the fever hospital."

"I dare not look at Winstanley," Baker replied.

"Then I will do so for you," Miss Edge offered. "There she is, with a look on her washed out face of weariness, and disgust, poor child. I do not know if we should not get rid of her as well," she ended, but in an uncertain voice.

"No really, dear, there must be limits."

"It is the risk of Infection again," Edge explained, all at once rather magisterial. "Jealousy is an epidemic, can even lead to crime."

"Now, Edge, I really should . . ."

"Yes, Baker, but there is so much which is unexplained. That is the reason I feel we must have a clearance, a real spring clean," Miss Edge interrupted. But, now the tension was relaxed, she spoke in almost languishing tones.

Miss Baker became unusually confident. The music, the dance, the air of festivity had loosened her tongue.

"So long as we ourselves don't get swept up into the dust pan along with the wet tea leaves," she said.

"Baker, surely that is rather fanciful," her colleague reproved, in an idle voice.

"This is hardly the time and place to discuss it," Miss Baker admitted. "Why, look at Mr Rock and Moira."

"Where? Dancing?"

"No, Edge, over in the doorway. Really he imagines he has particular manners, to use the Institute idiom."

"So long as they do not sample moonlight," Edge exclaimed.

Miss Baker laughed, then she said, "Of course if there was really anything of the sort I'd never hesitate. Out they'd all go, neck and crop. But until we have cleared Mary up, and got quite to the bottom of Merode, we mayn't be absolutely sure, you know. Even his turning up tonight with Elizabeth looks suspicious from a certain angle, I agree. Yet there's Mr Swaythling, not to mention Hargreaves. Both are old friends, remember."

"The way to handle all matters of this sort is to act in the name of the State at once, then congratulate the State on what has been done afterwards," Edge propounded, with a sudden dryness.

"My dear," Baker replied. "Those tactics may have served when we had to have another corridor of bathrooms, but I venture to think this an altogether different problem."

"I must have that cottage," Edge goodhumouredly insisted.

"And so you shall," Miss Baker promised, in the voice she would have used to a little girl who was wanting more chocolate, in the one day, than was proper. "Now, shall we postpone all this until tomorrow?"

"Very well," Edge agreed, content on the whole to let things slide this night of nights. "But I must just mention one thing, Baker," she added, as a last gesture, and in a rising voice, as though to yell defiance. "They can go too far," she shouted under the music, but kept her face expressionless. It was like a prisoner, confined with others to a workshop in which talk is forbidden, and who has learned to scream defiance as an unheard ventriloquist beneath the deafening, mechanical hammers. "They can outstretch themselves," (she was working herself up), "there is a Limit, and this," when, at that precise moment, the music stopped dead into a sighing silence, "this Rock" she continued, and could only go on, in a great voice, heard throughout the Hall, "upon which our Institute is Built," she recovered, and beamed at the Students.

"My dear, magnificent," Miss Baker approved, in praise of the recovery.

Mr Rock had had a grand time, so closely surrounded by children that he was protected even from Moira's pressing attentions.

Very likely because, on this occasion, it would be one way a girl could draw attention to herself, or, at any rate, that was how he explained it, he had been deluged by pretty, laughing invitations to be amongst his partners, all of which he had known how to refuse. It was enough that he had danced with Liz, would be ready again for Edge when the spirit moved her, and that he should be at hand if Liz lost her Sebastian even for a moment. One or two carefully done evenings like this, and she'd come right in no time. Nevertheless he was charmed with the fuss these children were making.

"Why don't you, Mr Rock, this once?"

"You might, you know. It's rather particular, with me I mean."

"We needn't finish the whole thing out. Come on, just three times round the floor."

After the dancing there had already been, these children were hot despite windows wide open onto sky-staring white Terraces, and, as several tugged at his old hands, Mr Rock could feel their moist fingers' skin, the tropic, anemone suction of soft palms over rheumatic, chalky knuckles.

"You do me honour. But no, I think not," he was saying.

"Why can't you leave the man be?" Moira demanded, on the outskirts.

"Well, it's not fair for you to have all," one objected.

"If I were fifty years younger," the old man fatuously said.

"I'll bet you were terrific, Mr Rock."

"Then what I say is, I wish I'd been about at the time," another cried.

"Now, will you let him alone?" Moira objected.

"All right, my dear, I'll call for help when I'm in need." Mr Rock told her.

"But you know you promised," she lied.

"What? Did I?" he asked, contrite at once. These last few years he had been nervous regarding his memory.

The others began to drift away, at this uncalled for intrusion of privacy.

"I wish poor Inglefield wouldn't hesitate so long between," one said.

"I'd something particular I wanted you to see below, now d'you remember?" Moira told him. She spoke right into his good ear, having to stand on her toes to reach.

"I'll not have that nonsense a second time," he said in a low, gruff voice.

"Oh I'm so sorry, and if you don't want, of course you shan't," she answered.

"Well, what is there?" he relented.

"Come and see."

"Certainly not."

"Then I'll never tell," she announced with a voice of authority, as she turned away.

"But need we go just the two of us?" he weakly asked. He considered the suggestion that another might come along must provide the impediment he sought.

"Naturally not. Whoever said?"

He misunderstood what he heard of this last.

"That's that, then," he concluded, much relieved.

She immediately caught hold of his hand once more.

"All right, come with me, tag on," she laughed. "Here, Melissa," she called, and lugged both off. "For better or worse," she ended.

"Where are we going?" he appealed, as soon as he was led into the pantry. A different girl stood guard.

He was ignored.

"Never those stairs again," Mr Rock weakly protested.

"Not much doing yet," the new child said, as she locked up behind.

"Why you managed last time like a bird," Moira said, with greater authority.

"Must I?" he pleaded, horrified at the thought that he could only make a fool of himself a second time on the scramble down. At his age it was a sort of rock climb.

"Yes," Moira insisted, Melissa laughed, and they began to whisper. As he painfully negotiated the steps, he thought his children were rough with him, but was too confused to protest. He could not understand, nor hear. When at last the thing had been managed, he was hurried along that dead silent, underground passage until, once again, they came to the green baize door and the upended case. As soon as Melissa had clambered up on this, he was so muddled he did not connect the action with what Moira had previously done, perhaps because neither of the girls had yet gone through the door. And he was painfully out of breath because he had been bustled. So, when the child said, "Come over," and Moira gave him a great shove in the back, he went forward, an old lamb offered up. Exactly the same recurred. Melissa laid a cheek against him, then rolled it over until her lips brushed his. "Stop," he demanded, stepping back, but not so far that he got whitewash on his clothes this time.

"Oh please don't be so dreadful, Mr Rock," Moira laughed. "It's only our Club rules and regulations. I must now enjoin you to silence," she recited.

"Mum's the word?" he asked like a fool, ashamed, blaming his deafness that he had been let in for this, afraid.

"You can talk all you want, you know, once we're inside," Melissa said as she jumped off the case. "Quiet a moment, just the same." She knocked on the door, which was opened forthwith. She gave what must have been the password. Upon which a child opened it wide, and all three came forward into a quick flicker of candlelight.

The first thing that arrested him was a notice, "INSTITUTE INN." The next he knew he was warmly surrounded by six or nine children, who clapped their hands, giggling. Then Moira stepped through them.

"My job's to welcome you," she said in a loud, formal voice. But she grew embarrassed, poor old Mr Rock did look pathetic. "Make yourself at home," she added on a much weaker note, at the verge of helpless giggles.

Melissa handed the old man a glass, as though it were a goblet.

"What is it?" he enquired, glad to be able to ask the familiar question.

"Will you be initiated now or later, Mr Rock?"

"You have to drink this down. The Club Special," Melissa told him.

"I'm not sure if you realise a single thing," a girl severely said. "But you're the first outside one has come down here. When we voted to ask you tonight, it was most particular."

"Yes, and when I'm caught, as will doubtless happen, I'll be the last," Mr Rock dryly said. He was recovering.

"That would be an honour," the child approved. "Oh, for us too," she corrected herself. "How idiotic."

"You're perfectly sweet," Moira assured him. "And we've our guard up top. They change every three quarters of an hour so they can get some dancing. She's got a bell up there. The moment the alarm goes, look here it is, we just lope out the back way. Though we've never had to yet, thank goodness."

"I see," he said, and at last sat down. He sipped what was in the glass. He judged it to be a kind of medicated syrup.

The girls having begun an argument, he was left to himself for the while. He looked around. He felt rather flattered. At the same time he began to have a gross feeling of immoderate amusement, such as had not come his way in years.

— What would those two idle, no good, boasting spinsters say to this, he wondered of the underground passage, widened here like a green bottle from its neck, and blocked off at the far end by a blue rug. More coverings in faded canvas had been hung to cover the walls. Pinned up in a continuous and beautiful arabesque, were single sprays of azalea filched from above stairs. In the light from a row of candles, on a trestle set back, so he found, too close for safety to the canvas, these flowers, laid flat against tarpaulin, cast each one a little shadow by which it was outlined from above; a medieval fancy, he thought; the sweet tented furnishing for a campaign the women followed, a camp in Flanders in an old war of bows and arrows, he opined, and smiled.

The children had come to an end of another of their discussions.

"Lord, it is slow, isn't it? Couldn't we have our music?" one demanded.

"Something's the matter with the thing. Margot's gone to fix that."

"Why don't we all go off, then?"

"Outside? Why Melissa, whatever for?"

"Haven't you heard, even yet?"

"Shut up," ordered another girl.

"Do you relay the music from above down here?" the old man enquired, and thought to identify himself with youth by the question.

"That ancient stuff?" Marion demanded. "You must think us properly out of date. Lord no. We get on to . . ." and she mentioned a source of which he had no knowledge. And he could not be sure he had caught the name.

"I do wish Mary might be with us," he remarked, suddenly regretting the child, ill at ease.

"Oh she's all right, don't you worry your head," Moira answered. Unseen by him, she pouted with jealousy.

"But where is she, then?" the old man persisted.

"I thought just everyone had a very good idea," Moira replied. "I'd not trouble myself if I was you. She's not worth it."

"She never bothered much where we were concerned," one of the others elaborated. "She put the whole show in danger. You wait until I catch Merode."

"No, but what has happened to Mary, please?" Mr Rock begged. He was frightened again.

"That's a secret. We're bound to silence, don't you realise?"

— How could one be certain these children were not simply prevaricating? Because he felt some true friend of Mary must get to her if she was hidden.

"Not an entirely intelligent mutism in that case," he tried, once more.

"It's the way it is," was all he got for his pains.

"Many of you see much of Adams, nowadays?" he next enquired, across the chatter they kept up at each other.

"Him?" Moira said, and laughed. "We call that man the answer to the virgin's prayer."

"Now Moira, duck," Melissa protested. "Who's gone too far this time?"

"Well, a person has only to look, haven't they? He's enough to bring on anyone a miscarriage."

"You're crazy."

"Am I?"

"What is the matter with Adams, if you will excuse my persistence?" Mr Rock tried once more, floundering after information.

"Look. Some of the girls in East block go out at night to find him."

"Oh no, Moira, it's too much," protested another.

"Not Club Members, of course," Moira admitted.

"But anyway, how are you sure?" the same child asked.

"Because I can afford to save my beauty sleep up, thank you, until I need. I mean, I don't have to go hogging it the whole night through in case I get pimples next morning on account of I stay awake," she proudly answered.

"Careful the stable clock doesn't toll midnight and catch you making faces at the horrid Adams, then. Under a new moon."

"Me?" Moira demanded. "I wouldn't be seen dead beside him."

Mr Rock was less than ever at ease. He began to ask himself how it would look if he were caught down here.

"But you do claim you have a lot on him," the first child insisted.

"Why shouldn't I? Who's to prevent me?" Moira demanded.

There was rather a pause at this last remark.

"After all's said and done, we're only young once," she said, with a trace of malice, at Mr Rock. But when she continued, it was after she had correctly interpreted the lines of distaste that had formed about his mouth. "Oh, you needn't pay attention, please," she said directly to the old man. "This is only a lot of talk. Fun and games," she added, as though to explain everything.

Upon which a couple of atomic cracks sounded from the amplifier up in an angle. Immediately followed, crescendo, by a polka which had been out of date even in the days when the old man had had his few months dancing. So he waited for a howl of protest from the children.

When none came, he looked up, and was amazed. With rapt expressions on their fair faces, they were already rocking to the ancient music.

"Isn't it marvellous?"

"Sh . . . Melissa. How can anyone listen if you . . ."

For the second time, Mr Rock was moved to suppress a smile despite his fears.

Then the apparatus stammered a few notes, gave out, broke down.

"Oh, isn't that just like this beastly hole?" Moira wailed.

"She's hopeless. She'd never repair a thing."

"Perhaps you'd like to go up and have a shot, then?"

"If I did, I wouldn't stop by the old apparatus, thanks. I'd find somewhere else, I expect, a little farther out."

"Will you shut up, Melissa, and for the last time?"

"I say, Mr Rock," Moira said. "If I asked, would you be dreadfully angry?"

"I can't say until you have tried, can I?" he answered.

"Oh, so you will. No then, I'd better not."

"Come on out with it. Get along with you," he said. He had not the slightest suspicion, was even beginning to be thoroughly amused again.

"We've all been so thrilled," Moira began. "In fact we don't know if it will be announced some time upstairs. And if she does, you might send word down, won't you? I mean we'd hate to miss that, through being stuck in the Inn, wouldn't we, girls?"

"What is this?" he demanded, at his most assured.

"Why, your granddaughter's engagement, of course. Don't pretend you haven't kept that dark from us when . . .", but his face so clouded over that Moira bit her fat lower lip. "Oh, Mr Rock, have I said something awful?" she meekly asked.

"Never heard such arrant nonsense in all my born days," he blustered. "Why, Elizabeth's a sick woman."

"I'm frightfully sorry, Mr Rock," Moira apologised, while the others watched, mouths open.

"Just gossip," Mr Rock thundered, rather white. He was furious. "Not a word of truth."

"Yes, Mr Rock," they said.

"And if you catch anyone repeating what you've just told I'd be glad if you would deny it, once and for all," he continued, trembling. Then he struggled up. "I'm tired. I shall go back home to bed."

"Oh, Mr Rock, it isn't anything we've said, surely?"

"We live in an ungrateful world," he replied. "I'm sorry, but there are times I have had enough."

He stalked off with dignity, and, for a short while, left behind a silence.

Then someone said, "oh Gosh," and laughed.

Mr Rock came away in a flustered rage. He banged on the stair door and a new girl immediately opened. She, also, was chewing. He thrust straight past, shambled off uglily and at speed to where they danced.

A white bunch of children, stood in the doorway, fell open to let him through like a huge dropped flower losing petals on a path. Then the thunderous, swinging room met him smack in his thick lenses, the hundred couples sweating glassily open-eyed now it was late; each child that pulled at her partner's waist to speed it, to gyrate quicker, get much more hot, to keep pace.

Elizabeth saw him. She considered if she would hide, but knew it might be wicked. Accordingly she yelled, "See Gapa, darling." Even then, Sebastian, cheek to her mouth, barely caught what she said. In any case, he paid no heed.

At the same moment the old man had a dark sight of them both. He made such an immense gesture to summon Liz, he almost smashed off his nose the spectacles that reflected reeling chandeliers. "In a minute," her lips shaped back across the shattering valse. He did not take this in, misunderstood it for impertinence.

But when, inevitably as tumbled water, the dance delivered them over, two leaves that touch beneath a weir, caught in the eddies, till they were by his side, she awoke Sebastian as she drew off from the young man's arms. He said,

"Why hullo, sir?"

"We must go. We are not welcome," the grandfather told Liz.

"Hush, Gapa," she said. But he walked away, they followed, and a second time that group of children opened, reclosed behind the couple trailing after, having parted as another vast bloom might that, torn by a wind in summer, lies collectedly dying on crushed fallen leaves, to be divided by one and then two walkers, only for a strain of wind to reassemble it, to be rolled back complete on the path once more, at the whim of autumnal airs again.

The three left music.

"Hush," she at last repeated, when he could hear.

"There is no use. We are not wanted," Mr Rock announced, in a low voice.

"Why? What? I insist, has anything happened?"

"We need never have demeaned ourselves," he said.

"Oh do say," she wailed. "Was it dreadful? But Gapa, you're making me nervous."

"No. We have to get out, that is all," he explained. "D'you hear?" And came to a halt.

"Don't go now, sir," Sebastian cravenly protested.

They stood, a miserable trio in black cloth, in the dank dark; music at their heels.

"What?" Mr Rock demanded.

"I said why just yet?" Birt asked, pale and obstinate.

"I've seen enough," the old man proclaimed. "Miserable children that they are. Too much freedom here. Lack of control. All they have to do is chatter," he ended.

"Was it about your lectures, then?" she enquired.

"They're downright illnatured," he replied, at a tangent. "And inclining towards a dangerous mentality in which I shall take no lot or part. I hope a man of my years would know better. Come out."

"But Gapa, don't you think, I mean mightn't it all look rather odd if we simply just walked off? Oughtn't we at least to say goodbye, you must agree?"

"Everything comes if one can bide one's time," Mr Rock said, to ignore her. — He's certainly waited long enough, Sebastian considered.

"Whatever you say, of course," Elizabeth consented. "But we must at least offer thanks, surely? And I'm sure I don't know where Miss Edge's got to, do you Seb? I've a notion I haven't set eyes on her this last half hour, have you?"

"I don't like it, I don't like any of it. I'll shake the dust from my feet," the old man insisted. He was very upset.

"Yes, Gapa, but at the same time, after all, when we're merely uninvited, I mean you can't just come in and out as you please, can you? We should thank them. Don't you feel we'd better? Come on, of course you . . . you know you do."

"Well then, where is Miss Edge?"

"Powdering her nose to pretend she's what she's not," Sebastian brought out in his parson's voice, to cheer them.

"Well, you can't chase after her in there, however you feel," Elizabeth protested, almost contemptuously, to the old man.

"Might I make a small suggestion?" Sebastian proposed, his own self again at last. "Could Liz and I finish this dance? We'd keep our eyes skinned for the guv'nor all the time."

— The old man seemed visibly deflated, he thought. He wondered what had punctured him. No more than some second-hand foolery about Mary, he decided, satisfied Mr Rock was now in such a state of tired confusion that he would swallow, entire, any ancient guff the girls chose to hand out.

"They're fiends," Mr Rock protested all at once. "Fiends. Every single one."

"It's the girls are, Gapa. You listen to a woman," Elizabeth said of herself. "Miss Baker and Miss Edge aren't so bad."

He glared. But he was not going to admit he agreed.

"So you won't come?" he challenged.

"Why, of course. Anything you want," she answered in a rude, spoilt voice. "But one must say thank you, surely?" she wheedled.

— You know full well I'm afraid outside, alone in the dark, the old man accused Liz, in his heart. Her carelessness for his feelings made him tired and sick, twice over.

"Then I'll seek Miss Edge for myself," he replied, and stamped off towards the sanctum. Sebastian made as if to follow.

But Elizabeth put a hand on the young man's arm. "Let Gapa be," she said. "It's his pride. Don't I know, oh so well, so often. I can tell you what's happened. One of those horrid children, and they're out to simply ruin our lives, darling, yours and mine, has mentioned something about his lectures. But tonight I don't care, I'll just not allow anything to come between. Let's nip back for a minute. Oh, this heavenly tune. He'll cool off. He doesn't mean to go."

So they slipped back into the whirlpool to forget, to join in again. But she soon found she could not put Mr Rock out of mind, not yet, not all at once at all events.

Edge had retired for the treat of the day, a cigarette. Because one of these made her feel she had both feet up on mantelpiece, she usually kept herself to the one, night and day. It was delicious, so bad for her heart she even had the sensation she was drunk, and this evening, in the Sanctum, as a special, exceptional indulgence, she had started on another immediately the first was finished. And had no sooner done so before she heard leather shuffled outside. Upon which, while she could hardly get so far for that heavenly lassitude she inhaled, she went over to the door, pushed it wide, and came face to face with the sage.

Light was dark in the passage. He must have had difficulty to get along it to collect the rubber boots. And, as she swayed at his unexpected appearance, she found, without suprise, she now had nothing but pity for the old man.

She leant, a lightweight against a doorjamb, he brittle and heavy against the wall over on the side away from her.

"I'm off home," he announced abruptly, curious, for his part, to find he no longer seemed to hate the woman, all the go gone out of him.

"Why so soon, Mr Rock?" she asked, the butterfly gently fluttering in a vein at one of her temples, from the cigarette.

"Passed my bedtime," he lied.

"Won't you come in for a minute?" she invited, by the entrance to the Sanctum, then took another long draw at the weed to exquisitely drain more blood from her thin limbs.

He made no move however.

"Can't help but worry about my cat," he replied, at random. "If I don't get her in she'll be out all night."

"Ah yes," she said, "the splendid creature."

"She comes over here such a deal," he added, rather petulant.

"So sweet," the Principal agreed, still with no trace of irony, speaking as though from another existence. Mr Rock was amazed. He had never known the woman so amenable. And then he himself could hear so well, away from the music.

"And has your granddaughter enjoyed it?" Edge enquired. — Ah well, he thought, day is done, this is a truce.

"Liz? Of course she is older than the others."

"I saw her take the floor with Sebastian," the Principal said, in an approving voice.

"Those two are great friends," Mr Rock agreed, cautiously.

"I'd much like to have a little chat with you one day about that young man," Edge suggested, gentle, undangerously soft. The sage was not yet to be drawn, however.

"Yes?" he asked, to gain time.

With a languorous gesture, Edge took one more anaesthetising puff.

"I would really appreciate your advice on Sebastian," she said, in the laziest voice he had heard her use.

"You would?" he countered. He almost surrendered then.

"My dear sir," she murmured. "Need we be too formal the one night of our Founder's Day Ball? I don't really fancy so, do you?"

There was a pause. The old man struggled with a lump in his throat. Then he let go, gave way.

"She's all I have," he said, given over to self pity.

"She loves you," Miss Edge dispassionately stated.

Mr Rock swallowed twice.

"But I can't care for him, ma'am," he admitted, still as if in spite of himself.

"Nor me," the lady answered readily. They looked at each other with great understanding.

"I can't stomach parlour tricks," the old man elaborated, stronger.

"So curiously unwise," Edge agreed. "A word which is out of fashion nowadays," she added. "The girls don't seem to know the meaning, but there, I bless them," she ended.

"Liz has been ill . . ." Mr Rock began, mistaking the object, prepared to take offence at once.

"Why I declare, after all," she soothed him. "I spoke of the man, the tutor, the untutored tutor, please. I trust you would not think . . ."

"My deafness," he explained, to cover the slip.

"D'you ever have treatment?"

"What's the good. I am too old."

"Never that, good heavens no," she countered, through a film of weakness.

"Well, there you are. I have to lump it," he said, and smiled.

"You of all men," she murmured.

"I've been most fortunate in my life," he admitted, weak as water yet again. All this sympathy was so unexpected.

"Look, come in, please. I can't tell what we are standing here for, could you?" she invited. "As a matter of fact, if you will keep our little secret, we've some sherry in the cupboard, Hermione and I."

He suddenly wondered if she could be drunk. He was not to connect the cigarette with her mood, because he had never previously seen the lady smoke. Yet it seemed he should be on guard. Nevertheless this was now a remarkable opportunity, he had to admit. He made up his mind. "And I, for my part," he said, for better or worse weakly entering the sanctum, "would appreciate if I could have two words with you? A domestic matter."

"My dear Mr Rock I make it my rule never to interfere." This was on the assumption that he could only be referring to Elizabeth.

"To do with your students, ma'am," he announced.

"Ah yes."

"They talk so."

"They do indeed," she languidly assented.

"There must be limits, after all," Mr. Rock argued. She slumped quickly down, in an elegant attitude, to hold her cigarette like a wand.

"Where would you draw them?" she asked, at ease.

"Where would I draw the line?" he echoed, but without conviction. Then he pulled himself together. "Yet there must be human decency," he said in a firmer voice. "The give and take of a civilised community," he said. "Justice," he ended.

"Of course," she admitted. "Naturally, of course." This time with her first trace of malice which, however, was lost on him.

"Yes," he said, in a muddled way of the girls below. "I mean, they can go too far, can't they?" He was desperate.

"Yes?" she enquired.

There was a pause. Came again the lump in his throat. Once more he surrendered.

"I love her. She's all I have," he said. He could have sobbed.

Edge was so distant, so absent that she had forgotten Mary and Merode. What she could do, and did without the slightest sense of shock, was to ask herself if he had meant Moira all along.

"My dear," she murmured. "As time goes on one clings to what one has."

"She's all I have," he repeated, still about his granddaughter, secure in self pity.

"But is it wise, or fair, to foul the nest you have built?" she archly enquired.

"In what way?" he demanded, at a loss.

"Weren't you complaining of the child's behaviour?"

"Never," he protested, of his granddaughter.

She remembered she had not brought out the sherry, but let this go. She was too tired.

"Believe me, I think sometimes you are inclined to misjudge us, Mr Rock," she said. "We have eyes in our grey heads. And we prize your friendship for the child," she lied, a white lie.

"I don't follow," he said.

"Why, Moira of course," she patiently explained.

"We are at cross purposes, ma'am," he concluded with pride, suddenly and finally disgusted. Then he noticed that she had finished the cigarette. He offered another from his case, as a matter of course. — She knew it to be madness, but how was she to refuse? So she lit up, as though this were the last action she would have strength for in life.

"We are just two old women trying our best, but we do have eyes in our heads," she repeated, obstinately gentle, unaware of the effect she had produced.

"Well, I don't think this Birt is up to any good here, either," the old man said, angry and tart. He had gone back to the doorway, so as to make good his escape, if need be, at a moment's notice.

"Where are you? I can't tell," she demanded.

— And only an hour since, she would insist she had no trouble at all with her eyes, joyfully he reminded himself.

"Are you sure you feel all right?" he asked, after he had narrowly regarded her. He almost hoped she would fall sideways, flat on an ear.

"I'll let you into a little secret," she said. "It's these smokes. My one small indulgence. They make me rather giddy. But it's true I had a nasty turn this afternoon."

"How was that, ma'am?"

"Where on earth have you got to, man?"

"Here," he replied, and came forward a second time, betrayed by curiosity, only to sit, without thinking, in her own place, behind the great desk of office.

She did not notice.

There was a pause.

"You had a fainting spell?" he hazarded. He had long since learned all about it. He thought,—perhaps she drinks all day.

"Oh, I've forgotten. Don't bother me," she said.

"Was it about this sorry disappearance, ma'am?" he persisted.

"Whose? Why, we've got to the bottom of Mary and Merode," she lied. "That did not take long. Absolutely nothing in their storm in a little teacup."

"Thank God," he said, anxious, of course, to learn about Mary.

"Why?" she dreamily wanted to know. "Can these children truly mean much to you?"

"Whatever occurs round this great place affects us all," he covered himself.

"Just one or two small points still to clear up," she emended, for, truth to say, she was superstitiously ashamed. "Believe me, Mr Rock, but now and again, at the end of a long day, I do get sick and tired of these girls. At their age they are terribly full of themselves, terribly."

Edge was being so revealing that Mr Rock once more decided he could not lose a minute of her present mood.

"Have you ever considered the fellow Adams?" he enquired.

"I had to see him this forenoon. Yes?"

"I thought he was hardly himself when we last met." — Like someone else I could mention, he added under his breath.

"I couldn't get sense out of him at all. But I meet so many, so many," she said. "There was a Mrs Manley," she added.

"It seemed as though he had something on his mind."

"Yes?" she airily replied.

"A widower who lives alone in his cottage," Mr Rock suggested.

There was a pause.

"Why, so he does," she said. Mr Rock could see the grey light begin to dawn within the woman.

"It had just occurred to me, that's all," he said.

"And so he does," she repeated, but not with quite the conviction for which he listened in her voice.

A silence fell.

"Then tell me," she demanded, back to her more usual tones. "We do so value your counsel." — And how often have you asked it, he commented to himself? "What would you propose?" she insinuated.

"I'm only an old fellow who's well passed his bedtime." Mr Rock countered. He had gone far enough. Yet he found that, if one tried, one could forgive this woman, and he wanted to bring the conversation back to himself.

"Oh, I'm tired too, deathly so," she idly agreed.

"I'm older than you. I'm older," he repeated.

She let this pass.

"I'm not much longer for this world," he said, on his dignity.

"Don't talk like that, Mr Rock, please. Tonight of all nights."

He sat, looking straight ahead.

"They will fiddle faddle so about themselves," Miss Edge went on, about the children. "It makes for such a deal of bother. I get no help from Baker, none at all," she ended.

He said no word.

"Strictly in confidence we are not certain of much about Mary yet," she went on, again in a most languid voice. "But we shall be tomorrow. I've had experience. Believe me. They will worry over trifles, but it all comes out in the wash, in the end."

He stayed silent. Contemplating his own death with disinterest, he did not catch what she said.

For her part, she felt so queer she hardly knew what she was doing, but found herself, somehow, committed to the following, — as though on top of a hill in a dream on a bicycle with no brakes. "Mr Rock," she began, — then experienced a last titter, or wobble, before it was too late. She threw the cigarette away which had been burning her forefingers. She missed the fireplace. Falling on a State Kidderminster rug it began to glow, unnoticed. "Mr Rock," she said, a second time. For she knew now she could not go back. "You really should have someone to take good care of you. Marry again," she said.

At this she giggled, once. — What a desperate expedient to gain possession of a cottage, she laughed to herself, almost completely out of control. She must be mad. But then, oh well, what harm was there? Things would all come out in the wash, be utterly forgotten come daylight.

"Why yes, yes," he said from the vast distance of his final, cold preoccupation, not having taken in the drift.

She dreamily excused herself to herself by thinking that, of course, he would not listen any more than he did now, which was not at all. This only proved, so she thought, that the kindest was to pack him off forthwith to an Academy of Science.

"I don't believe you bother with me," she rallied.

"How is that, then?" he asked, coming back to earth.

"I said, you must marry again." She spoke out with a slow simper which allowed of no misinterpretation. This, he at last saw, was an offer, and unconditional at that. He took it in his stride as entirely understandable; unthinkable of course, but not, in her pitiable circumstances, in the least surprising. He proudly ignored it.

At the same time he wished to let her down lightly, the safer course. He cast about him how to encompass this. And almost at once proceeded to discuss his health.

"I've been quite well the last few years. But there's none can dodge Father Time. Yet I sleep remarkably sound. I take care, naturally. Regular exercise every day, fetching Daisy's swill and so forth. No, it's just anno domini."

She despised him for not, as she thought, having heard. Or had he?

"What age are you really, then?" she asked.

"Seventy six next month."

"You don't look it," she lied. For she considered he looked more. — Too old, too old, she admitted, in another part of her head. But now it was up to him, she knew.

"Not bad for an old fellow," he said, pleased.

Oh, she must have lost her sanity just then, she thought, realising he did not intend to take her up. She would never, as long as she lived, ever indulge in so many cigarettes again. But was that, could it be, a smell of burning? And what had he meant, when all was said, discussing his health as he had?

"I keep a deal healthier, even, than she does," he remarked of Elizabeth.

"The child looks ever so much better," Edge agreed, dreamily, but with anguish. She still thought he referred to Moira. In a dazed state, she began to imagine larger and longer flames, as that smell came through.

"I am tired. I should go home," he said.

"In that case, goodnight," Edge answered from her deep chair, coldly, more of an enemy than ever. She had finally decided there would be nothing. "Look after yourself," she added with tired venom, while he dragged his body out of the Principal's rightful place, to take leave. She did not, of course, get to her feet when the old man came over. He, for his part, ignored the taste of burning. "Goodbye," she ended, gave him a slack hand. He turned his back to leave.

"Gracious," she remarked, as though to make conversation, having seen the cigarette at last. "Quite a blaze," she said. rose up in no haste, and stamped it well out.

Either he did not catch that, or could not be bothered, but he just stepped outside, closing the door behind him.

In the passage he gave one short, sharp laugh.

She heard.

5

NATHANAEL WEST *and* CYRIL CONNOLLY

If Adams and Eliot saw community breaking down, Nathanael West saw the next stage: nightmare mobs, public relations truth, celebrity souls, and nothing inside but chagrin and desolation and hysteria.

And then in 1945, there appeared a casebook called The Unquiet Grave, *as intelligent and undissembling a dossier on the soul, limits, and luck of twentieth-century man as anyone has published yet.*

from *The Day of the Locust*

[1939]

NATHANAEL WEST

When Tod reached the street, he saw a dozen great violet shafts of light moving across the evening sky in wide crazy sweeps. Whenever one of the fiery columns reached the lowest point of its arc, it lit for a moment the rose-colored domes and delicate minarets of Kahn's Persian Palace Theatre. The purpose of this display was to signal the world première of a new picture.

Turning his back on the searchlights, he started in the opposite direction, toward Homer's place. Before he had gone very far, he saw a clock that read a quarter past six and changed his mind about going back just yet. He might as well let the poor fellow sleep for another hour and kill some time by looking at the crowds.

When still a block from the theatre, he saw an enormous electric sign that hung over the middle of the street. In letters ten feet high he read that —

"MR. KAHN A PLEASURE DOME DECREED"

Although it was still several hours before the celebrities would arrive, thousands of people had already gathered. They stood facing the theatre with their backs toward the gutter in a thick line hundreds of feet long. A big squad of policemen was trying to keep a lane open between the front rank of the crowd and the façade of the theatre.

Tod entered the lane while the policeman guarding it was busy with a woman whose parcel had torn open, dropping oranges all over the place. Another policeman shouted for him to get the hell across the street, but he took a chance and kept going. They had enough to do without chasing him. He noticed how worried they looked and how careful they tried to be. If they had to arrest someone, they joked good-naturedly with the culprit, making light of it until they got him around the corner, then they whaled him with their clubs. Only so long as the man was actually part of the crowd did they have to be gentle.

Tod had walked only a short distance along the narrow lane when he began to get frightened. People shouted, commenting on his hat, his carriage, and his clothing. There was a continuous roar of catcalls, laughter and yells, pierced occasionally by a scream. The scream was usually followed by a sudden movement in the dense mass and part of it would surge forward wherever the police line was weakest. As soon as that part was rammed back, the bulge would pop out somewhere else.

The police force would have to be doubled when the stars started to arrive. At the sight of their heroes and heroines, the crowd would turn demoniac. Some little gesture, either too pleasing or too offensive, would start it moving and then nothing but machine guns would stop it. Individually the purpose of its members might simply be to get a souvenir, but collectively it would grab and rend.

A young man with a portable microphone was describing the scene. His rapid, hysterical voice was like that of a revivalist preacher whipping his congregation toward the ecstasy of fits.

"What a crowd, folks! What a crowd! There must be ten thousand excited, screaming fans outside Kahn's Persian tonight. The police can't hold them. Here, listen to them roar."

He held the microphone out and those near it obligingly roared for him.

"Did you hear it? It's a bedlam, folks. A veritable bedlam! What excitement! Of all the premières I've attended, this is the most . . . the most . . . stupendous, folks. Can the police hold them? Can they? It doesn't look so, folks . . . ."

Another squad of police came charging up. The sergeant pleaded with the announcer to stand further back so the people couldn't hear him. His men threw themselves at the crowd. It allowed itself to be hustled and shoved out of habit and because it lacked an objective. It tolerated the police, just as a bull elephant does when he allows a small boy to drive him with a light stick.

Tod could see very few people who looked tough, nor could he see any working men. The crowd was made up of the lower middle classes, every other person one of his torchbearers.

Just as he came near the end of the lane, it closed in front of him with a heave, and he had to fight his way through. Someone knocked his hat off and when he stooped to pick it up, someone kicked him. He whirled around angrily and found himself surrounded by people who were laughing at him. He knew enough to laugh with them. The crowd became sympathetic. A stout woman slapped him on the back, while a man handed him his hat, first brushing it carefully with his sleeve. Still another man shouted for a way to be cleared.

By a great deal of pushing and squirming, always trying to look as though he were enjoying himself, Tod finally managed to break into the open. After rearranging his clothes, he went over to a parking lot and sat down on the low retaining wall that ran along the front of it.

New groups, whole families, kept arriving. He could see a change come over them as soon as they had become part of the crowd. Until they reached the line, they looked difficult, almost furtive, but the moment they had become part of it, they turned arrogant and pugnacious. It was a mistake to think them harmless curiosity seekers. They were savage and bitter, especially the middle-aged and the old, and had been made so by boredom and disappointment.

All their lives they had slaved at some kind of dull, heavy labor, behind desks and counters, in the fields and at tedious machines of all sorts, saving their pennies and dreaming of the leisure that would be theirs when they had enough. Finally that day came. They could draw a weekly income of ten or fifteen dollars. Where else should they go but California, the land of sunshine and oranges?

Once there, they discover that sunshine isn't enough. They get tired of oranges, even of avocado pears and passion fruit. Nothing happens. They don't know what to do with their time. They haven't the mental equipment for leisure, the money nor the physical equipment for pleasure. Did they slave so long just to go to an occasional Iowa picnic? What else is there? They watch the waves come in at Venice. There wasn't any ocean where most of them came from, but after you've seen one wave, you've seen them all. The same is true of the airplanes at Glendale. If only a plane would crash once in a while so that they could watch the passengers being consumed in a "holocaust of flame," as the newspapers put it. But the planes never crash.

Their boredom becomes more and more terrible. They realize that they've been tricked and burn with resentment. Every day of their lives they read the newspapers and went to the movies. Both fed them on lynchings, murder, sex crimes, explosions, wrecks, love nests, fires, miracles, revolutions, war. This daily diet made sophisticates of them. The sun is a joke. Oranges can't titillate their jaded palates. Nothing can ever be violent enough to make taut their slack minds and bodies. They have been cheated and betrayed. They have slaved and saved for nothing.

Tod stood up. During the ten minutes he had been sitting on the wall, the crowd had grown thirty feet and he was afraid that his escape might be cut off if he loitered much longer. He crossed to the other side of the street and started back.

He was trying to figure what to do if he were unable to wake Homer when, suddenly he saw his head bobbing above the crowd. He hurried toward him. From his appearance, it was evident that there was something definitely wrong.

Homer walked more than ever like a badly made automaton and his features were set in a rigid, mechanical grin. He had his trousers on over his nightgown and part of it hung out of his open fly. In both of his hands were suitcases. With each step, he lurched to one side then the other, using the suitcases for balance weights.

Tod stopped directly in front of him, blocking his way.

"Where're you going?"

"Wayneville," he replied, using an extraordinary amount of jaw movement to get out this single word.

"That's fine. But you can't walk to the station from here. It's in Los Angeles."

Homer tried to get around him, but he caught his arm.

"We'll get a taxi. I'll go with you."

The cabs were all being routed around the block because of the preview. He explained this to Homer and tried to get him to walk to the corner.

"Come on, we're sure to get one on the next street."

Once Tod got him into a cab, he intended to tell the driver to go to the nearest hospital. But Homer wouldn't budge, no matter how hard he yanked and pleaded. People stopped to watch them, others turned their heads curiously. He decided to leave him and get a cab.

"I'll come right back," he said.

He couldn't tell from either Homer's eyes or expression whether he heard, for they both were empty of everything, even annoyance. At the corner he looked around and saw that Homer had started to cross the street, moving blindly. Brakes screeched and twice he was almost run over, but he didn't swerve or hurry. He moved in a straight diagonal. When he reached the other curb, he tried to get on the sidewalk at a point where the crowd was very thick and was shoved violently back. He made another attempt and this time a policeman grabbed him by the back of the neck and hustled him to the end of the line. When the policeman let go of him, he kept on walking as though nothing had happened.

Tod tried to get over to him, but was unable to cross until the traffic lights changed. When he reached the other side, he found Homer sitting on a bench, fifty or sixty feet from the outskirts of the crowd.

He put his arm around Homer's shoulder and suggested that they walk a few blocks further. When Homer didn't answer, he reached over to pick up one of the valises. Homer held on to it.

"I'll carry it for you," he said, tugging gently.

"Thief!"

Before Homer could repeat the shout, he jumped away. It would be extremely embarrassing if Homer shouted thief in front of a cop. He thought of phoning for an ambulance. But then, after all, how could he be sure that Homer was crazy? He was sitting quietly on the bench, minding his own business.

Tod decided to wait, then try again to get him into a cab. The crowd was growing in size all the time, but it would be at least half an hour before it over-ran the bench. Before that happened, he would think of some plan. He moved a short distance away and stood with his back to a store window so that he could watch Homer without attracting attention.

About ten feet from where Homer was sitting grew a large eucalyptus tree and behind the trunk of the tree was a little boy. Tod saw him peer around it with great caution, then suddenly jerk his head back. A minute later he repeated the maneuver. At first Tod thought he was playing hide and seek, then noticed that he had a string in his hand which was attached to an old purse that lay in front of Homer's bench. Every once in a while the child would jerk the string, making the purse hop like a sluggish toad. Its torn lining hung from its iron mouth like a furry tongue and a few uncertain flies hovered over it.

Tod knew the game the child was playing. He used to play it himself when he was small. If Homer reached to pick up the purse, thinking there was money in it, he would yank it away and scream with laughter.

When Tod went over to the tree, he was surprised to discover that it was Adore Loomis, the kid who lived across the street from Homer. Tod tried to chase him, but he dodged around the tree, thumbing his nose. He gave up and went back to his original position. The moment he left, Adore got busy with his purse again. Homer wasn't paying any attention to the child, so Tod decided to let him alone.

Mrs. Loomis must be somewhere in the crowd, he thought. Tonight when she found Adore, she would give him a hiding. He had torn the pocket of his jacket and his Buster Brown collar was smeared with grease.

Adore had a nasty temper. The completeness with which Homer ignored both him and his pocketbook made him frantic. He gave up dancing it at the end of the string and approached the bench on tiptoes, making ferocious faces, yet ready to run at Homer's first move. He stopped when about four feet away and stuck his tongue out. Homer ignored him. He took another step forward and ran through a series of insulting gestures.

If Tod had known that the boy held a stone in his hand, he would have interfered. But he felt sure that Homer wouldn't hurt the child and was waiting to see if he wouldn't move because of his pestering. When Adore raised his arm, it was too late. The stone hit Homer in the face. The boy turned to flee, but tripped and fell. Before he could scramble away, Homer landed on his back with both feet, then jumped again.

Tod yelled for him to stop and tried to yank him away. He shoved Tod and went on using his heels. Tod hit him as hard as he could, first in the belly, then in the face. He ignored the blows and continued to stamp on the boy. Tod hit him again and again, then threw both arms around him and tried to pull him off. He couldn't budge him. He was like a stone column.

The next thing Tod knew, he was torn loose from Homer and sent to his knees by a blow in the back of the head that spun him sideways. The crowd in front of the theatre had charged. He was surrounded by churning legs and feet. He pulled himself erect by grabbing a man's coat, then let himself be carried along backwards in a long, curving swoop. He saw Homer rise above the mass for a moment, shoved against the sky, his jaw hanging as though he wanted to scream but couldn't. A hand reached up and caught him by his open mouth and pulled him forward and down.

There was another dizzy rush. Tod closed his eyes and fought to keep upright. He was jostled about in a hacking cross surf of shoulders and backs, carried rapidly in one direction and then in the opposite. He kept pushing and hitting out at the people around him, trying to face in the direction he was going. Being carried backwards terrified him.

Using the eucalyptus tree as a landmark, he tried to work toward it by slipping sideways against the tide, pushing hard when carried away from it and riding the current when it moved toward his objective. He was within only a few feet of the tree when a sudden, driving rush carried him far past it. He struggled desperately for a moment, then gave up and let himself be swept along. He was the spearhead of a flying wedge when it collided with a mass going in the opposite direction. The impact turned him around. As the two forces ground against each other, he was turned again and again, like a grain between millstones. This didn't stop until he became part of the opposing force. The pressure continued to increase until he thought he must collapse. He was slowly being pushed into the air. Although relief for his cracking ribs could be gotten by continuing to rise, he fought to keep his feet on the ground. Not being able to touch was an even more dreadful sensation than being carried backwards.

There was another rush, shorter this time, and he found himself in a dead spot where the pressure was less and equal. He became conscious of a terrible pain in his left leg, just above the ankle, and tried to work it into a more comfortable position. He couldn't turn his body, but managed to get his head around. A very skinny boy, wearing a Western Union cap, had his back wedged against his shoulder. The pain continued to grow and his whole leg as high as the groin throbbed. He finally got his left arm free and took the back of the boy's neck in his fingers. He twisted as hard as he could. The boy began to jump up and down in his clothes. He managed to straighten his elbow, by pushing at the back of the boy's head, and so turn halfway around and free his leg. The pain didn't grow less.

There was another wild surge forward that ended in another dead spot. He now faced a young girl who was sobbing steadily. Her silk print dress had been torn down the front and her tiny brassiere hung from one strap. He tried by pressing back to give her room, but she moved with him every time he moved. Now and then, she would jerk violently and he wondered if she was going to have a fit. One of her thighs was between his legs. He struggled to get free of her, but she clung to him, moving with him and pressing against him.

She turned her head and said, "Stop, stop," to someone behind her.

He saw what the trouble was. An old man, wearing a Panama hat and horn-rimmed glasses, was hugging her. He had one of his hands inside her dress and was biting her neck.

Tod freed his right arm with a heave, reached over the girl and brought his fist down on the man's head. He couldn't hit very hard but managed to knock the man's hat off, also his glasses. The man tried to bury his face in the girl's shoulder, but Tod grabbed one of his ears and yanked. They started to move again. Tod held on to the ear as long as he could hoping that it would come away in his hand. The girl managed to twist under his arm. A piece of her dress tore, but she was free of her attacker.

Another spasm passed through the mob and he was carried toward the curb. He fought toward a lamp-post, but he was swept by before he could grasp it. He saw another man catch the girl with the torn dress. She screamed for help. He tried to get to her, but was carried in the opposite direction. This rush also ended in a dead spot. Here his neighbors were all shorter than he was. He turned his head upward toward the sky and tried to pull some fresh air into his aching lungs, but it was all heavily tainted with sweat.

In this part of the mob no one was hysterical. In fact, most of the people seemed to be enjoying themselves. Near him was a stout woman with a man pressing hard against her from in front. His chin was on her shoulder, and his arms were around her. She paid no attention to him and went on talking to the woman at her side.

"The first thing I knew," Tod heard her say, "there was a rush and I was in the middle."

"Yeah. Somebody hollered, 'Here comes Gary Cooper,' and then wham!"

"That ain't it," said a little man wearing a cloth cap and pullover sweater. "This is a riot you're in."

"Yeah," said a third woman, whose snaky gray hair was hanging over her face and shoulders. "A pervert attacked a child."

"He ought to be lynched."

Everybody agreed vehemently.

"I come from St. Louis," announced the stout woman, "and we had one of them pervert fellers in our neighborhood once. He ripped up a girl with a pair of scissors."

"He must have been crazy," said the man in the cap. "What kind of fun is that?"

Everybody laughed. The stout woman spoke to the man who was hugging her.

"Hey, you," she said. "I ain't no pillow."

The man smiled beatifically but didn't move. She laughed, making no effort to get out of his embrace.

"A fresh guy," she said.

The other woman laughed.

"Yeah," she said, "this is a regular free-for-all."

The man in the cap and sweater thought there was another laugh in his comment about the pervert.

"Ripping up a girl with scissors. That's the wrong tool."

He was right. They laughed even louder than the first time.

"You'd a done it different, eh, kid?" said a young man with a kidney-shaped head and waxed mustaches.

The two women laughed. This encouraged the man in the cap and he reached over and pinched the stout woman's friend. She squealed.

"Lay off that," she said good-naturedly.

"I was shoved," he said.

An ambulance siren screamed in the street. Its wailing moan started the crowd moving again and Tod was carried along in a slow, steady push. He closed his eyes and tried to protect his throbbing leg. This time, when the movement ended, he found himself with his back to the theatre wall. He kept his eyes closed and stood on his good leg. After what seemed like hours, the pack began to loosen and move again with a churning motion. It gathered momentum and rushed. He rode it until he was slammed against the base of an iron rail which fenced the driveway of the theatre from the street. He had the wind knocked out of him by the impact, but managed to cling to the rail. He held on desperately, fighting to keep from being sucked back. A woman caught him around the waist and tried to hang on. She was sobbing rhythmically. Tod felt his fingers slipping from the rail and kicked backwards as hard as he could. The woman let go.

Despite the agony in his leg, he was able to think clearly about his picture, "The Burning of Los Angeles." After his quarrel with Faye, he had worked on it continually to escape tormenting himself, and the way to it in his mind had become almost automatic.

As he stood on his good leg, clinging desperately to the iron rail, he could see all the rough charcoal strokes with which he had blocked it out on the big canvas. Across the top, parallel with the frame, he had drawn the burning city, a great bonfire of architectural styles, ranging from Egyptian to Cape Cod colonial. Through the center, winding from left to right, was a long hill street and down it, spilling into the middle foreground, came the mob carrying baseball bats and torches. For the faces of its members, he was using the innumerable sketches he had made of the people who come to California to die; the cultists of all sorts, economic as well as religious, the wave, airplane, funeral and preview watchers — all those poor devils who can only be stirred by the promise of miracles and then only to violence. A super "Dr. Know-All Pierce-All" had made the necessary promise and they were marching behind his banner in a great united front of screwballs and screwboxes to purify the land. No longer bored, they sang and danced joyously in the red light of the flames.

In the lower foreground, men and women fled wildly before the vanguard of the crusading mob. Among them were Faye, Harry, Homer, Claude and himself. Faye ran proudly, throwing her knees high. Harry stumbled along behind her, holding on to his beloved derby hat with both hands. Homer seemed to be falling out of the canvas, his face half-asleep, his big hands clawing the air in anguished pantomime. Claude turned his head as he ran to thumb his nose at his pursuers. Tod himself picked up a small stone to throw before continuing his flight.

He had almost forgotten both his legs and his predicament, and to make his escape still more complete he stood on a chair and worked at the flames in an upper corner of the canvas, modeling the tongues of fire so that they licked even more avidly at a corinthian column that held up the palmleaf roof of a nutburger stand.

He had finished one flame and was starting on another when he was brought back by someone shouting in his ear. He opened his eyes and saw a policeman trying to reach him from behind the rail to which he was clinging. He let go with his left hand and raised his arm. The policeman caught him by the wrist, but couldn't lift him. Tod was afraid to let go until another man came to aid the policeman and caught him by the back of his jacket. He let go of the rail and they hauled him up and over it.

When they saw that he couldn't stand, they let him down easily to the ground. He was in the theatre driveway. On the curb next to him sat a woman crying into her skirt. Along the wall were groups of other disheveled people. At the end of the driveway was an ambulance. A policeman asked him if he wanted to go to the hospital. He shook his head no. He then offered him a lift home. Tod had the presence of mind to give Claude's address.

He was carried through the exit to the back street and lifted into a police car. The siren began to scream and at first he thought he was making the noise himself. He felt his lips with his hands. They were clamped tight. He knew then it was the siren. For some reason this made him laugh and he began to imitate the siren as loud as he could.

Ecce Gubernator

from *The Unquiet Grave*

[1945]

CYRIL CONNOLLY

The more books we read, the clearer it becomes that the true function of a writer is to produce a masterpiece and that no other task is of any consequence. Obvious though this should be, how few writers will admit it, or having drawn the conclusion, will be prepared to lay aside the piece of iridescent mediocrity on which they have embarked! Writers always hope that their next book is going to be·their best, and will not acknowledge that they are prevented by their present way of life from ever creating anything different.

Every excursion into journalism, broadcasting, propaganda and writing for the films, however grandiose, will be doomed to disappointment. To put our best into these is another folly, since thereby we condemn good ideas as well as bad to oblivion. It is in the nature of such work not to last, and it should never be undertaken. Writers engrossed in any literary task which is not an assault on perfection are their own dupes and, unless these self-flatterers are content to dismiss such activity as their contribution to the war effort, they might as well be peeling potatoes.

.   .   .

What is a masterpiece? Let me name a few. The *Odes* and *Epistles* of Horace, the *Eclogues* and *Georgics* of Virgil, the *Testament* of Villon, the Essays of Montaigne, the Fables of La Fontaine, the Maxims of La Rochefoucauld and La Bruyère, the *Fleurs du Mal* and Intimate Journals of Baudelaire, the Poems of Pope and Leopardi, the *Illuminations* of Rimbaud, and Byron's *Don Juan*.

Such a catalogue reveals the maker. What is common in thought to these twelve writers? Love of life and nature; lack of belief in the idea of progress; interest in, mingled with contempt for humanity. All are what Palinurus has been called by a critic: "Earthbound"! Yet all are more adult and less romantic than he. These masterpieces then, (mostly high peaks of the secondary range), reflect either what he would like to be, or a self to which he is afraid of confessing. He would like to have written *Les Fleurs du Mal* or the *Saison en Enfer* without being Rimbaud or Baudelaire, that is without undergoing their mental suffering and without being diseased and poor.

In feeling, these works of art contain the maximum of emotion compatible with a classical sense of form.

Observe how they are written; many are short and compressed, fruit of reflective and contemplative natures, prose or poetry of great formal beauty and economy of phrase. There are no novels, plays or biographies included in the list and the poetry is of a kind which speculates about life. They have been chosen by one who most values the art which is distilled and crystallized out of a lucid, curious and passionate imagination. All these writers enjoy something in common, "jusqu'au sombre plaisir d'un cœur mélancolique": a sense of perfection and a faith in human dignity, combined with a tragic apprehending of our mortal situation, and our nearness to the Abyss.

We can deduce then that the compiler should set himself to write after these models. However unfavourable the conditions for the birth of a classic, he can at least attempt to work at the same level of intention as the Sacred Twelve. Spiritualize the Earthbound, Palinurus, and don't aim too high!

What follow are the doubts and reflections of a year, a word-cycle in three or four rhythms; art, love, nature and religion: an experiment in self-dismantling, a search for the obstruction which is blocking the flow from the well and whereby the name of Palinurus is becoming an archetype of frustration.

As we grow older we discover that what seemed at the time an absorbing interest or preoccupation which we had taken up and thrown over, was in reality an appetite or passion which had swept over us and passed on, until at last we come to see that our life has no more continuity than a pool in the rocks filled by the tide with foam and flotsam and then emptied. Nothing remains of the self but the sediment which this flux deposits; ambergris valuable only to those who know its use.

.   .   .

As we grow older, in fact, we discover that the lives of most human beings are worthless except in so far as they contribute to the enrichment and emancipation of the spirit. However attractive in our youth the animal graces may seem, if by our maturity they have not led us to emend one character in the corrupt text of existence, then our time has been wasted. No one over thirty-five is worth meeting who has not something to teach us, — something more than we could learn by ourselves, from a book.

.   .   .

There is no pain equal to that which two lovers can inflict on one another. This should be made clear to all who contemplate such a union. The avoidance of this pain is the beginning of wisdom, for it is strong enough to contaminate the rest of our lives: and since it can be minimized by obeying a few simple rules, rules which approximate to Christian marriage, they provide, even to the unbeliever, its *de facto* justification. It is when we begin to hurt those whom we love that the guilt with which we are born becomes intolerable, and since all those whom we love intensely and continuously grow part of us, and as we hate ourselves in them, so we torture ourselves and them together.

The object of Loving is a release from Love. We achieve this through a series of unfortunate love affairs or, without a death-rattle, through one that is happy.

Complete physical union between two people is the rarest sensation which life can provide — and yet not quite real, for it stops when the telephone rings. Such a passion can be maintained at full strength only by the admixture of more unhappiness (jealousy, rows, renunciation) or more and more artificiality (alcohol and other technical illusions). Who escapes this heaven may never have lived, who exists for it alone is soon extinguished.

We pay for vice by the knowledge that we are wicked: we pay for pleasure when we find out, too late, that we are disappearing.

.   .   .

Beneath a mask of selfish tranquillity nothing exists except bitterness and boredom. I am one of those whom suffering has made empty and frivolous: each night in my dreams I pull the scab off a wound; each day, vacuous and habit-ridden, I help it re-form.

When I contemplate the accumulation of guilt and remorse which, like a garbage-can, I carry through life, and which is fed not only by the lightest action but by the most harmless pleasure, I feel Man to be of all living things the most biologically incompetent and ill-organized. Why has he acquired a seventy-years' life-span only to poison it incurably by the mere being of himself? Why has he thrown Conscience, like a dead rat, to putrefy in the well?

It is no answer to say that we are meant to rid ourselves of the self: religions like Christianity and Buddhism are desperate stratagems of failure, the failure of men to be men. As escapes from the problem, as flights from guilt, they may be welcome, but they cannot turn out to be the revelation of our destiny. What should we think of dogs' monasteries, hermit cats, vegetarian tigers? Of birds who tore off their wings or bulls weeping with remorse? Surely it is in our nature to realize ourselves, yet there remains the deadly flaw by which we feel most guilty when we are most confidently human and are most to be pitied when most successful. Is this because Christianity is true? Or is it an ungrained effect of propaganda for the under-dog? When did the ego begin to stink? Those of us who were brought up as Christians and have lost our faith have retained the sense of sin without the saving belief in redemption. This poisons our thought and so paralyses us in action.

Communism is the new religion which denies original sin, though seldom do we meet a real Communist who seems either complete or happy. And yet Original Sin, what rubbish! The Expulsion from Eden is an act of vindictive womanish spite; the Fall of Man, as recounted in the Bible, comes nearer to the Fall of God.

When I consider what I believe, which I can do only by proceeding from what I do not, I seem in a minority of one, — and yet I know that there are thousands like me: Liberals without a belief in progress, Democrats who despise their fellow-men, Pagans who must live by Christian morals, Intellectuals who cannot find the intellect sufficient, — unsatisfied Materialists, we are as common as clay.

But there can be no going back to Christianity nor can I inhabit an edifice of truth which seems built upon a base of falsehood. The contradictions will out; hence the terrible record of the Church, which "brings not peace, but a sword" — her persecutions, her cupidity, her hypocrisy, her reaction. These are inherent in her nature as a jealous, worldly, and dogmatic body; and because of these the Church, whenever strong enough to do so, has always belied her spiritual claims.

.   .   .

For me success in life means survival. I believe that a ripe old age is nature's reward to those who have grasped her secret. I do not wish to die young or mad. The true pattern of existence can best be studied in a long life like Goethe's, — a life of reason interrupted at intervals by emotional outbursts, displacements, passions, follies. In youth the life of reason is not in itself sufficient; afterwards the life of emotion, except for short periods, becomes unbearable.

Sometimes at night I get a feeling of claustrophobia; of being smothered by my own personality, of choking through being in the world. During these moments the universe seems a prison wherein I lie fettered by the chains of my senses and blinded through being myself.

It is like being pinned underneath the hull of a capsized boat, yet being afraid to dive deeper and get clear. In those moments it seems that there must be a way out, and that through sloughing off the personality alone can it be taken.

We love but once, for once only are we perfectly equipped for loving: we may appear to ourselves to be as much in love at other times — so will a day in early September, though it be six hours shorter, seem as hot as one in June. And on how that first true love-affair will shape depends the pattern of our lives.

Two fears alternate in marriage, of loneliness and of bondage. The dread of loneliness being keener than the fear of bondage, we get married. For one person who fears being thus tied there are four who dread being set free. Yet the love of liberty is a noble passion and one to which most married people secretly aspire, — in moments when they are not neurotically dependent — but by then it is too late; the ox does not become a bull, nor the hen a falcon.

The fear of loneliness can be overcome, for it springs from weakness; human beings are intended to be free, and to be free is to be lonely, but the fear of bondage is the apprehension of a real danger, and so I find it all the more pathetic to watch young men and beautiful girls taking refuge in marriage from an imaginary danger, a sad loss to their friends and a sore trial to each other. First love is the one most worth having, yet the best marriage is often the second, for we should marry only when the desire for freedom be spent; not till then does a man know whether he is the kind who can settle down. The most tragic breakings-up are of those couples who have married young and who have enjoyed seven years of happiness, after which the banked fires of passion and independence explode — and without knowing why, for they still love each other, they set about accomplishing their common destruction.

When a love-affair is broken off, the heaviest blow is to the vanity of the one who is left. It is therefore reasonable to assume that, when a love-affair is beginning, the greatest source of satisfaction is also to the vanity. The first signs of a mutual attraction will induce even the inconsolable to live in the present.

Cracking tawny nuts, looking out at the tawny planes with their dappled festoons of yellow and green, reading the Tao Tê Ching by a log fire: such is the wisdom of October: autumn bliss; the equinoctial study of religions.

Jesus was a petulant man: his malediction on the barren fig tree was sheer spite, his attitude towards the Pharisees one of paranoiac wrath. He speaks of them as Hitler of the men who made the League of Nations. 'Those parables which all end "There shall be wailing and gnashing of teeth," — what a tone for a Redeemer! I find such incidents as the violence used on the man without a wedding garment or the praise of usury in the parable of the talents to be understandable only as outbursts of arrogance and bad temper. Though an inspired genius as a mystic and ethical reformer, Jesus is also completely a Jew; he does not wish to break away from the Jewish framework of the Old Testament, the Law and the Prophets, but to enrich their ethical content; consequently he imitates the intolerance of the Pharisees whom he condemns ("O ye generation of vipers") and maintains the avenging role of God the Father which he claims to have superseded.

Impression of Jesus Christ after re-reading the Gospels: He *thought* he was the son of God, he disliked his parents, was a prig, a high-spirited and serious young man (where was he, what was he doing, between the ages of twelve and twenty-nine?). He felt an especial hatred for the Pharisees, the family, his hometown and adultery, and he may have been illegitimate (Ben Pandere)[1]; he had a macabre sense of humour; was overwhelmingly grateful to those who believed in him ("Thou art Peter"), and extremely close to his elder cousin John, but though moulding himself on him, he was less ascetic. He was fond of wine and very partial to grapes and figs. More civilized than his cousin, he was yet deeply affected by his end, which warned him of what would be his own if he persisted. The death of John and the revelation of Messiahship at Cæsarea Philippi completely changed him: impatient, ironical and short-tempered, he was a true faith-healer, inspired by his sublime belief in himself and tragically betrayed by it. I can't believe in his divinity, yet it is impossible not to admire his greatness, his majesty, his fatalistic intuition and that mixture of practical wisdom with sublime vision which alone can save our world. His faith carried him through to the end, then wavered. Was there a secret understanding with John the Baptist? John the Baptist, I feel, holds many clues. About the miracles I suspend judgement. But not about the sermon on the Mount. Those loving dazzling teasing-tender promises are like the lifting of the human horror, the bursting of a great dam. How different he is from Buddha!

Buddha though a philosopher-king is too oriental. His courage in living to a great age, among ageing disciples, confers a pedagogic monotony on his teaching. Besides, we can never absorb his titles; they are ill-accommodated to the Western ear. The Chinese wisdom alone has a natural affinity for the West, the Chinese are always practical. And Tao — a religion without words, without a saviour, without a doubt a God or a future life, whose truth is in a hoof-mark filled with water — what more dare we ask? [2]

.   .   .

Forty, — sombre anniversary to the hedonist, — in seekers after truth like Buddha, Mahomet, Mencius, St. Ignatius, the turning-point of their lives.

The secret of happiness (and therefore of success) is to be in harmony with existence, to be always calm, always lucid, always willing, "to be joined to the universe without being more conscious of it than an idiot," to let each wave of life wash us a little farther up the shore.

But the secret of art? There have been so many Infernos and so few Paradises in European art that the Infernos would seem our true climate. Yet those who have survived Satanism, war or passion have cared only for Paradise. In that sense Religion is the sequel to art and the sequel to love, as *Paradise Regained* follows half-heartedly after *Paradise Lost*.

Two Modern Taoists

"I have never seen a man who had such creative quiet. It radiated from him as from the sun. His face was that of a man who knows about day and night, sky and sea and air. He did not speak about these things. He had no tongue to tell of them . . ."

"I have often seen Klee's window from the street, with his pale oval face, like a large egg, and his open eyes pressed to the window pane." – J. ADLER.

"The only thing in all my experience I cling to is my coolness and leisurely exhilarated contemplation. If I could influence you to achieve that *je t'aurais rendu un peu de service. J'y tiens TELLEMENT — si tu savais comme j'y tiens.* Let this advice be my perpetual and most solemn legacy to you." — w. SICKERT (to Nina Hamnett).

"The mind of the sage in repose becomes the mirror of the universe, the speculum of all creation." — CHUANG TZU.

Whether or not he produce anything, this contemplation is the hall-mark of the artist. It is his gelatine, his queen-bee jelly, the compost round his roots: the violent are drawn to such a man by the violence of his serenity.

.   .   .

There cannot be a personal God without a pessimistic religion. A personal God is a disappointing God; and Job, Omar Khayyam, Euripides, Palladas, Voltaire and Professor Housman will denounce him. With Buddhism, Taoism, Quietism, and the God of Spinoza there can be no disappointment, because there is no Appointment.

Yet no one can achieve Serenity until the glare of passion is past the meridian. There is no certain way of preserving chastity against the will of the body. Lao-Tsu succeeded. But then he was eighty and a Librarian. So he inveighed against books and book-learning, and left but one, shorter than the shortest gospel — a Kaleidoscope of the Void.

Action is the true end of Western religion, contemplation of Eastern; therefore the West is in need of Buddhism (or Taoism or Yoga) and the East of Communism (or muscular Christianity) — and this is just what both are getting. Undergoing the attraction of opposites, we translate the Tao Tê Ching and the Bhagavad-Gita, they learn the Communist Manifesto.

The moment a writer puts his pen to paper he is of his time; the moment he becomes of his time he ceases to appeal to other periods and so will be forgotten. He who would write a book that would last for ever must learn to use invisible ink. Yet if an author is of his age, parallel situations will recur which he may return to haunt. He will obsess the minds of living writers, prevent them from sleeping, crowd them out like the *Horla* and snatch the bread from their mouths.

Our minds do not come of age until we discover that the great writers of the past whom we patronize, dead though they be, are none the less far more intelligent than ourselves — Proust, James, Voltaire, Donne, Lucretius — how we would have bored them!

Fallen leaves lying on the grass in the November sun bring more happiness than daffodils. Spring is a call to action, hence to disillusion, therefore is April called "the cruellest month." Autumn is the mind's true Spring; what is there we have, "quidquid promiserat annus" and it is more than we expected.

.   .   .

A stone lies in a river; a piece of wood is jammed against it; dead leaves, drifting logs, and branches caked with mud collect; weeds settle there, and soon birds have made a nest and are feeding their young among the blossoming water plants. Then the river rises and the earth is washed away. The birds depart, the flowers wither, the branches are dislodged and drift downward; no trace is left of the floating island but a stone submerged by the water; — such is our personality.

If (as Christians, Buddhists, Mystics, Yogis, Platonists, believe), our life is vanity, the world unreal, personality non-existent, the senses deceivers, their perceptions and even reason and imagination false; then how tragic that from the Flesh are such deductions always made! If our mission in life is to evolve spiritually, then why are we provided with bodies so refractory that in many thousands of years we have not been able to improve them? Not one lust of the flesh, not one single illusion, not even our male nipples have been bred out of us; and still our new-born babies roll about in paroxysms of sensual cupidity and egomaniac wrath.

Three faults, which are found together and which infect every activity: laziness, vanity, cowardice. If one is too lazy to think, too vain to do a thing badly, too cowardly to admit it, one will never attain wisdom. Yet it is only the thinking which begins when habit-thinking leaves off, which is ignited by the logic of the train of thought, that is worth pursuing. A comfortable person can seldom follow up an original idea any further than a London pigeon can fly.

Complacent mental laziness is our national disease.

Today our literature is suffering from the decay of poetry and the decline of fiction, yet never have there been so many novelists and poets; this is

because neither will overcome the difficulties of their medium. Irrespon-
sible poets who simulate inspiration trample down the flower of a language as brutally as politician and journalist blunt and enfeeble with
their slovenliness the common run of words. Many war poets don't try;
they are like boys playing about on a billiard table who wonder what the
cues and pockets are for. Nor is it easier for novelists, who can no longer
develop character, situation or plot.

Flaubert, Henry James, Proust, Joyce and Virginia Woolf have finished
off the novel. Now all will have to be re-invented as from the beginning.
    Let us reflect whether there be any living writer whose silence we would
consider a literary disaster: one who, with three centuries more of art and
history to draw from, can sustain a comparison with, for example, Pascal.

Pascal's *Pensées* were written about 1660. Many of them are modern not
merely in thought, but in expression and force; they would be of overwhelming importance if they were now published for the first time. Such
a genius must invalidate the usual conception of human progress. Particularly modern are his rapidity, detachment and intellectual impatience.

.   .   .

Pascal and Leopardi (both died aged thirty-nine), depress and frighten
one because they were ill, almost deformed, and therefore because their
deformity renders suspect so much of their pessimism. They are the Grand
Inquisitors who break down our alibis of health and happiness. Are they
pessimistic because they are ill? Or does their illness act as a short cut to
reality — which is intrinsically tragic? [3] Or did their deformities encourage
the herd to treat them thoughtlessly, and so create in them a catastrophic
impression of human nature?

.   .   .

Christmas Eve: Dégoûté de tout. Midwinter cafard.

> La Nochebuena se viene
> la Nochebuena se va
> y nosotros nos iremos
> y no volveremos más.[4]

No opinions, no ideas, no true knowledge of anything, no ideals, no inspiration; a fat slothful, querulous, greedy, impotent carcass; a stump, a
decaying belly washed up on the shore. "Manes Palinuri esse placandos!"
Always tired, always bored, always hurt, always hating.

.   .   .

When we reflect on life we perceive that only through solitary communion with nature can we gain an idea of its richness and meaning. We
know that in such contemplation lies our true personality, and yet we
live in an age when we are told exactly the opposite and asked to believe
that the social and co-operative activity of humanity is the one way
through which life can be developed. Am I an exception, a herd-outcast?
There are also solitary bees, and it is not claimed that they are biologically
inferior. A planet of contemplators, each sunning himself before his door-
step like the mason-wasp; no one would help another, and no one would
need help!

Marriage: "An experience everyone should go through and then live his
own life" *or* "living one's own life — an experience everyone should go
through and then marry"?

The tragedy of modern marriage is that married couples no longer
enjoy the support of society, although marriage, difficult enough at any
time, requires social sanction. Thus, in the past, married women censured
the unmarried; the constant punished the inconstant; society outlawed
the divorced and the dwellers-in-sin. Now it does the opposite. The State
harries the human couple and takes both man and wife for its wars, society
quests impatiently for the first suspicion of mistress or lover, and neurotic
three-in-a-bedders, lonely and envious, make the young ménage their prey.

.   .   .

Human life is understandable only as a state of transition, as part of an
evolutionary process; we can take it to be a transition between the animal
world and some other form which we assume to be spiritual. Anxiety and
remorse are the results of failing to advance spiritually. For this reason
they follow close on pleasure, which is not necessarily harmful, but which,
since it does not bring advancement with it, outrages that part of us which
is concerned with growth. Such ways of passing time as chess, bridge, drink
and motoring accumulate guilt. But what constitutes the spiritual ideal?
Is it the Nietzschean Superman or his opposite, the Buddha? The spiritual
trend of human beings would seem to be towards pacifism, vegetarianism,
contemplative mysticism, the elimination of violent emotion and even of
self-reproduction. But is it impossible to improve animal-man so that
instead of being made to renounce his animal nature, he refines it? Can
anxiety and remorse be avoided in that way? Imagine a cow or a pig

which rejected the body for a "noble eight-fold way of self-enlightenment."
One would feel that the beast had made a false calculation. If our elaborate and dominating bodies are given us to be denied at every turn, if our
nature is always wrong and wicked, how ineffectual we are — like fishes
not meant to swim. Have the solitary, the chaste, the ascetic who have
been with us now for six thousand years, ever been proved to be right?
Has humanity shown any sign of evolving in their direction? As well as
Diogenes and the Stylite, there is also Aristippus and Epicurus as alternative to the Beast.[5]

And now we have a new conception: the Group Man. Man's spiritual
evolution, about which I prate, taking the form of a leap from the poorly
organized wolf-pack and sheep-flock into an insect society, a community
in which the individual is not merely a gregarious unit, but a cell in the
body itself. Community and individual are, in fact, indistinguishable.
How will you enjoy that, Palinurus?

.   .   .

As I waddle along in thick black overcoat and dark suit with a leather
brief-case under my arm, I smile to think how this costume officially disguises the wild and storm-tossed figure of Palinurus; who knows that a
poet is masquerading here as a whey-faced bureaucrat? And who should
ever know?

The secret of happiness lies in the avoidance of Angst (anxiety, spleen,
noia, fear, remorse, cafard). It is a mistake to consider happiness as a
positive state. By removing Angst, the condition of all unhappiness, we
are then prepared to receive such blessings as may come our way. We
know very little about Angst, which may even proceed from the birth
trauma, or be a primitive version of the sense of original sin, but we can
try to find out what makes it worse.[6]

Angst can take the form of remorse about the past, guilt about the
present, anxiety about the future. Often it is due to our acceptance
through an imperfect knowledge of ourselves of conventional habits of
living. Thus to keep someone waiting or to be kept waiting is a cause of
Angst which is out of all proportion to the minor fault of unpunctuality.
Therefore we may assume that we keep people waiting symbolically because we do not wish to see them and that our anxiety is due not to being
late, but lest our hostility be detected. The chronically unpunctual should
cancel all engagements for a definite period. Similarly, anxiety at being
kept waiting is a form of jealousy, a fear that we are not liked.

Fatigue is one cause of Angst which may disappear if the tired person is able to lie down; bad air is another, or seeing a tube train move out as one reaches the platform.

To sit in a restaurant (especially when one has to pay the bill) or over a long meal after a cocktail party is particularly conducive to Angst, which does not affect us after snacks taken in an armchair with a book. The business lunch is another meal from which we would prefer to be driven away in a coffin. Certainly a frequent cause of Angst is an awareness of the waste of our time and ability, such as may be witnessed among people kept waiting by a hairdresser.

Further considerations on cowardice, sloth and vanity; vices which do small harm to other people but which prevent one from doing any good and which poison and enfeeble all the virtues. Sloth rots the intelligence, cowardice destroys all power at the source, while vanity inhibits us from facing any fact which might teach us something; it dulls all other sensation.

.   .   .

I see the world as a kind of Black Hole of Calcutta, where we are all milling about in darkness and slime; now and then the mere being in the world is enough to cause violent claustrophobia (or is it a physical shortness of breath which creates the sensation of claustrophobia and therefore the image of the Black Hole?). And then I know that it is only by some desperate escape, like Pascal's, that I can breathe; but cowardice and sloth prevent me from escaping.

> Who have escaped?
> "Those who know don't speak;
> Those who speak don't know."

On the American desert are horses which eat loco-weed and some are driven mad by it; their vision is affected, they take enormous leaps to cross a tuft of grass or tumble blindly into rivers. The horses which have become thus addicted are shunned by the rest and will never rejoin the herd. So it is with human beings: those who are conscious of another world, the world of the spirit, acquire an outlook which distorts the values of ordinary life; they are consumed by the weed of non-attachment. Curiosity is their one excess and therefore they are recognized not by what they do but by what they refrain from doing, like those Araphants or disciples of Buddha who were pledged to the "Nine Incapabilities." Thus they do not take life, they do not compete, they do not boast, they do not join groups of more than six, they do not condemn others; they are "abandoners of revels, mute, contemplative" who are depressed by gossip, gaiety and equals, who wait to be telephoned to, who neither speak in public nor keep up with their friends nor take revenge on their enemies. Self-knowledge has taught them to abandon hate and blame and envy in their lives until they look sadder than they are. They seldom make positive assertions because they see, outlined against any statement, (as a painter sees a complementary colour), the image of its opposite. Most psychological questionnaires are designed to search out these moonlings and ensure their non-employment. They divine each other by a warm indifference for they know that they are not intended to foregather, but, like stumps of phosphorus in the world's wood, each to give forth his misleading radiance.

The two errors: We can either have a spiritual or a materialist view of life. If we believe in the spirit then we make an assumption which permits a whole chain down to a belief in fairies, witches, astrology, black magic, ghosts, and treasure-divining; the point at which we stop believing is dictated by our temperament or by our mood at a given moment. Thus the early Christians believed in the miracles of false prophets, and regarded the pagan gods as devils who had entrenched themselves in secure positions. They were more pagan than I am. On the other hand a completely materialist view leads to its own excesses, such as a belief in Behaviorism, in the economic basis of art, in the social foundation of ethics and the biological nature of psychology, in fact to the justification of expediency and therefore ultimately to the Ends-Means fallacy of which our civilization is perishing.

If we believe in a supernatural or superhuman intelligence creating the universe, then we end by stocking our library with the prophecies of Nostradamus and the calculations on the Great Pyramid. If instead we choose to travel viâ Montaigne and Voltaire, then we choke among the brimstone aridities of the Left Book Club.

It is a significant comment on the victory of science over magic that were someone to say "if I put this pill in your beer it will explode," we might believe them; but were they to cry "if I pronounce this spell over your beer it will go flat," we should remain incredulous and Paracelsus, the Alchemists, Aleister Crowley and all the Magi have lived in vain. Yet when I read science I turn magical; when I study magic, scientific.

We cannot say that truth lies in the centre between the spiritual and material conception, since life must be one thing or the other. But can it

be both? Supposing life were created by an act of God willing the accidental combination of chemicals to form a cell; created in fact, by deliberate accident. Then, in the confidence of youth when the body seems
self-sufficing, it would be natural to emphasize the materialist nature of
phenomena, and in old age, when the body begins to betray us, to
abandon our sensual outlook for a more spiritual cosmorama, — and both
times we should be right.

Sunshine streams through the room, the dove grinds her love-song on the
roof, out in the square the grass turns green, the earth has been cleared
round the daffodils as a stage is cleared for the dancers, and under a
rinsed blue sky the streets remember Canaletto; London spring is on its
way.
    Spring, season of massacre and offensives, of warm days and flowing
blood, of flowers and bombs. Out with the hyacinths, on with the
slaughter! Glorious weather for tanks and land-mines!

The creative moment of a writer comes with the autumn. The winter is
the time for reading, revision, preparation of the soil; the spring for
thawing back to life; the summer is for the open air, for satiating the
body with health and action, but from October to Christmas for the
release of mental energy, the hard crown of the year.

The duality of man is the heresy of Paul and Plato, heresy because the
concept of soul and body is bound to imply a struggle between them
which leads on the one hand to asceticism and puritanism, on the other to
excess of materialism and sensuality. The greatness of Christ and Buddha
sprang from the abandonment of asceticism for the Middle Path.
    The spiritual life of man is the flowering of his bodily existence: there
is a physical life which remains the perfect way of living for natural man,
a life in close contact with nature, with the sun and the passage of the
seasons, and one rich in opportunities for equinoctial migrations and
home-comings. This life has now become artificial, out of reach of all but
the rich or the obstinately free, yet until we can return to it we are unable
to appreciate the potentialities of living. (Whales, branded in the Arctic,
are found cruising in Antarctic waters; men, ringed in childhood, are
observed, seventy years later, under the same stone.) We may compare a
human being to a fruit-tree whose purpose is its fruit, fruit out of all
proportion to the tree's value; yet, unless the tree receives its years of
leisure, its requirements of sun and rain, the fruit will not ripen. So it is
with the spiritual virtues of man, for we have divided man into two

kinds; those whose soil is so poor or the climate of whose lives so unsuitable that they can never bear, or those who are forced and cramped
under glass, whose lives are so constricted by responsibility that they
become all fruit; hasty, artificial and without flavour.

We progress through an intensifying of the power generated by the
physical satisfaction of natural man, whose two worst enemies are apathy
and delirium; the apathy which spreads outward from the mechanical
life, the delirium which results from the violent methods we use to escape.

Happiness lies in the fulfilment of the spirit through the body. Thus
humanity has already evolved from an animal life to one more civilized.
There can be no complete return to nature, to nudism or desert-islandry:
city life is the subtlest ingredient in the human climate. But we have
gone wrong over the size of our cities and over the kind of life we lead
in them; in the past the clods were the peasants, now the brute mass of
ignorance is urban. The village idiot walks in Leicester Square. To live
according to nature we should pass a considerable time in cities for they
are the glory of human nature, but they should never contain more than
two hundred thousand inhabitants; it is our artificial enslavement to the
large city, too sprawling to leave, too enormous for human dignity, which
is responsible for half our sickness and misery. Slums may well be
breeding-grounds of crime, but middle-class suburbs are incubators of
apathy and delirium. No city should be too large for a man to walk out
of in a morning.[7]

Surrealism is a typical city-delirium movement, a violent explosion of
urban claustrophobia; one cannot imagine Surrealists except in vast
cities, "paysans de Paris" or New York. The nihilism of Céline and Miller
is another by-product, and so are those mass-movers, Marx with his car-
buncles, Hitler with his Beer-Hall. The English masses are lovable: they
are kind, decent, tolerant, practical and not stupid. The tragedy is that
there are too many of them, and that they are aimless, having outgrown
the servile functions for which they were encouraged to multiply. One
day these huge crowds will have to seize power because there will be
nothing else for them to do, and yet they neither demand power nor are
ready to make use of it; they will learn only to be bored in a new way.
Sooner or later the population of England will turn Communist, and
then take over. Some form of State Socialism is the only effective religion
for the working class; its coming is therefore as inevitable as was that of
Christianity. The Liberal Die-hard then grows to occupy historically the

same position as the "good Pagan": he is doomed to extinction.

While we re-live the horrors of the Dark Ages, of absolute States and ideological wars, the old platitudes of liberalism loom up in all their glory, familiar streets as we reel home furious in the dawn.

Wisdom of de Quincey
de Quincey: decadent English essayist who, at the age of seventy-five, was carried off by half a century of opium-eating.

"Marriage had corrupted itself through the facility of divorce and through the consequences of that facility (viz. levity in choosing and fickleness in adhering to the choice) into so exquisite a traffic of selfishness that it could not yield so much as a phantom model of sanctity."

"By the law I came to know sin."

On the first time he took opium in 1804: "It was Sunday afternoon, wet and cheerless; and a duller spectacle this earth of ours has not to show than a rainy Sunday in London."

The mystery of drugs: How did savages all over the world, in every climate, discover in frozen tundras or remote jungles the one plant, indistinguishable from so many others of the same species, which could, by a most elaborate process, bring them fantasies, intoxication, and freedom from care? How unless by help from the plants themselves? Opium-smokers in the East become surrounded by cats, dogs, birds and even spiders, who are attracted by the smell. The craving for the drug proceeds from the brain-cells which revolt and overrule the will. The Siberian tribes who eat Agaric say, "The Agaric orders me to do this or that" — the Hashish chewers experience a like sensation. Horses and cattle which become "indigo eaters" continue to gorge till they drop dead. Though one of the rarest and most obscure drugs, Peotl gave its name to a range of uninhabited mountains where it is found.
    The Greeks and Romans looked on alcohol and opium as lovely twin reconcilers to living and dying presented to man by Dionysus and Morpheus, — God-given because of their extraordinary sympathy to us and because of the mystery attending their discovery. If man be part of nature, then his parasites may well understand him better than he knows.

Everything is a dangerous drug to me except reality, which is unendurable.

Happiness is in the imagination. What we perform is always inferior to what we imagine; yet day-dreaming brings guilt; there is no happiness except through freedom from Angst and only creative work, communion with nature and helping others are Anxiety-free.

Fraternity is the State's bribe to the individual; it is the one virtue which can bring courage to members of a materialist society. All State propaganda exalts comradeship for it is this gregarious herd-sense and herd-smell which keep people from thinking and so reconcile them to the destruction of their private lives. A problem for government writers or for the war artists in their war cemeteries: how to convert Fraternity into an æsthetic emotion?

Subversive thought for the year: "Every man is to be respected as an absolute end in himself; and it is a crime against the dignity that belongs to him to use him as a mere means to some external purpose."—KANT.

"If I had to choose between betraying my country and betraying my friend, I hope I should have the guts to betray my country." This statement by Mr. E. M. Forster reminds us how far we have wandered from the ancient conception of friendship, of treating a kindred soul as an end not a means. "The Chinese poet recommends himself as a friend, the Western poet as a lover," writes Arthur Waley; but the Western prose-writer also used to recommend himself as a friend; the seventeenth and eighteenth centuries elaborated friendship and all but made it their religion. In the circle of Johnson, of Walpole and Madame du Deffand or of the Encyclopædists nobody could live without his friend. They loved them and even a misanthropic philosopher like La Bruyère could grow sentimental over the theme. Only the invalid Pascal demolished friendship on the ground that if we could read each other's thoughts it would disappear.

Now the industrialization of the world, the totalitarian State, and the egotism of materialism have made an end to friendship; the first through speeding up the tempo of human communication to the point where no one is indispensable, the second by making such demands on the individual that comradeship can be practised between workers and colleagues only for the period of their co-operation and the last by emphasizing whatever is fundamentally selfish and nasty in people, so that we are unkind about our friends and resentful of their intimacy because of something which is rotting in ourselves. We have developed sympathy at the expense of loyalty.

How many people drop in on us? That is a criterion of friendship. Or may tell us our faults? To how many do we give unexpected presents? With whom can we remain silent? The egocentric personality requires, alas, a changing audience, not a constant scrutiny. Romantic lovers are disloyal and, by making fun of old friends, they hit upon a congenial way of entertaining each other.

.   .   .

Masterplay

Three requisites for a work of art: validity of the myth, vigour of belief, intensity of vocation. Examples of valid myths: The Gods of Olympus in Ancient Greece; the City of Rome and afterwards the Roman Empire; Christianity; the discovery of Man in the Renaissance with its conse-quence, the Age of Reason; the myths of Romanticism and of Material Progress (how powerful is the myth of bourgeois life in the work of the Im-pressionist painters!). The belief in a myth whose validity is diminishing will not produce such great art as the belief in one which is valid, and none are valid today. Yet no myth is ever quite worthless as long as there remains one artist to honour it with his faith.

O for the past, when a masterpiece was enough to maintain a reputation for life! All Catullus, Tibullus and Propertius fit into the same volume; Horace and Virgil require but one tome, so do La Fontaine and La Bruyère. One book for each lifetime and the rest is fame, ease and free-dom from Angst. Nature was so indulgent; if we could but write one good book every twelve years we would have done as well as Flaubert. Voltaire wrote *Candide* when he was sixty-five, Peacock wrote *Gryll Grange* at seventy-five, at eighty Joinville began his *Life of St. Louis.* Waste is a law of art as it is of nature. There is always time.

Every good writer must discover the yawning crevasse which separates Man's finite destiny from his infinite potentialities. It is afterwards that he will reveal his artistic courage and so register the protest which is a final plea for order, his *Gulliver's Travels,* his *Maxims,* his *Songs of Experience,* his *Saison en Enfer,* his *Fleurs du Mal.* The rest either pretend that they have seen nothing, and that all is well, or else howl with self-pity. Optim-ism and self-pity are the positive and negative poles of contemporary cowardice.

What makes the great writers of the past vivid to us is the extent of their misery; the despair of Pascal, the bitterness of La Rochefoucauld, the ennui of Flaubert, the "noia" of Leopardi, the "spleen" of Baudelaire, — none but the truths which have been extracted under mental torture appeal to us. We live in so desperate an age that any happiness which we possess must be hidden like a deformity, for we know that, though all our nature revolt, we can create only through what we suffer.

"We are all conceived in close prison . . . and then all our life is but a going out to the place of execution, to death. Nor was there any man seen to sleep in the cart between Newgate and Tyburn — between prison and the place of execution, does any man sleep? But we sleep all the way; from the womb to the grave we are never thoroughly awake."—DONNE.

A modern Rune: "Pooey on the war!" No one can pronounce these four words and not feel a tremor of earth-shaking dimension. And not until the two thousand and fifty million belligerents can thunder them in unison, will the war be over.

A Rune for the very bored: When very bored recite: "It was during the next twenty minutes that there occurred one of those tiny incidents which revolutionize the whole course of our life and alter the face of history. Truly we are the playthings of enormous fates."

The ten-year torture of two faces. "The tyranny of the human face." When we see a friend in the depth of despair because they have been left by someone whom we know to be insignificant, we must remember that there is a way of leaving and yet of not leaving; of hinting that one loves and is willing to return, yet never coming back and so preserving a relationship in a lingering decay. This technique can be learnt like a hold in jiu-jitsu. The person who has been abandoned is always psychologically groggy; the ego is wounded in its most tender part and is forced back on the separation and rejection phobias of infancy. Someone who knows how to prolong this state and to reproduce it at will can be quite insignificant, — so is the sand-wasp which stings a grub in the nerve-centre where it will be paralysed, yet remain alive.

Axiom: There is no happiness to be obtained by the destruction of another's. To take wife away from husband or husband from wife, is a kind of murder; guilt turns lovers into bad accomplices and the wrecking of a home destroys the wreckers. As we leave others, so shall we be left.

There is immunity in reading, immunity in formal society, in office routine, in the company of old friends and in the giving of officious help

to strangers, but there is no sanctuary in one bed from the memory of another. The past with its anguish will break through every defence-line of
custom and habit; we must sleep and therefore we must dream.

And in our dreams, as in the vacant afternoons of London week-ends,
there enter the excluded, the disinherited, the heartbroken, the heart-
breakers, the saboteurs and wrecking crews of our daylight selves. Θύραζέ
κῆρες.[8] Bone-crushing hyenas!

The harbour of Cassis on a bright winter morning; a gull is floating a few
yards from the quay, unable to rise because its wings are fouled with oil.
The fisher-children pelt it with stones. I drive them off; laughing they
run across to the farther side and begin again, the stones falling around
the dying bird as it bobs on the water like a painted decoy.

> "While under its storm-beaten breast
> Cried out the hollows of the sea."

Causes of Angst: Angst is inherent in the uncoiling of the ego, the tape-
worm, the *ver solitaire*. It dwells in the *Lacrimœ Rerum,* in the contrast-
ing of the Past with the present. It lurks in old loves and old letters or in
our despair at the complexity of modern life.

Effect: Misery, disgust, tears, guilt.

Temporary cures: (1) Lunch with a new friend, gossip, literary talk,
i.e. appeals to vanity; (2) Art (Renoir landscapes), the true escape into
Timelessness; (3) The office personality (Alibi Ike); (4) Old friends,
(relationships which date from before the Fall.)

Angoisse des Gares: A particularly violent form of Angst. Bad when we
meet someone at the station, but worse when we are seeing them off; not
present when we are departing ourselves, but unbearable when arriving
in London, if only from a day in Brighton. Since all Angst is identical,
we may learn something from these station-fears: Arrival-Angst is closely
connected with guilt, with the dread of something terrible having happened during our absence. Death of parents. Entry of bailiffs. Flight of
loved one. Sensation worse at arriving in the evening than in the morning,
and much worse at Victoria and Waterloo than at Paddington. This may
have been due in my case to my way of going abroad every vacation and
therefore returning to London with guilt-feelings about having spent my
money or not written to my parents, and to endless worry over work and
debt.[9] Going to London as a schoolboy was a treat, as an undergraduate
an ordeal, a surrender to justice. Later on the trips abroad grew longer,
and returns were painful because of neglected household worries, and

through a particularly strong guilt-feeling about not being at work, out-distanced by successful stay-at-home friends. But this is not all, for much of our anxiety is caused by horror of London itself; of the hideous entrails seen from the southern approaches, the high cost of living, the slums where we may die, embodiment of ugly and unnatural urban existence. When living in France, I began to have a similar feeling about Paris, though it has none of the same associations. I therefore deduce, that though it is wrong for us to live and work in great cities, to live away from them *without working* is worse. Angst begins at Reading, Woking or Croydon, or even in Paris, when we see the first grisly English faces home-ward bound at the Gare du Nord.

If, instead of Time's notorious and incompetent remedy, there was an operation by which we could be cured of loving, how many of us would not rush to have it!

To be kept for six months in a refrigerator or to hibernate in deep narcotic sleep, to be given new drugs, new glands, a new heart, and then to wake up with the memory swept clear of farewells and accusations, never more to be haunted by the grief-stricken eyes of our assassinated murderers!

But Angst descends; I wake up in anxiety; like a fog it overlays all my action, and my days are muffled with anguish. Somewhere in the mind are crossed the wires of fear and lust and all day long nature's burglar-alarm shrills out in confusion. I dread the bell, the post, the telephone, the sight of an acquaintance. Anguish, anxiety, remorse and guilt: TOUT EST DE-GOUT ET MISERE. When even despair ceases to serve any creative purpose, then surely we are justified in suicide. For what better ground for self-destruction can there be than to go on making the same series of false moves which invariably lead to the same disaster, and to repeat a pattern without knowing what it is or wherein lies the flaw? And yet to perceive that in ourselves there revolves a cycle of activity which is certain to end in paralysis of the will, desertion, panic and despair — always to go on loving those who have ceased to love us, those who have quite lost all resemblance to the beings whom once we loved! Suicide is catching: what if the agony which self-murderers go through while being driven to take their own lives, the conviction that all is lost, be infectious also? And if you have contracted it. Palinurus, if it has sought you out?

PART

II

Breaking Up

It is art that *makes* life.

—*Henry James, 1915*

Make it new.

—*Ezra Pound, 1934*

1

MARCEL PROUST *and* JAMES JOYCE

During the years of the First World War, two extraordinary men were obscurely at work. Proust was in a cork-lined room in Paris, Joyce was in a pension in Zurich. Proust was asthmatic, Joyce nearly blind. Both were secreting novels that were as much acts of faith as works of art. They practiced very different methods, and preached very different doctrines, but for both, Henry James' reply to H. G. Wells' charge of preciosity would have been gospel: "It is art that makes *life!"*

from *The Past Recaptured*
[1927]

MARCEL PROUST

And lastly, this idea of time had a final value for me; it was like a goad, reminding me that it was time to begin if I wished to achieve what I had occasionally in the course of my life sensed in brief flashes, along the Guermantes way or while driving with Mme. de Villeparisis, and which had encouraged me to regard life as worth living. How much more so it appeared to me now that I felt it possible to shed light on this life which we live in darkness and to bring back to its former true character this life which we distort unceasingly — in short, extract the real essence of life in a book. Happy the man who could write such a book, I thought to myself, what a mighty task before him! To convey an idea of it, one would have to go to the noblest and most varied arts for comparisons; for this writer, who, moreover, would have to shew the most contradictory sides of each of his characters in order to give his volume the effect of a solid, would need to prepare it with minute care, constantly regrouping his forces as if for an attack, endure it like an exhausting task, accept it like a rule of conduct, build it like a church, follow it like a regimen, overcome it like an obstacle, win it like a friendship, feed it intensively like a child, create it like a world, without overlooking those mysteries whose explanation is probably to be found only in other worlds and the presentiment of which is the quality in life and art which moves us most deeply. And in those great books there are certain portions which there has been time only to sketch in and which no doubt will never be completed because of the very magnitude of the architect's plan. How many great cathedrals remain unfinished! Such a book one nourishes over a long period of time, builds up its weaker parts, keeps it safe from harm; but later it is the book itself that grows up, selects our tomb, protects it against false rumours and somewhat against oblivion. But to return to myself — I had a more modest opinion of my book and it would be incorrect to say even that I was thinking of those who might read it as "my readers." For, as I have already shewn, they would not be my readers but readers of themselves, my book serving merely as a sort of magnifying glass, such as the optician of Combray used to offer a customer, so that through my book I would give them the means of reading in their own selves. Consequently, I would not ask them to praise or dispraise me but only to tell me if it is as I say, if the words they read in themselves are, indeed, the same as I have written (any possible discrepancies in this respect not being always attributable, by the way, to any mistake on my part but to the fact that the reader's eyes would not be of the type which my book would "fit" for comfortably reading in one's own self). And constantly changing the simile as I obtained a better and more material conception of the task to which I was going to devote myself, I thought how I would work at my book on my large, white-pine table, with Frànçoise looking on. As all the unpretentious persons who live close beside us acquire a certain intuitive comprehension of our work and as I had forgotten Albertine sufficiently to forgive Françoise for whatever she might have done to injure her, I would work near her and almost in her manner — at least, as she used to, for she was now so old she could scarcely see any more — for, pinning on an extra sheet here and there, I would construct my book, I dare not say ambitiously "like a cathedral," but simply like a dress. And if I did not have at hand all my papers — my "old rubbish," as Françoise called it — and just the one I needed was missing, Françoise would understand perfectly my exasperation, since she herself always used to say she could not sew unless she had the size thread and the buttons she needed and also because she had lived my life so long that she had developed a sort of instinctive understanding of literary work

more correct than that possessed by many intelligent persons and, *a
fortiori,* by stupid people. In the same way, years before, when I was
writing my article for *Le Figaro,* whereas the old butler, with that sympathetic expression which always somewhat overestimates the arduousness
of a kind of work one is not accustomed to performing and of which one
has not even a clear conception — or even the discomfort of a habit one
is free from, like the folk who say, "How it must tire you to sneeze like
that" — used to pity writers sincerely, saying "How you must have to rack
your brains over that work," Françoise, on the contrary, sensed my happiness and respected my work. She got angry only when I told Bloch about
my articles beforehand, because she was afraid he would steal my ideas.
"All these people," she would say, "you trust them too much; they're a lot
of copy-cats." And Bloch, as a matter of fact, would establish a retroactive
alibi for himself, whenever I outlined something he thought was good, by
saying, "Why, that's funny, I've written something almost exactly like
that. I must read it to you." (He could not have read it to me then and
there but would go and write it that very evening.)

My papers — what Françoise called my "old rubbish" — by dint of being
continually pasted together, would get torn here and there. When
necessary, Françoise would help me mend them in the same way as she
put patches on the worn parts of her dresses or, while waiting for the
glazier (just as I was waiting for the printer) pasted a piece of newspaper
over the broken pane of the kitchen window.

Pointing to my notebooks, eaten away like wood an insect has gotten
into, she would exclaim, "It's all moth-eaten; it's too bad; here's a piece of
a page that's all in ribbons." And, examining it like a tailor, "I don't
think I can fix that; it's too far gone. It's a pity; maybe that's your finest
ideas. As they say at Combray, there aren't any furriers who know their
business as well as the moths do. They always get into the best materials."

Moreover, since in this book the individual entities, human or otherwise, would be constructed from numerous impressions which, derived
from many young girls, many churches, many sonatas, would go to make
up a single sonata, a single church, a single young girl, would I not
be making my book the way Françoise made her *boeuf à la mode* so
liked by M. de Norpois, the jelly of which was enriched by so many carefully selected pieces of meat? And I would realise what I had so much
longed for in my walks along the Guermantes way but had believed impossible, just as I had believed it would be impossible when I went home
ever to get accustomed to going to bed without kissing my mother, or,
later, to the idea that Albertine loved women, an idea I finally adjusted
to without even being aware of its presence, for our gravest apprehensions,

as well as our fondest hopes, are not beyond our strength and we are able in the end to overcome the former and realise the latter. — Yes, this conception of time which I had just formulated warned me that I must at once set myself to this work. It was high time; this justified the anxiety which had come over me the moment I entered the drawing-room, when the made-up faces gave me a sense of the time lost. But was there yet time? The mind also has its landscapes which it is allowed to contemplate only for a moment. I had lived like a painter climbing a road overlooking a lake, which is hidden from his eyes by a curtain of rocks and trees. Through a breach he catches sight of it, has it all before him, takes out his brushes. But already night is coming on when painting will be impossible, the night on which day will never dawn!

One prerequisite to my book, such as I had conceived it just now in the library, was that I plumb to the very bottom impressions which I should first have to re-create with the aid of my memory. But my memory was exhausted. Then, too, as long as nothing had been begun, I could, indeed, be uneasy, even if I thought that at my age I still had several years before me, for my hour might strike in a few minutes. As a matter of fact, I must start from the idea that I had a body, in other words, that I was continually under the threat of a two-fold danger, external and internal. But even there I spoke in that way only for convenience of expression. For the internal danger, such as a cerebral hemorrhage, is external, being of the body. And having a body constitutes the principal danger that threatens the mind. The life of the thinking human being — which certainly is to be described less as a perfecting of physical, animal life than as an imperfect creation, still as rudimentary as the communal existence of protozoa in polyparies or the body of the whale and so on — is such, in the organisation of the spiritual life, that the body imprisons the mind in a fortress; soon the fortress is besieged on all sides and in the end the mind must capitulate. But, admitting this distinction between the two kinds of danger that threaten the mind, and beginning with the external one, I recalled that, many times in my past life, in moments of mental stimulation, when some circumstance had suspended all physical activity for me — for instance when, half-intoxicated, I was leaving the restaurant at Rivebelle in a carriage to go to some nearby casino, it had happened to me to feel very definitely within myself the momentary subject of my thoughts and to understand that it was a mere matter of chance, not only that this subject had come into my mind at all but also that it had not been annihilated at that time along with my body. This mattered little to me. My gaiety was neither foresighted nor apprehensive. That this joy left me in a second and disappeared into thin air was of little consequence to me. But it was no longer the same now, the reason being that the happiness I felt did not come from a purely subjective tension of the nerves, which isolates us from the past, but on the contrary from a broadening out of my mind in which the past took shape again, became vividly present and gave me — but, alas, only for a moment — a sense of eternity. I fain would have bequeathed this last to those whom I might have enriched with my treasure. What I had felt in the library and sought to preserve was pleasure, it is true, but no longer selfish or, if so, then with a selfishness which could be made profitable to others — for all the fruitful forms of altruism in nature follow a selfish pattern in their development; human altruism which is not selfish is sterile, like that of the writer who interrupts his work to receive an unhappy friend, accept a public function or write propaganda articles.

The indifference I used to feel on my way back from Rivebelle was gone; I felt myself pregnant with the work which I was carrying within me, like some precious and fragile object which had been entrusted to me and which I desired to transmit intact to the other persons for whom it was destined. And to think that, when I went home presently, an accidental shock would suffice to destroy my body and force my mind, from which the life would be withdrawn, to abandon forever the ideas it was at this moment clasping to its bosom and shielding anxiously with its quivering flesh, not yet having had time to put them out of harm's way in a book. Now the feeling that I was the bearer of a literary work made an accident in which I might meet with death more to be dreaded, even absurd (in proportion as this work appeared to me necessary and enduring) inimical to my desire and to the eager aspiration of my thoughts, but none the less possible for all that, since accidents, being the product of material causes, may perfectly well take place when very different intentions, which they destroy without knowing what they are, make them most objectionable, as happens every day in the simplest incidents of life, as when, though we desire with all our heart not to make any noise on account of a sleeping friend, a carafe, placed too near the edge of a table, falls and wakes him.

I knew very well that my brain was a rich mineral basin where there was a vast area of extremely varied precious deposits. But would I have time to exploit them? I was the only person able to do this, for two reasons: with my death there would disappear, not only the one miner able to extract the minerals but the deposit itself; now, when I returned home presently, a collision between the auto I took and another would suffice to destroy my body and to force my mind to abandon my new ideas for all time. And, by a strange coincidence, this rational fear of danger was developing in me at a time when the idea of death had been for only a short while a matter of indifference to me. The fear of ceasing to be myself, had formerly caused me horror and especially with each new love that came to me — for Gilberte, for Albertine — because I could not endure the idea that one day he who loved them would exist no longer, which would be a sort of death. But, after this fear had recurred many times, it was naturally transmitted into a confident serenity.

While the idea of death had thus in those days cast a shadow over love for me, for a long time now the remembrance of love had aided me to contemplate death without fear, for I understood that it was no new thing to die but that, on the contrary, I had already died many times since childhood. To take the most recent period — had I not clung to Albertine even more than to life itself? Could I at that time have conceived of myself without my love for her continuing to form part of me? Now, I no longer loved her; I was, not the person who used to love her but a different person who did not love her; I had ceased to love her when I had become another person. But I did not suffer on account of having become this other person and having ceased to love Albertine; and, assuredly, some day no longer to have my body could in no wise appear to me as sad a thing as formerly had seemed to me the idea of some day no longer loving Albertine. And yet how unimportant it now appeared to me not to love her any more. These successive deaths, so dreaded by the "me" they were to obliterate, but so gentle and inconsequential once they had become a fact and when he who had feared them was no longer there to feel them, had a while before made me realise how unintelligent it would be to be afraid of death. And it was now, shortly after I had become indifferent to death, that I was beginning anew to fear it — under another form, it is true, and not for myself but for my book, to the full flowering of which this life, menaced by so many dangers, was, at least for a while, indispensable. Victor Hugo said,

Il faut que l'herbe pousse et que les enfants meurent.

But I say that it is the cruel law of art that human beings should die and that we ourselves must die after exhausting the gamut of suffering so that the grass, not of oblivion but of eternal life, may grow, the thick grass of fecund works of art, on which future generations will come and gaily have their "picnic lunch," without a thought for those who sleep beneath. I said "external dangers," but there are internal dangers also. If I escaped an accident from without, who knows whether I might not be prevented from making full use of this merciful favour through some mischance occurring within myself, some internal catastrophe, some cerebral accident, before the months had passed that were needed for the writing of this book?

Even the cerebral accident was not necessary. Some symptoms — indicated to me by a peculiar mental void and a tendency to forget things and have them come back to me only by accident, just as, when you are putting certain objects in order, you come across one you had forgotten and had not even thought to look for — made me feel like a miser whose broken treasure chest had allowed his riches to slip away one by one.

When I should return home presently through the Champs-Elysées, what guarantee had I that I would not be struck with the same malady as was my grandmother one afternoon when she had come there with me for a stroll which was to be her last, without her suspecting it, unconscious, as are we all, that the minute-hand now stands over the very point where the spring will be released to strike the hour? Possibly the fear of having already consumed almost the entire minute which precedes the first stroke of the hour and during which the stroke is making ready to fall, possibly the fear that it was about to be set in motion in my brain, was a sort of obscure sense of what was going to happen, a reflexion in the consciousness, so to speak, of the precarious condition of the brain, the arteries of which are about to give way — which is no more impossible than the sudden conviction of approaching death which many a wounded man has so clearly that, although he has retained his mental lucidity and both the physician and his own desire to live seek to deceive him, he says, foreseeing what is going to happen, "I am going to die, I am ready," and he writes his farewell to his wife.

This obscure sense of what was going to happen was conveyed to me by the strange thing which occured before I had begun my book and which befell me in a manner I would never have expected. When I went out one evening, my friends thought me looking better than before; they expressed surprise that my hair was still black. But three times I nearly fell as I went down the stairs. I was away only two hours and yet, when I got home, I felt as if I had no memory, no power to think, no strength, no life at all. If someone had come to see me, to proclaim me king, to lay hold of me, to arrest me, I would have let them do to me whatever they wished without uttering a word or opening my eyes, like the people crossing the Caspian Sea who are taken with the worst form of seasickness and do not even make a feeble gesture of resistance when they are told they are going to be thrown overboard. Strictly speaking, I had no particular illness but I felt as though I had become incapable of anything, as frequently happens to an old man who, active the day before, breaks his hip or has an attack of indigestion and may for some time to come lead a bedridden existence which is only a more or less long preparation for the now inevitable end. One of my various selves—the one who used to go to those barbaric banquets called formal dinners, where for the white-shirted men and the semi-nude, feather-bedecked women values are so reversed that anyone who does not come, after accepting the invitation, or does not arrive until the roast is being served commits a more reprehensible act than the immoral conduct discussed so lightly in the course of the dinner along with recent deaths, and where death or serious illness are the only excuses for not coming (and then only provided you notify your hostess of your dying condition in time for her to invite a fourteenth person) — that self within me had kept his society scruples and lost his memory. My other self, on the contrary, the one who had reached a clear conception of his task, had not forgotten. I had received an invitation from Mme. Molé and had learned that Mme. Sazerat's son was dead. I made up my mind to waste in sending apologies to Mme. Molé and condolences to Mme. Sazerat one of those hours after which, my tongue paralysed, as was the case with my grandmother during her last illness, I would no longer be able to utter a word or even swallow some milk. But a few minutes later I had forgotten that I was to do this. Fortunate forgetfulness, as the remembrance of my work was vigilant and would employ in laying the first foundations the hour of extra existence which had thus reverted to me. Unluckily, as I took up a notebook to start writing, Mme. Molé's card of invitation slipped in front of me. Straightway my forgetful self which, however, took precedence over the other, as happens with all scrupulous barbarians who attend formal dinners, pushed the notebook aside and wrote to Mme. Molé — who, by the way, would doubtless have thought very highly of me for it, had she learned that I had put my reply to her invitation ahead of my architectural labours. Suddenly a remark in my reply reminded me that Mme. Sazerat had lost her son; I wrote to her also. Then, having sacrificed a real duty to the fictitious obligation of shewing myself courteous and sympathetic, I fell back exhausted, closed my eyes and for a week I merely vegetated. And yet, while all my useless duties to which I was ready to sacrifice the real one went out of my head in a few minutes, the idea of the thing I was to construct did not leave me for an instant. I knew not whether it would be a church in which the true believers would be able little by little to learn some truths and discover some harmonies, the great, comprehensive plan, or would stand, forever unvisited, on the summit of an island, like a druid monument. But I had decided to devote to it all my strength, which was leaving me slowly, as though reluctant and wishing to allow me time, having completed the outer structure, to close the funereal door. Soon I was able to shew a few sketches. No one understood a word. Even those who were favourable to my conception of the truths which I intended later to carve within the temple congratulated me on having discovered them with a microscope when I had, on the contrary, used a telescope to perceive things which, it is true, were very small but situated afar off and each of them a world in itself. Whereas I had sought great laws, they called me one who grubs for petty details. Moreover, what was the use of my undertaking it? I had had a certain facility as a young man and Bergotte had declared my schoolboy writings "perfect" [1]; but instead of working, I had lived in idleness, in the dissipation of a life of pleasure, amid sickness, care of my health and strange humours, and I was taking up my work on the eve of my death, with no knowledge of my craft. I no longer felt equal to facing either my obligations to human beings or my duties to my thought and work — still less to both. As for the former, my task was somewhat simplified by my habit of forgetting the letters I had to write. The loss of my memory aided me a little by cutting out some of my obligations; my work filled their place. But suddenly at the end of a month the association of ideas brought back my memory, together with my remorse, and I was crushed with a sense of my own impotence. I was astonished to find myself indifferent to the criticism made of me but the truth is that, from the day when my legs had trembled so as I descended the stairs, I had become indifferent to everything; I craved nothing now but rest, while waiting for the long rest that would eventually come. My unconcern over the approval of the élite of my own time was not due to the expectation that my work would not receive until after my death the admiration which it seemed to me to deserve. Those who came after me might think what they wished. I was just as little concerned about that. In reality, if I thought of my work and not at all of the letters to be answered, this was no longer because I recognised any great difference in importance between the two objects, as I had done in the days of my idleness and then in the time of my active work up to the evening when I was obliged to seize hold of the railing of the staircase. The organisation of my memory and my preoccupations was closely bound up with my work, perhaps because, whereas the letters were forgotten immediately after being received, the idea of my work was in my mind, always the same, in a perpetual state of development. But it also had become irksome to me. It was to me like a son whose dying mother must still take upon herself the fatigue of looking after him between injections and cuppings. Possibly she still loves him but she now knows it only through the exhausting obligation she is under to take care of him. In me the powers of the writer were no longer equal to the inconsiderate demands of the work. Since that day on the staircase, nothing concerning the social world, no happiness, whether it came from the friendliness of people, the progress of my work, the hope of fame, any longer penetrated to my consciousness except as such a pale ray of sunlight that it no longer had the power to warm me, put life into me, give me any desire whatsoever; and even at that, wan though it was, it was still too dazzling for my eyes and I preferred to close them and turn my head toward the wall. It seems to me, as far as I was able to feel the movement of my lips, that I must have had an imperceptible little smile at one corner of my mouth when a lady wrote me, "I was *surprised* not to get a reply to my letter." Nevertheless, that reminded me of the letter and I answered her. In order that I might not be thought an ingrate, I tried to place my present courtesy on a par with the courtesy people might have had for me. And I was crushed under the superhumanly wearisome burdens of life which I imposed upon my existence as it ebbed to its agonising close.

This idea of death took up its permanent abode within me as does love for a woman. Not that I loved death, I detested it. But, doubtless because I had pondered over it from time to time as over a woman one does not yet love, now the thought of it adhered to the deepest stratum of my brain so completely that I could not turn my attention to anything without first relating it to the idea of death and, even if I was not occupied with anything but was in a state of complete repose, the idea of death was with me as continuously as the idea of myself. I do not think that, on the day I became half-dead, it was the accompanying symptoms, such as my inability to descend the staircase, to recall a name, to get up, which gave rise, even by an unconscious process of reasoning, to the idea of death, the idea that I was already nearly dead, but rather that all this had come at the same time, that inevitably the great mirror of the mind was reflecting a new reality. And yet I did not see how one could pass without warning from the ills I was enduring to actual death. But then I thought of others, of all those who die every day without the hiatus between their illness and their death seeming to us extraordinary. I even thought it was only because I saw them from within (still more than through the consequent disappointment of my hopes) that certain ailments did not appear to me fatal when considered singly, although I believed in my death, just as those who are the most firmly convinced that their term has come are nevertheless easily persuaded that, if they cannot pronounce certain words, it has nothing to do with a stroke or an attack of aphasia, but comes from a fatigue of the tongue, from a nervous affection akin to stammering or from exhaustion consequent upon an attack of indigestion.

As for me, it was something quite other than a dying man's farewell to his wife which I had to write, something long and addressed to more than one person. Long to write! Only in the daytime, at best, might I try to sleep. If I worked, it would be only at night. But I should need many nights, possibly a hundred, possibly a thousand. And I would live in the anxiety of not knowing whether the master of my destiny, less indulgent than the Sultan Sheriar, when I interrupted my story in the morning, would permit me to take up the continuation of it the following evening. Not that I intended to reproduce in any respect *The Arabian Nights,* any more than the *Mémoires of Saint-Simon,* which likewise were written at night, any more than any of the books I had loved so deeply that, superstitiously devoted to them as to the women I loved, I could not, in my childish *naïveté,* imagine without horror a book that might be different from them. But like Elstir and Chardin, one cannot reproduce what one loves without abandoning it. Doubtless my books also, like my earthly being, would finally some day die. But one must resign oneself to the idea of death. One accepts the idea that in ten years one's self, and in a hundred years one's books, will no longer exist. Eternal existence is not promised to books any more than to men. It might be a book as long as *The Arabian Nights* but entirely different. It is quite true that, when one is enamoured of a book, one would like to create something exactly like it but one must sacrifice one's love of the moment and think, not of one's predilection but of a truth which does not ask our preferences and forbids us to give them a thought. And it is only by following this truth that one happens occasionally to come upon what one abandoned and, even while keeping them out of one's mind, to write the *Arabian Nights* or the *Mémoires of Saint-Simon* of another period. But had I still time? Was it not too late?

In any event, if I still had the strength to accomplish my work, I realised that the nature of the circumstances which to-day, even during the progress of this reception at the Princesse de Guermantes', had given me at one and the same time the idea of my work and the fear of not being able to carry it out would assuredly before all else imprint upon it the form I had once dimly sensed in the church at Combray, during certain days which had deeply influenced me, a form which usually remains invisible to us, the form of Time. This dimension of Time which I had once vaguely felt in the church at Combray I would try to make continually perceptible in a transcription of human life necessarily very different from that conveyed to us by our deceptive senses. There are, it is true — this was proven to me, as has been seen, by sundry episodes in this narrative — many other errors of our senses which distort for us the true aspect of this world. But after all, in the more accurate transcription which I would do

my utmost to give, I would at least be able not to change the location of
sounds, to take care not to detach them from their cause, with which the
intelligence retroactively associates them — although to make rain hum in
the middle of a room and our boiling *tisane* come down in torrents in the
courtyard cannot, when all is said and done, be more disconcerting than
what artists have so often done in representing as very near us or very
far away, according as the laws of perspective, the intensity of the colours
and the illusion of the first glance make them appear to us, a sail or a
mountain peak which our reason will later move, sometimes an enormous
distance, farther away or nearer to us.

I might, although this error is more serious, continue, as is customary, to
assign features to the countenance of a passing woman character, whereas,
in place of the nose, cheeks and chin, there should at the very most be a
vacant space on which would play the light of our desires. And even if I
did not have the leisure for that far more important matter, namely, to
prepare the hundred masks that needs must be attached to a single face —
even if one would merely portray it according to the various pairs of
eyes that look at it and the meanings they read into its features and, in
the case of one and the same pair of eyes, according to the hope and
fear (or, on the contrary, the love and confidence) which over so many
years hide the changes due to age; even, moreover, if I did not (although
my liaison with Albertine sufficed to prove to me that otherwise all is
spurious and deceitful) undertake to represent certain persons, not outwardly but as they exist within us, where their slightest acts may induce
fatal disturbances, and did not undertake also to vary the lighting from the
subjective sky according to the variations in pressure of our sensitiveness
or according to the serenity of our confidence, which makes an object
seem so small, whereas the mere shadow of a risk instantly multiplies its
size; even if I could not introduce these changes and many others (the
necessity for which, if one desires to paint things as they really are, has
become apparent in the course of this narrative) into the transcription of a
universe which required to be entirely redrawn, at any rate I would not
fail, above all else, to describe man as having the length, not of his body
but of his years, which he must drag about with him from place
to place, an ever increasing burden which overcomes him in the end.
Moreover, everyone realises that we occupy a steadily growing place in
Time and this universality could not fail to rejoice me, since it was truth,
the truth vaguely sensed by each, which I must seek to make clear to all.
Not only is everyone conscious that we occupy a place in Time, but
this place even the most simple-minded person measures approximately,
just as he would measure the place we occupy in space. True, the measur-

ing is often incorrect, but the fact that it was considered possible shews that age was thought of as something measurable.

I also asked myself, "Not only have I still time, but am I going to be able to complete my work?" By forcing me, like a stern spiritual adviser, to declare myself dead to the world, illness had done me a great service — for, an the grain of wheat die not after it hath been sown, it will abide alone; but if it die, it will bear much fruit — and after indolence had protected me from my facility in writing, ill health was perhaps going to save me from my indolence; but this same illness had exhausted my mental faculties and (as I had noticed long before, when I ceased to love Albertine) also the power of my memory. But re-creating through the memory impressions which must then be plumbed to their depths, brought into the light and transformed into intellectual equivalents, was this not one of the pre-requisites, almost the very essence, of a work of art such as I had conceived it in the library a few moments ago? Ah, if only I still had the mental power that was intact on that evening the memory of which I evoked when my eye fell on *François le Champi!* It was that evening, when my mother abdicated her authority, which marked the commencement of the waning of my will-power and my health, as well as the beginning of my grand-mother's lingering death. Everything was predetermined from the moment when, unable any longer to endure the idea of waiting until the morning to press a kiss upon my mother's face, I made up my mind, jumped out of bed and, in my nightshirt, went and sat by the window through which the moonlight came, until I heard M. Swann leave. My parents had accompanied him to the door; I heard the door open, the bell tinkle and the door shut again. Even at this moment, in the mansion of the Prince de Guermantes, I heard the sound of my parents' footsteps as they ac-companied M. Swann and the reverberating, ferruginous, interminable, sharp, jangling tinkle of the little bell which announced to me that at last M. Swann had gone and Mamma was going to come upstairs — I heard these sounds again, the very identical sounds themselves, although situated so far back in the past. Then, thinking over all the events that necessarily ranged themselves between the moment when I heard those sounds and the Guermantes reception, I was startled at the thought that it was, indeed, this bell which was still tinkling within me and that I could in no wise change its sharp janglings, since, having forgotten just how they died away, to recapture it and hear it distinctly, I was forced to close my ears to the sound of the conversations the masks were carrying on around me. To endeavour to listen to it from nearby, I had to descend again into my own consciousness. It must be, then, that this tinkling was still there and also, between it and the present moment, all the infinitely unrolling past which I had been unconsciously carrying within me. When the bell tinkled, I was already in existence and, since that night, for me to have been able to hear the sound again, there must have been no break of continuity, not a moment of rest for me, no cessation of existence, of thought, of consciousness of myself, since this distant moment still clung to me and I could recapture it, go back to it, merely by descending more deeply within myself. It was this conception of time as incarnate, of past years as still close held within us, which I was now determined to bring out into such bold relief in my book. And it is because they thus contain all the hours of days gone by that human bodies can do such injury to those who love them, because they contain so many past memories, joys and desires, already effaced for them but so cruel for one who contemplates and carries back in the domain of Time the cherished body of which he is jealous, jealous even to the point of desiring its destruction. For after death Time withdraws from the body, and the memories — so pale and in-significant — are effaced from her who no longer exists, and soon will be from him whom they still torture, and the memories themselves will perish in the end when the desire of a living body is no longer there to keep them alive.

There came over me a feeling of profound fatigue at the realisation that all this long stretch of time not only had been uninterruptedly lived, thought, secreted by me, that it was my life, my very self, but also that I must, every minute of my life, keep it closely by me, that it upheld me, that I was perched on its dizzying summit, that I could not move without carrying it about with me.

The date when I heard the sound — so distant and yet so deep within me — of the little bell in the garden at Combray was a landmark I did not know I had available in this enormous dimension of Time. My head swam to see so many years below me, and yet within me, as if I were thousands of leagues in height.

I now understood why it was that the Duc de Guermantes, whom, as I looked at him sitting in a chair, I marvelled to find shewing his age so little, although he had so many more years than I beneath him, as soon as he rose and tried to stand erect, had tottered on trembling limbs (like those of aged archbishops who have nothing solid on them except their metallic cross, with the young divinity students flocking assiduously about them) and had wavered as he made his way along the difficult summit of his eighty-three years, as if men were perched on giant stilts, sometimes taller than church spires, constantly growing and finally rendering their progress so difficult and perilous that they suddenly fall. I was alarmed that mine were already so tall beneath my feet; it did not seem as if I should have the strength to carry much longer attached to me that past which already extended so far down and which I was bearing so painfully within me! If, at least, there were granted me time enough to complete my work, I would not fail to stamp it with the seal of that Time the understanding of which was this day so forcibly impressing itself upon me, and I would therein describe men — even should that give them the semblance of monstrous creatures — as occupying in Time a place far more considerable than the so restricted one allotted them in space, a place, on the contrary, extending boundlessly since, giant-like, reaching far back into the years, they touch simultaneously epochs of their lives — with countless intervening days between — so widely separated from one another in Time.

from *A Portrait of the Artist as a Young Man*

[1916]

JAMES JOYCE

— To finish what I was saying about beauty — said Stephen — the most satisfying relations of the sensible must therefore correspond to the necessary phases of artistic apprehension. Find these and you find the qualities of universal beauty. Aquinas says: *Ad pulcritudinem tria requiruntur integritas, consonantia, claritas.* I translate it so: *Three things are needed for beauty, wholeness, harmony and radiance.* Do these correspond to the phases of apprehension? Are you following? —

— Of course, I am — said Lynch. — If you think I have an excrementitious intelligence run after Donovan and ask him to listen to you. —

Stephen pointed to a basket which a butcher's boy had slung inverted on his head.

— Look at that basket — he said.

— I see it — said Lynch.

— In order to see that basket — said Stephen — your mind first of all separates the basket from the rest of the visible universe which is not the basket. The first phase of apprehension is a bounding line drawn about the object to be apprehended. An esthetic image is presented to us either in space or in time. What is audible is presented in time, what is visible is presented in space. But temporal or spatial, the esthetic image is first luminously apprehended as selfbounded and selfcontained upon the immeasurable background of space or time which is not it. You apprehended it as *one* thing. You see it as one whole. You apprehend its wholeness. That is *integritas*. —

— Bull's eye! — said Lynch, laughing — Go on. —

— Then — said Stephen — you pass from point to point, led by its formal lines; you apprehend it as balanced part against part within its limits; you feel the rhythm of its structure. In other words, the synthesis of immediate perception is followed by the analysis of apprehension. Having first felt that it is *one* thing you feel now that it is a *thing*. You apprehend it as complex, multiple, divisible, separable, made up of its parts, the result of its parts and their sum, harmonious. That is *consonantia*. —

— Bull's eye again! — said Lynch wittily. — Tell me now what is claritas and you win the cigar. —

— The connotation of the word — Stephen said — is rather vague. Aquinas uses a term which seems to be inexact. It baffled me for a long time. It would lead you to believe that he had in mind symbolism or idealism, the supreme quality of beauty being a light from some other world, the idea of which the matter was but the shadow, the reality of which it was but the symbol. I thought he might mean that *claritas* was the artistic discovery and representation of the divine purpose in anything or a force of generalization which would make the esthetic image a universal one, make it outshine its proper conditions. But that is literary talk. I understand it so. When you have apprehended that basket as one thing and have then analysed it according to its form and apprehended it as a thing you make the only synthesis which is logically and esthetically permissible. You see that it is that thing which it is and no other thing. The radiance of which he speaks in the scholastic *quidditas,* the *whatness* of a thing. This supreme quality is felt by the artist when the esthetic image is first conceived in his imagination. The mind in that mysterious instant Shelley likened beautifully to a fading coal. The instant wherein that supreme quality of beauty, the clear radiance of the esthetic image, is apprehended luminously by the mind which has been arrested by its wholeness and fascinated by its harmony is the luminous silent stasis of esthetic pleasure, a spiritual state very like to that cardiac condition which the Italian physiologist Luigi Galvani, using a phrase almost as beautiful as Shelley's, called the enchantment of the heart. —

Stephen paused and, though his companion did not speak, felt that his words had called up around them a thought enchanted silence.

— What I have said — he began again — refers to beauty in the wider sense of the word, in the sense which the word has in the literary tradition. In the market place it has another sense. When we speak of beauty in the second sense of the term our judgment is influenced in the first place by the art itself and by the form of that art. The image, it is clear, must be set between the mind or senses of the artist himself and the mind or senses of others. If you bear this in memory you will see that art necessarily divides itself into three forms progressing from one to the next. These forms are: the lyrical form, the form wherein the artist presents his image in immediate relation to himself; the epical form, the form wherein he presents his image in mediate relation to himself and to others; the dramatic form, the form wherein he presents his image in immediate relation to others. —

— That you told me a few nights ago — said Lynch — and we began the famous discussion. —

— I have a book at home — said Stephen — in which I have written down questions which are more amusing than yours were. In finding the answers to them I found the theory of the esthetic which I am trying to explain. Here are some questions I set myself: *Is a chair finely made tragic or comic? Is the portrait of Mona Lisa good if I desire to see it? Is the bust of Sir Philip Crampton lyrical, epical or dramatic? If not, why not?* —

— Why not, indeed? — said Lynch, laughing.

— *If a man hacking in fury at a block of wood* — Stephen continued — *make there an image of a cow, is that image a work of art? If not, why not?* —

— That's a lovely one — said Lynch, laughing again. — That has the true scholastic stink. —

— Lessing — said Stephen — should not have taken a group of statues to write of. The art, being inferior, does not present the forms I spoke of distinguished clearly one from another. Even in literature, the highest and most spiritual art, the forms are often confused. The lyrical form is in fact the simplest verbal vesture of an instant of emotion, a rhythmical cry such as ages ago cheered on the man who pulled at the oar or dragged stones up a slope. He who utters it is more conscious of the instant of emotion than of himself as feeling emotion. The simplest epical form is seen emerging out of lyrical literature when the artist prolongs and broods upon himself as the centre of an epical event and this form progresses till the centre of emotional gravity is equidistant from the artist himself and from others. The narrative is no longer purely personal. The personality of the artist passes into the narration itself, flowing round and round the persons and the action like a vital sea. This progress you will see easily in that old English ballad *Turpin Hero,* which begins in the first person and ends in the third person. The dramatic form is reached when the vitality which has flowed and eddied round each person fills every person with such vital force that he or she assumes a proper and intangible esthetic life. The personality of the artist, at first a cry or a cadence or a mood and then a fluid and lambent narrative, finally refines itself out of existence, impersonalizes itself, so to speak. The esthetic image in the dramatic form is life purified in and reprojected from the human imagination. The mystery of esthetic like that of material creation is accomplished. The artist, like the God of the creation, remains within or behind or beyond or above his handiwork, invisible, refined out of existence, indifferent, paring his fingernails. —

from *Finnegans Wake*

[1939]

JAMES JOYCE

Well, you know or don't you kennet or haven't I told you every telling has a taling and that's the he and the she of it. Look, look, the dusk is growing. My branches lofty are taking root. And my cold cher's gone ashley. Fieluhr? Filou! What age is at? It saon is late. 'Tis endless now senne eye or erewone last saw Waterhouse's clogh. They took it asunder, I hurd thum sigh. When will they reassemble it? O, my back, my back, my bach! I'd want to go to Aches-les-Pains. Pingpong! There's the Belle for Sexaloitez! And Concepta de Send-us-pray! Pang! Wring out the clothes! Wring in the dew! Godavari, vert the showers! And grant thaya grace! Aman. Will we spread them here now? Ay, we will. Flip! Spread on your bank and I'll spread mine on mine. Flep! It's what I'm doing. Spread! It's churning chill. Der went is rising. I'll lay a few stones on the hostel sheets. A man and his bride embraced between them. Else I'd have sprinkled and folded them only. And I'll tie my butcher's apron here. It's suety yet. The strollers will pass it by. Six shifts, ten kerchiefs, nine to hold to the fire and this for the code, the convent napkins, twelve, one baby's shawl. Good mother Jossiph knows, she said. Whose head? Mutter snores? Deataceas! Wharnow are alle her childer, say? In kingdome gone or power to come or gloria be to them farther? Allalivial, allalluvial! Some here, more no more, more again lost alla stranger. I've heard tell that same brooch of the Shannons was married into a family in Spain. And all the Dunders de Dunnes in Markland's Vineland beyond Brendan's herring pool takes number nine in yangsee's hats. And one of Biddy's beads went bobbing till she rounded up lost histereve with a marigold and a cobbler's candle in a side strain of a main drain of a manzinahurries off Bachelor's Walk. But all that's left to the last of the Meaghers in the loup of the years prefixed and between is one kneebuckle and two hooks in the front. Do you tell me that now? I do in troth. Orara por Orbe and poor Las Animas! Ussa, Ulla, we're umbas all! Mezha, didn't you hear it a deluge of times, ufer and ufer, respund to spond? You deed, you deed! I need, I need! It's that irrawaddyng I've stoke in my aars. It all but husheth the lethest zswound. Oronoko! What's your trouble? Is that the great Finnleader himself in his joakimono on his statue riding the high horse there forehengist? Father of Otters, it is himself! Yonne there! Isset that? On Fallareen Common? You're thinking of Astley's Amphitheayter where the bobby restrained you making sugarstuck pouts to the ghostwhite horse of the Peppers. Throw the cobwebs from your eyes, woman, and spread your washing proper. It's well I know your sort of slop. Flap! Ireland sober is Ireland stiff. Lord help you, Maria, full of grease, the load is with me! Your prayers. I sonht zo! Madammangut! Were you lifting your elbow, tell us, glazy cheeks, in Conway's Carrigacurra canteen? Was I what, hobbledyhips? Flop! Your rere gait's creakorheuman bitts your butts disagrees. Amn't I up since the damp dawn, marthared mary allacook, with Corrigan's pulse and varicoarse veins, my pramaxle smashed, Alice Jane in decline and my oneeyed mongrel twice run over, soaking and bleaching boiler rags, and sweating cold, a widow like me, for to deck my tennis champion son, the laundryman with the lavandier flannels? You won your limpopo limp fron the husky hussars when Collars and Cuffs was heir to the town and your slur gave the stink to Carlow. Holy Scamander, I sar it again! Near the golden falls. Icis on us! Seints of light! Zezere! Subdue your noise, you hamble creature! What is it but a blackburry growth or the dwyergray ass them four old codgers owns. Are you meanam Tarpey and Lyons and Gregory? I meyne now, thank all, the four of them, and the roar of them, that draves that stray in the mist and old Johnny MacDougal along with them. Is that the Poolbeg flasher beyant, pharphar, or a fireboat coasting nyar the Kishtna or a glow I behold within a hedge or my Garry come back from the Indes? Wait till the honeying of the lune, love! Die eve, little eve, die! We see that wonder in your eye. We'll meet again, we'll part once more. The spot I'll seek if the hour you'll find. My chart shines high where the blue milk's upset. Forgivemequick, I'm going! Bubye! And you, pluck your watch, forgetmenot. Your evenlode. So save to jurna's end! My sights are swimming thicker on me by the shadows to this place. I sow home slowly now by own way, moyvalley way. Towy I too, rathmine.

Ah, but she was the queer old skeowsha anyhow, Anna Livia, trinkettoes! And sure he was the quare old buntz too, Dear Dirty Dumpling, foostherfather of fingalls and dottergills. Gammer and gaffer we're all their gangsters. Hadn't he seven dams to wive him? And every dam had her seven crutches. And every crutch had its seven hues. And each hue had a differing cry. Sudds for me and supper for you and the doctor's bill for Joe John. Befor! Bifur! He married his markets, cheap by foul, I know, like any Etrurian Catholic Heathen, in their pinky limony creamy birnies and their turkiss indienne mauves. But at milkidmass who was the spouse? Then all that was was fair. Tys Elvenland! Teems of times and happy returns. The seim anew. Ordovico or viricordo. Anna was, Livia is, Plurabelle's to be. Northmen's thing made southfolk's place but howmulty plurators made eachone in person? Latin me that, my trinity scholard, out of eure sanscreed into oure eryan. *Hircus Civis Eblanensis!* He had buckgoat paps on him, soft ones for orphans. Ho, Lord! Twins of his bosom. Lord save us! And ho! Hey? What all men. Hot? His tittering daughters of. Whawk?

Can't hear with the waters of. The chittering waters of. Flittering bats, fieldmice bawk talk. Ho! Are you not gone ahome? What Thom Malone? Can't hear with bawk of bats, all thim liffeying waters of. Ho, talk save us! My foos won't moos. I feel as old as yonder elm. A tale told of Shaun or Shem? All Livia's daughtersons. Dark hawks hear us. Night! Night! My ho head halls. I feel as heavy as yonder stone. Tell me of John or Shaun? Who were Shem and Shaun the living sons or daughters of? Night now! Tell me, tell me, tell me, elm! Night night! Telmetale of stem or stone. Beside the rivering waters of, hitherandthithering waters of. Night!

2

EZRA POUND *and* JEAN COCTEAU

*At no time in history did the Arts have a more passionate
patriot than Ezra Pound (he was their Patrick Henry, crying
"Give me Poetry, or give me Death!" — which he nearly got,
at one point, though for other reasons); nor a more seductive
Pied Piper than Jean Cocteau. They were poets themselves,
and much more original in their own right than it is yet possible to see, probably. But at the least, they already stand as
the century's most inspired, tireless and resourceful "public
relations" men on behalf of the Arts. Cocteau's "clients" included Picasso, Stravinsky, Apollinaire, Proust, Gide, de
Chirico; Pound's included Yeats, Eliot, Joyce, Brancusi, Frost,
Henry James; and between them, in one way or another, their
precept and example inflamed three generations of literate
youth and will go on doing so indefinitely.*

How to Read

[1928]

EZRA POUND

PART ONE: INTRODUCTION

*Largely Autobiographical, Touching the Present, and More or Less
Immediately Past, "State of Affairs."*

Literary instruction in our "institutions of learning" was, at the
beginning of this century, cumbrous and inefficient. I dare say it still is.
Certain more or less mildly exceptional professors were affected by the
"beauties" of various authors (usually deceased), but the system, as a
whole, lacked sense and co-ordination. I dare say it still does. When
studying physics we are not asked to investigate the biographies of all the
disciples of Newton who showed interest in science, but who failed to
make any discovery. Neither are their unrewarded gropings, hopes, passions, laundry bills, or erotic experiences thrust on the hurried student or
considered germane to the subject.

The general contempt of "scholarship," especially any part of it connected with subjects included in university "Arts" courses; the shrinking
of people in general from any book supposed to be "good"; and, in another mode, the flamboyant advertisements telling "how to seem to know
it when you don't," might long since have indicated to the sensitive that
there is something defective in the contemporary methods of purveying
letters.

As the general reader has but a vague idea of what these methods are
at the "centre," i.e. for the specialist who is expected to serve the general
reader, I shall lapse or plunge into autobiography.

In my university I found various men interested (or uninterested) in
their subjects, but, I think, no man with a view of literature as a whole,
or with any idea whatsoever of the relation of the part he himself taught
to any other part.

Those professors who regarded their "subject" as a drill manual rose
most rapidly to positions of executive responsibility (one case is now a

provost). Those professors who had some natural aptitude for comprehending their authors and for communicating a general sense of comfort in the presence of literary masterwork remained obscurely in their less exalted positions.

A professor of Romanics admitted that the *Chanson de Roland* was inferior to the *Odyssey,* but then the Middle Ages were expected to present themselves with apologies, and this was, if I remember rightly, an isolated exception. English novelists were not compared with the French. "Sources" were discussed; forty versions of a Chaucerian anecdote were "compared," but not on points of respective literary merit. The whole field was full of redundance. I mean that what one had learned in one class, in the study of one literature, one was told again in some other.

One was asked to remember what some critic (deceased) had said, scarcely to consider whether his views were still valid, or ever had been very intelligent.

In defence of this dead and uncorrelated system, it may be urged that authors like Spengler, who attempt a synthesis, often do so before they have attained sufficient knowledge of detail: that they stuff expandable and compressible objects into rubber-bag categories, and that they limit their reference and interest by supposing that the pedagogic follies which they have themselves encountered, constitute an error universally distributed, and encountered by every one else. In extenuation of their miscalculations we may admit that any error or clumsiness of method that has sunk into, or been hammered into one man, over a period of years, probably continues as an error — not merely passively, but as an error still being propagated, consciously or unconsciously, by a number of educators, from laziness, from habits, or from natural cussedness.

"Comparative literature" sometimes figures in university curricula, but very few people know what they mean by the term, or approach it with a considered conscious method.

To tranquillize the low-brow reader, let me say at once that I do not wish to muddle him by making him read more books, but to allow him to read fewer with greater result. (I am willing to discuss this privately with the book trade.) I have been accused of wanting to make people read all the classics; which is not so. I have been accused of wishing to provide a "portable substitute for the British Museum," which I would do, like a shot, were it possible. It isn't.

American "taste" is less official than English taste, but more derivative. When I arrived in England (A.D. 1908), I found a greater darkness in the British "serious press" than had obtained on the banks of the Schuylkill. Already in my young and ignorant years they considered me "learned."

It was impossible, at first, to see why and whence the current opinion of British weeklies. It was incredible that literate men — men literate enough, that is, to write the orderly paragraphs that they did write constantly in their papers — believed the stupidities that appeared there with such regularity. (Later, for two years, we ran fortnightly in the *Egoist,* the sort of fool-column that the French call a *sottisier,* needing nothing for it but quotations from the *Times Literary Supplement.* Two issues of the *Supplement* yielding, easily, one page of the *Egoist.*) For years I awaited enlightenment. One winter I had lodgings in Sussex. On the mantelpiece of the humble country cottage I found books of an earlier era, among them an anthology printed in 1830, and yet another dated 1795, and there, there by the sox of Jehosaphat was the British taste of this century, 1910, 1915, and even the present, A.D. 1931.

I had read Stendhal's remark that it takes eighty years for anything to reach the general public, and looking out on the waste heath, under the December drizzle, I believed him. But that is not all of the story. Embedded in that naïve innocence that does, to their credit, pervade our universities, I ascribed the delay to mere time. I still thought: With the attrition of decades, ah, yes, in another seventy, in another, perhaps, ninety years, they will admit that . . . etc.

I mean that I thought they wanted to, but were hindered.

Later it struck me that the best history of painting in London was the National Gallery, and that the best history of literature, more particularly of poetry, would be a twelve-volume anthology in which each poem was chosen not merely because it was a nice poem or a poem Aunt Hepsy liked, but because it contained an invention, a definite contribution to the art of verbal expression. With this in mind, I approached a respected agent. He was courteous, he was even openly amazed at the list of three hundred items which I offered as an indication of outline. No autochthonous Briton had ever, to his professed belief, displayed such familiarity with so vast a range, but he was too indolent to recast my introductory letter into a form suited to commerce. He, as they say, "repaired" to an equally august and long-established publishing house (which had already served his and my interest). In two days came a hasty summons: would I see him in person. I found him awed, as if one had killed a cat in the sacristy. Did I know what I had said in my letter? I did. Yes, but about Palgrave? I did. I had said: "It is time we had something to replace that doddard Palgrave." "But don't you know," came the awstruck tones, "that the whole fortune of X & Co. is founded on Palgrave's *Golden Treasury?*"

From that day onward no book of mine received a British imprimatur until the appearance of Eliot's castrated edition of my poems.

I perceived that there were thousands of pounds sterling invested in electro-plate, and the least change in the public taste, let alone swift, catastrophic changes, would depreciate the value of those electros (of Hemans, let us say, or of Collins, Cowper, and of Churchill, who wrote the satiric verses, and of later less blatant cases, touched with a slighter flavour of mustiness).

I sought the banks of the Seine. Against ignorance one might struggle, and even against organic stupidity, but against a so vast vested interest the lone odds were too heavy.

Two years later a still more august academic press reopened the question. *They* had ventured to challenge Palgrave: they had been "interested" — would I send back my prospectus? I did. They found the plan "too ambitious." They said they might do "something," but that if they did it would "be more in the nature of gems."

For a Method

Nevertheless, the method I had proposed was simple, it is perhaps the only one that can give a man an orderly arrangement of his perception in the matter of letters. In opposition to it, there are the forces of super-stition, of hang-over. People regard literature as something vastly more flabby and floating and complicated and indefinite than, let us say, mathematics. Its subject-matter, the human consciousness, is more complicated than are number and space. It is not, however, more complicated than biology, and no one ever supposed that it was. We apply a loose-leaf system to book-keeping so as to have the live items separated from the dead ones. In the study of physics we begin with simple mechanisms, wedge, lever and fulcrum, pulley and inclined plane, all of them still as useful as when they were first invented. We proceed by a study of dis-coveries. We are not asked to memorize a list of the parts of a side-wheeler engine.

And we could, presumably, apply to the study of literature a little of the common sense that we currently apply to physics or to biology. In poetry there are simple procedures, and there are known discoveries, clearly marked. As I have said in various places in my unorganized and fragmentary volumes: in each age one or two men of genius find some-thing, and express it. It may be in only a line or in two lines, or in some quality of a cadence; and thereafter two dozen, or two hundred, or two or more thousand followers repeat and dilute and modify.

And if the instructor would select his specimens from works that con-tain these discoveries and solely on the basis of discovery — which may

lie in the dimension of depth, not merely of some novelty on the surface
— he would aid his student far more than by presenting his authors at
random, and talking about them *in toto*.

Needless to say, this presentation would be entirely independent of
consideration as to whether the given passages tended to make the student
a better republican, monarchist, monist, dualist, rotarian, or other sec-
tarian. To avoid confusion, one should state at once that such method has
nothing to do with those allegedly scientific methods which approach
literature as if it were something *not literature,* or with scientists'
attempts to sub-divide the elements in literature according to some non-
literary categoric division.

You do not divide physics or chemistry according to racial or religious
categories. You do not put discoveries by Methodists and Germans into
one category, and discoveries by Episcopalians or Americans or Italians
into another.

Defective Relativities

It is said that in America nothing is ever consciously related to anything
else. I have cited as an exception the forty versions of the Chaucerian
anecdote; they and the great edition of Horace with the careful list and
parallel display of Greek sources for such line or such paragraph, show
how the associative faculty can be side-tracked. Or at any rate they indi-
cate the first gropings of association. Let us grant that some bits of literature have been, in special cases, displayed in relation to some other bits;
usually some verbose gentleman writes a trilogy of essays, on three grandiose figures, comparing their "philosophy" or personal habits.

Let us by all means glance at "philology" and the "germanic system."
Speaking as an historian, "we" may say that this system was designed to
inhibit thought. After 1848 it was, in Germany, observed that some people
thought. It was necessary to curtail this pernicious activity, the thinkists
were given a china egg labelled scholarship, and were gradually unfitted
for active life, or for any contact with life in general. Literature was permitted as a subject of study. And its study was so designed as to draw the
mind of the student away from literature into inanity.

Why Books?

I

This simple first question was never asked.

The study of literature, or more probably of morphology, verb-roots,
etc., was permitted the German professor in, let us say, 1880–1905, to keep
his mind off life in general, and off public life in particular.

In America it was permitted from precedent; it was known to be permitted in Germany; Germany had a "great university tradition," which it behoved America to equal and perhaps to surpass.

This study, or some weaker variety of it, was also known to be permitted at Oxford, and supposed to have a refining influence on the student.

II

The practice of literary composition in private has been permitted since "age immemorial," like knitting, crocheting, etc. It occupies the practitioner, and, so long as he keeps it to himself, *ne nuit pas aux autres,* it does not transgress the definition of liberty which we find in the declaration of the *Droits de l'Homme:* Liberty is the right to do anything which harms not others. All of which is rather negative and unsatisfactory.

III

It appears to me quite tenable that the function of literature as a generated prize-worthy force is precisely that it does incite humanity to continue living; that it eases the mind of strain, and feeds it, I mean definitely as *nutrition of impulse.*

This idea may worry lovers of order. Just as good literature does often worry them. They regard it as dangerous, chaotic, subversive. They try every idiotic and degrading wheeze to tame it down. They try to make a bog, a marasmus, a great putridity in place of a sane and active ebullience. And they do this from sheer simian and pig-like stupidity, and from their failure to understand the function of letters.

IV

Has literature a function in the state, in the aggregation of humans, in the republic, in the *res publica,* which ought to mean the public convenience (despite the slime of bureaucracy, and the execrable taste of the populace in selecting its rulers)? It has.

And this function is *not* the coercing or emotionally persuading, or bullying or suppressing people into the acceptance of any one set or any six sets of opinions as opposed to any other one set or half-dozen sets of opinions.

It has to do with the clarity and vigour of "any and every" thought and opinion. It has to do with maintaining the very cleanliness of the tools, the health of the very matter of thought itself. Save in the rare and limited instances of invention in the plastic arts, or in mathematics, the individual cannot think and communicate his thought, the governor and legislator cannot act effectively or frame his laws, without words, and the solidity and validity of these words is in the care of the damned and despised *litterati*. When their work goes rotten — by that I do not mean when they express indecorous thoughts — but when their very medium, the very essence of their work, the application of word to thing goes rotten, i.e. becomes slushy and inexact, or excessive or bloated, the whole machinery of social and of individual thought and order goes to pot. This is a lesson of history, and a lesson not yet half learned.

The great writers need no debunking.

The pap is not in them, and doesn't need to be squeezed out. They do not lend themselves to imperial and sentimental exploitations. A civilization was founded on Homer, civilization not a mere bloated empire. The Macedonian domination rose and grew after the sophists. It also subsided.

It is not only a question of rhetoric, of loose expression, but also of the loose use of individual words. What the renaissance gained in direct examination of natural phenomena, it in part lost in losing the feel and desire for exact descriptive terms. I mean that the medieval mind had little but words to deal with, and it was more careful in its definitions and verbiage. It did not define a gun in terms that would just as well define an explosion, nor explosions in terms that would define triggers.

Misquoting Confucius, one might say: It does not matter whether the author desire the good of the race or acts merely from personal vanity. The thing is mechanical in action. In proportion as his work is exact, i.e., true to human consciousness and to the nature of man, as it is exact in formulation of desire, so is it durable and so is it "useful"; I mean it maintains the precision and clarity of thought, not merely for the benefit of a few dilettantes and "lovers of literature," but maintains the health of thought outside literary circles and in non-literary existence, in general individual and communal life.

Or *"dans ce genre on n'émeut que par la clarté."* One "moves" the reader only by clarity. In depicting the motions of the "human heart" the durability of the writing depends on the exactitude. It is the thing that is true and stays true that keeps fresh for the new reader.

With this general view in mind, and subsequent to the events already set forth in this narrative, I proposed (from the left bank of the Seine, and to an American publishing house), not the twelve-volume anthology, but a short guide to the subject. That was after a few years of "pause and reflection." The subject was pleasantly received and considered with amity, but the house finally decided that it would pay neither them to print nor me to write the book, because we "weren't in the text-book ring." For the thing would have been a text-book, its circulation would have depended on educators, and educators have been defined as "men with no intellectual interests."

Hence, after a lapse of four years, this essay, dedicated to Mr Glenn Frank, and other starters of ideal universities, though not with any great hope that it will rouse them.

PART II: OR WHAT MAY BE
AN INTRODUCTION TO METHOD

It is as important for the purpose of thought to keep language efficient as it is in surgery to keep tetanus bacilli out of one's bandages.

In introducing a person to literature one would do well to have him examine works where language is efficiently used; to devise a system for getting directly and expeditiously at such works, despite the smokescreens erected by half-knowing and half-thinking critics. To get at them, despite the mass of dead matter that these people have heaped up and conserved round about them in the proportion: one barrel of sawdust to each half-bunch of grapes.

Great literature is simply language charged with meaning to the utmost possible degree.

When we set about examining it we find that this charging has been done by several clearly definable sorts of people, and by a periphery of less determinate sorts.

(*a*) *The inventors*, discoverers of a particular process or of more than one mode and process. Sometimes these people are known, or discoverable; for example, we know, with reasonable certitude, that Arnaut Daniel introduced certain methods of rhyming, and we know that certain fine-nesses of perception appeared first in such a troubadour or in G. Cavalcanti. We do not know, and are not likely to know, anything definite about the precursors of Homer.

(*b*) *The masters*. This is a very small class, and there are very few real ones. The term is properly applied to inventors who, apart from their own inventions, are able to assimilate and co-ordinate a large number of preceding inventions. I mean to say they either start with a core of their own and accumulate adjuncts, or they digest a vast mass of subject-matter, apply a number of known modes of expression, and succeed in pervading the whole with some special quality or some special character of their own, and bring the whole to a state of homogeneous fullness.

(*c*) *The diluters*, these who follow either the inventors or the "great writers," and who produce something of lower intensity, some flabbier variant, some diffuseness or tumidity in the wake of the valid.

(*d*) (And this class produces the great bulk of all writing.) The men who do more or less good work in the more or less good style of a period. Of these the delightful anthologies, the song books, are full, and choice among them is the matter of taste, for you prefer Wyatt to Donne, Donne to Herrick, Drummond of Hawthornden to Browne, in response to some purely personal sympathy, these people add but some slight personal flavour, some minor variant of a mode, without affecting the main course of the story.

At their faintest *"Ils n'existent pas, leur ambiance leur confert une existence."* They do not exist: their ambience confers existence upon them. When they are most prolific they produce dubious cases like Virgil and Petrarch, who probably pass, among the less exigeant, for colossi.

(*e*) *Belles Lettres.* Longus, Prévost, Benjamin Constant, who are not exactly "great masters," who can hardly be said to have originated a form, but who have nevertheless brought some mode to a very high development.

(*f*) And there is a supplementary or sixth class of writers, the starters of crazes, the Ossianic McPhersons, the Gongoras [1] whose wave of fashion flows over writing for a few centuries or a few decades, and then subsides, leaving things as they were.

It will be seen that the first two classes are the more sharply defined: that the difficulty of classification for particular lesser authors increases as one descends the list, save for the last class, which is again fairly clear.

The point is, that if a man knows the facts about the first two categories, he can evaluate almost any unfamiliar book at first sight. I mean he can form a just estimate of its worth, and see how and where it belongs in this schema.

As to crazes, the number of possible diseases in literature is perhaps not very great, the same afflictions crop up in widely separated countries without any previous communication. The good physician will recognize a known malady, even if the manifestation be superficially different.

The fact that six different critics will each have a different view concerning what author belongs in which of the categories here given, does not in the least invalidate the categories. When a man knows the facts about the first two categories, the reading of work in the other categories will not greatly change his opinion about those in the first two.

Language

Obviously this knowledge cannot be acquired without knowledge of various tongues. The same discoveries have served a number of races. If a man has not time to learn different languages he can at least, and with very little delay, be told what the discoveries were. If he wish to be a good critic he will have to look for himself.

Bad critics have prolonged the use of demoded terminology, usually a terminology originally invented to describe what had been done before 300 B.C., and to describe it in a rather exterior fashion. Writers of second order have often tried to produce works to fit some category or term not yet occupied in their own local literature. If we chuck out the classifications which apply to the outer shape of the work, or to its occasion, and if we look at what actually happens, in, let us say, poetry, we will find that the language is charged or energized in various manners.

That is to say, there are three "kinds of poetry":

MELOPŒIA, wherein the words are charged, over and above their plain meaning, with some musical property, which directs the bearing or trend of that meaning.

PHANOPŒIA, which is a casting of images upon the visual imagination.

LOGOPŒIA, "the dance of the intellect among words," that is to say, it employs words not only for their direct meaning, but it takes count in a special way of habits of usage, of the context we *expect* to find with the word, its usual concomitants, of its known acceptances, and of ironical play. It holds the aesthetic content which is peculiarly the domain of verbal manifestation, and cannot possibly be contained in plastic or in music. It is the latest come, and perhaps most tricky and undependable mode.

The *melopœia* can be appreciated by a foreigner with a sensitive ear, even though he be ignorant of the language in which the poem is written. It is practically impossible to transfer or translate it from one language to another, save perhaps by divine accident, and for half a line at a time.

Phanopœia can, on the other hand, be translated almost, or wholly, intact. When it is good enough, it is practically impossible for the translator to destroy it save by very crass bungling, and the neglect of perfectly well-known and formulative rules.

Logopœia does not translate; though the attitude of mind it expresses may pass through a paraphrase. Or one might say, you can *not* translate it "locally," but having determined the original author's state of mind, you may or may not be able to find a derivative or an equivalent.

Prose

The language of prose is much less highly charged, that is perhaps the only availing distinction between prose and poesy. Prose permits greater factual presentation, explicitness, but a much greater amount of language is needed. During the last century or century and a half, prose has, perhaps for the first time, perhaps for the second or third time, arisen to

challenge the poetic pre-eminence. That is to say, *Cœur Simple,* by Flaubert, is probably more important than Théophile Gautier's *Carmen,* etc.

The total charge in certain nineteenth-century prose works possibly
surpasses the total charge found in individual poems of that period; but
that merely indicates that the author has been able to get his effect
cumulatively, by a greater heaping up of factual data; imagined fact, if
you will, but nevertheless expressed in factual manner.

By using several hundred pages of prose, Flaubert, by force of architectonics, manages to attain an intensity comparable to that in Villon's
Heaulmière, or his prayer for his mother. This does not invalidate my
dissociation of the two terms: poetry, prose.

In *Phanopœia* we find the greatest drive toward utter precision of word;
this art exists almost exclusively by it.

In *melopœia* we find a contrary current, a force tending often to lull, or
to distract the reader from the exact sense of the language. It is poetry
on the borders of music and music is perhaps the bridge between consciousness and the unthinking sentient or even insentient universe.

All writing is built up of these three elements, plus "architectonics" or
"the form of the whole," and to know anything about the relative effi-
ciency of various works one must have some knowledge of the maximum
already attained by various authors, irrespective of where and when.

It is not enough to know that the Greeks attained to the greatest skill
in melopœia, or even that the Provençaux added certain diverse developments and that some quite minor, nineteenth-century Frenchmen achieved
certain elaborations.

It is not quite enough to have the general idea that the Chinese (more
particularly Rihaku and Omakitsu) attained the known maximum of
phanopœia, due perhaps to the nature of their written ideograph, or to
wonder whether Rimbaud is, at rare moments, their equal. One wants
one's knowledge in more definite terms.

It is an error to think that vast reading will automatically produce any
such knowledge or understanding. Neither Chaucer with his forty books,
nor Shakespeare with perhaps half a dozen, in folio, can be considered
illiterate. A man can learn more music by working on a Bach fugue until
he can take it apart and put it together, than by playing through ten
dozen heterogeneous albums.

You may say that for twenty-seven years I have thought consciously
about this particular matter, and read or read at a great many books, and
that with the subject never really out of my mind, I don't yet know half
there is to know about *melopœia.*

There are, on the other hand, a few books that I still keep on my desk, and a great number that I shall never open again. But the books that a man needs to know in order to "get his bearings," in order to have a sound judgement of any bit of writing that may come before him, are very few. The list is so short, indeed, that one wonders that people, professional writers in particular, are willing to leave them ignored and to continue dangling in mid-chaos emitting the most imbecile estimates, and often vitiating their whole lifetime's production.

Limiting ourselves to the authors who actually invented something, or who are the "first known examples" of the process in working order, we find:

OF THE GREEKS: Homer, Sappho. (The "great dramatists" decline from Homer, and depend immensely on him for their effects; their "charge," at its highest potential, depends so often, and so greatly on their being able to count on their audience's knowledge of the *Iliad*. Even Æschylus is rhetorical.)

OF THE ROMANS: As we have lost Philetas, and most of Callimachus, we may suppose that the Romans added a certain sophistication; at any rate, Catullus, Ovid, Propertius, all give us something we cannot find now in Greek authors.

A specialist may read Horace if he is interested in learning the precise demarcation between what can be learned about writing, and what cannot. I mean that Horace is the perfect example of a man who acquired all that is acquirable, without having the root. I beg the reader to observe that I am being exceedingly iconoclastic, that I am omitting thirty established names for every two I include. I am chucking out Pindar, and Virgil, without the slightest compunction. I do not suggest a "course" in Greek or Latin literature, I name a few isolated writers; five or six pages of Sappho. One can throw out at least one-third of Ovid. That is to say, I am omitting the authors who can teach us no new or no more effective method of "charging" words.

OF THE MIDDLE AGES: The Anglo-Saxon Seafarer, and some more cursory notice of some medieval narrative, it does not so greatly matter what narrative, possibly the *Beowulf,* the *Poema del Cid,* and the sagas of *Grettir* and *Burnt Nial.* And then, in contrast, troubadours, perhaps thirty poems in Provençal, and for comparison with them a few songs by Von Morungen, or Wolfram von Essenbach, and von der Vogelweide; and then Bion's *Death of Adonis.*

From which mixture, taken in this order, the reader will get his bearings on the art of poetry made to be sung; for there are three kinds of *melopœia:* (1) that made to be sung to a tune; (2) that made to be intoned or sung to a sort of chant; and (3) that made to be spoken; and the art of joining words in each of these kinds is different, and cannot be clearly understood until the reader knows that there are three different objectives.

OF THE ITALIANS: Guido Cavalcanti and Dante; perhaps a dozen and a half poems of Guido's, and a dozen poems by his contemporaries, and the *Divina Commedia*.

In Italy, around the year 1300, there were new values established, things said that had not been said in Greece, or in Rome or elsewhere.

VILLON: After Villon and for several centuries, poetry can be considered as *fioritura,* as an efflorescence, almost an effervescence, and without any new roots. Chaucer is an enrichment, one might say a more creamy version of the "matter of France," and he in some measure preceded the verbal richness of the classic revival, but beginning with the Italians after Dante, coming through the Latin writers of the Renaissance, French, Spanish, English, Tasso, Ariosto, etc., the Italians always a little in the lead, the whole is elaboration, medieval basis, and wash after wash of Roman or Hellenic influence. I mean one need not read any particular part of it for purpose of learning one's comparative values.

If one were studying history and not poetry, one might discover the medieval mind more directly in the opening of Mussato's *Ecerinus* than even in Dante. The culture of Chaucer is the same as that which went contemporaneously into Ferrara, with the tongue called *"francoveneto."*

One must emphasize one's contrasts in the quattrocento. One can take Villon as pivot for understanding them. After Villon, and having begun before his time, we find this *fioritura,* and for centuries we find little else. Even in Marlowe and Shakespeare there is this embroidery of language, this talk about the matter, rather than presentation. I doubt if anyone ever acquired discrimination in studying "The Elizabethans." You have grace, richness of language, abundance, but you have probably nothing that isn't replaceable by something else, no ornament that wouldn't have done just as well in some other connection, or for which some other figure of rhetoric couldn't have served, or which couldn't have been distilled from literary antecedents.

The "language" had not been heard on the London stage, but it had been heard in the Italian law courts, etc.; there were local attempts, all over Europe, to teach the public (in Spain, Italy, England) Latin diction. "Poetry" was considered to be (as it still is considered by a great number of drivelling imbeciles) synonymous with "lofty and flowery language."

One Elizabethan specialist has suggested that Shakespeare, disgusted with his efforts, or at least despairing of success, as a poet, took to the stage. The drama is a mixed art; it does not rely on the charge that can be put into the word, but calls on gesture and mimicry and "impersonation" for assistance. The actor must do a good half of the work. One does no favour to drama by muddling the two sets of problems.

Apologists for the drama are continually telling us in one way or another that drama either cannot use at all, or can make but a very limited use of words charged to their highest potential. This is perfectly true. Let us try to keep our minds on the problem we started with, i.e., the art of writing, the art of "charging" language with meaning.

After 1450 we have the age of *fioritura;* after Marlowe and Shakespeare came what was called a "classic" movement, a movement that restrained without inventing. Anything that happens to mind in England has usually happened somewhere else first. Someone invents something, then someone develops, or some dozens develop a frothy or at any rate creamy enthusiasm or over-abundance, then someone tries to tidy things up. For example, the estimable Pleiad emasculating the French tongue, and the French classicists, and the English classicists, etc., all of which things should be relegated to the subsidiary zone: period interest, historical interest, bric-à-brac for museums.

At this point someone says: "O, but the ballads." All right, I will allow the voracious peruser a half-hour for ballads (English and Spanish, or Scottish, Border, and Spanish). There is nothing easier than to be distracted from one's point, or from the main drive of one's subject by a desire for utterly flawless equity and omniscience.

Let us say, but directly in parenthesis, that there was a very limited sort of *logopœia* in seventeenth- and eighteenth-century satire. And that Rochester and Dorset may have introduced a new note, or more probably re-introduced an old one, that reappears later in Heine.

Let us also cut loose from minor details and minor exceptions: the main fact is that we "have come" or that "humanity came" to a point where verse-writing can or could no longer be clearly understood without the study of prose-writing.

Say, for the sake of argument, that after the slump of the Middle Ages, prose "came to" again in Machiavelli; admit that various sorts of prose had existed, in fact nearly all sorts had existed. Herodotus wrote history that is literature. Thucydides was a journalist. (It is a modern folly to suppose that vulgarity and cheapness have the merit of novelty; they have always existed, and are of no interest in themselves.)

There have been bombast, oratory, legal speech, balanced sentences, Ciceronian impressiveness; Petronius had written a satiric novel, Longus had written a delicate nouvelle. The prose of the Renaissance leaves us

Rabelais, Brantôme, Montaigne. A determined specialist can dig interesting passages, or sumptuous passages, or even subtle passages out of
Pico, the medieval mystics, scholastics, platonists, none of which will be the
least use to a man trying to learn the art of "changing language."

I mean to say that from the beginning of literature up to A.D. 1750
poetry was the superior art, and was so considered to be, and if we read
books written before that date we find the number of interesting books in
verse at least equal to the number of prose books still readable; and the
poetry contains the quintessence. When we want to know what people
were like before 1750, when we want to know that they had blood and
bones like ourselves, we go to the poetry of the period.

But, as I have said, the *"fioritura* business"* set in. And one morning
Monsieur Stendhal, not thinking of Homer, or Villon, or Catullus, but
having a very keen sense of actuality, noticed that "poetry," *la poésie,* as
the term was then understood, the stuff written by his French contemporaries, or sonorously rolled at him from the French stage, was a damn
nuisance. And he remarked that poetry, with its bagwigs and its bob-
wigs, and its padded calves and its periwigs, its "fustian à la Louis XIV,"
was greatly inferior to prose for conveying a clear idea of the diverse
states of our consciousness ("les mouvements du cœur").

And at that moment the serious art of writing "went over to prose,"
and for some time the important developments of language as means of
expression were the developments of prose. And a man cannot clearly
understand or justly judge the value of verse, modern verse, any verse,
unless he has grasped this.

PART III: CONCLUSIONS, EXCEPTIONS, CURRICULA

Before Stendhal there is probably nothing in prose that does not also
exist in verse or that can't be done by verse just as well as by prose. Even
the method of annihilating imbecility employed by Voltaire, Bayle, and
Lorenzo Valla can be managed quite as well in rhymed couplets.

Beginning with the Renaissance, or perhaps with Boccaccio, we have
prose that is quite necessary to the clear comprehension of things in
general: with Rabelais, Brantôme, Montaigne, Fielding, Sterne, we begin
to find prose recording states of consciousness that their verse-writing
contemporaries scamp. And this fuller consciousness, in more delicate
modes, appears in l'Abbé Prévost, Benjamin Constant, Jane Austen. So
that Stendhal had already "something back of him" when he made his
remarks about the inferiority of *"La Poésie."*

During the nineteenth century the superiority, if temporary, is at any rate obvious, and to such degree that I believe no man can now write really good verse unless he knows Stendhal and Flaubert. Or, let us say, *Le Rouge et le Noir,* the first half of *La Chartreuse, Madame Bovary, L'Education, Les Trois Contes, Bouvard et Pécuchet.* To put it perhaps more strongly, he will learn more about the art of charging words from Flaubert than he will from the floribund sixteenth-century dramatists.

The main expression of nineteenth-century consciousness is in prose. The art continues in Maupassant, who slicked up the Flaubertian mode. The art of popular success lies simply in never putting more on any one page than the most ordinary reader can lick off it in his normally rapid, half-attentive skim-over. The Goncourts struggled with praiseworthy sobriety, noble, but sometimes dull. Henry James was the first person to add anything to the art of the nineteenth-century novel not already known to the French.

Thought was churned up by Darwin, by science, by industrial machines, Nietzsche made a temporary commotion, but these things are extraneous to our subject, which is the *art of getting meaning into words.* There is an "influence of Ibsen," all for the good, but now exploited by cheap-jacks. Fabre and Frazer are both essential to contemporary clear thinking. I am not talking about the books that have poured something into the general consciousness, but of books that show *how* the pouring is done or display the implements, newly discovered, by which one can pour.

The nineteenth-century novel is such an implement. The Ibsen play is, or perhaps we must say was, such an implement.

It is for us to think whether these implements are more effective than poetry: *(a)* as known before 1800; *(b)* as known during the nineteenth century and up to the present.

France

The decline of England began on the day when Landor packed his trunks and departed to Tuscany. Up till then England had been able to contain her best authors; after that we see Shelley, Keats, Byron, Beddoes on the Continent, and still later observe the edifying spectacle of Browning in Italy and Tennyson in Buckingham Palace.

In France, as the novel developed, spurred on, shall we say, by the activity in the prose-media, the versifiers were not idle.

Departing from Albertus, Gautier developed the medium we find in the *Emaux et Camées.* England in the 'nineties had got no further than the method of the *Albertus.* If Corbière invented no process he at any rate restored French verse to the vigour of Villon and to an intensity that no Frenchman had touched during the intervening four centuries.

Unless I am right in discovering *logopœia* in Propertius (which means unless the academic teaching of Latin displays crass insensitivity as it probably does), we must almost say that Laforgue invented *logopœia* observing that there had been a very limited range of *logopœia* in all satire, and that Heine occasionally employs something like it, together with a dash of bitters, such as can (though he may not have known it) be found in a few verses of Dorset and Rochester. At any rate Laforgue found or refound *logopœia*. And Rimbaud brought back to *phanopœia* its clarity and directness.

All four of these poets, Gautier, Corbière, Laforgue, Rimbaud, redeem poetry from Stendhal's condemnation. There is in Corbière something one finds nowhere before him, unless in Villon.

Laforgue is not like any preceding poet. He is not ubiquitously like Propertius.

In Rimbaud the image stands clean, unencumbered by non-functioning words; to get anything like this directness of presentation one must go back to Catullus, perhaps to the poem which contains *dentes habet*.

If a man is too lazy to read the brief works of these poets, he cannot hope to understand writing, verse writing, prose writing, any writing.

England

Against this serious action England can offer only Robert Browning. He has no French or European parallel. He has, indubitably, grave limitations, but *The Ring and the Book* is serious experimentation. He is a better poet than Landor, who was perhaps the only complete and serious man of letters ever born in these islands.

We are so encumbered by having British literature in our foreground that even in this brief survey one must speak of it in disproportion. It was kept alive during the last century by a series of exotic injections. Swinburne read Greek and took English metric in hand; Rossetti brought in the Italian primitives; FitzGerald made the only good poem of the time that has gone to the people; it is called, and is to a great extent, a trans- or mistrans-lation.

There was a faint waft of early French influence. Morris translated sagas, the Irish took over the business for a few years; Henry James led, or rather preceded, the novelists, and then the Britons resigned *en bloc;* the language is now in the keeping of the Irish (Yeats and Joyce); apart from Yeats, since the death of Hardy, poetry is being written by Americans. All the developments in English verse since 1910 are due almost wholly to Americans. In fact, there is no longer any reason to call it English verse, and there is no present reason to think of England at all.

We speak a language that was English. When Richard Cœur de Lion first heard Turkish he said: "He spik lak a fole Britain." From which orthography one judges that Richard himself probably spoke like a French-Canadian.

It is a magnificent language, and there is no need of, or advantage in, minimizing the debt we owe to Englishmen who died before 1620. Neither is there any point in studying the "History of English Literature" as taught. Curiously enough, the histories of Spanish and Italian literature always take count of translators. Histories of English literature always slide over translation — I suppose it is inferiority complex — yet some of the best books in English are translations. This is important for two reasons. First, the reader who has been appalled by the preceding parts and said, "Oh, but I can't learn all these languages," may in some measure be comforted. He can learn the art of writing precisely where so many great local lights learned it; if not from the definite poems I have listed, at least from the men who learned it from those poems in the first place.

We may count the *Seafarer,* the *Beowulf,* and the remaining Anglo-Saxon fragments as indigenous art; at least, they dealt with a native subject, and by an art not newly borrowed. Whether alliterative metre owes anything to Latin hexameter is a question open to debate; we have no present means of tracing the debt. Landor suggests the problem in his dialogue of Ovid and the Prince of the Gaetae.

After this period English literature lives on translation, it is fed by translation; every new exuberance, every new heave is stimulated by translation, every allegedly great age is an age of translations, beginning with Geoffrey Chaucer, Le Grand Translateur, translator of the *Romaunt of the Rose,* paraphraser of Virgil and Ovid, condenser of old stories he had found in Latin, French, and Italian.

After him even the ballads that tell a local tale tell it in art indebted to Europe. It is the natural spreading ripple that moves from the civilized Mediterranean centre out through the half-civilized and into the barbarous peoples.

The Britons never have shed barbarism; they are proud to tell you that Tacitus said the last word about Germans. When Mary Queen of Scots went to Edinburgh she bewailed going out among savages, and she herself went from a sixteenth-century court that held but a barbarous, or rather a drivelling and idiotic and superficial travesty of the Italian culture as it had been before the débâcle of 1527. The men who tried to civilize these shaggy and uncouth marginalians by bringing them news of civilization have left a certain number of translations that are better reading today than are the works of the ignorant islanders who were too proud to translate. After Chaucer we have Gavin Douglas's *Eneados,* better than the original, as Douglas had heard the sea. Golding's *Metamorphoses,* from which Shakespeare learned so much of his trade. Marlowe's translation of Ovid's *Amores.* We have no satisfactory translation of any Greek author. Chapman and Pope have left Iliads that are of interest to specialists; so far as I know, the only translation of Homer that one can read with continued pleasure is in early French by Hugues Salel; he, at least, was intent on telling the story, and not wholly muddled with accessories. I have discussed the merits of these translators elsewhere. I am now trying to tell the reader what he can learn of comparative literature through translations that are in themselves better reading than the "original verse" of their periods. He can study the whole local development, or, we had better say, the sequence of local fashion in British verse by studying the translations of Horace that have poured in uninterrupted sequence from the British Press since 1650. That is work for a specialist, an historian, not for a man who wants simply to establish his axes of reference by knowing *the best of each kind* of written thing; as he would establish his axes of reference for painting by knowing a few pictures by Cimabue, Giotto, Piero della Francesca, Ambrogio de Predis, etc.; Velasquez, Goya, etc.

It is one thing to be able to spot the best painting and quite another and far less vital thing to know just where some secondary or tertiary painter learned certain defects.

Apart from these early translations, a man may enlarge his view of international poetry by looking at Swinburne's Greek adaptations. The Greeks stimulated Swinburne; if he had defects, let us remember that, apart from Homer, the Greeks often were rather Swinburnian. Catullus wasn't, or was but seldom. From which one may learn the nature of the Latin, non-Greek contribution to the art of expression.[2]

Swinburne's Villon is not Villon very exactly, but it is perhaps the best Swinburne we have. Rossetti's translations were perhaps better than Rossetti, and his *Vita Nuova* and early Italian poets guide one to originals, which he has now and again improved. Our contact with Oriental poetry begins with FitzGerald's Rubáiyát. Fenollosa's essay on the Chinese written character opens a door that the earlier students had, if not "howled without," at least been unable to open.

In mentioning these translations, I don't in the least admit or imply that any man in our time can think with only one language. He may be able to invent a new carburettor, or even work effectively in a biological laboratory, but he probably won't even try to do the latter without study of at least one foreign tongue. Modern science has always been multilingual. A good scientist simply would not be bothered to limit himself to one language and be held up for news of discoveries. The writer or reader who is content with such ignorance simply admits that his particular mind is of less importance than his kidneys or his automobile. The French who know no English are as fragmentary as the Americans who know no French. One simply leaves half of one's thought untouched in their company.

Different languages — I mean the actual vocabularies, the idioms — have worked out certain mechanisms of communication and registration. No one language is complete. A master may be continually expanding his own tongue, rendering it fit to bear some charge hitherto borne only by some other alien tongue, but the process does not stop with any one man. While Proust is learning Henry James, preparatory to breaking through certain French paste board partitions, the whole American speech is churning and chugging, and every other tongue doing likewise.

To be "possible" in mentally active company the American has to learn French, the Frenchman has to learn English or American. The Italian has for some time learned French. The man who does not know the Italian of the duocento and trecento has in him a painful lacuna, not necessarily painful to himself, but there are simply certain things he don't know, and can't; it is as if he were blind to some part of the spectrum. Because of the determined attempt of the patriotic Latinists of Italy in the renaissance to "conquer" Greek by putting every Greek author effectively into Latin it is now possible to get a good deal of Greek through Latin cribs. The disuse of Latin cribs in Greek study, beginning, I suppose, about 1820, has caused no end of damage to the general distribution of "classic culture."

Another point miscomprehended by people who are clumsy at languages is that one does not need to learn a whole language in order to understand some one or some dozen poems. It is often enough to understand thoroughly the poem, and every one of the few dozen or few hundred words that compose it.

This is what we start to do as small children when we memorize some lyric of Goethe or Heine. Incidentally, this process leaves us for life with a measuring rod *(a)* for a certain type of lyric, *(b)* for the German language, so that, however bored we may be by the *Grundriss von Groeber,* we never wholly forget the feel of the language.

Vaccine

Do I suggest a remedy? I do. I suggest several remedies. I suggest that we throw out all critics who use vague general terms. Not merely those who use vague terms because they are too ignorant to have a meaning; but the critics who use vague terms to *conceal* their meaning, and all critics who use terms so vaguely that the reader can think he agrees with them or assents to their statements when he doesn't.

The first credential we should demand of a critic is *his* ideograph of the good; of what he considers valid writing, and indeed of all his general terms. Then we know where he is. He cannot simply stay in London writing of French pictures that his readers have not seen. He must begin by stating that such and such *particular* works seem to him "good," "best," "indifferent," "valid," "non-valid." I suggest a definite curriculum in place of the present *émiettements,* of breaking the subject up into crumbs quickly dryable. A curriculum for instructors, for obstreperous students who wish to annoy dull instructors, for men who haven't had time for systematized college courses. Call it the minimum basis for a sound and liberal education in letters (with French and English "aids" in parenthesis).

Confucius — In full (there being no complete and intelligent English version, one would have either to learn Chinese or make use of the French version by Pauthier).

Homer — in full (Latin cribs, Hugues Salel in French, no satisfactory English, though Chapman can be used as reference).

Ovid — And the Latin "personal" poets, Catullus and Propertius. (Golding's *Metamorphoses,* Marlowe's *Amores.* There is no useful English version of Catullus.)

A Provençal Song Book — With cross reference to Minnesingers, and to Bion, perhaps thirty poems in all.

Dante — "And his circle"; that is to say Dante, and thirty poems by his contemporaries, mostly by Guido Cavalcanti.

Villon —

Parenthetically — Some other medieval matter might be added, and some general outline of history of thought through the Renaissance.

Voltaire — That is to say, some incursion into his critical writings, not into his attempts at fiction and drama, and some dip into his contemporaries (prose).

Stendhal — (At least a book and half).

Flaubert (omitting *Salammbô* and the *Tentation*) — And the Goncourts.

Gautier, Corbière, Rimbaud.

This would not overburden the three- or four-year student. After this inoculation he could be "with safety exposed" to modernity or anything else in literature. I mean he wouldn't lose his head or ascribe ridiculous values to works of secondary intensity. He would have axes of reference and would, I think, find them dependable.

For the purposes of general education we could omit all study of monistic totemism and voodoo for at least fifty years and study of Shakespeare for thirty on the ground that acquaintance with these subjects is already very widely diffused, and that one absorbs quite enough knowledge of them from boring circumjacent conversation.

This list does not, obviously, contain the names of every author who has ever written a good poem or a good octave or sestet. It is the result of twenty-seven years' thought on the subject and a résumé of conclusions. That may be a reason for giving it some consideration. It is not a reason for accepting it as a finality. Swallowed whole it is useless. For practical class work the instructor should try, and incite his students to try, to pry out some element that I have included and to substitute for it something more valid. The intelligent lay reader will instinctively try to do this for himself.

I merely insist that *without* this minimum the critic has almost no chance of sound judgment. Judgment will gain one more chance of soundness if he can be persuaded to consider Fenollosa's essay or some other, and to me unknown but equally effective, elucidation of the Chinese written charater.

Before I die I hope to see at least a few of the best Chinese works printed bilingually, in the form that Mori and Ariga prepared certain texts for Fenollosa, a "crib," the picture of each letter accompanied by a full explanation.

For practical contact with all past poetry that was actually *sung* in its own day I suggest that each dozen universities combine in employing a couple of singers who understand the meaning of words. Men like Yves Tinayre and Robert Maitland are available. A half-dozen hours spent in listening to the lyrics actually performed would give the student more knowledge of that sort of *melopœia* than a year's work in philology. The Kennedy-Frasers have dug up music that fits the *Beowulf*. It was being used for heroic song in the Hebrides. There is other available music, plenty of it, from at least the time of Faidit (A.D. 1190).

I cannot repeat too often or too forcibly my caution against so-called critics who talk "all around the matter," and who do not define their terms, and who won't say frankly that certain authors are demnition bores. Make a man tell you *first* and specially what writers he thinks are good writers, after that you can listen to his explanation.

Naturally, certain professors who have invested all their intellectual capital, i.e., spent a lot of time on some perfectly dead period, don't

like to admit they've been sold, and they haven't often the courage to cut
a loss. There is no use in following them into the shadows.

In the above list I take full responsibility for my omissions. I have
omitted "the Rhooshuns." All right. Let a man judge them after he has
encountered Charles Bovary; he will read them with better balance. I have
omitted practically all the fustian included in curricula of French literature in American universities (Bossuet, Corneille, etc.) and in so doing I
have not committed an oversight. I have touched German in what most
of you will consider an insufficient degree. All right. I have done it. I
rest my case.

If one finds it convenient to think in chronological cycles, and wants
to "relate literature to history," I suggest the three convenient "breaks"
or collapses. The fall of Alexander's Macedonian empire; the fall of the
Roman empire; the collapse of Italy after 1500, the fall of Lodovico
Moro, and the sack of Rome. That is to say, human lucidity appears to
have approached several times a sort of maximum, and then suffered a
set-back.

The great break in the use of language occurs, however, with the
change from inflected to uninflected speech. It can't be too clearly understood that certain procedures are good for a language in which every word
has a little final tag telling what part of speech it is, and what case it is in,
and whether it is a subject, or an object or an accessory; and that these
procedures are not good in English or French. Milton got into a mess
trying to write English as if it were Latin. Lack of this dissociation is
largely responsible for late renaissance floridity. One cannot at this point
study all the maladies and all their variations. The study of misguided
Latinization needs a treatise to itself.

from *Professional Secrets*

[1925]

JEAN COCTEAU

The following notes were written in solitude; a circumstance which
has influenced them both for good and bad. If they have gained in frank-
ness, they are lacking in those qualities of prudence and politeness which

we acquire by living in great cities, and without which our authority is
no better than a boor's.

.   .   .

I know a small boy who used to ask old ladies their age. Sometimes it
was seventy, sometimes eighty. "Oh," said he with an icy stare, "then you
haven't much longer to live."

An enormity of this kind, which leaves all the fragile conventions of
civilization far behind, does not astonish one who is used to solitude. For
he thinks to himself, no less ingenuously, "My works will live."

.   .   .

Style can never be a starting-point; it is a result. What is style? Many
people think it is a complicated way of saying something very simple.
According to us, it is a very simple way of saying something complicated.
A Stendhal, even a Balzac (the Balzac of "Le Père Goriot," or "La Cousine
Bette") are chiefly concerned to hit the bull's-eye. Nine times out of ten,
they succeed, without minding how they do it. It is just this "not
minding how," a sort of quickly improvised method of their own which
they adopt according to the results obtained — this way of shouldering the
rifle, aiming, and shooting quick and true, which I call style.

A Flaubert only thinks about shouldering his arm; the target doesn't
interest him; he lavishes all his attention on the weapon. The lady of the
shooting-gallery, who has her back turned to the targets, is watching him.
What a handsome fellow he is! What a sportsman! What style! Little she
cares whether the marksman hits the "bull," provided he takes a long
aim, has a graceful style, and most important of all, takes plenty of time
over the job.

The target? The target is ten yards away — an infinite distance for short-
sighted people and those who refuse to look further than the end of
their own noses — in other words, the *élite*. So many of the so-called
"realistic" scenes of Flaubert have very little to do with reality. "Madame
Bovary," for example, every page of which reveals the writer's concern to
"shoulder" effectively, is a mass of unreality — a series of Salon pictures.

.   .   .

A mannerism, no matter how distinguished, can never constitute style.

To cultivate one's thought — to learn to shape and handle it — is to culti-vate one's style. Looked at from any other point of view, style merely makes for obscurity and acts as a drag.

Your true writer is all bone and muscle. The others are either fat or lean. Those who go in for "stunts" (and are always in the fashion) exhibit a dreadful mixture of fat *and* lean.

.   .   .

Writing, especially writing poetry, is like perspiring. The poem, or book, is a kind of sweat. It would be unhealthy to walk, or run, or play games, or practise athletics without sweating. The only things that inter-est me are the man himself and the kind of exercise he takes. That is why most works by living artists leave me cold. What I look for in the work of a dead artist — in the fragrance, as it were, of his sweat — is a proof of activity. The Louvre is like the Morgue; one goes there to identify one's friends. We like to show off, and sell our own sweat. Both the masses and the fastidious like nothing better than to intoxicate themselves with sweat; but they take no interest in the exercise, or sport, itself.

Rimbaud, when he was at Harrar, is an example of a poetical athlete who does not sweat. But then he had ceased to run about. If one is going to run about (granted that one agrees to put up with the inconvenience), then one ought to sweat as little as possible, and so to speak, sweat dry.

(P.S. — When I speak of "exercise" or "sport," I do not mean that way of living which Wilde used to say was his masterpiece. I refer to the life of the intellect.)

.   .   .

The "modern style," "modern poet" and "modern spirit" have all been invented. There is no more sense in saying "I am modern" than there is in the expression "We mediaeval knights." (Allusion to a well-known farce.) The confusion arises because man, like the primitive nigger he is, is dazzled by "progress" — in the form of aeroplanes, the telephone, and the cinematograph. He can't get over them. He talks about them in the same way as M. Jourdain telling everybody that he expressed himself in prose.

This is what simple people, mistaking words for a state of mind, call "modern poetry." They give the first place to mere accessories.

The part played by the things of everyday life should neither be ignored, nor given undue prominence. The poet should make the same use of them as he does of anything else.

As for the man who will have modernism at any price, and startles the public by offering them an orgy of colour and sensations grafted on to the old material, instead of weaving a new tissue altogether — he will soon be left behind by progress.

Everything goes out of fashion sooner or later, you tell me. That is another question. A masterpiece is not hailed as such, but it transforms everything. It is profoundly in the fashion. Everybody follows it without knowing. It is bound to go out of fashion: another masterpiece drives it out. Finally, it begins by being picturesque, and then, having ceased to be just an old-fashioned gown, it takes its place in the costumes museum.

.   .   .

So much the worse for those who only recognize a poet from external signs. The shape of his thought, a limited number of problems, the angle of his vision (which is what style really is), these are the qualities which distinguish him from the others, and this is his way of saying: This is what I am. The rest — what commonly passes for style — must be made to follow unobtrusively the outline of this individual silhouette. Show a connoisseur ten quite dissimilar pieces of tapestry. He looks at the back and pronounces them all to have been woven in the same factory.

A good writer always strikes in the same place, but each time with a hammer of a different size and substance. The sound varies; he treats the nail with care. If he always used the same hammer, he would end by smashing the nail-head, driving nothing in, and merely making an empty noise. That is the noise our big-wigs make. But be careful! He who upsets expectations gives offence. The public was not prepared for what the true poet offers it. It is disappointed. It considers that he has not kept his promise.

What have I promised you? When will you learn that a good book is never what it is expected to be? It should never come up to your expectations; it should cause you to bristle with marks of interrogation.

.   .   .

Ours is an age infected with literature. Not only that, but following on a recent attack of convulsions, and by dint of running down literature, an anti-literary literature has been engendered by this very attitude of romantic disgust.

A destructive spirit is romantic, and betrays a taste for ruins, and a pessimism which I condemn.

The antidote for intelligence is stupidity. But stupidity is not as common as you would think — still less madness. Here again we see the unhappy muse with her dishevelled hair. . . .

Now I endeavour to be as un-literary as possible — and that, to the *littérateur* is an unforgivable sin. But a *littérateur* will flirt with Dadaism, which is literature *par excellence*. He is tickled, intrigued, excited, and a good deal troubled by it.

"What do you mean by literature?" asks some carping person.

"Mannerisms, style treated as a starting-point, and everything that constitutes 'genre.' "

"Then you are for the poetry of ideas?"

Not at all — and here we see how the secret, inner forms of poetry are unlike anything which can be explained. I remarked elsewhere that what I ask of the musician is that he should see that his work *resembles* something — it should resemble the original movements which urged him to develop them thematically, even if it is only a simple case of musical mathematics.

The same thing is true of painting. When Picasso has finished a picture its beauty is due to the intensity of its resemblance, even if our eyes are unable to distinguish each separate object which called it into being. The reason is that Picasso, saturated in the methods and technique of the great masters of painting, and for ever turning up new ground, is conscious of the inferiority of arabesques and "spots," which he leaves to mere decorators.

When he looks at a group of objects, he digests them, and gradually transports them into a world of his own, of which he is the ruler, he never embroiders, and never loses sight of their objective force. In this way he does away with slavish imitation, but maintains the resemblance between these objects — a resemblance conceived on another plane, but forming the same sum-total. Instead of deceiving the eye he deceives the mind. His picture is a picture; it has an independent existence; it tells you nothing about anything else.

.   .   .

What is commonly called genius is rarely accompanied by intelligence. But there is no harm in intelligence, as far as I can see. Stendhal and Nietzsche are types of intelligent geniuses. True, Zarathustra is often no better than an old guide turned phrase-maker through leading a

lonely life in the Alps. None the less, there is nothing that his diamond
does not cut. Nietzsche denounced, saw, and foretold everything. He
sensed the approach of a Dionysian pessimism; and that describes our
present state. Who is aware of it?

.   .   .

When you hear it said of an artist or of a woman that they are angelic,
do not expect to see them looking like the pictures you had when you
made your first Communion.

Disinterested, selfish, tender, pitying, cruel, shrinking from contacts,
pure in the midst of debauchery, taking a violent delight in, and at the
same time despising, earthly pleasures, naïvely a-moral — make no mistake,
these are the signs of that state which we call angelic — signs by which you
may recognize all true poets, be they writers, painters, sculptors or
musicians. . . .

A true poet does not bother to be poetical. Nor does a nursery gardener
scent his roses. What he does is to subject them to treatment which en-
sures them having the finest colour and the sweetest scent. Paul Valéry
takes a pride in being a versifier and in exercising himself in this art. It is
lucky for us he is a poet. But this mystery does not concern him.

If, however, you may observe, all a poet has to do is to play a sort of
game of chess with himself, it will still be necessary to have rules. Valéry
writes in verse. What can you claim on behalf of this game of yours, which
we don't understand at all? To begin with, the more I realize the prestige
of the commonplace, the more inclined I am to think that the mind is the
more readily stimulated when the means at its disposal are most limited,
and so I am increasingly attracted by verse, which is like an old uniform,
always the same, but which each one of us wears in a different way.

Friends often imagine our poems to be just notes, jotted down haphazard, which we have been prevented by laziness from carrying any
further. Now, in spite of all their invisible architecture, the effort of concentration, and the sacrifices that the writing of these poems entailed, I
admit that it is impossible for even the most enlightened reader to be
penetrated by the same rhythm as the writer, or be conscious of all his
smallest reactions.

Since, therefore, everyone works for himself and creates his own rules,
I am unable to believe in the advent of any one new rule, and can only
see in this state of general disorder, which is made up of individual order,
the signs of an intellectual quickening, and emancipation. After impres-
sionism, *vers libre;* it is impossible for the mind to dispense altogether

with so valuable an asset. And so everyone prunes and models and disciplines it in his own way. It is thus that our age, anarchist in appearance, is escaping from anarchy, and returning, in a new spirit, to the path of the law.

.   .   .

Putting the verb in its right place, arranging for masculine and feminine terminations, establishing the rhythmic beat, submitting to a discipline of incredible severity (which the reader mistakes for laziness) — all these processes take place slowly and painfully, straining the nervous system to breaking-point. It is absolutely essential that one's thought should beat as one's heart beats, with its systole, diastole, and syncopes which prove that it is not a machine.

Even while the poet is in the act of creation, his poem runs a thousand mortal risks.

A bather in danger of drowning, and not knowing how to swim, invents the art of swimming. A poet, in order to save his poem, re-invents all the old familiar devices. He remembers how to work them, and begins again. He is possessed by a thousand devils whom he must obey. These mysterious laws stand in the same relation to the old laws of versification as do ten games of chess played simultaneously to a game of dominoes. But our player involves himself in increasingly subtle combinations where no one can follow him, and amongst which he is himself in danger of getting lost one day. He develops various systems; either he gets intrigued, finds an artificial stimulant in the rewriting of a text, and endeavours to recreate or destroy its inner proportions, or else he refines curiously on the game of acrostics.

Some think he is playing the fool, others that he is ill, but there are some who feel the tragic beauty of the game and take pleasure in it without wanting to know why.

.   .   .

Do you remember also the picture in the books for children, of Franklin, armed with a whip, chasing the lightning out of his room, like a dog?

But neither the lightning-conductor nor the electric lamp tell us anything about the soul of electricity.

And, of course, it is no longer a question of inspiration. Inspiration will be a matter of more or less electric current, or of a strong or weak discharge.

We do not pretend to be able to analyse an occult power which permeates the universe, and does not only reveal itself through the medium of artists. This power may move us to tears through the medium of phenomena quite unconnected with art. For example, a certain firework display a few days before the war, a wounded seagull falling from the sky, my first sight of the moon through a telescope, the disaster of the "Titanic" read in a newspaper, a crowd trying to catch a thief in the rue de la Bourse, a steam roundabout on the Place du Trône, the gallop of a horse slowed down on the film, or, on the other hand, the accelerated blossoming of a rose — I mention here a few things I happen to remember which seemed charged with an accumulation of poetic fluid like a gathering storm, filling me with feelings of uneasiness, presentiment, and poetry.

Let us, then, for the sake of simplicity, call this fluid poetry; and let us call the more or less successful methods we employ to domesticate it art. Herein lies the function of the artist. But "if Heaven did not make a poet of him at his birth," in the words of the excellent Boileau, it will be no good his laying the necessary wires — his lamp will never light.

Poetry in its raw state is a source of life to those in whom it arouses a feeling of nausea. This sort of moral nausea is caused by death. Death is at the back of life. That is why we cannot imagine what it is like, but we are always obsessed with the idea that it forms the lining of the tissue that is ourselves. We may even sometimes establish a sort of contact with our dead, but in a way which precludes any kind of communication. Imagine a text of which we can never get to know the continuation, because it is printed at the back of a page of which we can only read the front. Now, although the words "back" and "front," useful though they may be for the purposes of human expression, probably mean nothing at all where the superhuman is concerned, the idea of this mysterious "underneath" makes every one of our actions, words, even our slightest gestures, seem as though they were suspended in a void, which makes the soul as dizzy as looking over a precipice may make the head.

Poetry aggravates this uneasiness, and mixes it with the emotions aroused in us by scenery, love, sleep, and our pleasures in general.

The poet does not dream; he counts. But he is walking on a quicksand, and from time to time plunges his leg into the jaws of death.

He gets used to this, however, and soon looks upon it as quite normal — just as people with heart disease are not alarmed by the severest attack of palpitations.

Poetry, then, implies a predisposition to the supernatural. The hyper-sensitive atmosphere in which it envelops us sharpens our secret sensibili-ties, and causes us to put out feelers which probe into depths which our official senses ignore. The scents which rise from these forbidden regions make our official senses jealous. They rise in revolt, exhaust themselves, attempt to do work which is beyond their power, and the individual is overcome by a marvellous confusion. Beware! Whoever finds himself in such a state may see miracles in everything.

Poets live on miracles. They happen on the slightest pretext *à propos* of anything, great or small. Objects, desires, sympathies place themselves spontaneously under their hands. For their sake the incoherencies of fate take on a rhythm of their own. They live for a time like kings. But let a miracle fail to happen, and their nervous tension relaxes, their senses calm down again. It is as if the magic ring had fallen from their suddenly shrunken finger. These are painful periods. Poetry, like a drug, continues to act, but turns against the poet and torments him with a series of mis-adventures. The consciousness of death, which was to him what the pleasure of giddiness is to speed, sickens him with the spasm of a sudden fall.

One day the finger grows fat again, the ring returns to its place, and miracles happen once more.

We are here in the presence of phenomena of quite a special character over which we have no control, and which stand in the same relation to tame poetry as occultism does to science.

Poetry, though it may form part of the mechanism of dreams, is in no sense a cause of dreams, or of a dreamy state of mind. What it does some-times is to invest dreams with a certain relief, combined with a critical intensity and the super-position of one background on another, recollec-tions of which, added to memories of what are known as "waking dreams," increase that feeling of moral nausea which poetry always brings.

Dreaming and dreaminess may be left to the poet who has no poetry in him. For poetry in no way excludes liveliness, childish pranks, penny toys, practical jokes, and the wild laughter in which poets indulge in the most incredibly melancholy way.

As you will perceive, we are not very far from the spirit of religion, or from what Charles Péguy called "the missionary's laugh." [1]

Religion is something different again. I have no means of knowing in what way poetry may bring us nearer to God or the reverse. I refer the reader to Paul Claudel's preface to the complete works of Arthur Rim-baud — despite the fact that his love for both the Church and the poet oblige him to reconcile them at all costs.

Far be it from us to accuse Claudel of interpreting to his own advantage the delirium of a dying man as recorded by a very pious sister. But such a confusion would be quite justifiable precisely on account of this poetical spirit reaching its highest possible pitch of development at such a supreme moment. The spirit of poetry equals the spirit of religion — as distinct from any given religious system — which is no doubt what Paul Claudel means when he says so justly that Rimbaud was "a mystic in the raw." ("Un mystique à l'état sauvage.")

The poet is a believer. In what? In everything.

Hence Renan, who is saturated with our fluid, is undoubtedly a religious nature, unlike Voltaire, whom poetry shuns, just as a silken thread is shunned by electricity.

.   .   .

In the old days the priests commanded and the artisan obeyed. Was the latter a real artist? His work in those days had the double merit of being both outwardly beautiful and at the same time full of profound meaning. Thus the Jews were Egypt's true sculptors. At the present day, art vegetates exclusively in the hands of artisans. The artisan-priest is extremely rare. It is to him we are looking to-day. The public is content to admire doors which lead nowhere. But, like the game of chess which, it appears, derives its distorted rules from the itinerary of the Ark of the Covenant, is there anything into which the ancient game of art does not plunge its roots? The most insignificant player sets more mystery afoot than appears on the surface. This is another of the reasons why this game intrigues us, and is a source of so much uneasiness, surprise, sorrow, and consolations.

It is none the less a game which is essentially human, earthly, and in a sense, humble. It is dangerous in the same way as was the Holy Ark — that mighty electrical machine around which surged a people ignorant of electricity. The cowherd who brushes against it while driving his cattle on the road to Jerusalem falls dead, struck down by the hand of God, perhaps, but above all a victim of his own imprudence. Depend upon it, the priests never touched it before cutting off the current. Similarly, the secrets of art are also man's concern.

Moreover, man is entitled to play this game. This is not the case, however, as regards science and metaphysics, to which it almost always leads. The poet, whose range is unlimited, sometimes brings back a pearl from depths into which the man of science *proves* it is impossible to descend. Metaphysics and primary causes are intently engaged in a leisurely game of hide-and-seek. The poet goes for a stroll and discovers their hiding-place. But though he is always the first to discover things, the poet never exploits his discovery. He sees and passes on. He does not worry or chase after the unknown.

And yet it is precisely owing to this faculty of being able to penetrate to the core of things, more deeply than any science, that art seems to be enveloped in an atmosphere of punishment. Science, who moves slowly and counts her steps, makes mistakes. She does not appear to be a cause of much inconvenience to the Unknown. And the Unknown leaves her pretty well alone. She is sometimes useful to man, and never disturbs the gods.

The Unknown is a sea which "we are forbidden to explore." Science, philosophy, and spiritualism bathe in it, and paddle on its shores.

The artist builds a ship, or a villa on the beach.

He who plays the game of art is doing something which concerns him, but with the risk of opening a breach onto something which is not his concern at all. The discoveries of an Einstein outstrip our limited capacities, but do not reach the feet of the gods. He exhausts himself in empty space.

An Einstein proves the existence of errors, and opens the door to fresh ones. If you want to expose errors without appearing ridiculous, you ought to place yourself at such an altitude that you are out of all human earshot. The fact of remaining within limits accessible to a mass of good medium intelligences is enough to invalidate any theory.

.   .   .

I am looking at a solid object, say an old nail. Its matter is made up of molecules, which have no connection with each other, and which are whirling about at wild speeds. Imagine one of these molecules to be inhabited by rational beings like ourselves, gravitating, living and dreaming, surrounded by empty space, and seeing at varying distances in this pseudo-space other molecules from which they derive warmth and light, and which are gravitating like themselves. It is likely that their pride will allow them to believe that they are merely an infinitesimal fraction of an enormous nail-head?

The metals contained in our atmosphere lead me to believe that our eyes and our ether form one of those spaces which separate the molecules of a solid object.

I attain the conviction that the earth, sun, moon, and stars are fractions

of a nail-head on an earth which again is itself, etc. . . . . A lot of good
that does me!

What discomfort, what loneliness!

I go back to the games which console me.

It is therefore for disciplinary reasons that I advise artists not to mix
up art, and science, and philosophy, and occultism. Such mixtures lead
either to laziness, or to the kind of pedantry peculiar to learned women.
The art of Picasso, so simple and so instructive, and the lessons which may
be learnt from it are obscured, not only by the term "cubist," but also by
futile discussions in which, instead of talking about painting, people talk
about Poincaré, Bergson, the Fourth Dimension, and the pineal gland.

.   .   .

If I must now make a *résumé* of, and cast a comprehensive glance backwards over what I have said, these are my conclusions:—

That form should be understood as meaning mental form. Not a way
of saying things, but a way of *thinking* them;

That the need to express oneself in public is a form of secretion which
cannot be excused, unless one is born with it and finds it incurable;

That one must either coincide, or commit suicide — the state of mind of
a spectator who finds a play absurd, but stays in the theatre to warm
himself and then makes a disturbance, whistling and preventing other
people from hearing, being inadmissible;

That there are always very few people who really belong to their own
epoch, seeing that there is no such thing as a precursor — one such so-
called precursor — that is to say, the only man who really expresses his
epoch, whether it likes it or not — being capable of making a whole
epoch, although quite unaware of the fact, seem to be lagging behind him;

That stupidity, insensitiveness, and spiritual scepticism protect a country's finest individuals by failing to recognise their true value. They act
as a kind of refrigerator for the preservation of our finest fruit. A too
curious, or a too serious, or a too amiable, or a too indulgent attitude
results in the fruit being passed from hand to hand, and finally losing its
bloom;

That fighting stimulates us, whereas a kindly-disposed public sends us
to sleep;

That we continually need a wall, as in the game of "pelota," in order
to carry on our game, either alone, or with or against others. It is this
that brings down on us the reproach, now of arrogance if the wall we have

selected is a masterpiece universally respected — now of maliciousness if our wall is a "master."

.   .   .

That the poet resembles the dead, inasmuch as he walks about invisibly amongst the living who only vaguely perceive him after he is dead — that is to say, when they speak of the dead as ghosts;

That poems, poetical forms, and poetry are quite different things, and that the fact that there are excellent lightning-conductors which never attract lightning in no way discredits storms;

That it is when poetry assumes a confused — as we see it — and as it were a stormy shape, that it becomes capable of producing a collective effect on a great many different kinds of people;

That this cattle-like herding together under the storm gives rise to artificial caresses, which are a source of misunderstanding and friction;

That shipwrecks, and occasions when one's country or one's purse are in danger, are fertile in poetry of this description;

That poetry ceases to be obvious to all as soon as it begins to mean something to a few;

That the fact of abandoning rhyme and fixed rules in favour of other intuitive rules brings us back to fixed rules and to rhyme with renewed respect;

That, for example, a poet who has been brought back in this way concentrates in a single line what he would have previously spread out over four stanzas;

That when an infidelity brings us back to our first love it binds us thereto so strongly that it is rendered indestructible; whereas in a love exempt from the slightest kind of infidelity all the germs of infidelity are latent;

That "grace" exists in the sense that there are inventors of new vehicles, or simple drivers of old ones who never manage to get hold of the "fluid," but that "grace" is a mystery which does not concern mankind, from whom we need not demand any mystical activity outside the sphere of religion;

That music, painting, sculpture, architecture, dancing, poetry, the drama, and that muse I call "Cinema, tenth Muse," are all so many traps in which man endeavours to capture poetry for our use;

That few of these traps work, and few are the lamps which can be made to light; and all the time the majority of mankind go strutting about in the dark and imagine that their houses are magnificently illuminated.

Translated by Rollo H. Myers

11. Constantin Brancusi, *The New-Born* (1920).

Make it new.   EZRA POUND

12. Alexander Calder,
*Lobster Trap and
Fish Tail* (1939).

13. Henri Matisse, *The Red Studio* (1911).

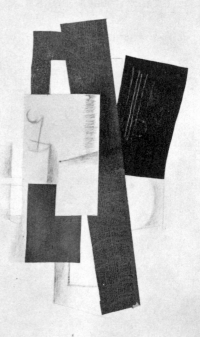

Art is made to disturb.

GEORGES BRAQUE

14. George Braque,
Guitar (1913–1914).

15. Jean (Hans) Arp.
*Collage with Squares Arranged
According to the Law of Chance*
(1916–1917).

M. Languevin: But how do you measure these things?
Einstein: These things are not measurable.

. . . *1923*

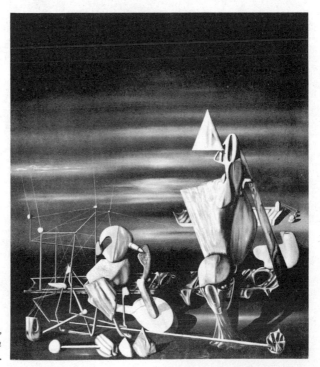

16. Yves Tanguy,
Slowly Toward the North
(1942).

17. Wassily Kandinsky,
Composition (4) (1914).

18. Piet Mondrian, *Composition
with Red, Yellow and Blue*
(1935–1943).

It is art that makes life. HENRY JAMES

Abstract art . . . is dominated by desire for perfection and for
total liberation in the same spirit that has produced saints,
heroes, and madmen. Extreme as it is, only a few creators and
admirers can sustain it . . . FERNAND LÉGER

19. Robert Motherwell, *Elegy to the Spanish Republic, 70* (1961).

20. Jackson Pollock, *Grayed Rainbow* (1953).

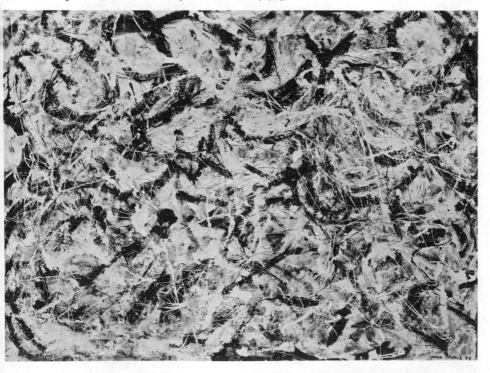

21. Frank Lloyd Wright, *Project for Roger Lacy Hotel,* Dallas, Texas (1947).

22. Buckminster Fuller, *Geodesic Dome,* Honolulu, Hawaii.

Only connect. E. M. FORSTER

23. Arnold Schoenberg,
from *Drei Klavierstücke*
(Op. 11).

Aufführungsrecht vorbehalten
Droits d'exécution réservés

1.

Arnold Schoenberg, Op. 11 Nr. 1.

We have only one absolute duty to music,
and that is to invent it. IGOR STRAVINSKY

24. Karlheinz Stockhausen, from *Etude II.*

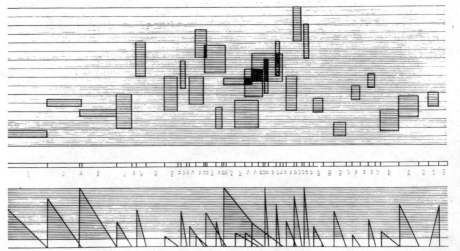

25. Jean Cocteau himself, as Heurtebise in *Orpheus*.

Cultivate that which the public reproaches you for—it's you.

JEAN COCTEAU

26. Bertolt Brecht, scene from *Mother Courage* with Helene Weigel.

We must identify ourselves with what we are.
The world is full of people thinking of myths. CESARE ZAVATINI

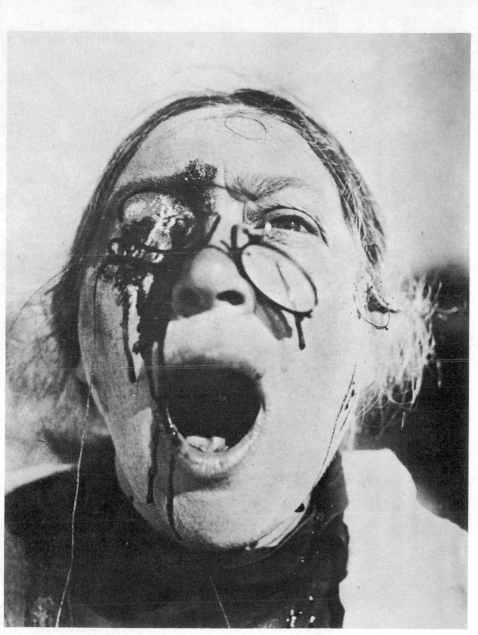

27. Sergei Eisenstein, scene from *Potemkin*.

... the stage will have to give way to the cinema.   MAX REINHARDT

28. Martha Graham and Company in *Primitive Mysteries*.

I—I—I—how we have lost the secret of saying that. VIRGINIA WOOLF

3

GERTRUDE STEIN *and* PAUL VALÉRY

Gertrude Stein wrote novels and Paul Valéry wrote verse, but both, like so many of the creative people of their generation, were more interested in theory than practice, in how the creative consciousness worked than in its mere artifacts. Monsieur Teste *is a portrait of self-awareness which is autotelic.* Composition as Explanation *tells, as graphically as a short story, what is happening when a sentence is made.*

Composition as Explanation
[1926]

GERTRUDE STEIN

There is singularly nothing that makes a difference a difference in beginning and in the middle and in ending except that each generation has something different at which they are all looking. By this I mean so simply that anybody knows it that composition is the difference which makes each and all of them then different from other generations and this is what makes everything different otherwise they are all alike and everybody knows it because everybody says it.

It is very likely that nearly every one has been very nearly certain that something that is interesting is interesting them. Can they and do they. It is very interesting that nothing inside in them, that is when you consider the very long history of how every one ever acted or has felt, it is very interesting that nothing inside in them in all of them makes it connectedly different. By this I mean this. The only thing that is different from one time to another is what is seen and what is seen depends upon

how everybody is doing everything. This makes the thing we are looking
at very different and this makes what those who describe it make of it,
it makes a composition, it confuses, it shows, it is, it looks, it likes it as it
is, and this makes what is seen as it is seen. Nothing changes from generation to generation except the thing seen and that makes a composition.
Lord Grey remarked that when the generals before the war talked about
the war they talked about it as a nineteenth century war although to be
fought with twentieth century weapons. That is because war is a thing
that decides how it is to be when it is to be done. It is prepared and to
that degree it is like all academies it is not a thing made by being made
it is a thing prepared. Writing and painting and all that, is like that, for
those who occupy themselves with it and don't make it as it is made. Now
the few who make it as it is made, and it is to be remarked that the most
decided of them usually are prepared just as the world around them is
preparing, do it in this way and so I if you do not mind I will tell you
how it happens. Naturally one does not know how it happened until it
is well over beginning happening.

   To come back to the part that the only thing that is different is what
is seen when it seems to be being seen, in other words, composition and
time-sense.

   No one is ahead of his time, it is only that the particular variety of
creating his time is the one that his contemporaries who also are creating
their own time refuse to accept. And they refuse to accept it for a very
simple reason and that is that they do not have to accept it for any
reason. They themselves that is everybody in their entering the modern
composition and they do enter it, if they do not enter it they are not so
to speak in it they are out of it and so they do enter it; but in as you may
say the non-competitive efforts where if you are not in it nothing is lost
except nothing at all except what is not had, there are naturally all the
refusals, and the things refused are only important if unexpectedly somebody happens to need them. In the case of the arts it is very definite.
Those who are creating the modern composition authentically are naturally only of importance when they are dead because by that time the
modern composition having become past is classified and the description
of it is classical. That is the reason why the creator of the new composition in the arts is an outlaw until he is a classic, there is hardly a moment
in between and it is really too bad very much too bad naturally for the
creator but also very much too bad for the enjoyer, they all really would
enjoy the created so much better just after it has been made than when
it is already a classic, but it is perfectly simple that there is no reason why

the contemporaries should see, because it would not make any difference as they lead their lives in the new composition anyway, and as every one is naturally indolent why naturally they don't see. For this reason as in quoting Lord Grey it is quite certain that nations not actively threatened are at least several generations behind themselves militarily so aesthetically they are more than several generations behind themselves and it is very much too bad, it is so very much more exciting and satisfactory for everybody if one can have contemporaries, if all one's contemporaries could be one's contemporaries.

There is almost not an interval.

For a very long time everybody refuses and then almost without a pause almost everybody accepts. In the history of the refused in the arts and literature the rapidity of the change is always startling. Now the only difficulty with the *volte-face* concerning the arts is this. When the acceptance comes, by that acceptance the thing created becomes a classic. It is a natural phenomena a rather extraordinary natural phenomena that a thing accepted becomes a classic. And what is the characteristic quality of a classic. The characteristic quality of a classic is that it is beautiful. Now of course it is perfectly true that a more or less first rate work of art is beautiful but the trouble is that when that first rate work of art becomes a classic because it is accepted the only thing that is important from then on to the majority of the acceptors the enormous majority, the most intelligent majority of the acceptors is that it is so wonderfully beautiful. Of course it is wonderfully beautiful, only when it is still a thing irritating annoying stimulating then all quality of beauty is denied to it.

Of course it is beautiful but first all beauty in it is denied and then all the beauty of it is accepted. If every one were not so indolent they would realise that beauty is beauty even when it is irritating and stimulating not only when it is accepted and classic. Of course it is extremely difficult nothing more so than to remember back to its not being beautiful once it has become beautiful. This makes it so much more difficult to realise its beauty when the work is being refused and prevents every one from realising that they were convinced that beauty was denied, once the work is accepted. Automatically with the acceptance of the time-sense comes the recognition of the beauty and once the beauty is accepted the beauty never fails any one.

Beginning again and again is a natural thing even when there is a series.

Beginning again and again and again explaining composition and time is a natural thing.

It is understood by this time that everything is the same except composition and time, composition and the time of the composition and the time in the composition.

Everything is the same except composition and as the composition is different and always going to be different everything is not the same. Everything is not the same as the time when of the composition and the time in the composition is different. The composition is different, that is certain.

The composition is the thing seen by every one living in the living they are doing, they are the composing of the composition that at the time they are living is the composition of the time in which they are living. It is that that makes living a thing they are doing. Nothing else is different, of that almost any one can be certain. The time when and the time of and the time in that composition is the natural phenomena of that composition and of that perhaps every one can be certain.

No one thinks these things when they are making when they are creating what is the composition, naturally no one thinks, that is no one formulates until what is to be formulated has been made.

Composition is not there, it is going to be there and we are here. This is some time ago for us naturally.

The only thing that is different from one time to another is what is seen and what is seen depends upon how everybody is doing everything. This makes the thing we are looking at very different and this makes what those who describe it make of it, it makes a composition, it confuses, it shows, it is, it looks, it likes it as it is, and this makes what is seen as it is seen. Nothing changes from generation to generation except the thing seen and that makes a composition.

Now the few who make writing as it is made and it is to be remarked that the most decided of them are those that are prepared by preparing, are prepared just as the world around them is prepared and is preparing to do it in this way and so if you do not mind I will again tell you how it happens. Naturally one does not know how it happened until it is well over beginning happening.

Each period of living differs from any other period of living not in the way life is but in the way life is conducted and that authentically speaking is composition. After life has been conducted in a certain way everybody knows it but nobody knows it, little by little, nobody knows it as long as nobody knows it. Any one creating the composition in the arts does not know it either, they are conducting life and that makes their composition what it is, it makes their work compose as it does.

Their influence and their influences are the same as that of all of their contemporaries only it must always be remembered that the analogy is not obvious until as I say the composition of a time has become so pronounced that it is past and the artistic composition of it is a classic.

And now to begin as if to begin. Composition is not there, it is going to be there and we are here. This is some time ago for us naturally. There is something to be added afterwards.

Just how much my work is known to you I do not know. I feel that perhaps it would be just as well to tell the whole of it.

In beginning writing I wrote a book called *Three Lives* this was written in 1905. I wrote a negro story called *Melanctha*. In that there was a constant recurring and beginning there was a marked direction in the direction of being in the present although naturally I had been accustomed to past present and future, and why, because the composition forming around me was a prolonged present. A composition of a prolonged present is a natural composition in the world as it has been these thirty years it was more and more a prolonged present. I created then a prolonged present naturally I knew nothing of a continuous present but it came naturally to me to make one, it was simple it was clear to me and nobody knew why it was done like that, I did not myself although naturally to me it was natural.

After that I did a book called *The Making of Americans* it is a long book about a thousand pages.

Here again it was all so natural to me and more and more complicatedly a continuous present. A continuous present is a continuous present. I made almost a thousand pages of a continuous present.

Continuous present is one thing and beginning again and again is another thing. These are both things. And then there is using everything.

This brings us again to composition this the using everything. The using everything brings us to composition and to this composition. A continuous present and using everything and beginning again. In these two books there was elaboration of the complexities of using everything and of a continuous present and of beginning again and again and again.

In the first book there was a groping for a continuous present and for using everything by beginning again and again.

There was a groping for using everything and there was a groping for a continuous present and there was an inevitable beginning of beginning again and again and again.

Having naturally done this I naturally was a little troubled with it when I read it. I became then like the others who read it. One does, you know, excepting that when I reread it myself I lost myself in it again. Then I said to myself this time it will be different and I began. I did not begin again I just began.

In this beginning naturally since I at once went on and on very soon there were pages and pages and pages more and more elaborated creating a more and more continuous present including more and more using of everything and continuing more and more beginning and beginning and beginning.

I went on and on to a thousand pages of it.

In the meantime to naturally begin I commenced making portraits of anybody and anything. In making these portraits I naturally made a continuous present an including everything and a beginning again and again within a very small thing. That started me into composing anything into one thing. So then naturally it was natural that one thing an enormously long thing was not everything an enormously short thing was also not everything nor was it all of it a continuous present thing nor was it always and always beginning again. Naturally I would then begin again. I would begin again I would naturally begin. I did naturally begin. This brings me to a great deal that has been begun.

And after that what changes what changes after that, after that what changes and what changes after that and after that and what changes and after that and what changes after that.

The problem from this time on became more definite.

It was all so nearly alike it must be different and it is different, it is natural that if everything is used and there is a continuous present and a beginning again and again if it is all so alike it must be simply different and everything simply different was the natural way of creating it then.

In this natural way of creating it then that it was simply different everything being alike it was simply different, this kept on leading one to lists. Lists naturally for a while and by lists I mean a series. More and more in going back over what was done at this time I find that I naturally kept simply different as an intention. Whether there was or whether there was not a continuous present did not then any longer trouble me there was or there was, and using everything no longer troubled me if everything is alike using everything could no longer trouble me and beginning again and again could no longer trouble me because if lists were inevitable if series were inevitable and the whole of it was inevitable beginning again and again could not trouble me so then with nothing to trouble me I very completely began naturally since everything is alike making it as simply different naturally as simply different as possible. I began doing natural phenomena what I call natural phenomena and natural phenomena naturally everything being alike natural phenomena are making things be naturally simply different. This found its culmination later, in the beginning it began in a center confused with lists with series with geography with returning portraits and with particularly often four and three and often with five and four. It is easy to see that in the beginning such a conception as everything being naturally different would be very inarticulate and very slowly it began to emerge and take the form of anything, and then naturally if anything that is simply different is simply different what follows will follow.

So far then the progress of my conceptions was the natural progress entirely in accordance with my epoch as I am sure is to be quite easily realised if you think over the scene that was before us all from year to year.

As I said in the beginning, there is the long history of how every one ever acted or has felt and that nothing inside in them in all of them makes it connectedly different. By this I mean all this.

The only thing that is different from one time to another is what is seen and what is seen depends upon how everybody is doing everything.

It is understood by this time that everything is the same except composition and time, composition and the time of the composition and the time in the composition.

Everything is the same except composition and as the composition is different and always going to be different everything is not the same. So then I as a contemporary creating the composition in the beginning was groping toward a continuous present, a using everything a beginning again and again and then everything being alike then everything very simply everything was naturally simply different and so I as a contemporary was creating everything being alike was creating everything naturally being naturally simply different, everything being alike. This then was the period that brings me to the period of the beginning of 1914. Everything being alike everything naturally would be simply different and war came and everything being alike and everything being simply different brings everything being simply different brings it to romanticism.

Romanticism is then when everything being alike everything is naturally simply different, and romanticism.

Then for four years this was more and more different even though this was, was everything alike. Everything alike naturally everything was simply different and this is and was romanticism and this is and was war. Everything being alike everything naturally everything is different simply different naturally simply different.

And so there was the natural phenomena that was war, which had been, before war came, several generations behind the contemporary composition, because it became war and so completely needed to be contemporary became completely contemporary and so created the completed recognition of the contemporary composition. Every one but one may say every one became consciously became aware of the existence of the authenticity of the modern composition. This then the contemporary recognition, because of the academic thing known as war having been forced to become contemporary made every one not only contemporary in act not only contemporary in thought but contemporary in self-consciousness made every one contemporary with the modern composition. And so the art creation of the contemporary composition which would have been outlawed normally outlawed several generations more behind even than war, war having been brought so to speak up to date art so to speak was allowed not completely to be up to date, but nearly up to date, in other words we who created the expression of the modern composition were to be recognised before we were dead some of us even quite a long time before we were dead. And so war may be said to have advanced a general recognition of the expression of the contemporary composition by almost thirty years.

And now after that there is no more of that in other words there is peace and something comes then and it follows coming then.

And so now one finds oneself interesting oneself in an equilibration, that of course means words as well as things and distribution as well as between themselves between the words and themselves and the things and themselves, a distribution as distribution. This makes what follows what follows and now there is every reason why there should be an arrangement made. Distribution is interesting and equilibration is interesting when a continuous present and a beginning again and again and using everything and everything alike and everything naturally simply different has been done.

After all this, there is that, there has been that that there is a composition and that nothing changes except composition the composition and the time of and the time in the composition.

The time of the composition is a natural thing and the time in the composition is a natural thing it is a natural thing and it is a contemporary thing.

The time of the composition is the time of the composition. It has been at times a present thing it has been at times a past thing it has been at times a future thing it has been at times an endeavour at parts or all of these things. In my beginning it was a continuous present a beginning again and again and again and again, it was a series it was a list it was a similarity and everything different it was a distribution and an equilibration. That is all of the time some of the time of the composition.

Now there is still something else the time-sense in the composition. This is what is always a fear a doubt and a judgement and a conviction. The quality in the creation of expression the quality in a composition that makes it go dead just after it has been made is very troublesome.

The time in the composition is a thing that is very troublesome. If the time in the composition is very troublesome it is because there must even if there is no time at all in the composition there must be time in the composition which is in its quality of distribution and equilibration. In the beginning there was the time in the composition that naturally was in the composition but time in the composition comes now and this is what is now troubling every one the time in the composition is now a part of distribution and equilibration. In the beginning there was confusion there was a continuous present and later there was romanticism which was not a confusion but an extrication and now there is either succeeding or failing there must be distribution and equilibration there must be time that is distributed and equilibrated. This is the thing that is at present the most troubling and if there is the time that is at present the most troublesome the time-sense that is at present the most troubling is the thing that makes the present the most troubling. There is at present there is distribution, by this I mean expression and time, and in this way at present composition is time that is the reason that at present the time-sense is troubling that is the reason why at present the time-sense in the composition is the composition that is making what there is in composition.

And afterwards.

Now that is all.

from *Monsieur Teste*

[before 1926]

PAUL VALÉRY

Preface

This imaginary character, whose author I became in my partly
literary, partly wayward or . . . inward youth, has lived, it seems, since
that faded time, with a certain life — with which his reticences more than
his avowals have induced a few readers to endow him.

Teste was created — in a room where Auguste Comte spent his early
years — at a moment when I was drunk with my own will, and subject to
strange excesses of insight into myself.

I was affected with the acute malady of precision. I was straining toward
the extreme of the reckless desire to understand, seeking in myself the
critical limits of my powers of attention.

I was doing what I could in this way to increase a little the duration of
a few thoughts. Everything that came easy was indifferent and almost
offensive to me. The sense of effort seemed to me the thing to be sought,
and I did not value happy results which are no more than the natural
fruits of our native powers. That is to say, results in general, and consequently works, were much less important to me than the energy of the
workman — the substance of things he hopes to make. This proves that
theology occurs nearly everywhere.

I was suspicious of literature, even of the fairly precise demands of
work in poetry. The act of writing always requires a certain "sacrifice of
the intellect." It is quite clear, for instance, that the conditions of literary
reading do not allow for an excessive precision of language. The intellect
would readily exact of ordinary language certain perfections and purities
that are not in its power. But rare are the readers who find pleasure only
when their minds are tense. We get their attention only by offering a bit
of amusement; and this kind of attention is passive.

I thought it unworthy, moreover, to divide my ambition between the effort to produce an effect on others, and the passion to know and acknowledge myself just as I was, without omissions, pretenses, or indulgence.

I put away not only Literature but nearly all of Philosophy as well among those Vague Things and Impure Things which I rejected with all my heart. The traditional objects of speculation stirred me so little that I thought something was wrong, with philosophers or with me. I had not yet learned that the loftiest problems hardly press themselves upon us, and that they get much of their prestige and their attraction from certain *conventions* which we must know and accept if we are to be received by philosophers. Youth is a time when conventions are, and must be, ill understood; either blindly rejected or blindly obeyed. It is impossible to conceive, at the beginning of the reflective life, that only arbitrary decisions enable man to *found* anything at all: language, societies, knowledge, works of art. As for me, I could so little conceive it, that I made it a rule secretly to hold as null or contemptible all opinions and habits of mind which grow out of life in common, out of our external relations with other men, and which disappear in voluntary solitude. I could think only with disgust of all ideas and feelings that are induced or roused in man only by his ills and fears, his hopes and terrors, and not freely as when he purely looks at things and into himself.

I was thus trying to reduce myself to my *real* qualities. I had little confidence in my means, and found within me, with no trouble at all, all I needed to despise myself, but I was strong in my infinite desire for clarity, in my contempt for convictions and idols, in my distaste for facility, and in the sense of my limitations. I had made myself an inner island, and spent my time exploring and fortifying it.

M. Teste was born one day of a memory, then recent, of those moods.

It is in this that he resembles me, much as a child resembles a father who at the moment of conceiving him was himself undergoing a profound change of being, and was not himself.

Perhaps from time to time we do thrust into life the exceptional creature of an exceptional moment. It is not impossible, after all, that the singularity of certain men, the qualities of their difference, good or bad, may sometimes be due to the momentary condition of their begetters. It may be that the transitory is thus transmitted and given career. Moreover, is this not, in matters of the mind, just the function of our works, the act of talent, the very object of our labor, and in short, *the essence of that strange instinct to make our rarest finds survive us.*

Coming back to M. Teste, and observing that the existence of a creature of this kind could hardly be prolonged into the real much above an hour, I say that the very problem of his existence, and of its duration, is sufficient to give him a kind of life. This problem is a germ. A germ is a living thing, but some germs are incapable of growth. These latter *attempt* to live, become deformed, and die. In fact, we know them only by this *remarkable property* of being unable to endure. *Abnormal* are those beings which have a little less future than the *normal*. They are like many of our thoughts, that contain hidden contradictions. Such thoughts occur to the mind, seem just and fertile, but their consequences ruin them, and their very presence is soon deadly to themselves.

Who knows but that most of the prodigious ideas over which so many great men, and a multitude of lesser ones, have for centuries turned gray, may be psychological deformities — *Monster Ideas* — spawned by the naïve exercise of our questioning faculties, which we carelessly apply here and there — without realizing that we should reasonably question only what can in fact give us an answer?

But the monsters of flesh rapidly perish. Yet not without having existed for a while. Nothing is more instructive than to meditate on their destiny.

Why is M. Teste impossible? That question is the *soul* of him. *It turns you into M. Teste.* For he is no other than the very demon of possibility. Regard for the sum total of what he can do rules him. He watches himself, he maneuvers, he is unwilling to be maneuvered. He knows only two values, two categories, those of consciousness reduced to its acts: *the possible* and *the impossible*. In this strange head, where philosophy has little credit, where language is always on trial, there is scarcely a thought that is not accompanied by the feeling that it is tentative; there exists hardly more than the anticipation and execution of definite operations. The short, intense life of this brain is spent in supervising the mechanism by which the relations of the known and the unknown are established and organized. It even uses its obscure and transcendent powers in the obstinate pretense that it is an isolated system in which the infinite has no part.

To give some idea of such a monster, to portray his appearance and habits, to sketch at least a Hippogriff, a Chimera of the mythology of intellect, requires — and therefore excuses — the use if not the invention of a forced language, at times energetically abstract. It requires also a tone of familiarity and even a few traces of that vulgarity or triviality which we use with ourselves. We are not reserved toward the one who is in us.

A text subject to these very special conditions is certainly not easy reading in the original. All the more must it present to whoever tries to put it into a foreign language almost insurmountable difficulties. . . .

Vita cartesii res est simplicissima. . . .

AN EVENING WITH M. TESTE

Stupidity is not my strong point. I have seen many persons; I have visited several nations; I have taken part in divers enterprises without liking them; I have eaten nearly every day; I have had to do with women. I now recall several hundred faces, two or three great events, and perhaps the substance of twenty books. I have not retained the best nor the worst of these things. What could stick, did.

This bit of arithmetic spares me surprise at getting old. I could also add up the victorious moments of my mind, and imagine them joined and soldered, composing a *happy* life. . . . But I think I have always been a good judge of myself. I have rarely lost sight of myself; I have detested, and adored myself — and so, we have grown old together.

Often I have supposed that all was over for me, and I would begin ending with all my strength, anxious to exhaust and clear up some painful situation. This has made me realize that we interpret our own thought too much according to the *expression* of other people's! Since then, the thousands of words that have buzzed in my ears have rarely shaken me with what they were meant to mean. And all those I have myself spoken to others, I could always feel them become distinct from my thought — for they were becoming *invariable*.

If I had gone on as most men do, not only would I have believed myself their superior, but would have seemed so. I have preferred myself. What they call a superior being is one who has deceived himself. To wonder at him, we have to see him — and to be seen, he has to show himself. And he shows me that he has a silly obsession with his own name. Every great man is thus flawed with an error. Every mind considered powerful begins with the fault that makes it known. In exchange for a public fee, it gives the time necessary to make itself knowable, the energy spent in transmitting itself and in preparing the alien satisfaction. It even goes so far as to compare the formless games of glory to the joy of feeling unique — the great private pleasure.

And so I have surmised that the strongest heads, the most sagacious inventors, the most exacting connoisseurs of thought, must be unknown men, misers, who die without giving up their secret. Their existence was revealed to me by just those showy, somewhat less *solid* individuals.

This induction was so easy that I could see it taking shape from one moment to the next. It was only necessary to imagine ordinary great men pure of their first error, or to take this error itself as a basis for conceiving a higher degree of consciousness, a fuller sense of the freed mind. Such a simple process opened curious vistas before me, as if I had gone down into the sea. I thought that I perceived there, dimmed by the brilliance of published discoveries, but side by side with the unsung inventions recorded every day by business, fear, boredom, and poverty, *many inner masterpieces.* I amused myself with smothering known history beneath the annals of anonymity.

Here they were, solitary figures, invisible in their limpid lives, but knowing beyond anyone in the world. They seemed in their obscurity twice, three times, many times greater than any celebrated person — they, in their disdain for making known their lucky finds and private achievements. I believe they would have refused to consider themselves as anything but things. . . .

These ideas came to me during October of 93, at those moments of leisure when thought practices simply existing.

I was beginning to think no more about them, when I made the acquaintance of M. Teste. (I am now thinking of the traces a man leaves in the little space through which he moves each day.) Before I knew M. Teste, I was attracted by his rather special manner. I studied his eyes, his clothes, his slightest low word to the waiter at the café where I used to see him. I wonder whether he felt observed. I would turn my eyes quickly away from his, only to catch my own following me. I would pick up the newspapers he had just been reading, and go over in my mind the sober gestures that rose from him; I noticed that no one paid any attention to him.

I had nothing more of this kind to learn when our relations began. I never saw him except at night. Once in a kind of b——; often at the theater. I heard that he lived on modest weekly speculations at the Bourse. He used to take his meals at a small restaurant on the rue Vivienne. Here, he would eat as if he were taking a purgative, with the same rush. From time to time he would go elsewhere and allow himself a fine, leisurely meal.

M. Teste was perhaps forty years old. His speech was extraordinarily rapid, and his voice quiet. Everything about him was fading, his eyes, his hands. His shoulders, however, were military, and his step had a regularity that was amazing. When he spoke he never raised an arm or a finger: he had *killed his puppet.* He did not smile, and said neither hello nor good-by. He seemed not to hear a "How do you do?"

His memory gave me much to think about. Signs that I could judge by led me to imagine in him unequaled intellectual gymnastics. It was not

that this faculty in him was excessive — it was rather trained or transformed. These are his own words: "I have not had a book for twenty
years. I have burned my papers also. I scribble in the flesh. . . . I can
retain what I wish. That is not the difficulty. *It is rather to retain what I
shall want tomorrow!* I have tried to invent a mechanical sieve. . . ."

Thinking about it convinced me that M. Teste had managed to discover laws of the mind we know nothing of. Surely he must have devoted
years to this research: even more surely, other years, and many more
years, had been given to maturing his findings, making them into instincts.
Discovery is nothing. The difficulty is to acquire what we discover.

The delicate art of duration: time, its distribution and regulation —
expending it upon well chosen objects, to give them special nourishment
— was one of M. Teste's main preoccupations. He watched for the repetition of certain ideas; he watered them with number. This served to make
the application of his conscious studies in the end mechanical. He even
sought to sum up this whole effort. He often said: *"Maturare!"* . . .

Certainly his singular memory must have retained for him exclusively
those impressions which the imagination by itself is powerless to construct.
If we imagine an ascent in a balloon, we can, with sagacity and vigor,
produce many of the probable sensations of an aeronaut; but there will
always remain something peculiar to a real ascent, which by contrast with
our imagined one shows the value of the methods of an Edmond Teste.

This man had early known the importance of what might be called
human *plasticity.* He had tried to find out its limits and its laws. How
deeply he must have thought about his own malleability!

In him I sensed feelings that made me shudder, a terrible obstinacy in
delirious experience. He was a being absorbed in his own variation, one
who becomes his own system, who gives himself up wholly to the frightful
discipline of the free mind, and who sets his joys to killing one another,
the stronger killing the weaker — the milder, the temporal, the joy of a
moment, of an hour just begun, killed by the fundamental — by hope for
the fundamental.

And I felt that he was master of his thought: I write down this
absurdity here. The expression of a feeling is always absurd.

M. Teste had no opinions. I believe he could become impassioned at
will, and to attain a definite end. What had he done with his personality?
How did he regard himself? . . . He never laughed, never a look of unhappiness on his face. He hated melancholy.

He spoke, and one felt oneself confounded with *things* in his mind:
one felt withdrawn, mingled with houses, with the grandeurs of space,
with the shuffled colors of the street, with street corners. . . . And the most

cleverly touching words — the very ones that bring their author closer to us than any other man, those that make us believe the eternal wall between minds is falling — could come to him. He knew wonderfully that they would have moved *anyone else*. He spoke, and without being able to tell precisely the motives or the extent of the proscription, one knew that a large number of words had been banished from his discourse. The ones he used were sometimes so curiously held by his voice or lighted by his phrase that their weight was altered, their value new. Sometimes they would lose all sense, they seemed to serve only to fill an empty place for which the proper term was still in doubt or not provided by the language. I have heard him designate a simple object by a group of abstract words and proper names.

To what he said, there was nothing to reply. He killed polite assent. Conversation was kept going in leaps that were no surprise to him.

If this man had reversed the direction of his inward meditations, if he had turned against the world the regular power of his mind, nothing could have resisted him. I am sorry to speak of him as we speak of those we make statues of. I am well aware that between "genius" and him, there is a quantity of weakness. He, so genuine! So new! So free of all trickery and magic, so hard! My own enthusiasm spoils him for me. . . .

How is it possible not to feel enthusiasm for a man who never said anything *vague?* for a man who calmly declared: "In all things I am interested only in the *facility* or *difficulty* of knowing them, of doing them. I give extreme care to measuring the degree of each quality, and to not getting attached to the problem. . . . What do I care for what I know quite well already?"

How is it possible not to be won over to a being whose mind seemed to transform to its own use all that is, a mind tha*t performed* everything suggested to it. I imagined this mind managing, mixing, making variations, connections, and throughout the whole field of its knowledge able to intercept and shunt, to guide, to freeze this and warm that, to drown, to raise, to name what has no name, to forget what it wished, to put to sleep or to color this and that. . . .

I am grossly simplifying his impenetrable powers. I do not dare say all my object tells me. Logic stops me. But, within me, every time the problem of Teste arises, curious formations appear.

On certain days I can recover him quite clearly. He reappears in my memory, beside me. I breathe the smoke of our cigars, I listen to him, I am wary. Sometimes, in reading a newspaper I encounter his thought, which some event has just justified. And I try again some of those illusory experiments that used to delight me during our evenings together. That is, I imagine him doing what I have not seen him do. What is M. Teste like when he is sick? How does he reason when he is in love! Is it possible for him to be sad? What would he be afraid of? What could make him tremble? . . . I wondered. I kept before me the complete image of this rigorous man, trying to make it answer my questions. . . . But it kept changing.

He loves, he suffers, he is bored. People all imitate themselves. But he must combine in his sigh, in his elemental moan, the rules and forms of his whole mind.

Exactly two years and three months ago this evening, I was at the theater with him, in a box someone had offered us. I have thought about this all day today.

I can still see him standing with the golden column of the Opera; together.

He looked only at the audience. He was *breathing in* the great blast of brilliance, on the edge of the pit. He was red.

An immense copper girl stood between us and a group murmuring beyond the dazzlement. Deep in the haze shone a naked bit of woman, smooth as a pebble. A number of independent fans were breathing over the crowd, dim and clear, that foamed up to the level of the top lights. My eyes spelled a thousand little faces, settled on a sad head, ran along arms, over people, and finally flickered out.

Each one was in his place, freed by a slight movement. I tasted the system of classification, the almost theoretical simplicity of the audience, the social order. I had the delicious sensation that everything breathing in this cube was going to follow its laws, flare up with laughter in great circles, be moved in rows, feel as a mass *intimate*, even *unique* things, secret urges, be lifted to the unavowable! I strayed over these layers of men, from level to level, in orbits, fancying that I could join ideally together all those with the same illness, or the same theory, or the same vice. . . . One music moved us all, swelled, and then became quite small.

It disappeared. M. Teste was murmuring: "We are *beautiful*, extraordinary, only to others! *We* are eaten by others!"

The last word stood out in the silence created by the orchestra. Teste drew a deep breath.

His fiery face, glowing with heat and color, his broad shoulders, his dark figure bronzed by the lights, the form of the whole clothed mass of him propped by the heavy column, took hold of me again. He lost not an atom of all that at each moment became perceptible in that grandeur of red and gold.

I watched his skull making acquaintance with the angles of the capital, his right hand refreshing itself among the gilt ornaments; and, in the purple shadow, his large feet. From a distant part of the theater his eyes came back to me; his mouth said: "Discipline is not bad. . . . It is at least a beginning. . . ."

I did not know what to answer. He said in his low quick voice: "Let them enjoy and obey!"

He fixed his eyes for a long time on a young man opposite us, then on a lady, then on a whole group in the higher galleries — overflowing the balcony in five or six burning faces — and then on everybody, the whole theater full as the heavens, ardent, held by the stage which we could not see. The stupor they were all in showed us that something or other sublime was going on. We watched the light dying from all the faces in the audience. And when it was quite low, when the light no longer shone, there remained only the vast phosphorescence of those thousand faces. I saw that this twilight made these beings passive. Their attention and the darkness mounting together formed a continuous equilibrium. I was myself attentive, *necessarily,* to all this attention.

M. Teste said: "The supreme simplifies *them*. I bet they are all thinking, more and more, *toward* the same thing. They will be equal at the crisis, the common limit. Besides, the law is not so simple . . . since it does not include me — and — I am here."

He added: "The lighting is what holds them."

I said, laughing: "You too?"

He replied: "You too."

"What a dramatist you would make," I said to him. "You seem to be watching some experiment going on beyond the limits of all the sciences! I would like to see a theater inspired by your meditations."

He said: "No one meditates."

The applause and the house lights drove us out. We circled, and went down. The passers-by seemed set free. M. Teste complained slightly of the midnight coolness. He alluded to old pains.

As we walked along, almost incoherent phrases sprang from him. Despite my efforts, I could follow his words only with great difficulty, finally deciding merely to remember them. The incoherence of speech depends on the one listening to it. The mind seems to me so made that it cannot be incoherent to itself. For that reason I refused to consider Teste as mad. Anyway, I could vaguely make out the thread of his ideas, and I saw no contradiction in them; also, I would have been wary of too simple a solution.

We went through streets quieted by the night, we turned corners, in the void, by instinct finding our way — wider, narrower, wider. His military step subdued mine. . . .

"Yet, *I replied,* how can we escape a music so powerful! And why should we? I find in it a peculiar excitement. Must I reject this? I find in it the illusion of an immense effort, which suddenly might become possible. . . . It gives me *abstract sensations,* delightful images of everything I love — change, movement, mixture, flux, transformation. . . . Will you deny that certain things are anæsthetic? That there are trees that intoxicate us, men that give us strength, girls that paralyze us, skies that stop our speech?"

M. Teste put in, in a rather loud voice:

". . . But, sir, what is the 'talent' of your trees — or of anyone! . . . to me! I am at home in MYSELF, I speak my language, I hate extraordinary things. Only weak minds need them. Believe me literally: *genius* is *easy, divinity* is *easy.* . . . I mean simply — that I know how it is conceived. It is *easy.*

"Long ago — at least twenty years — the least thing out of the ordinary that some other man accomplished was for me a personal defeat. I used to see only ideas stolen from me! What nonsense! . . . Imagine thinking our own image is not indifferent to us! In our imaginary struggles, we treat ourselves *too well* or *too ill! . . .*"

He coughed. He said to himself: "What can a man do? . . . What can a man do? . . ." He said to me: "You know a man who knows that he does not know what he is saying!"

We were at his door. He asked me to come in and smoke a cigar with him.

On the top floor of the house we went into a very small "furnished" apartment. I did not see a book. Nothing indicated the traditional manner of work, at a table, under a lamp, in the midst of papers and pens.

In the greenish bedroom, smelling of mint, there was only a candle and, sitting around it, the dull abstract furniture — the bed, the clock, the wardrobe with a mirror, two armchairs — like rational beings. On the mantel, a few newspapers, a dozen visiting cards covered with figures, and a medicine bottle. I have never had a stronger impression of the *ordinary.* It was *any lodging,* like geometry's *any point* — and perhaps as useful. My host existed in the most general interior. I thought of the hours he had spent in that armchair. I was frightened at the infinite drabness possible in this pure and banal room. I have lived in such rooms. I have never been able to believe them final, without horror.

M. Teste talked of money. I do not know how to reproduce his special eloquence: it seemed less precise than usual. Fatigue, the silence becoming deeper with the late hour, the bitter cigars, the abandon of night seemed to overtake him. I can still hear his voice, lowered and slow, making the flame dance above the single candle that burned between us, as he recited very large numbers, wearily. Eight hundred ten million seventy-five thousand five hundred fifty. . . . I listened to this unheard-of music without following the calculation. He conveyed to me the fever of the Bourse, and these long series of names of numbers gripped me like poetry. He correlated news events, industrial phenomena, public taste and the passions, and still more figures, one with another. He was saying: "Gold is, as it were, the mind of society."

Suddenly he stopped. He was in pain.

I again scanned the cold room, the nullity of the furnishings, to keep from looking at him. He took out his little bottle and drank. I got up to go.

"Stay awhile longer," he said. "You don't mind. I am going to get in bed. In a few moments I'll be asleep. You can take the candle to go down."

He undressed quietly. His gaunt body bathed in the covers, and lay still. Then he turned over and plunged farther down in the bed, too short for him.

He smiled and said to me: "I am like a plank. I am floating! . . . I feel an imperceptible rolling under me — an immense movement? I sleep an hour or two at the very most; I adore navigating the night. Often I can not distinguish thought before from sleep. I do not know whether I have slept. It used to be, when I dozed, I thought of all those who had afforded me pleasure; faces, things, minutes. I would summon them so that my thought might be as sweet as possible, easy as the bed. . . . I am old. I can show you that I feel old. . . . You remember! When we are children we *discover* ourselves, we slowly discover the extent of our bodies, we express the particularity of our bodies by a series of efforts, I suppose? We squirm and discover or recover ourselves, and are surprised! We touch a heel, grasp the right foot with the left hand, take a cold foot in a warm palm! . . . Now I know myself by heart. Even my heart. Bah! the world is all marked off, all the flags are flying over all territories. . . . My bed remains. I love this stream of sleep and linen: this linen that stretches and folds, or crumples — runs over me like sand, when I lie still — curdles around me in sleep. . . . It is a very complex bit of mechanics. In the direction of the woof or the warp, a very slight deviation. . . . Ah!"

He was in pain.

"What is it?" I said. "I can . . ."

"Nothing . . . much," he said. "Nothing but . . . a tenth of a second appearing. . . . Wait. . . . At certain moments my body is illuminated. . . . It is very curious. Suddenly I see into myself . . . I can make out the depth of the layers of my flesh; and I feel zones of pain, rings, poles, plumes of pain. Do you see these living figures, this geometry of my suffering? Some of these flashes are exactly like ideas. They make me understand — from here, to there. . . . And yet they leave me *uncertain*. Uncertain is not the word. . . . When *it* is about to appear, I find in myself something confused or diffused. Areas that are . . . hazy, occur in my being, wide spaces suddenly make their appearance. Then I choose a question from my memory, any problem at all . . . and I plunge into it. I count grains of sand . . . and so long as I can see them . . . My increasing pain forces me to observe it. I think about it! I only await my cry, and as soon as I have heard it — the *object*, the terrible *object*, getting smaller, and still smaller, escapes from my inner sight. . . .

"What is possible, what can a man do? I can withstand anything — except the suffering of my body, beyond a certain intensity. Yet, that is where I ought to begin. For, to suffer is to give supreme attention to something, and I am somewhat a man of attention. You know, I had foreseen my future illness. I had visualized precisely what everybody now knows. I believe the vision of a manifest portion of the future should be part of our education. Yes, I foresaw what is now beginning. At that time, it was just an idea like any other. So, I was able to follow it."

He grew calm.

He turned over on his side, lowered his eyes; and after a moment, was talking again. He was beginning to lose himself. His voice was only a murmur in the pillow. His reddening hand was already asleep.

He was still saying: "I think, and it doesn't bother at all. I am alone. How comfortable solitude is! Not the slightest thing weighs on me. . . . The same reverie here as in the ship's cabin, the same at the Café Lambert. . . . If some Bertha's arms take on importance, I am robbed — as by pain. . . . If anyone says something and doesn't prove it — he's an enemy. I prefer the sound of the least fact, happening. I am being and seeing myself, seeing me see myself, and so forth. . . . Let's think very closely. Bah! you can fall asleep on any subject. . . . Sleep can continue any idea. . . ."

He was snoring softly. A little more softly still, I took the candle, and went out on tiptoe.

Translated by Jackson Matthews

4

PABLO PICASSO *and* IGOR STRAVINSKY

Two of the mightiest, most long-lasting producers of any century, Picasso and Stravinsky are pythons, eclectics-extraordinary, who can assimilate and nourish themselves upon the whole history of art; and in fact, if we can speak of a "tradition of the new," it is the example of their tirelessly changing "periods" and "styles" which authorizes the paradox.

Statements

[1923]

PABLO PICASSO

I can hardly understand the importance given to the word *research* in connection with modern painting. In my opinion to search means nothing in painting. To find, is the thing. Nobody is interested in following a man who, with his eyes fixed on the ground, spends his life looking for the pocket book that fortune should put in his path. The one who finds something no matter what it might be, even if his intention were not to search for it, at least arouses our curiosity, if not our admiration.

Among the several sins that I have been accused of committing, none is more false than the one that I have, as the principal objective in my work, the spirit of research. When I paint my object is to show what I have found and not what I am looking for. In art intentions are not sufficient and, as we say in Spanish: love must be proved by facts and not by reasons. What one does is what counts and not what one had the intention of doing.

We all know that art is not truth. Art is a lie that makes us realize truth, at least the truth that is given us to understand. The artist must know the manner whereby to convince others of the truthfulness of his lies. If he only shows in his work that he has searched, and re-searched, for the way to put over his lies, he would never accomplish anything.

The idea of research has often made painting go astray, and made the artist lose himself in mental lucubrations. Perhaps this has been the principal fault of modern art. The spirit of research has poisoned those who have not fully understood all the positive and conclusive elements in modern art and has made them attempt to paint the invisible and, therefore, the unpaintable.

They speak of naturalism in opposition to modern painting. I would like to know if anyone has ever seen a natural work of art. Nature and art, being two different things, cannot be the same thing. Through art we express our conception of what nature is not.

Velasquez left us his idea of the people of his epoch. Undoubtedly they were different from what he painted them, but we cannot conceive a Philip IV in any other way than the one Velasquez painted. Rubens also made a portrait of the same king and in Rubens' portrait he seems to be quite another person. We believe in the one painted by Velasquez, for he convinces us by his right of might.

From the painters of the origins, the primitives, whose work is obviously different from nature, down to those artists who, like David, Ingres and even Bouguereau, believed in painting nature as it is, art has always been art and not nature. And from the point of view of art there are no concrete or abstract forms, but only forms which are more or less convincing lies. That those lies are necessary to our mental selves is beyond any doubt, as it is through them that we form our esthetic point of view of life.

Cubism is no different from any other school of painting. The same principles and the same elements are common to all. The fact that for a long time cubism has not been understood and that even today there are people who cannot see anything in it, means nothing. I do not read English, an English book is a blank book to me. This does not mean that the English language does not exist, and why should I blame anybody else but myself if I cannot understand what I know nothing about?

I also often hear the word evolution. Repeatedly I am asked to explain how my painting evolved. To me there is no past or future in art. If a work of art cannot live always in the present it must not be considered at all. The art of the Greeks, of the Egyptians, of the great painters who lived in other times, is not an art of the past; perhaps it is more alive today than it ever was. Art does not evolve by itself, the ideas of people change and with them their mode of expression. When I hear people speak of the evolution of an artist, it seems to me that they are considering him standing between two mirrors that face each other and reproduce his image an infinite number of times, and that they contemplate the successive images of one mirror as his past, and the images of the other mirror as his future, while his real image is taken as his present. They do not consider that they all are the same images in different planes.

Variation does not mean evolution. If an artist varies his mode of expression this only means that he has changed his manner of thinking, and in changing, it might be for the better or it might be for the worse.

The several manners I have used in my art must not be considered as an evolution, or as steps toward an unknown ideal of painting. All I have ever made was made for the present and with the hope that it will always remain in the present. I have never taken into consideration the spirit of research. When I have found something to express, I have done it without thinking of the past or of the future. I do not believe I have used radically different elements in the different manners I have used in painting. If the subjects I have wanted to express have suggested different ways of expression I have never hesitated to adopt them. I have never made trials nor experiments. Whenever I had something to say, I have said it in the manner in which I have felt it ought to be said. Different motives inevitably require different methods of expression. This does not imply either evolution or progress, but an adaptation of the idea one wants to express and the means to express that idea.

Arts of transition do not exist. In the chronological history of art there are periods which are more positive, more complete than others. This means that there are periods in which there are better artists than in others. If the history of art could be graphically represented, as in a chart used by a nurse to mark the changes of temperature of her patient, the same silhouettes of mountains would be shown, proving that in art there is no ascendant progress, but that it follows certain ups and downs that might occur at any time. The same occurs with the work of an individual artist.

Many think that cubism is an art of transition, an experiment which is to bring ulterior results. Those who think that way have not understood it. Cubism is not either a seed or a foetus, but an art dealing primarily with forms, and when a form is realized it is there to live its own life. A mineral substance, having geometric formation, is not made so for transitory purposes, it is to remain what it is and will always have its own form. But if we are to apply the law of evolution and transformism to art, then we have to admit that all art is transitory. On the contrary, art does not enter into these philosophic absolutisms. If cubism is an art of transition I am sure that the only thing that will come out of it is another form of cubism.

Mathematics, trigonometry, chemistry, psychoanalysis, music, and whatnot, have been related to cubism to give it an easier interpretation. All this has been pure literature, not to say nonsense, which brought bad results, blinding people with theories.

Cubism has kept itself within the limits and limitations of painting, never pretending to go beyond it. Drawing, design and color are understood and practiced in cubism in the same spirit and manner that they are understood and practiced in all other schools. Our subjects might be different, as we have introduced into painting objects and forms that were formerly ignored. We have kept our eyes open to our surroundings, and also our brains.

We give to form and color all their individual significance, as far as we can see it; in our subjects we keep the joy of discovery, the pleasure of the unexpected; our subject itself must be a source of interest. But of what use is it to say what we do when everybody can see it if he wants to?

[*1935*]

In the old days pictures went forward toward completion by stages. Every day brought something new. A picture used to be a sum of additions. In my case a picture is a sum of destructions. I do a picture — then I destroy it. In the end, though, nothing is lost: the red I took away from one place turns up somewhere else.

It would be very interesting to preserve photographically, not the stages, but the metamorphoses of a picture. Possibly one might then discover the path followed by the brain in materializing a dream. But there is one very odd thing — to notice that basically a picture doesn't change, that the first "vision" remains almost intact, in spite of appearances. I often ponder on a light and a dark when I have put them into a picture; I try hard to break them up by interpolating a color that will create a different effect. When the work is photographed, I note that what I put in to correct my first vision has disappeared, and that, after all, the photographic image corresponds with my first vision before the transformation I insisted on.

A picture is not thought out and settled beforehand. While it is being done it changes as one's thoughts change. And when it is finished, it still goes on changing, according to the state of mind of whoever is looking at it. A picture lives a life like a living creature, undergoing the changes imposed on us by our life from day to day. This is natural enough, as the picture lives only through the man who is looking at it.

At the actual time that I am painting a picture I may think of white and put down white. But I can't go on working all the time thinking of white and painting it. Colors, like features, follow the changes of the emotions. You've seen the sketch I did for a picture with all the colors indicated on it. What is left of them? Certainly the white I thought of and the green I thought of are there in the picture, but not in the places I intended, nor in the same quantities. Of course, you can paint pictures by matching up different parts of them so that they go quite nicely together, but they'll lack any kind of drama.

I want to get to the stage where nobody can tell how a picture of mine is done. What's the point of that? Simply that I want nothing but emotion to be given off by it.

Work is a necessity for man.

A horse does not go between the shafts of its own accord.

Man invented the alarm clock.

.   .   .

There is no abstract art. You must always start with something. Afterward you can remove all traces of reality. There's no danger then, anyway, because the idea of the object will have left an indelible mark. It is what started the artist off, excited his ideas, and stirred up his emotions. Ideas and emotions will in the end be prisoners in his work. Whatever they do, they can't escape from the picture. They form an integral part of it, even when their presence is no longer discernible. Whether he likes it or not, man is the instrument of nature. It forces on him its character and appearance. In my Dinard pictures and in my Pourville pictures I expressed very much the same vision. However, you yourself have noticed how different the atmosphere of those painted in Brittany is from those pointed in Normandy, because you recognize the light of the Dieppe cliffs. I didn't *copy* this light nor did I pay it any special attention. I was simply soaked in it. My eyes saw it and my subconscious registered what they saw: my hand fixed the impression. One cannot go against nature. It is stronger than the strongest man. It is pretty much to our interest to be on good terms with it! We may allow ourselves certain liberties, but only in details.

Nor is there any "figurative" and "non-figurative" art. Everything appears to us in the guise of a "figure." Even in metaphysics ideas are expressed by means of symbolic "figures." See how ridiculous it is then to think of painting without "figuration." A person, an object, a circle are all "figures"; they react to us more or less intensely. Some are nearer our sensations and produce emotions that touch our affective faculties; others appeal more directly to the intellect. They all should be allowed a place because I find my spirit has quite as much need of emotion as my senses. Do you think it concerns me that a particular picture of mine represents two people? Though these two people once existed for me, they exist no longer. The "vision" of them gave me a preliminary emotion; then little by little their actual presences became blurred; they developed into a fiction and then disappeared altogether, or rather they were transformed into all kinds of problems. They are no longer two people, you see, but forms and colors: forms and colors that have taken on, meanwhile, the *idea* of two people and preserve the vibration of their life.

I deal with painting as I deal with things. I paint a window just as I look out of a window. If an open window looks wrong in a picture, I draw the curtain and shut it, just as I would in my own room. In painting, as in life, you must act directly. Certainly, painting has its conventions, and it is essential to reckon with them. Indeed, you can't do anything else. And so you always ought to keep an eye on real life.

The artist is a receptacle for emotions that come from all over the place: from the sky, from the earth, from a scrap of paper, from a passing shape, from a spider's web. That is why we must not discriminate between things. Where things are concerned there are no class distinctions. We must pick out what is good for us where we can find it — except from our own works. I have a horror of copying myself. But when I am shown a portfolio of old drawings, for instance, I have no qualms about taking anything I want from them.

When we invented cubism we had no intention whatever of inventing cubism. We wanted simply to express what was in us. Not one of us drew up a plan of campaign, and our friends, the poets, followed our efforts attentively, but they never dictated to us. Young painters today often draw up a program to follow, and apply themselves like diligent students to performing their tasks.

.   .   .

Academic training in beauty is a sham. We have been deceived, but so well deceived that we can scarcely get back even a shadow of the truth. The beauties of the Parthenon, Venuses, Nymphs, Narcissuses, are so many lies. Art is not the application of a canon of beauty but what the instinct and the brain can conceive beyond any canon. When we love a

woman we don't start measuring her limbs. We love with our desires —
although everything has been done to try and apply a canon even to love.
The Parthenon is really only a farmyard over which someone put a
roof; colonnades and sculptures were added because there were people
in Athens who happened to be working, and wanted to express themselves.
It's not what the artist *does* that counts, but what he *is*. Cézanne would
never have interested me a bit if he had lived and thought like Jacques
Emile Blanche, even if the apple he painted had been ten times as beautiful. What forces our interest is Cézanne's anxiety — that's Cézanne's
lesson; the torments of van Gogh — that is the actual drama of the man.
The rest is a sham.

Everyone wants to understand art. Why not try to understand the song
of a bird? Why does one love the night, flowers, everything around one,
without trying to understand them? But in the case of a painting people
have to *understand*. If only they would realize above all that an artist
works of necessity, that he himself is only a trifling bit of the world, and
that no more importance should be attached to him than to plenty of
other things which please us in the world, though we can't explain them.
People who try to explain pictures are usually barking up the wrong tree.
Gertrude Stein joyfully announced to me the other day that she had at
last understood what my picture of the three musicians was meant to be.
It was a still life! . . .

The Composition of Music
from *Poetics of Music*
[1939]

IGOR STRAVINSKY

We are living at a time when the status of man is undergoing profound upheavals. Modern man is progressively losing his understanding
of values and his sense of proportions. This failure to understand essential realities is extremely serious. It leads us infallibly to the violation
of the fundamental laws of human equilibrium. In the domain of music,
the consequences of this misunderstanding are these: on one hand there
is a tendency to turn the mind away from what I shall call the higher
mathematics of music in order to degrade music to servile employment,

and to vulgarize it by adapting it to the requirements of an elementary utilitarianism — as we shall soon see on examining Soviet music. On the other hand, since the mind itself is ailing, the music of our time, and particularly the music that calls itself and believes itself *pure,* carries within it the symptoms of a pathologic blemish and spreads the germs of a new original sin. The old original sin was chiefly a sin of knowledge; the new original sin, if I may speak in these terms, is first and foremost a sin of non-acknowledgement — a refusal to acknowledge the truth and the laws that proceed therefrom, laws that we have called fundamental. What then is the truth in the domain of music? And what are its repercussions on creative activity?

Let us not forget that it is written: "Spiritus ubi vult spirat" (St. John, 3:8). What we must retain in this proposition is above all the word WILL. The Spirit is thus endowed with the capacity of willing. The principle of speculative volition is a fact.

Now it is just this fact that is too often disputed. People question the direction that the wind of the Spirit is taking, not the rightness of the artisan's work. In so doing, whatever may be your feelings about ontology or whatever your own philosophy and beliefs may be, you must admit that you are making an attack on the very freedom of the spirit — whether you begin this large word with a capital or not. If a believer in Christian philosophy, you would then also have to refuse to accept the idea of the Holy Spirit. If an agnostic or atheist, you would have to do nothing less than refuse to be a *free-thinker* . . .

It should be noted that there is never any dispute when the listener takes pleasure in the work he hears. The least informed of music-lovers readily clings to the periphery of a work; it pleases him for reasons that are most often entirely foreign to the essence of music. This pleasure is enough for him and calls for no justification. But if it happens that the music displeases him, our music-lover will ask you for an explanation of his discomfiture. He will demand that we explain something that is in its essence ineffable.

By its fruit we judge the tree. Judge the tree by its fruit then, and do not meddle with the roots. Function justifies an organ, no matter how strange the organ may appear in the eyes of those who are not accustomed to see it functioning. Snobbish circles are cluttered with persons who, like one of Montesquieu's characters, wonder how one can possibly be a Persian. They make me think unfailingly of the story of the peasant who, on seeing a dromedary in the zoo for the first time, examines it at length, shakes his head and, turning to leave, says, to the great delight of those present: "It isn't true."

It is through the unhampered play of its functions, then, that a work is revealed and justified. We are free to accept or reject this play, but no one has the right to question the fact of its existence. To judge, dispute, and criticize the principle of speculative volition which is at the origin of all creation is thus manifestly useless. In the pure state, music is free speculation. Artists of all epochs have unceasingly testified to this concept. For myself, I see no reason for not trying to do as they did. Since I myself was created, I cannot help having the desire to create. What sets this desire in motion, and what can I do to make it productive?

The study of the creative process is an extremely delicate one. In truth, it is impossible to observe the inner workings of this process from the outside. It is futile to try and follow its successive phases in someone else's work. It is likewise very difficult to observe one's self. Yet it is only by enlisting the aid of introspection that I may have any chance at all of guiding you in this essentially fluctuating matter.

Most music-lovers believe that what sets the composer's creative imagination in motion is a certain emotive disturbance generally designated by the name of *inspiration.*

I have no thought of denying to inspiration the outstanding role that has developed upon it in the generative process we are studying; I simply maintain that inspiration is in no way a prescribed condition of the creative act, but rather a manifestation that is chronologically secondary.

Inspiration, art, artist — so many words, hazy at least, that keep us from seeing clearly in a field where everything is balance and calculation through which the breath of the speculative spirit blows. It is afterwards, and only afterwards, that the emotive disturbance which is at the root of inspiriation may arise — an emotive disturbance about which people talk so indelicately by conferring upon it a meaning that is shocking to us and that compromises the term itself. Is it not clear that this emotion is merely a reaction on the part of the creator grappling with that unknown entity which is still only the object of his creating and which is to become a work of art? Step by step, link by link, it will be granted him to discover the work. It is this chain of discoveries, as well as each individual discovery, that give rise to the emotion — an almost physiological reflex, like that of the appetite causing a flow of saliva — this emotion which invariably follows closely the phases of the creative process.

All creation presupposes at its origin a sort of appetite that is brought on by the foretaste of discovery. This foretaste of the creative act accompanies the intuitive grasp of an unknown entity already possessed but not yet intelligible, an entity that will not take definite shape except by the action of a constantly vigilant technique.

This appetite that is aroused in me at the mere thought of putting in order musical elements that have attracted my attention is not at all a fortuitous thing like inspiration, but as habitual and periodic, if not as constant, as a natural need.

This premonition of an obligation, this foretaste of a pleasure, this conditioned reflex, as a modern physiologist would say, shows clearly that it is the idea of discovery and hard work that attracts me.

The very act of putting my work on paper, of, as we say, kneading the dough, is for me inseparable from the pleasure of creation. So far as I am concerned, I cannot separate the spiritual effort from the psychological and physical effort; they confront me on the same level and do not present a hierarchy.

The word *artist* which, as it is most generally understood today, bestows on its bearer the highest intellectual prestige, the privilege of being accepted as a pure mind — this pretentious term is in my view entirely incompatible with the role of the *homo faber*.

At this point it should be remembered that, whatever field of endeavor has fallen to our lot, if it is true that we are *intellectuals,* we are called upon not to cogitate, but to perform.

The philosopher Jacques Maritain reminds us that in the mighty structure of medieval civilization, the artist held only the rank of an artisan. "And his individualism was forbidden any sort of anarchic development, because a natural social discipline imposed certain limitative conditions upon him from without." It was the Renaissance that invented the artist, distinguished him from the artisan and began to exalt the former at the expense of the latter.

At the outset the name artist was given only to the Masters of Arts: philosophers, alchemists, magicians; but painters, sculptors, musicians, and poets had the right to be qualified only as artisans.

> Plying divers implements,
> The subtile artizan implants
> Life in marble, copper, bronze,

says the poet Du Bellay. And Montaigne enumerates in his *Essays* the "painters, poets and other artizans." And even in the seventeenth century, La Fontaine hails a painter with the name of *artisan* and draws a sharp rebuke from an ill-tempered critic who might have been the ancestor of most of our present-day critics.

The idea of work to be done is for me so closely bound up with the idea of the arranging of materials and of the pleasure that the actual doing of the work affords us that, should the impossible happen and my work suddenly be given to me in a perfectly completed form, I should be embarrassed and nonplussed by it, as by a hoax.

We have a duty towards music, namely, to invent it. I recall once during the war when I was crossing the French border a gendarme asked me what my profession was. I told him quite naturally that I was an inventor of music. The gendarme, then verifying my passport, asked me why I was listed as a composer. I told him that the expression "inventor of music" seemed to me to fit my profession more exactly than the term applied to me in the documents authorizing me to cross borders.

Invention presupposes imagination but should not be confused with it. For the act of invention implies the necessity of a lucky find and of achieving full realization of this find. What we imagine does not necessarily take on a concrete form and may remain in a state of virtuality, whereas invention is not conceivable apart from its actual being worked out.

Thus, what concerns us here is not imagination in itself, but rather creative imagination: the faculty that helps us to pass from the level of conception to the level of realization.

In the course of my labors I suddenly stumble upon something unexpected. This unexpected element strikes me. I make a note of it. At the proper time I put it to profitable use. This gift of chance must not be confused with that capriciousness of imagination that is commonly called fancy. Fancy implies a predetermined will to abandon one's self to caprice. The aforementioned assistance of the unexpected is something quite different. It is a collaboration which is immanently bound up with the inertia of the creative process and is heavy with possibilities which are unsolicited and come most appositely to temper the inevitable over-rigorousness of the naked will. And it is good that this is so.

"In everything that yields gracefully," G. K. Chesterton says somewhere, "there must be resistance. Bows are beautiful when they bend only because they seek to remain rigid. Rigidity that slightly yields, like Justice swayed by Pity, is all the beauty of earth. Everything seeks to grow straight, and happily, nothing succeeds in so growing. Try to grow straight and life will bend you."

The faculty of creating is never given to us all by itself. It always goes hand in hand with the gift of observation. And the true creator may be recognized by his ability always to find about him, in the commonest and humblest thing, items worthy of note. He does not have to concern himself with a beautiful landscape, he does not need to surround himself with rare and precious objects. He does not have to put forth in search of discoveries: they are always within his reach. He will have only to cast a glance about him. Familiar things, things that are everywhere, attract his attention. The least accident holds his interest and guides his operations. If his finger slips, he will notice it; on occasion, he may draw profit from something unforeseen that a momentary lapse reveals to him.

One does not contrive an accident: one observes it to draw inspiration therefrom. An accident is perhaps the only thing that really inspires us. A composer improvises aimlessly the way an animal grubs about. Both of them go grubbing about because they yield to a compulsion to seek things out. What urge of the composer is satisfied by this investigation? The rules with which, like a penitent, he is burdened? No: he is in quest of his pleasure. He seeks a satisfaction that he fully knows he will not find without first striving for it. One cannot force one's self to love; but love presupposes understanding, and in order to understand, one must exert one's self.

It is the same problem that was posed in the Middle Ages by the theologians of pure love. To understand in order to love; to love in order to understand: we are here not going around in a vicious circle; we are rising spirally, providing we have made an initial effort, have even just gone through a routine exercise.

Pascal has specifically this in mind when he writes that custom "controls the automaton, which in its turn unthinkingly controls the mind. For there must be no mistake," continues Pascal, "we are automatons just as much as we are minds . . ."

So we grub about in expectation of our pleasure, guided by our scent, and suddenly we stumble against an unknown obstacle. It gives us a jolt, a shock, and this shock fecundates our creative power.

The faculty of observation and of making something out of what is observed belongs only to the person who at least possesses, in his particular field of endeavor, an acquired culture and an innate taste. A dealer, an art-lover who is the first to buy the canvases of an unknown painter who will be famous twenty-five years later under the name of Cézanne — doesn't such a person give us a clear example of this innate taste? What else guides him in his choice? A flair, an instinct from which this taste proceeds, a completely spontaneous faculty anterior to reflection.

As for culture, it is a sort of upbringing which, in the social sphere, confers polish upon education, sustains and rounds out academic instruction. This upbringing is just as important in the sphere of taste and is essential to the creator who must ceaselessly refine his taste or run the risk of losing his perspicacity. Our mind, as well as our body, requires continual exercise. It atrophies if we do not cultivate it.

It is culture that brings out the full value of taste and gives it a chance to prove its worth simply by its application. The artist imposes a culture upon himself and ends by imposing it upon others. That is how tradition becomes established.

Tradition is entirely different from habit, even from an excellent habit, since habit is by definition an unconscious acquisition and tends to become mechanical, whereas tradition results from a conscious and deliberate acceptance. A real tradition is not the relic of a past that is irretrievably gone; it is a living force that animates and informs the present. In this sense the paradox which banteringly maintains that everything which is not tradition is plagiarism, is true . . .

Far from implying the repetition of what has been, tradition presupposes the reality of what endures. It appears as an heirloom, a heritage that one receives on condition of making it bear fruit before passing it on to one's descendants.

Brahms was born sixty years after Beethoven. From the one to the other, and from every aspect, the distance is great; they do not dress the same way, but Brahms follows the tradition of Beethoven without borrowing one of his habiliments. For the borrowing of a method has nothing to do with observing a tradition. "A method is replaced: a tradition is carried forward in order to produce something new." Tradition thus assures the continuity of creation. The example that I have just cited does not constitute an exception but is one proof out of a hundred of a constant law. This sense of tradition which is a natural need must not be confused with the desire which the composer feels to affirm the kinship he finds across the centuries with some master of the past.

My opera *Mavra* was born of a natural sympathy for the body of melodic tendencies, for the vocal style and conventional language which I came to admire more and more in the old Russo-Italian opera. This sympathy guided me quite naturally along the path of a tradition that seemed to be lost at the moment when the attention of musical circles was turned entirely towards the music drama, which represented no tradition at all from the historical point of view and which fulfilled no necessity at all from the musical point of view. The vogue of the music drama had a pathological origin. Alas, even the admirable music of *Pélléas et Mélisande,* so fresh in its modesty, was unable to get us into the open, in spite of so many characteristics with which it shook off the tyranny of the Wagnerian system.

The music of *Mavra* stays within the tradition of Glinka and Dargomisky. I had not the slightest intention of reëstablishing this tradition. I simply wanted in my turn to try my hand at the living form of the *opéra-bouffe* which was so well suited to the Pushkin tale which gave me my subject. *Mavra* is dedicated to the memory of composers, not one of whom, I am sure, would have recognized as valid such a manifestation of the tradition they created, because of the novelty of the language my music speaks a hundred years after its models flourished. But I wanted to renew the style of these dialogues-in-music whose voices had been reviled and drowned out by the clang and clatter of the music drama. So a hundred years had to pass before the freshness of the Russo-Italian tradition could again be appreciated, a tradition that continued to live apart from the main stream of the present, and in which circulated a salubrious air, well adapted to delivering us from the miasmic vapors of the music drama, the inflated arrogance of which could not conceal its vacuity.

I am not without motive in provoking a quarrel with the notorious Synthesis of the Arts. I do not merely condemn it for its lack of tradition, its *nouveau riche* smugness. What makes its case much worse is the fact that the application of its theories has inflicted a terrible blow upon music itself. In every period of spiritual anarchy wherein man, having lost his feeling and taste for ontology, takes fright at himself and at his destiny, there always appears one of these gnosticisms which serve as a religion for those who no longer have a religion, just as in periods of international crises an army of soothsayers, fakirs, and clairvoyants monopolize journalistic publicity. We can speak of these things all the more freely in view of the fact that the halcyon days of Wagnerism are past and that the distance which separates us from them permits us to set matters straight again. Sound minds, moreover, never believed in the paradise of the Synthesis of the Arts and have always recognized its enchantments at their true worth.

I have said that I never saw any necessity for music to adopt such a dramatic system. I shall add something more: I hold that this system, far from having raised the level of musical culture, has never ceased to undermine it and finally to debase it in the most paradoxical fashion. In the past one went to the opera for the diversion offered by facile musical works. Later on one returned to it in order to yawn at dramas in which music, arbitrarily paralyzed by constraints foreign to its own laws, could not help tiring out the most attentive audience in spite of the great talent displayed by Wagner.

So, from music shamelessly considered as a purely sensual delight, we passed without transition to the murky inanities of the Art-Religion, with its heroic hardware, its arsenal of warrior-mysticism and its vocabulary seasoned with an adulterated religiosity. So that as soon as music ceased to be scorned, it was only to find itself smothered under literary flowers. It succeeded in getting a hearing from the cultured public thanks only to a misunderstanding which tended to turn drama into a hodgepodge of symbols, and music itself into an object of philosophical speculation. That is how the speculative spirit came to lose its course and how it came to betray music while ostensibly trying to serve it the better.

Music based upon the opposite principles has, unfortunately, not yet given proofs of its worth in our own period. It is curious to note that it was a musician who proclaimed himself a Wagnerian, the Frenchman Chabrier, who was able to maintain the sound tradition of dramatic art in those difficult times and who excelled in the French *opéra comique* along with a few of his compatriots, at the very height of the Wagnerian vogue. Is not this the tradition that is continued in the sparkling group of masterpieces that are called *Le Médecin malgré lui, La Colombe, Philémon et Baucis* of Gounod; *Lakmé, Coppélia, Sylvia* of Léo Delibes; *Carmen* by Bizet; *Le Roi malgré lui, L'Etoile* of Chabrier; *La Béarnaise, Véronique* of Messager — to which has just recently been added the *Chartreuse de Parme* by the young Henri Sauguet?

Think how subtle and clinging the poison of the music drama was to have insinuated itself even into the veins of the colossus Verdi.

How can we help regretting that this master of the traditional opera, at the end of a long life studded with so many authentic masterpieces, climaxed his career with *Falstaff* which, if it is not Wagner's best work, is not Verdi's best opera either?

I know that I am going counter to the general opinion that sees Verdi's best work in the deterioration of the genius that gave us *Rigoletto, Il Trovatore, Aïda,* and *La Traviata.* I know I am defending precisely what the elite of the recent past belittled in the works of this great composer. I regret having to say so; but I maintain that there is more substance and true invention in the aria *La donna è mobile,* for example, in which this elite saw nothing but deplorable facility, than in the rhetoric and vociferations of the *Ring.*

Whether we admit it or not, the Wagnerian drama reveals continual bombast. Its brilliant improvisations inflate the symphony beyond all proportion and give it less real substance than the invention, at once modest and aristocratic, that blossoms forth on every page of Verdi.

At the beginning of my course I gave notice that I would continually come back to the necessity for order and discipline; and here I must weary you again by returning to the same theme.

Richard Wagner's music is more improvised than constructed, in the specific musical sense. Arias, ensembles, and their reciprocal relationships in the structure of an opera confer upon the whole work a coherence that is merely the external and visible manifestation of an internal and profound order.

The antagonism of Wagner and Verdi very neatly illustrates my thoughts on this subject.

While Verdi was being relegated to the organ-grinder's repertory, it was fashionable to hail in Wagner the typical revolutionary. Nothing is more significant than this relegation of order to the muse of the street corners at the moment when one found sublimity in the cult of disorder.

Wagner's work corresponds to a tendency that is not, properly speaking, a disorder, but one which tries to compensate for a lack of order. The principle of the endless melody perfectly illustrates this tendency. It is the perpetual becoming of a music that never had any reason for starting, any more than it has any reason for ending. Endless melody thus appears as an insult to the dignity and to the very function of melody which, as we have said, is the musical intonation of a cadenced phrase. Under the influence of Wagner the laws that secure the life of song found themselves violated, and music lost its melodic smile. Perhaps his method of doing things answered a need; but this need was not compatible with the possibilities of musical art, for musical art is limited in its expression in a measure corresponding exactly to the limitations of the organ that perceives it. A mode of composition that does not assign itself limits becomes pure fantasy. The effects it produces may accidentally amuse but are not capable of being repeated. I cannot conceive of a fantasy that is repeated, for it can be repeated only to its detriment.

Let us understand each other in regard to this word fantasy. We are not using the word in the sense in which it is connected with a definite musical form, but in the acceptation which presupposes an abandonment of one's self to the caprices of imagination. And this presupposes that the composer's will is voluntarily paralyzed. For imagination is not only the mother of caprice but the servant and handmaiden of the creative will as well.

The creator's function is to sift the elements he receives from her, for human activity must impose limits upon itself. The more art is controlled, limited, worked over, the more it is free.

As for myself, I experience a sort of terror when, at the moment of setting to work and finding myself before the infinitude of possibilities that present themselves, I have the feeling that everything is permissible to me. If everything is permissible to me, the best and the worst; if nothing offers me any resistance, then any effort is inconceivable, and I cannot use anything as a basis, and consequently every undertaking becomes futile.

Will I then have to lose myself in this abyss of freedom? To what shall I cling in order to escape the dizziness that seizes me before the virtuality of this infinitude? However, I shall not succumb. I shall overcome my terror and shall be reassured by the thought that I have the seven notes of the scale and its chromatic intervals at my disposal, that strong and weak accents are within my reach, and that in all of these I possess solid and concrete elements which offer me a field of experience just as vast as the upsetting and dizzy infinitude that had just frightened me. It is into this field that I shall sink my roots, fully convinced that combinations which have at their disposal twelve sounds in each octave and all possible rhythmic varieties promise me riches that all the activity of human genius will never exhaust.

What delivers me from the anguish into which an unrestricted freedom plunges me is the fact that I am always able to turn immediately to the concrete things that are here in question. I have no use for a theoretic freedom. Let me have something finite, definite — matter that can lend itself to my operation only insofar as it is commensurate with my possibilities. And such matter presents itself to me together with its limitations. I must in turn impose mine upon it. So here we are, whether we like it or not, in the realm of necessity. And yet which of us has ever heard talk of art as other than a realm of freedom? This sort of heresy is uniformly widespread because it is imagined that art is outside the bounds of ordinary activity. Well, in art as in everything else, one can build only upon a resisting foundation: whatever constantly gives way to pressure, constantly renders movement impossible.

My freedom thus consists in my moving about within the narrow frame that I have assigned myself for each one of my undertakings.

I shall go even further: my freedom will be so much the greater and more meaningful the more narrowly I limit my field of action and the more I surround myself with obstacles. Whatever diminishes constraint, diminishes strength. The more constraints one imposes, the more one frees one's self of the chains that shackle the spirit.

To the voice that commands me to create I first respond with fright; then I reassure myself by taking up as weapons those things participating in creation but as yet outside of it; and the arbitrariness of the constraint serves only to obtain precision of execution.

From all this we shall conclude the necessity of dogmatizing on pain of missing our goal. If these words annoy us and seem harsh, we can abstain from pronouncing them. For all that, they nonetheless contain the secret of salvation: "It is evident," writes Baudelaire, "that rhetorics and prosodies are not arbitrarily invented tyrannies, but a collection of rules demanded by the very organization of the spiritual being, and never have prosodies and rhetorics kept originality from fully manifesting itself. The contrary, that is to say, that they have aided the flowering of originality, would be infinitely more true."

5

GLENWAY WESCOTT *and* W. B. YEATS

Thornton Wilder once quoted Freud as saying to him: "The poets have always sensed what psychoanalysis has discovered. Now that this sphere of knowledge, which used to belong to them exclusively, has been illuminated by Science and has become available to every normally endowed person, the poets ought to submerge themselves in new depths of darkness."

If in our century the poets began to do just this, if literature were becoming a faute de mieux *priesthood, then could its makers be only concerned with their novelty of means, with experimental forms and surprising styles?*

Hardly. They must learn, said Glenway Wescott, that of all words, "the shortest and most potent is the personal pronoun: I." And they must realize, said Yeats, that "faith is the highest achievement of the human intellect, the only gift man can make to God."

from *The Moral of Scott Fitzgerald*

[1941]

GLENWAY WESCOTT

The great thing about Fitzgerald was his candor; verbal courage; simplicity. One little man with eyes really witnessing; objective in all he uttered, even about himself in a subjective slump; arrogant in just one connection, for one purpose only, to make his meaning clear. The thing, I think, that a number of recent critics have most disliked about him is his confessional way, the personal tone, the *tête-à-tête* or man-to-man style, first person singular. He remarked it himself in *The Crack-Up:*

256

"There are always those to whom all self-revelation is contemptible."

I on the other hand feel a real approval and emulation of just that; and I recommend that all our writers give it serious consideration. It might be the next esthetic issue and new mode of American letters. It is American enough; our greatest fellows, such as Franklin and Audubon and Thoreau and Whitman, were self-expressers in so far as they knew themselves. This is a time of greater knowledge, otherwise worse; an era which has as many evil earmarks as, for example, the Renaissance: awful political genius running amok and clashing, migrations, races whipped together as it were by a titanic egg-beater, impatient sexuality and love of stimulants and cruelty, sacks, burnings and plagues. Fine things eventually may be achieved amid all this, as in that other century. I suggest revelation of man as he appears to himself in his mirror — not as he poses or wishes or idealizes — as one thing to try a revival of, this time. Naked truth about man's nature in unmistakable English.

In the Renaissance they had anatomy: Vesalius in Paris at midnight under the gallows-tree, bitten by the dogs as he disputed with them the hanged cadavers which they wanted to eat and he wanted to cut up. They had anatomy and we have psychology. The throws of dice in our world — at least the several dead-weights with which the dice appear to be loaded against us — are moral matters; and no one ever learns much about all that except in his own person, at any rate in private. In public, in the nation and the inter nation and the anti-nation, one just suffers the weight of the morality of others like a dumb brute. This has been a dishonest century above all: literature lagging as far behind modern habits as behind modern history; democratic statesmanship all vitiated by good form, understatement, optimism; and the nations which could not afford democracy, finally developing their supremacy all on a basis of the deliberate lie. And now is the end, or another beginning.

Writers in this country still can give their little examples of truth-telling; little exercises for their fellow citizens, to develop their ability to distinguish truth from untruth in other connections when it really is important. The importance arises as desperately in the public interest as in private life. Even light fiction can help a society get together and agree upon its vocabulary; little strokes of the tuning-fork, for harmony's sake. And for clarity's sake, let us often use, and sanction the use of, words of one syllable. The shortest and most potent is the personal pronoun: I. The sanctified priest knows that, he says *credo;* and the trustworthy physician only gives his opinion, not a panacea. The witness in the courtroom does not indulge in the editorial we; the judge and the lawyers will not allow it; and indeed, if the case is important, if there is life or liberty or even a large amount of money at stake, not even supposition or hearsay is admitted as evidence. Our worldwide case is important.

Not only is Anglo-Saxondom all at war with the rest of the world in defense of its accustomed power and prosperity, and of the luxuries of the spirit such as free speech, free publication, free faith — for the time being, the United States is the likeliest place for the preservation of the Mediterranean and French ideal of fine art and writing: which puts a new, peculiar obligation upon us ex-expatriates. The land of the free should become and is becoming a city of refuge; but there is cultural peril even in that. France has merely committed her tradition to our keeping, by default; whereas Germany has exiled to us her most important professors and brilliant writers. Perhaps the latter are bound to introduce into our current literature a little of that mystically philosophic, obscurely scientific mode which somewhat misled or betrayed them as a nation. Therefore we must keep up more strictly and energetically than ever, our native specific skeptical habit of mind; our plainer and therefore safer style.

In any consideration of the gravity of the work of art and letters — and upon any solemn occasion such as the death of a good writer like Scott Fitzgerald — I think of Faust, and that labor he dreamed of when he was blind and dying, keeping the devil waiting. It was the drainage of a stinking sea-marsh and the construction of a strong dyke. Fresh fields amid the eternally besieging sea: room for a million men to live, not in security — Goethe expressly ruled out that hope of which we moderns have been too fond — but free to do the best they could for themselves. Does it seem absurd to compare a deceased best seller with that mythic man: former wholesome Germany's demigod? There must always be some pretentiousness about literature, or else no one would take its pains or endure its disappointments. Throughout this article I have mixed bathos with pathos, joking with tenderness, in order to venture here and there a higher claim for literary art than is customary now. I am in dead earnest. Bad writing is in fact a rank feverish unnecessary slough. Good writing is a dyke, in which there is a leak for every one of our weary hands. And honestly I do see the very devil standing worldwide in the decade to come, bound to get some of us. I realize that I have given an exaggerated impression of Fitzgerald's tragedy in recent years: all the above is based on his confession of 1936, and he was not so nearly finished as he thought. But fear of death is one prophecy that never fails; and now his strength is only in print, and his weakness of no account, except for our instruction.

from *Fear and Trembling*

[1932]

GLENWAY WESCOTT

The great doctors and psychologists of the first part of our century, regarded as indecent in their youth, are also inclined in their old age to frown upon scandal, shaming the poor poet or rebel with clever categorical words. They never did care for art much; but it is even less certain than before that their analytical cures accomplish as much as the mere burning and cleansing and shocking of the written word; and by the late war and the present peace, the ideal of manhood for which they laboured has been somewhat discredited. Their ideally able man with lots of money and lots of children, knowing how to assert himself and compel respect, the *bourgeois*, the *Bürger*, the normal good citizen, has made a mess of his world (too much unsound money, precisely, and too many children) and does not know what to do about it. If the word *neurotic* is to be used, may we say that it is the neurotic's turn?

We should not expect too much of the old men. They have lived ardently and kindly, if not perspicaciously, and have a right to rest. Besides, it is not they who are in danger; they are not likely to live to see the next war, the next revolution. A certain number of millions of the rest of us probably will. Already, in imagination, embittered, it is our war; it can be our revolution, if we get started at it in time and avert the war; it is our unripe salvation that is dangling, you might say, on the tree of life.

So long as the old secretiveness lasts, so long as we are expected positively not to face the facts of what we all do and, in spirit and flesh, all that privately happens, how can we learn to face and quietly deal with the new state of affairs?

We may as well begin at the beginning, at birth, from birth, even before, and up to death; begin by knowing more and more, hearing, saying, learning more. More about that beginning and end in one — death, in respect to which morbid means wholesome: how health and sickness interweave and wind all about us. How the one collaborates with the other to house the soul and feed it and quench its thirst (health being its water, sickness its wine). How the momentary victory of health is advantageous to the soul, but the supremacy of sickness in the end is even more necessary — for man must die. How hard and loving a gaze is required if we are to recognize both God's hands at work, and press them both to our lips, with due enthusiasm.

More about birth and its flowery mechanism, the products and the by-products, the seed to sprout and the fruit just to be eaten. Amid spontaneous laughter, rippling up and down being as a whole, and sometimes ideal weeping — pains and rewards, noble and ignoble lessons: in the past, may we say, God was wise enough, working in and by accident; He peopled the world well enough, moderately (by the act of darkness, as it was called, when, for simple needs of society, one could see well enough in the dark); now and then, also He depopulated it sufficiently, without too much harming the residue. How miserable is man, not to say woman, now that they must know what they are doing, and still cannot decide! It is so advantageous to the soul not to feel sterile or defeated; yet it seems that certain sterilities and surrenders are necessary — for man must eat, and eat his new costly healthy meals in peace. How miserable, man and woman, now that they can no longer safely live for the old purposes alone (the aggrandizement of the family, the victories of the state, etc.) and are still unable to see new purposes! Love-impulses may be misapplied, outside the home circle or love circle — that they have seen, to their sorrow; they may be well applied also; how? Instinct may be deformed for the worse, but also for the better; how? If instinct is to be kept intact at all costs, other faculties around it may be deformed, and so it may bring about precisely what it is supposed to prevent: the undoing of the species and its way of life. What else is there? How else?

More of praise and more of blame will provoke in man all that, unbeknown to himself, he knows.

There is no use our aspiring, either for our way of thinking or our way of working, to an innocence of troubadours and church-builders, the plain, radiant embodiment of overflowing impulse, beauties of angelic animal and inspired child; that was the day of faith. It is hopeless to envy the courtesies of Versailles, its glorious understatement, throne-room grace; that was the age of government. When we cry for faith, we do not mean quite what the word classically meant: that listening in every nerve to an infinite absent concert, that sensibility as of some prehistoric temple vibrating and making a little melodious uproar toward the still unrisen sun, that mild Gothic madness about the unknown — but rather interest,

in love of, and courage about what we already know, more or less scien-
tifically. And before we have ceased our Alexandrian ambitions and
Carthaginian conquests, until we have settled down (literally and figura-
tively) to defend our borders, what right have we to the dignity of
governors, to a royal literature, subtle and well-dressed?

This is an age of seeing and learning; an age of sciences all absorbed
by meetings of matter with ghost of matter (it might be Hamlet and his
father, on laboratory ramparts); in the spiritual traits of flesh and intellect's carnal being; in the soul of radium, the body of lead, for example;
in marriages of ideas with tissues in all that exists, as in ourselves. If we
are to do anything at all, beyond these adventures in mathematics,
chemistry, surgery, physics, etc., if we are to last long enough to have
been anything, among history's various masterpieces, it must be by admitting, learning from, imagining — well, the plain truth. The whole
plain truth: evidently there is, can be, no other God for us, not in any
case until that one has got His work done.

A mere age of prudery, of double standards and flattery and personal
discretion, is necessarily an age of chiefs of state, modest-looking and
mealy-mouthed, incapable of plain speech as of adequate action, and of
masses swept by regular plagues of ignorant feeling, all-powerful and
altogether helpless; an age, naturally, of paper currency based just on optimism, of equivocal banking and secret diplomacy, of world-imprudence
and world-war finally, with any old revolution bungling in among the
cadavers — just such an age as this, in fact, if it goes on as it has begun.
Shall we let it go on? We young or youngish ones, shall we hold back our
hands from scrapping the whole dubious system, from breaking the
honourable chain of habits and habits of thought? Are we just being
crude and petulant when we say that we are sick of old fellows and old
ideals? Look what they have done and are about to do.

No — (it is a cry of hope as well as exasperation). It shall be an age of
telling the truth. A worldly age, if you like, a carnal age, all infatuated
with mere man, never more than life-size: it must, indeed, bore some
people. An age of confessions and curiosities: yes, it must shock some
people. An adolescent age, undressing and looking and showing-off — oh,
well, there were also Daphnis and Chloe. Not so lovely a couple this time,
no doubt, amid our flocks of half-domesticated machines, undoing merely
stylish shepherd's rags around rather asymmetrical figures — but side by
side, as before, hand in hand, and a bit closer still presently, when they
know what there is to know: how each may have his pleasure, yet keep
from doing the other harm, and how (in spite of the lively imagination)
oh, how to be content. Then once more, under the swaying international

leaves, in almost the same sun and shadow as in the world's early morning, there may be a little more whispering, whistling, bargaining, and peace, a little longer.

Anima Hominis
from *Per Amica Silentia Lunae*
[1917]

W. B. YEATS

We make out of the quarrel with others, rhetoric, but of the quarrel with ourselves, poetry. Unlike the rhetoricians, who get a confident voice from remembering the crowd they have won or may win, we sing amid our uncertainty; and, smitten even in the presence of the most high beauty by the knowledge of our solitude, our rhythm shudders. I think, too, that no fine poet, no matter how disordered his life, has ever, even in his mere life, had pleasure for his end. Johnson and Dowson, friends of my youth, were dissipated men, the one a drunkard, the other a drunkard and mad about women, and yet they had the gravity of men who had found life out and were awakening from the dream; and both, one in life and art and one in art and less in life, had a continual pre-occupation with religion. Nor has any poet I have read of or heard of or met with been a sentimentalist. The other self, the anti-self or the antithetical self, as one may choose to name it, comes but to those who are no longer deceived, whose passion is reality. The sentimentalists are practical men who believe in money, in position, in a marriage bell, and whose understanding of happiness is to be so busy whether at work or at play, that all is forgotten but the momentary aim. They find their pleasure in a cup that is filled from Lethe's wharf, and for the awakening, for the vision, for the revelation of reality, tradition offers us a different word — ecstasy. An old artist wrote to me of his wanderings by the quays of New York, and how he found there a woman nursing a sick child, and drew her story from her. She spoke, too, of other children who had died: a long tragic story. "I wanted to paint her," he wrote; "if I denied myself any of the pain I could not believe in my own ecstasy." We must not make a false faith by hiding from our thoughts the causes of doubt, for faith is the highest achievement of the human intellect, the only gift man can make to God, and therefore it must be offered in sincerity. Neither must we create, by hiding ugliness, a false beauty as our offering to the world. He only can create the greatest imaginable beauty who has endured all imaginable pangs, for only when we have seen and foreseen what we dread shall we be rewarded by that dazzling unforeseen wing-footed wanderer. We could not find him if he were not in some sense of our being and yet of our being but as water with fire, a noise with silence. He is of all things not impossible the most difficult, for that only which comes easily can never be a portion of our being, "Soon got, soon gone," as the proverb says. I shall find the dark grow luminous, the void fruitful when I understand I have nothing, that the ringers in the tower have appointed for the hymen of the soul a passing bell.

The last knowledge has often come most quickly to turbulent men, and for a season brought new turbulence. When life puts away her conjuring tricks one by one, those that deceive us longest may well be the wine-cup and the sensual kiss, for our Chambers of Commerce and of Commons have not the divine architecture of the body, nor has their frenzy been ripened by the sun. The poet, because he may not stand within the sacred house but lives amid the whirlwinds that beset its threshold, may find his pardon.

I think the Christian saint and hero, instead of being merely dissatisfied, make deliberate sacrifice. I remember reading once an autobiography of a man who had made a daring journey in disguise to Russian exiles in Siberia, and his telling how, very timid as a child, he schooled himself by wandering at night through dangerous streets. Saint and hero cannot be content to pass at moments to that hollow image and after become their heterogeneous selves, but would always, if they could, resemble the antithetical self. There is a shadow of type on type, for in all great poetical styles there is saint or hero, but when it is all over Dante can return to his chambering and Shakespeare to his "pottle pot." They sought no impossible perfection but when they handled paper or parchment. So too will saint or hero, because he works in his own flesh and blood and not in paper or parchment, have more deliberate understanding of that other flesh and blood.

Some years ago I began to believe that our culture, with its doctrine of sincerity and self-realisation, made us gentle and passive, and that the Middle Ages and the Renaissance were right to found theirs upon the imitation of Christ or of some classic hero. St. Francis and Cæsar Borgia made themselves over-mastering, creative persons by turning from the mirror to meditation upon a mask. When I had this thought I could see nothing else in life. I could not write the play I had planned, for all became allegorical, and though I tore up hundreds of pages in my endeavour to escape from allegory, my imagination became sterile for nearly five years and I only escaped at last when I had mocked in a comedy my own thought. I was always thinking of the element of imitation in style and in life, and of the life beyond heroic imitation. I find in an old diary: "I think all happiness depends on the energy to assume the mask of some other life, on a re-birth as something not one's self, something created in a moment and perpetually renewed; in playing a game like that of a child where one loses the infinite pain of self-realisation, in a grotesque or solemn painted face put on that one may hide from the terror of judgment. . . . Perhaps all the sins and energies of the world are but the world's flight from an infinite blinding beam"; and again at an earlier date: "If we cannot imagine ourselves as different from what we are, and try to assume that second self, we cannot impose a discipline upon ourselves though we may accept one from others. Active virtue, as distinguished from the passive acceptance of a code, is therefore theatrical, consciously dramatic, the wearing of a mask. . . . Wordsworth, great poet though he be, is so often flat and heavy partly because his moral sense, being a discipline he had not created, a mere obedience, has no theatrical element. This increases his popularity with the better kind of journalists and politicians who have written books."

I thought the hero found hanging upon some oak of Dodona an ancient mask, where perhaps there lingered something of Egypt, and that he changed it to his fancy, touching it a little here and there, gilding the eyebrows or putting a gilt line where the cheekbone comes; that when at last he looked out of his eyes he knew another's breath came and went within his breath upon the carven lips, and that his eyes were upon the instant fixed upon a visionary world: how else could the god have come to us in the forest? The good, unlearned books say that He who keeps the distant stars within His fold comes without intermediary, but Plutarch's precepts and the experience of old women in Soho, ministering their witchcraft to servant girls at a shilling a piece, will have it that a strange living man may win for Daemon [1] an illustrious dead man; but now I add another thought: the Daemon comes not as like to like but seeking its own opposite, for man and Daemon feed the hunger in one another's hearts. Because the ghost is simple, the man heterogeneous and confused, they are but knit together when the man has found a mask whose lineaments permit the expression of all the man most lacks, and it may be dreads, and of that only.

The more insatiable in all desire, the more resolute to refuse deception or an easy victory, the more close will be the bond, the more violent and definite the antipathy.

I think that all religious men have believed that there is a hand not ours in the events of life, and that, as somebody says in *Wilhelm Meister,* accident is destiny; and I think it was Heraclitus who said: the Daemon is our destiny. When I think of life as a struggle with the Daemon who would ever set us to the hardest work among those not impossible, I understand why there is a deep enmity between a man and his destiny, and why a man loves nothing but his destiny. In an Anglo-Saxon poem a certain man is called, as though to call him something that summed up all heroism, "Doom eager." I am persuaded that the Daemon delivers and deceives us, and that he wove that netting from the stars and threw the net from his shoulder. Then my imagination runs from Daemon to sweetheart, and I divine an analogy that evades the intellect. I remember that Greek antiquity has bid us look for the principal stars, that govern enemy and sweetheart alike, among those that are about to set, in the Seventh House as the astrologers say; and that it may be "sexual love," which is "founded upon spiritual hate," is an image of the warfare of man and Daemon; and I even wonder if there may not be some secret communion, some whispering in the dark between Daemon and sweetheart. I remember how often women when in love, grow superstitious, and believe that they can bring their lovers good luck; and I remember an old Irish story of three young men who went seeking for help in battle into the house of the gods at Slieve-na-mon. "You must first be married," some god told them, "because a man's good or evil luck comes to him through a woman."

I sometimes fence for half an hour at the day's end, and when I close my eyes upon the pillow I see a foil playing before me the button to my face. We meet always in the deep of the mind, whatever our work, wherever our reverie carries us, that other Will.

The poet finds and makes his mask in disappointment, the hero in defeat. The desire that is satisfied is not a great desire, nor has the shoulder used all its might that an unbreakable gate has never strained. The saint alone is not deceived, neither thrusting with his shoulder nor holding out unsatisfied hands. He would climb without wandering to the antithetical self of the world, the Indian narrowing his thought in meditation or driving it away in contemplation, the Christian copying Christ, the antithetical self of the classic world. For a hero loves the world till it breaks him, and the poet till it has broken faith; but while the world was yet debonair, the saint has turned away, and because he renounced Experience itself, he will wear his mask as he finds it. The poet or the hero, no matter upon what bark they found their mask, so teeming their fancy, somewhat change its lineaments, but the saint, whose life is but a round of customary duty, needs nothing the whole world does not need, and day by day he scourges in his body the Roman and Christian conquerors; Alexander and Caesar are famished in his cell. His nativity is neither in disappointment nor in defeat, but in a temptation like that of Christ in the Wilderness, a contemplation in a single instant perpetually renewed of the Kingdoms of the World; all — because all renounced — continually present showing their empty thrones. Edwin Ellis, remembering that Christ also measured the sacrifice, imagined himself in a fine poem as meeting at Golgotha the phantom of "Christ the Less," the Christ who might have lived a prosperous life without the knowledge of sin, and who now wanders "companionless a weary spectre day and night."

> I saw him go and cried to him
> "Eli, thou hast forsaken me."
> The nails were burning through each limb,
> He fled to find felicity.

And yet is the saint spared — despite his martyr's crown and his vigil of desire — defeat, disappointed love, and the sorrow of parting.

> O Night, that did'st lead thus,
> O Night, more lovely than the dawn of light,
> O Night, that broughtest us
> Lover to lover's sight,
> Lover with loved in marriage of delight!
>
> Upon my flowery breast,
> Wholly for him, and save himself for none,
> There did I give sweet rest
> To my beloved one;
> The fanning of the cedars breathed thereon.
>
> When the first morning air
> Blew from the tower, and waved his locks aside,
> His hand, with gentle care,
> Did wound me in the side,
> And in my body all my senses died.
>
> All things I then forgot,
> My cheek on him who for my coming came;

> All ceased and I was not,
> Leaving my cares and shame
> Among the lilies, and forgetting them.[2]

It is not permitted to a man, who takes up pen or chisel, to seek originality, for passion is his only business, and he cannot but mould or sing after a new fashion because no disaster is like another. He is like those phantom lovers in the Japanese play who, compelled to wander side by side and never mingle, cry: "We neither wake nor sleep and passing our nights in a sorrow which is in the end a vision, what are these scenes of spring to us?" If when we have found a mask we fancy that it will not match our mood till we have touched with gold the cheek, we do it furtively, and only where the oaks of Dodona cast their deepest shadow, for could he see our handiwork the Daemon would fling himself out, being our enemy.

Many years ago I saw, between sleeping and waking, a woman of incredible beauty shooting an arrow into the sky, and from the moment when I made my first guess at her meaning I have thought much of the difference between the winding movement of nature and the straight line, which is called in Balzac's *Seraphita* the "Mark of Man," but is better described as the mark of saint or sage. I think that we who are poets and artists, not being permitted to shoot beyond the tangible, must go from desire to weariness and so to desire again, and live but for the moment when vision comes to our weariness like terrible lightning, in the humility of the brutes. I do not doubt those heaving circles, those winding arcs, whether in one man's life or in that of an age, are mathematical, and that some in the world, or beyond the world, have foreknown the event and pricked upon the calendar the life-span of a Christ, a Buddha, a Napoleon: that every movement, in feeling or in thought, prepares in the dark by its own increasing clarity and confidence its own executioner. We seek reality with the slow toil of our weakness and are smitten from the boundless and the unforeseen. Only when we are saint or sage, and renounce Experience itself, can we, in imagery of the Christian Cabala, leave the sudden lightning and the path of the serpent and become the bowman who aims his arrow at the centre of the sun.

The doctors of medicine have discovered that certain dreams of the night, for I do not grant them all, are the day's unfulfilled desire, and that our terror of desires condemned by the conscience has distorted and disturbed our dreams. They have only studied the breaking into dream of elements that have remained unsatisfied without purifying discouragement. We can satisfy in life a few of our passions and each passion but a little, and our characters indeed but differ because no two men bargain alike. The bargain, the compromise, is always threatened, and when it is broken we become mad or hysterical or are in some way deluded; and so when a starved or banished passion shows in a dream we, before awakening, break the logic that had given it the capacity of action and throw it into chaos again. But the passions, when we know that they cannot find fulfilment, become vision; and a vision, whether we wake or sleep, prolongs its power by rhythm and pattern, the wheel where the world is butterfly. We need no protection but it does, for if we become interested in ourselves, in our own lives, we pass out of the vision. Whether it is we or the vision that create the pattern, who set the wheel turning, it is hard to say, but certainly we have a hundred ways of keeping it near us: we select our images from past times, we turn from our own age and try to feel Chaucer nearer than the daily paper. It compels us to cover all it cannot incorporate, and would carry us when it comes in sleep to that moment when even sleep closes her eyes and dreams begin to dream; and we are taken up into a clear light and are forgetful even of our own names and actions and yet in perfect possession of ourselves murmur like Faust, "Stay, moment," and murmur in vain.

A poet, when he is growing old, will ask himself if he cannot keep his mask and his vision without new bitterness, new disappointment. Could he if he would, knowing how frail his vigour from youth up, copy Landor who lived loving and hating, ridiculous and unconquered, into extreme old age, all lost but the favour of his muses?

> The mother of the muses we are taught
> Is memory; she has left me; they remain
> And shake my shoulder urging me to sing.

Surely, he may think, now that I have found vision and mask I need not suffer any longer. He will buy perhaps some small old house where like Ariosto he can dig his garden, and think that in the return of birds and leaves, or moon and sun, and in the evening flight of the rooks he may discover rhythm and pattern like those in sleep and so never awake out of vision. Then he will remember Wordsworth withering into eighty years, honoured and empty-witted, and climb to some waste room and find, forgotten there by youth, some bitter crust.

III

Breaking Through

Aloneness is man's real condition.
> —*W. H. Auden, 1941*

A cage went in search of a bird.
> —*Franz Kafka, 1917*

1

SIGMUND FREUD *and* GEORG GRODDECK

The farther we get from Freud the more his truth seems like a personal, poetic vision, rather than an impersonal, scientific investigation. Is the Oedipus complex as universal as he thought? Or has it, after all, some local relation to his own background of the Viennese middle class, with its particular morals and economy?

But it makes no difference. For the first time, he turned our attention to the lustrum it is hardest to remember, demonstrating its radical importance, and even defining religion itself as "the recapitulation and the solution of the problems of one's first four years that have been covered over by amnesia." And when not abused, when not reduced to a cold, academic formula, the Psychoanalytic Method is not only a means of recovering and accepting these years, but a two-way, Samaritan act of human caring and loving which, unlike the Confessional, is not necessarily impersonal.

Along with other things, Freud's account of the origins of his Method is the record of as lonely a quest as any twentieth-century man has left us. It was this loneliness, perhaps, which later prompted him to work so patiently to establish the dignity of a world Psychoanalytic Movement, at the cost, inevitably, of some of the original fire. This, in turn, may have been why he invited a younger colleague who called himself "a wild analyst" to write something which would introduce the general point of view of psychoanalysis to the lay public.

The result, anyway, was Georg Groddeck's The Book of the It, *a unique series of imaginary letters which most professional analysts still regard with uneasiness and exasperation, yet which poets (including Freud) have cherished — and chiefly for the dangerous reason Karen Horney cited when she first read it in 1923:*

"What pleased me most is the grandiose candor with which you include yourself in this whole confusion. This is splendid . . ."

from *The History of the Psychoanalytic Movement*

SIGMUND FREUD

Fluctuat nec mergitur. [It is storm-tossed, but it does not sink.]

No one need be surprised to find a subjective element in the contribution I propose to make here to the history of the psychoanalytic movement, nor need anyone wonder at the part I play in it. For psychoanalysis is my creation; I was for ten years the only person who concerned himself with it, and all the dissatisfaction which the new doctrine aroused in my contemporaries has been poured forth in the form of criticisms on my head. Although it is long now since I was the only psychoanalyst, I regard myself as justified in maintaining that even to-day no one can know better than I what psychoanalysis is, how it differs from other ways of investigating the life of the mind, and precisely what should be called psychoanalysis and what would better be described by some other name. . . .

In 1909, in the lecture hall of an American university, I had my first opportunity of speaking in public about psychoanalysis; the occasion was a momentous one for my work, and moved by this thought I then declared that it was not I who had brought psychoanalysis into existence. The credit for this was due to another, to Josef Breuer, whose work had been done at a time when I was still a student occupied with my examinations (1880–82). Since I gave those lectures, however, well-meaning friends have suggested to me a doubt whether my gratitude should not have been expressed less extravagantly on that occasion. According to them, I should have done as I had previously been accustomed to do, and regarded Breuer's "cathartic procedure" as a forerunner of psychoanalysis, the latter beginning with my discarding the hypnotic method and introducing that of free association. It is of no great importance in any case whether the history of psychoanalysis is reckoned as beginning with the cathartic method or with my modification of it; I refer to this uninteresting point merely because certain opponents of psychoanalysis have the habit of recollecting occasionally that the art of psychoanalysis was after all not invented by me, but by Breuer. This of course happens only when for once in a way they are able to find something worthy of attention in it; when they impose no such limits to their general rejection of it, however, psychoanalysis is always without question my work alone. I have never heard that Breuer's great share in psychoanalysis has earned him a corresponding measure of criticism and abuse; 'and as it is long ago now since I recognized that to stir up contradiction and arouse bitterness is the inevitable fate of psychoanalysis, I conclude that I must be the real originator of all that is particularly characteristic in it. I am happy to be able to add that none of the efforts to minimize my part in creating this much-reviled analysis have ever come from Breuer himself or have met with any support from him.

Breuer's discovery has so often been described that I can dispense with discussing it in detail here. The fundamental fact was that the symptoms of hysterical patients are founded upon highly significant, but forgotten, scenes in their past lives (traumas); the therapy founded upon this consisted in causing them to remember and reproduce these scenes in a state of hypnosis (catharsis); and the fragment of theory inferred from this was that these symptoms represented an abnormal form of discharge for quantities of excitation which had not been disposed of otherwise (conversion). Whenever Breuer . . . referred to this process of conversion, he always added my name in brackets after it, as though the priority for this first attempt at theoretic evaluation belonged to me. I believe that actually this distinction relates only to the name, and that the conception was evolved by us simultaneously together.

It is well known, too, that after Breuer made his first discovery of the cathartic method he let it rest for a number of years, and took it up again only after I returned from studying with Charcot and induced him to do so. He had a large consulting practice in medicine which made great claims on him; I had only unwillingly taken up the profession of medicine, but I had at that time a strong motive for helping nervous persons or at least for wishing to understand something about nervous states. I had already devoted myself to physical therapy, and had felt absolutely helpless after the disappointing results I had experienced with Erb's "electrotherapy," which was so full of detailed indications. If I did not at the time arrive on my own account at the conclusion which Möbius later established, that the successes of electrical treatment in nervous patients are the effects of suggestion, certainly only the total absence of these promised successes was to blame. Treatment by suggestion during deep hypnosis, which I learned from Liébeault's and Bernheim's highly impressive demonstrations, then seemed to offer a satisfactory substitute for the failure of electrical treatment. But the method of investigating patients in a state of hypnosis, which I learned of from Breuer — with its automatic effectiveness and the satisfaction it afforded to scientific interest — was bound to be incomparably more attractive than the monotonous, arbitrary prohibitions used in treatment by suggestion, which stood in the way of all research.

We have lately received an admonition purporting to represent one of the latest developments of psychoanalysis, to the effect that the current conflict and the exciting cause of illness are to be brought into the foreground in the analysis. Now this is exactly what Breuer and I used to do at the beginning of our work with the cathartic method. We led the patient's attention directly to the traumatic scene in which the symptom had arisen, endeavoured to find the mental conflict inherent in it and to release the suppressed affect. In the course of this we discovered the mental process, so characteristic of the neuroses, which I later named regression. The patient's associations led back from the scene which one was trying to elucidate to earlier experiences, and compelled the analysis, which had to correct the present, to occupy itself with the past. This regression led constantly further backwards; at first it seemed regularly to bring us to puberty; later on, failures and points which still awaited explanation beckoned the analytic work still further back into years of childhood which had hitherto been inaccessible to any kind of exploration. This regressing trend became an important character of analysis. It appeared that psychoanalysis could explain nothing current without referring back to something past; more, that every pathogenic experience implied a previous one which, though not in itself pathogenic, had yet endowed the later one with its pathogenic quality. The temptation to confine attention to the known actual exciting cause was so strong, however, that even in later analyses I gave way to it. In the analysis of the patient I named "Dora," carried out in 1899, I had knowledge of the event which occasioned the outbreak of the actual illness. I tried innumerable times to analyse this experience, but even direct demands always failed to produce from her anything more than the same meagre and incomplete description of it. Not until a long détour, leading back over her earliest childhood, had been traversed, did a dream present itself which on analysis brought to mind the hitherto forgotten details of this scene, so that comprehension and a solution of the current conflict became finally possible.

This one example shows how very misleading is the advice just now referred to, and what a degree of scientific regression is represented by the neglect of regression in analytic technique thus enjoined upon us.

The first difference between Breuer and myself came to light in regard to a question concerning the finer psychical mechanism of hysteria. He gave preference to a theory which was still to some extent physiological, as one might call it; he wished to explain the mental dissociation of hysteria by the absence of communication between various psychical states (states of consciousness, as we called them at that time), and he therefore constructed the theory of "hypnoid" states, the effects of which were supposed to penetrate into waking consciousness like unassimilated foreign bodies. I had taken the matter less academically; everywhere I seemed to discern motives and tendencies analogous to those of everyday life, and I looked upon mental dissociation itself as an effect of a process of rejection which at that time I called *defence,* and later called *repression.* I made a shortlived attempt to allow the two mechanisms a separate existence side by side, but as observation showed me always and only one thing, it was not long before my "defence" doctrine took up its stand opposite his "hypnoid" theory.

I am quite sure, however, that this opposition between our views had nothing to do with the severance of our relations which followed shortly after. This severance had deeper causes, but it came about in such a way that at first I did not understand it; it was only later that I learnt from many sure indications how to account for it. It will be remembered that Breuer said of his famous first patient that the sexual element was amazingly undeveloped in her and had contributed nothing to the very rich clinical picture of the case. I have always wondered why the critics did not more often cite this assurance of Breuer's as an argument against my contention of a sexual aetiology in the neuroses, and even to-day I do not know whether I should regard the omission as evidence of tact or of carelessness on their part. Anyone who reads the history of Breuer's case now in the light of the knowledge gained in the last twenty years will at once perceive the symbolism in it — the snake, the stiffening, the disabling of the arm — and, on taking into account the situation at the bedside of the sick father, will easily guess the real interpretation of her symptom-formation; his opinion of the part played by sexuality in the young woman's mental life will then be very different from that of her physician. In his treatment of her case, Breuer could make use of a very intense suggestible *rapport* on the part of the patient, which may serve us as a prototype of what we call "transference" to-day. Now I have strong reasons for surmising that after all her symptoms had been relieved Breuer must have discovered from further indications the sexual motivation of this transference, but that the universal nature of this unexpected phenomenon escaped him, with the result that, as though confronted by an "untoward event," he broke off all further investigation. He never told me this in so many words, but he gave me at various times indications enough to justify this reconstruction of what happened. When I later began more and more resolutely to put forward the significance of sexuality in the aetiology of neurosis, he was the first to show that reaction of distaste and repudiation which was later to become so familiar to me, but which at that time I had not yet learnt to recognize as my inevitable fate.

The fact of transference appearing, although neither desired nor induced by either physician or patient, in every neurotic who comes under treatment, in its crude sexual, or affectionate, or hostile form, has always seemed to me the most irrefragable proof that the source of the propelling forces of neurosis lies in the sexual life. This argument has never received anything approaching the degree of attention that it merits, for if it had, there would really be no choice but acceptance. In my own conviction of the truth it remains, beside and above the more specific results of analytic work, the decisive factor.

There was some consolation for the bad reception accorded even among my intimate friends to my contention of a sexual aetiology in the neuroses — a vacuum rapidly formed itself about my person — in the thought that I was taking up the fight for a new and original idea. But, one day, certain memories collected in my mind which disturbed this pleasing notion, and gave me instead a valuable insight into the processes of human activity and the nature of human knowledge. The idea for which I was being made responsible had by no means originated with me. It had been imparted to me by no less than three people whose opinion had commanded my deepest respect — by Breuer himself, by Charcot, and by the gynaecologist of Vienna University, Chrobak, perhaps the most eminent of all our Viennese physicians. These three men had all communicated to me a piece of knowledge which, strictly speaking, they themselves did not possess. Two of them later denied having done so when I reminded them of the fact; the third (Charcot) would probably have done the same if it had been granted to me to see him again. But these three identical opinions, which I had heard without understanding, had lain dormant in my mind for years until one day they awoke in the form of an apparently original idea.

One day when I was a young house-physician I was walking with Breuer through the town, when a man came up who evidently wished urgently to speak to him. I fell back; as soon as Breuer was free, he told me in his friendly instructive way that this man was the husband of a patient and had brought him some news of her. The wife, he added, was behaving in such an extraordinary way in society that she had been brought to him for treatment as nervous. Then he concluded: "These things are always *secrets d'alcove!*" Astonished, I asked him what he meant, and he answered by telling me the meaning of the word *alcove* (marriage-bed), for he did not realize how extraordinary his remark had seemed to me.

Some years later, at one of Charcot's evening receptions, I happened to be standing near the great teacher at a moment when he appeared to be telling Brouardel some very interesting story from his day's work. I hardly heard the beginning, but gradually my attention was seized by what he was saying. A young married couple from the far East: the woman a confirmed invalid: the man either impotent or exceedingly awkward. *"Tâchez donc,"* I heard Charcot repeating, *"je vous assure, vous y arriverez."* Brouardel, who spoke less loudly, must have expressed his astonishment that symptoms such as the wife's could have been produced in such circumstances. For Charcot suddenly broke in with great animation, *"Mais, dans des cas pareils c'est toujours la chose génitale, toujours . . . toujours . . . toujours"*; and he crossed his arms over his stomach, hugging himself and jumping up and down on his toes several times in his own characteristic lively way. I know that for one second I was almost paralyzed with amazement and said to myself, "Well, but if he knows that, why does he never say so?" But the impression was soon forgotten; brain anatomy and the experimental induction of hysterical paralyses absorbed all available interest.

A year later, I had begun medical practice in Vienna as a *Privatdozent* for nervous diseases, and in everything relating to the aetiology of the neuroses I was still as ignorant and innocent as one could only expect of a promising student trained at a university. One day I had a friendly message from Chrobak, asking me to take a patient of his to whom he could not give enough time, owing to his new appointment as University lecturer. I arrived at the patient's house before he did and found that she was suffering from attacks of insensate anxiety, and could only be soothed by the most detailed information about where her physician was at every moment of the day. When Chrobak arrived he took me aside and told me that the patient's anxiety was due to the fact that although she had been married for eighteen years she was still *virgo intacta*. The husband was absolutely impotent. In such cases, he said, there was nothing for a medical man to do but to shield this domestic misfortune with his own reputation, and put up with it if people shrugged their shoulders and said of him, "He is no good if he can't cure her after so many years." The sole prescription for such a malady, he added, is familiar enough to us, but we cannot order it. It runs:

> R.   Penis normalis
>   dosim
>   repetatur!

I had never heard of such a prescription and would have liked to shake my head over my kind friend's cynicism.

I have certainly not disclosed the illustrious parentage of this scandalous idea in order to saddle others with the responsibility for it. I am well aware that it is one thing once or twice, or even oftener, to give words to an idea that comes in the form of a fleeting inspiration, and quite another to intend it seriously, to take it literally, to pursue it in spite of all difficulties into every detail and to win it a place among accepted truths. It is the difference between a casual flirtation and solemn matrimony with all its duties and difficulties. "To be wedded to an idea" is not an uncommon figure of speech.

Among the other new factors which were added to the cathartic procedure as a result of my work, transforming it into psychoanalysis, I should mention particularly: The doctrine of repression and resistance, the recognition of infantile sexuality, and the interpreting and making use of dreams as a source of knowledge of the unconscious.

The doctrine of repression quite certainly came to me independently of any other source; I know of no outside impression which might have suggested it to me, and for a long time I imagined it to be entirely my own, until Otto Rank showed us the passage in Schopenhauer's *World as Will and Idea* in which the philosopher is trying to give an explanation of insanity. What he says there about the struggle against acceptance of a painful part of reality fits my conception of repression so completely that I am again indebted for having made a discovery to not being a wide reader. And yet others have read the passage and passed it by without making this discovery, and perhaps the same would have happened to me if in my young days I had had more taste for reading philosophical works. In later years I have denied myself the very great pleasure of reading the works of Nietzsche from a deliberate resolve not to be hampered in working out the impressions received in psychoanalysis by any sort of expectation derived from without. I have to be prepared, therefore — and am so, gladly — to forego all claim to priority in the many instances in which laborious psychoanalytic investigation can merely confirm the truths which this philosopher recognized intuitively.

The doctrine of repression is the foundation-stone on which the whole structure of psychoanalysis rests, the most essential part of it, and yet it is nothing but a theoretical formulation of a phenomenon which may be observed to recur as often as one undertakes an analysis of a neurotic without resorting to hypnosis. One notices a resistance then making itself evident in opposition to the work of analysis and inducing a failure to recall memories in order to frustrate it. The use of hypnosis is bound to hide this resistance; the history of psychoanalysis proper, therefore, begins with the new technique that dispenses with hypnosis. Considered theoretically, the fact that this resistance coincides with an amnesia leads inevitably to that view of unconscious mental activity which is peculiar to psychoanalysis and after all distinguishes it quite clearly from philosophical speculations about the unconscious. It may thus be said that the theory of psychoanalysis is an attempt to account for two observed facts that strike one conspicuously and unexpectedly whenever an attempt is made to trace the symptoms of a neurotic back to their sources in his past life: the facts of transference and of resistance. Any line of investigation, no matter what its direction, which recognizes these two facts and takes them as the starting-point of its work may call itself psychoanalysis, though it arrives at results other than my own. But anyone who takes up other sides of the problem while avoiding these two premises will hardly escape the charge of misappropriating by attempted impersonation, if he persists in calling himself a psychoanalyst.

If anyone should seek to regard the theory of repression and of resistance as assumptions instead of as results following from psychoanalysis, I should oppose him most emphatically. Such assumptions of a general psychological and biological nature do exist, and it would be useful to consider them on some other occasion; but the doctrine of repression is the outcome of psychoanalytic work, a theoretic inference legitimately drawn from innumerable observations. The formulation of infantile sexuality is another of these products, acquired, however, at a much later date; in the early days of tentative investigation by analysis no such thing was thought of. At first one merely remarked that the effect of current experiences had to be traced back to something in the past. Only, "enquirers often find more than they bargain for." One was drawn further and further back into the past; one hoped at last to be able to halt at puberty, the period in which sexuality is traditionally supposed to awake. But in vain; the tracks led on still further backwards, into childhood and into its earliest years. On the way an obstacle had to be overcome that was almost fatal to the young science. Influenced by Charcot's view of the traumatic origin of hysteria, one was readily inclined to accept as true and aetiologically significant the statements made by patients in which they ascribed their symptoms to passive sexual experiences in early childhood — broadly speaking, to seduction. When this aetiology broke down under its own improbability and under contradiction in definitely ascertainable circumstances, the result at first was helpless bewilderment. Analysis had led by the right paths back to these sexual traumas, and yet they were not true. Reality was lost from under one's feet. At that time I would gladly have given up the whole thing, just as my esteemed predecessor, Breuer, had done when he made his unwelcome discovery. Perhaps I persevered only because I had no choice and could not then begin again at anything else. At last came the reflection that, after all, one has no right to despair because one has been deceived in one's expectations; one must revise them. If hysterics trace back their symptoms to fictitious traumas, this new fact signifies that they create such scenes in phantasy, and psychical reality requires to be taken into account alongside actual reality. This was soon followed by the recognition that these phantasies were intended to cover up the auto-erotic activity of early childhood, to gloss it over and raise it to a higher level; and then, from behind the phantasies, the whole range of the child's sexual life came to light.

With this sexual activity during early childhood the inherited constitution at last came into its own. Predisposition and experience were here linked up in an indissoluble aetiological unity; impressions which were entirely commonplace, and would otherwise have had no effect, became exaggerated by the predisposition into traumas giving rise to excitation and fixations; while experiences stimulated factors in the disposition which, without them, might have remained long dormant and perhaps never have awakened. The last word on the subject of traumatic aetiology was spoken later by Abraham, when he pointed out that the peculiarity of the sexual constitution in children is precisely calculated to provoke sexual experiences of a certain kind, namely, traumas.

In the beginning my formulations regarding infantile sexuality were founded almost exclusively upon the results of analysis in adults, leading as they did back into the past. I had no opportunity of direct observations on children. It was therefore a very great triumph when it became possible years later to confirm almost all my inferences by direct observation and analysis of children, a triumph that lost some of its magnitude as one gradually realized that the nature of the discovery was such that one should really be ashamed of having to make it. The further one carried these observations on children, the more self-evident the facts became, and the more astonishing was it too that so much trouble was taken to overlook them.

Such a certain conviction of the existence and significance of infantile sexuality can, it is true, only be obtained by the path of analysis, pursuing the symptoms and peculiarities of neurotics back to their ultimate sources, the discovery of which then explains whatever is explicable in them and enables whatever is modifiable in them to be changed. I can understand that one would arrive at different results if, as C. G. Jung has recently done, one first forms a theoretical conception of the nature of the sexual instinct and then seeks to explain the life of children on this basis. A conception of this kind is bound to be selected arbitrarily or in accordance with secondary considerations, and runs the risk of not corresponding adequately to the field in which it is applied. It is true that the road of analysis leads also to certain final difficulties and obscurities in regard to sexuality and its relation to the whole life of the individual: but these problems cannot be dealt with by speculation; they must await solution by other observations or by observations in other fields.

I need say little about the interpretation of dreams. It came as the first-fruits of the new technique, when, following a dim presentiment, I had decided to exchange hypnosis for free association. My desire for knowledge had not been directed to start with towards understanding dreams. I do not know of any outside influence which drew my interest to them or inspired me with any helpful expectations. Before Breuer and I ceased to meet there had only just been time for me to tell him in one sentence that I now understood how to translate dreams. Since this was how the discovery came about, it followed that the symbolism in the language of dreams was almost the last thing to become clear to me, for the dreamer's associations help very little towards understanding symbols. I have held fast to the habit of always studying things themselves before looking for information about them in books, and therefore I was able to establish the symbolism of dreams for myself before I was led to it by Scherner's work on the subject. It was only later that I came to appreciate to its full extent this mode of expression in dreams — partly through the influence of Stekel, who at first did such very creditable work but afterwards went totally astray. The close connection between psychoanalytic dream-interpretation and the art of interpreting dreams as practised and held in such high esteem by the ancients only became clear to me much later. I found the essential characteristic and most significant part of my dream theory — the reduction of dream-distortion to an inner conflict, a kind of inward dishonesty — later in a writer who was familiar with philosophy though not with medicine, the engineer J. Popper, who published his *Phantasien eines Realisten* under the name of Lynkeus.

The interpretation of dreams became a solace and a support to me in those arduous first years of analysis, when I had to master the technology, clinical phenomena and therapy of the neuroses all at the same time; I was then completely isolated, and in the network of problems and accumulation of difficulties often dreaded losing my way and also my confidence. It was often a long time before the test of my hypothesis, that a neurosis must become intelligible by analysis, was realized in the patient; in their dreams, which might be regarded as analogues of their symptoms, this hypothesis was confirmed almost without exception.

It was only my success in this direction that enabled me to persevere. The result is that I have acquired the habit of gauging the measure of a psychologist's understanding by his attitude to dream-interpretation; and have observed with satisfaction that most of the opponents of psychoanalysis avoid this question altogether or else display remarkable clumsiness if they attempt to deal with it. I soon saw the necessity of an analysis of myself and this I carried out with the help of a series of my own dreams which led me back through all the events of my childhood; I am still to-day of the opinion that this kind of analysis may suffice for anyone who is a prolific dreamer and not too abnormal.

I think that by narrating this history of its development I have shown what psychoanalysis is better than by a systematic description of it. I did not at first perceive the peculiar nature of what I had discovered. Without thinking, I sacrificed at its inception my popularity as a physician, and the growth of a large consulting practice among nervous patients, by enquiries relating to the sexual factors involved in the causation of their neuroses; this brought me a great many new facts which definitely confirmed my conviction of the practical importance of the sexual factor. Unsuspectingly, I spoke before the Vienna Neurological Society, then under the presidency of Krafft-Ebing, expecting to be compensated by the interest and recognition of my colleagues for the material losses I had willingly undergone. I treated my discoveries as ordinary contributions to science and hoped to be met in the same spirit. But the silence with which my addresses were received, the void which formed itself about me, the insinuations that found their way to me, caused me gradually to realize that one cannot count upon views about the part played by sexuality in the aetiology of the neuroses meeting with the same reception as other communications. I understood that from now onwards I belonged to those who have "disturbed the sleep of the world," as Hebbel says, and that I could not reckon upon objectivity and tolerance. Since, however, my conviction of the general accuracy of my observations and conclusions grew and grew, and as my confidence in my own judgement was by no means slight, any more than my moral courage, there could be no doubt about the outcome of the situation. I made up my mind that it had been my fortune to discover particularly important connections, and was prepared to accept the fate that sometimes accompanies such discoveries.

I imagined the future somewhat as follows: I should probably succeed in sustaining myself by means of the therapeutic success of the new method, but science would ignore me entirely during my lifetime. Some decades later, someone else would infallibly come upon the same things — for which the time was not yet ripe —, would achieve recognition for them and bring me to honour as a forerunner whose failure had been inevitable. Meanwhile I settled down, like Robinson, as comfortably as possible on my lonely island. When I look back to those lonely years, away from the pressure and preoccupations of to-day, it seems to me like a glorious "heroic era"; my "splendid isolation" was not lacking in advantages and in charms. I had not to read any publications, nor to listen to any ill-informed opponents; I was not subject to influence from any quarter; no one attempted to hurry me. I learnt to restrain speculative tendencies and to follow the unforgotten advice of my master, Charcot — to look at the same things again and again until they themselves begin to speak. There was no need for my writings, for which with some difficulty I found a publisher, to keep pace with my knowledge; they could be postponed as long as I pleased; there was no doubtful "priority" to be secured. *Die Traumdeutung,* for instance, was complete in all essentials at the beginning of 1896; it was not written out until the summer of 1899. The analysis of "Dora" was over at the end of 1899; the case was noted down in the next two weeks, but not published until 1905. All this time my writings were not reviewed in the medical journals, or, if by an exception this happened, they were scouted with contemptuous or pitying arrogance. Occasionally a colleague would make some reference to me in one of his publications; it would be very short and not at all flattering — such as "eccentric," "extreme," "very peculiar ideas." It happened once that an assistant at the clinic in Vienna where I gave lectures asked me for permission to attend one of the courses. He listened very attentively and said nothing; after the last lecture was over he offered to accompany me. As we walked, he told me that with the knowledge of his chief he had written a book against my views, but regretted very much that he had not first learnt more about them from my lectures, as in that case he would have written very differently. He had indeed enquired at the clinic whether he had not better first read the *Die Traumdeutung;* but had

been advised against it, as it was not worth the trouble. He then himself
compared the solidity of the structure of my doctrine with that of the
Catholic church. In the interests of his salvation I take this as an expression of acknowledgement. But, he concluded by saying, it was too late to
alter anything; his book was already printed. Nor did this man think it
necessary later on to make known anything of the change in his opinion
of psychoanalysis, but in his capacity of reviewer for a medical journal
chose rather to follow its development with flippant comments.

Whatever personal sensitiveness I possessed was blunted in those years,
to my advantage. From embitterment I was saved, however, by one circumstance that is not always present to help lonely discoverers. Many a
one is tormented by the need to account for the lack of sympathy or the
repudiation expressed by his contemporaries, and feels their attitude
painfully as a contradiction of his own secure conviction. There was no
need for me to feel so; for psychoanalytical principles enabled me to
understand this attitude in my contemporaries and to see it as a necessary
consequence of fundamental analytic premises. If it was true that the
associated connections I had discovered were kept from the knowledge
of patients by inward resistances of an affective kind, then these resistances
would be bound to appear in the healthy also, as soon as, from some
external source, they became confronted with what is repressed. It was not
surprising that they should be able to justify on intellectual grounds this
rejection of my ideas though it was actually affective in nature. The
same thing happened just as often in patients, and the arguments they
advanced were just the same and not precisely brilliant — reasons are as
plenty as blackberries, as Falstaff says. The only difference was that with
patients one was in a position to bring pressure to bear on them, so as to
induce them to realize their resistances and overcome them, but had to do
without this advantage in dealing with those who were apparently healthy.
How to compel these normal persons to examine the matter in a cool,
objective scientific spirit was an insoluble problem which was best left
to time to accomplish. . . .

Translated by Joan Riviere

from *The Book of the It*

[1923]

GEORG GRODDECK

Letter I

So, my dear, you want me to write to you, and it is to be nothing personal or gossipy. I am not to make fine phrases but to be serious, instructive, and, as far as possible, scientific. That's tiresome! For what has my humble self to do with science? The small amount one needs as a practising physician I cannot well display to you, or you would see the holes in the gown with which, as qualified physicians, we are officially endowed. Perhaps, however, I shall meet your wishes if I tell you why I became a doctor, and how I was led to reject the claims of science.

I do not remember that as a boy I had any special liking for the profession of medicine, and I am very certain that, neither then nor later, did I bring any humanitarian feeling into it; if, as may well be, I used to deck myself out with such noble sentiments, you must look upon my lying with a lenient eye — the truth is I became a doctor just because my father was one. He had forbidden all my brothers to follow that career, probably because he wanted to convince himself and other people that his financial difficulties were due to a doctor's wretched remuneration, which was certainly not the case, since his praises were sung by young and old alike and he was correspondingly rewarded. But he liked, just as his son does, and indeed every one of us, to look for outside causes when he knew that something was out of harmony within himself. One day he asked me — I don't know why — whether I would not like to be a doctor, and because I looked upon this enquiry as a mark of distinction which set me above my brothers, I said yes. With that my fate was sealed, both as to my choice of a profession and as to the manner in which I have followed it, for from that moment I consciously imitated my father to such a degree that an old friend of his, when she came to know me many years later, broke out with the words: "Just your father over again, only without a spark of his genius!"

On this occasion my father related to me a story which later, when doubts arose as to my medical capacity, kept me fast to my work. Perhaps I had already heard it before, but I know that it made a deep impression upon me while I was in that exalted mood, fancying myself like Joseph, raised above my brothers. He had watched me, he said, when as a three-year-old I was playing at dolls with my sister, a little older than myself and my constant playfellow. Lina wanted to pile still another garment on the doll and, after a long dispute, I gave in to her with the words "All right, but you'll see she'll be smothered!" From this he concluded that I had a gift for medicine, and I myself drew the same conclusion from these slender grounds.

I have mentioned this trivial incident to you because it gives me the opportunity to speak of a propensity of mine to fall a prey to anxiety about quite insignificant matters, suddenly, and without apparent cause. As you know, anxiety is the result of a repressed wish; in that moment when I uttered the thought "The doll will be smothered," the wish must have been in me to kill someone represented by the doll. Who that was I do not know, but one may surmise that it was this very sister; her delicacy secured for her many privileges from my mother which I, as the baby of the family, wanted for myself. There you have the essential quality of the doctor, a propensity to cruelty which has been just so far repressed as to be useful, and which has for its warder the dread of causing pain. It would be worth while to pursue this subtle interplay between cruelty and anxiety in mankind, for it is extremely important in life, but for the purpose of this letter it is sufficient to establish quite clearly the fact that my relation to my sister had a great deal to do with the development and with the taming of my desire to cause pain. Our favourite game was "Mother and Child," in which the child was naughty and was slapped. My sister's delicacy compelled us to do this gently, and the manner in which I have carried on my professional work reflects our childhood's play. Nearly as great as my aversion from the surgeon's bloody trade is my dislike of the assorted poisons of the pharmacopoeia, and so I came to massage and to mental treatment; these are both not less cruel, but they adapt themselves better to any particular man's desire to suffer. Out of the constantly changing demands made by Lina's heart-trouble upon my unconscious sensitivity, there grew the preference for dealing with chronic cases, acute illness making me impatient.

That is, roughly, what I can tell you about my choice of a profession. But if you will only reflect a little, all sorts of things will occur to you in connection with my attitude to science, for anyone who from childhood upwards has had his attention directed to one particular invalid will find it difficult to learn how to classify things systematically according to the rubric. And then, too, there is that very important question of imitation. My father was a heretic in medicine; he was his own authority, went his own ways, right or wrong, and showed no respect for science either in word or in deed. I still remember how he scoffed at the hopes that were raised by the discovery of the tubercle and the cholera bacilli, and with what glee he recounted how, against all physiological teaching, he had fed an infant for a whole year on bouillon. The first medical book which he put into my hands — I was at that time still a lad at the Gymnasium — was the empirical teaching of Rademacher, and since in that book the points conflicting with scientific teaching are heavily underlined and plentifully sprinkled with marginal comments, it is no matter for surprise if already from the beginning of my studies I was disposed to doubt.

This disposition to doubt was in yet other ways determined. When I was six years old I lost for a time the exclusive companionship of my sister. She gave her affection to a school friend called Alma, and, what was terribly hard to bear, she taught our little childish sadistic games to this new friend and shut me out from them. On one solitary occasion I managed to overhear the two girls while they were at their favourite occupation of telling stories. Alma was making up a tale about an angry mother who punished her disobedient child by putting it into a privy-pit (one must picture for this a primitive country closet). To this day it sticks in my memory that I did not hear the conclusion of that story. The friendship between the two little girls came to an end, and my sister returned to me, but that period of loneliness was enough to inspire me with a deep distaste for the name of Alma.

And here I must certainly remind you that a university calls itself Alma Mater. That gave me a strong prejudice against science, all the greater because the term "alma mater" was also used of the Gymnasium in which I followed my classical studies, and where I suffered much that I should have to tell you of, if it were my purpose to make you understand the unfolding of my nature. That, however, is not what is in my mind, but only the fact that I attributed all the hatred and the suffering of my schooldays to science, because it is more convenient to ascribe one's depression to external events than to seek its roots in the depths of the unconscious.

.   .   .

Letter II

Fair lady, you are not pleased; is there too much of the personal in my letter, and you would have me objective? But I thought I had been! Let us see then; what I wrote about was the choice of a profession, certain aversions, and an inner conflict which lasted from childhood onwards. Certainly I spoke of myself, but these experiences are typical, and if you apply them to others there is much that you will learn to understand. One thing above all will become clear to you, that our lives are governed by forces that do not lie open to the day, but must needs be laboriously sought out. I wanted to show by an example, by my own example, that a great deal goes on in us which lies outside our accustomed thought. But perhaps it would be better if I made my purpose quite clear, and then you will be able to decide whether the theme is sufficiently serious. If once I drop into chit chat or into fine writing, you must tell me; that will help both of us.

I hold the view that man is animated by the Unknown, that there is within him an "Es," an "It," some wondrous force which directs both what he himself does, and what happens to him. The affirmation "I live" is only conditionally correct, it expresses only a small and superficial part of the fundamental principle "Man is lived by the It." With this Unknown, this It, my letters will be concerned. Are you agreed?

Yet one thing more. Of the It, we know only so much as lies within our consciousness. Beyond that the greater part of its territory is unattainable, but by search and effort we can extend the limits of our consciousness, and press far into the realm of the unconscious, if we can bring ourselves no more to desire knowledge but only to fantasy. Come then, my pretty Dr. Faust, the mantle is spread for the flight. Forth into the Unknown. . . .

Is it not strange that we should know hardly anything of our three first years of life? Now and then a man produces some faint remembrance of a face, a door, a wallpaper or whatnot, which he claims to have seen in his infancy, but never yet have I met anyone who remembered his first steps, or the manner in which he learned to talk, to eat, to see or to hear. Yet these are all vital experiences. I can well imagine that a child in stumbling across a room for the first time receives a deeper impression than his elders would from a visit to Italy. I can well imagine that a child who realises for the first time that the person with the kind smile over there is his mother, is more completely gripped by his emotion than the husband who leads his bride home. Why do we forget it all?

There is much to say on that, but one point must be made clear before proceeding to the answer. The question is wrongly put. It is not that we forget those three first years, only the remembrance of them is shut out from our consciousness; in the Unconscious it goes on living, and continues to be so active that all we do is fed from this unknown treasure-heap of memory: we walk as we then learned to walk, we eat, we speak, we feel just as we did then. There are matters, then, which are cast out of consciousness although they are essential to life, which, just because they are essential to life, are preserved in regions of our being which have been named the Unconscious. But why does the conscious mind forget experiences without which mankind could not exist?

May I leave the question open? I shall often have to put it again. But now it is more in my mind to enquire from you, as a woman, why mothers know so little of their children, and why they too forget the substance of those three first years? Perhaps mothers only act as if they had forgotten it? Or perhaps with them also the essential things do not reach consciousness?

You will chide because once more I am making merry over mothers, but how else can I help myself? A yearning is in me: when I am sad my heart cries for my mother, and she is not to be found. Am I then to grumble at God's world? Better to laugh at myself, at this childishness from which we never emerge, for never do we quite grow up; we manage it rarely, and then only on the surface; we merely play at being grown up as a child plays at being big. So soon as we live intensely we become children. For the It, age does not exist, and in the It is our own real life. Do but look upon someone in his moments of deepest sorrow or of highest joy: his face is like that of a child, his gestures too, his voice is flexible again, his heart leaps as it did in childhood, his eyes glisten or cloud over. Certainly we attempt to hide all this, but it is clearly there, and if we pay attention we observe it, only we fail to notice in other people those signs that tell so much because we do not want to perceive them in ourselves. No one cries any more after he is grown up? But that is only because it is not the custom, because some silly idiot or other sent it out of fashion. I have always joked about Mars shrieking like ten thousand men when he was wounded, and it is only in the eyes of the would-be great that Achilles is dishonoured by his tears over the body of Patroclus. We play the hypocrite, that is the whole story, and never once dare to give a genuine laugh. Still, that does not prevent our looking like schoolboys when we are up against something we can't do, from wearing the same anxious expression as we did in childhood, from showing always the same little mannerisms in walking, lying, speaking, which cry to everyone who has eyes to see, "Behold the child!" Watch anyone when he thinks he is alone; at once you see the child come to the surface, sometimes in very comical fashion. He yawns, or, without embarrassment, he scratches his head or his bottom, or he picks his nose, or even — yes, it has got to be said — he lets out wind. The daintiest lady will do so! Or notice people who are absorbed in thought or in some task; look at lovers, at the sick, at the aged. All of them are children now and again.

If we like, we can think of life as a masquerade at which we don a disguise, perhaps many different disguises, at which nevertheless we retain our own proper characters, remaining ourselves amidst the other revellers in spite of our disguise, and from which we depart exactly as we were when we came. Life begins with childhood, and by a thousand devious paths through maturity attains its single goal, once more to be a child, and the one and only difference between people lies in the fact that some grow childish, and some child-like.

.   .   .

Letter XXXI

My vanity prevented me from interesting myself in scientific psychoanalysis for a long time. Later on I tried to repair my fault, with a fair amount of success, I venture to hope, although there yet remains a weed here and there which I have not uprooted from my analytical theory and procedure. But my wilful refusal to learn has also held a certain advantage. In that blind struggle, unimpeded by previous knowledge, I came by chance upon the idea that in addition to the unconscious of the thinking brain, there is an analogous unconscious of other organs, cells, tissues, etc., and that through the intimate connection of these separate unconscious-units with the organism as a whole, a beneficial influence may be directed upon the individual units by means of the analysis of the brain-unconscious.

You must not think that I feel quite easy in my mind as I write down these views. I have the uncomfortable feeling that they will not survive your kindly criticism, let alone the serious examination of an expert. But since it has become easier for me to give an opinion than to give proof, I will take refuge in opinion here too, and say: "Every sickness of the organism, whether it is physical or psychic, is to be influenced by analysis. Whether in a given case one should have recourse to analytical methods, or surgical, or mechanical, whether one should prescribe medicine or a special dietary, depends upon what one is aiming at. Of itself, there is no department of medicine in which Freud's discovery cannot prove its worth."

Your reference to the fact that I am a practising physician and claim the title of doctor is so very trenchant, my dear, that I feel myself obliged to brag a little more about how I imagine I understand and cure disease. But first we must come to some agreement over what we shall call "disease." I think we won't worry about what other people understand by the term, but will make sure of what we mean ourselves, and I therefore propose to enunciate quite definitely, "Disease is a vital expression of the human organism." Take a little time to think whether you agree with this formula or not, and meanwhile I will continue as if you approved it.

Perhaps you do not consider the question particularly important, but if you had been trying for thirty years, as I have, to get a certain number of people every day to grasp this simple statement, and day by day for thirty years had found that it could by no means be driven into people's heads, then you would consent at least, when I emphasized its value, to understand it.

Whoever, like me, sees in illness a vital expression of the organism, will no longer see it as an enemy. It will no longer be his purpose to fight the illness, he no longer tries to cure it, he does not treat it at all. It would be just as absurd for me to treat disease as it would be to try to answer your teasing by pointing out the little naughtinesses in your letters very nicely and delicately, without answering it.

In the moment that I realize that the disease is a creation of the patient, it becomes for me the same sort of thing as his manner of walking, his mode of speech, his facial expression, the movements of his hands, the drawing he has made, the house he has built, the business he has settled, or the way his thoughts go: a significant symbol of the powers that rule him and that I try to influence when I deem it right. Disease is then no longer anything abnormal but something conditioned by the nature of this one man who is ill and wishes to be treated by me. One difference exists in the case of disease, namely that the creations of the It to which we are accustomed to give the name of disease are under certain conditions inconvenient for the creator himself, or for those surrounding him. But after all, a shrill voice or illegible handwriting can also be intolerable to one's fellow men, and an unsuitable house needs just as much rebuilding as a lung that is inflamed, so in the end there is no essential difference to be found between disease and speaking, or writing, or building. In other words I can no longer make up my mind to proceed with a sick man otherwise than with someone who wrote or spoke or built badly. I should try to make out why, and to what end, his It made use of the bad writing, speaking, building; of his sick state, what it was it wanted to express in this way. I should inquire from the It itself what grounds it had for acting in a way that was disagreeable, for me as well as for itself — I would discuss these and then view the result. And if one discussion was not enough I should repeat it again ten times, twenty times, a hundred times, until at last the It found this talking tedious, and either changed its behaviour or compelled its creature, the patient, to depart from me, whether by breaking off the treatment or by dying.

Now I grant you it may be necessary, is so in most cases, to reconstruct or to pull down a badly built house as quickly as possible, to put a man to bed with pneumonia and nurse him, to get rid of the oedema in a nephritic patient perhaps with digitalis, to set and immobilize a broken bone, and to amputate a gangrenous limb. Yes, and I have that same well-founded hope that the architect whose new building is reconstructed or pulled down immediately after he has handed it over to the owner, will examine himself, see his mistake and avoid it in future or give up his calling altogether, as that an It, when it has damaged its own work, lungs or bones, and thereby suffered pain and trouble, will be reasonable, and will have learned its lesson for the future. In other words the It can convince itself, by its own experiences, that it is foolish to spend its strength in producing disease instead of using it to compose a song, to carry on a business, to empty the bladder or to achieve the sexual act. But all this does not relieve me, whom my It has made into a physician, from the necessity of listening, when time permits, to the reasons of the disease-seeking It of a fellow man, of weighing them, and when it is possible and desirable, of refuting them.

The matter is important enough, looked at again from another point of view. We are usually accustomed to search for the causes of our experiences, according to whether they are pleasing or not, in the world outside, or within ourselves. If we slip in the street we look for and find some orange peel, or a stone, the external cause of our fall. On the other hand, if we take a pistol and put a bullet through our heads, we are of the opinion that we are acting from inward reasons, with intention. If someone gets pneumonia, we attribute this to infection, but if we rise from our chair, walk across the room and take some morphia from a cupboard in order to drink it, then we think we are being moved by causes within. I, as you know, have always believed I knew better than other people, and if someone has held forth to me about the well known piece of orange peel that suddenly appeared on the path, despite all the police warning, and caused Frau Lange's broken arm, I have gone down to her and asked, "What was your purpose in breaking your arm?" And if anyone told me Herr Treiner had taken morphia the night before because he couldn't sleep, I have asked, "How and by what means did the idea of morphia become so overpowering in you yesterday, that you made yourself sleepless in order to have the excuse for taking it?" So far an answer to such questions has always been forthcoming, which after all is not so very wonderful. Since everything has two sides, we can always consider it from two points of view, and shall find, if we take the trouble, that for every event in life there is both an external and an internal cause.

This amusement of the would-be wiseacre has had some strange results. In its exercise I have been led more and more to seek out the internal cause, partly because I was born into a time which prated of the bacillus and only of the bacillus, even if it did not still bow down before the words "chill" and "disorder of the stomach," partly because the wish awoke in me very early — probably owing to Troll arrogance — to find within myself an It, a God, whom I could make responsible for everything. Since I had not been so badly trained as to claim omnipotence for myself alone, I attributed it to other people also, invented for them also this, to you, so offensive It, and was now able to maintain, "Illness does not come from without; man creates it for himself, uses the outer world merely as the instrument with which to make himself ill, selects from that inexhaustible supply to be found in the wide world, now the spirochaete of syphilis, to-day a piece of orange peel, to-morrow the bullet of a revolver, the day after a chill, so that he may pile on his woes. And always for the sake of getting pleasure out of it, because as a human being he finds a natural pleasure in suffering: because as a human being he has by nature a feeling of guilt, and wants to remove it by self-punishment; because he wants to escape from something or other that is uncomfortable." For the most part these strange causes are all unknown to him, indeed they are all removed from the conscious mind, locked up in the depths of the It, into which we can never look. Between the bottomless depths of the It and our sane human intellect, however, there are layers of the unconscious which are attainable by the conscious mind, layers which Freud deemed capable of becoming conscious, and in which all sorts of nice things are to be found. And the strangest thing of all is that if one rummages through this, it not infrequently happens that we suddenly come upon what we call healing too, — by chance it seems to be. "Not all our worth, nor all our pride." I must be forever repeating that.

.   .   .

Letter XXXII

I ought now to tell you something about the onset of diseases, but on this subject I know nothing. And about their cure, I ought to speak, if I am to do what you wish. And of that, too, I know just nothing at all. I take both of them as given facts. At the utmost, I can say something about the treatment, and that I will now do.

The aim of the treatment, of all medical treatment, is to gain some influence over the It. It is the usual custom for this purpose to give direct treatment to groups of the It-units; we reach them with the knife, or with chemical substances, with light and air, heat or cold, electric currents, or some sort of rays. No one is able to try more than one method or another, the results of which nobody can foretell. What the It will make of such a means can often be judged with some degree of precision; often again, we merely entertain some vague hope that the It will be good, will call our action satisfactory, and for its part will set the healing forces in motion. But mostly it is a groping in the dark, to which not even the most indulgent of critics can attribute any intention. This has always been the common practice, and the experience of thousands of years shows that it can achieve results, favourable results. Only one must not forget that recovery is brought about not by the physician, but by the sick man himself. He heals himself, by his own power, exactly as he walks by means of his own power, or eats, or thinks, breathes or sleeps.

Generally speaking, people have been content with this method of treatment, called "symptomatic treatment" because it deals with the phenomena of disease, the symptoms. And nobody will assert that they were wrong. But we physicians, because we are compelled by our calling to play at being God Almighty, and consequently to entertain overwhelming desires, long to invent a treatment which will do away not with the symptoms but with the cause of the disease. We want to develop causal therapy, as we call it. In this attempt we look around for a cause, and first theoretically establish, under the disguise of many words, that there are apparently two essentially different causes, an inner one, *causa interna,* which the man contributes of himself, and an outer one, *causa externa,* which springs from his environment. And accepting this clear distinction, we have thrown ourselves with raging force upon the external causes, such as bacilli, chills, overeating, overdrinking, work, and anything else. And the *causa interna,* that we have forgotten. Why? Because it is not pleasant to look within ourselves — and it is only in oneself that one finds some tiny sparks which can lighten the darkness of the inner causes, the "disposition" — because there is something which Freudian analysis calls the resistance of the complexes, the Oedipus complex, the impotence and masturbation complexes, etc., and because these complexes are terrifying. Nevertheless, in every age there have always been physicians who raised their voices to declare that man himself produces his diseases, that in him are to be found the *causæ internæ*; he is the cause of the disease and we need seek none other. To this claim people have assented, they have repeated it, and then they have again attacked the outer causes with prophylaxis, disinfection, and so on. Then some people

came along with very loud voices, and never ceased to cry "Immunize!"
This only emphasized the truth that the sick man himself creates his
disease. But when it came to the practical application of immunization,
once again people applied themselves to the symptoms, and what was
ostensibly a causal treatment grew into a symptomatic treatment una-
wares. The same thing has happened with suggestion, and admit it at
once, with psycho-analysis. Even this method uses the symptoms, and
nothing but the symptoms, although its practitioners know that the man
alone is the cause of the disease.

And there I have my jumping-off point. One cannot treat in any other
way than causally. For both ideas are the same; no difference exists between them. Whoever is treating, is treating the *causa interna,* the man
who has created the disease out of his own It, and in order to treat him the
physician must watch the symptoms, whether he works with stethoscope
and Röntgen rays, or looks to see if a tongue is furred, the urine cloudy, or
whether he judges by a dirty shirt or a few cut-off hairs. It is the same
thing in essence, whether one goes carefully through all the signs of the
disease, or contents oneself with reading a letter written by the sick man,
or with looking at the lines of his hand, or with dealing with him while he
is in a somnambulistic condition. Always it is a treatment of the man and
therefore of his symptoms. For the man, as he appears, is a symptom of the
It, which is the object of the whole treatment; his ear is just as much a
symptom as the rustling in his lungs; his eye is a symptom, an expression of
the It, just as is the eruption of scarlet fever; his leg is a symptom, in the
same sense as the grating of the bones which indicates the broken condition
of this leg.

If then it's all the same thing, what sort of purpose is there in Patrik
Troll's writing such a long book, full of statements sounding as if they
claimed to be new thoughts? No, they make no such claim, they merely
sound like that. In truth I am convinced that, in analysing, I do no
differently from what I did before, when I ordered hot baths, gave
massage, and issued masterful commands, all of which I still do. The new
thing is merely the point of attack in the treatment, the symptom which
appears to me to be there in all circumstances, the "I." My treatment, in
so far as it is different from what it used to be, consists of the attempt to
make conscious the unconscious complexes of the "I," to do this systematically and with all the cunning and all the strength at my command.
That is certainly something new, but it originated not with me, but with
Freud; all that I have done in the matter is to apply this method to organic
diseases. Because I hold the view that the object of all medical treatment
is the It; because I hold the view that this It, with its own masterly

power, forms the nose, inflames the lungs, makes a man nervous, prescribes his breathing, his gait, his activities; because, furthermore, I believe that the It can be just as much influenced by the making conscious of the unconscious "I"-complexes, as by an abdominal operation; for these reasons I fail to understand — or rather, I no longer understand — how anybody at all can believe that psycho-analysis is applicable only to neurotics, and that organic diseases must be helped by other methods.

You must let me have my laugh over that!

Ever your

Patrik Troll.

Translated by V. M. E. Collins

2

ANDRÉ GIDE *and* SAUL BELLOW

Well into the century, we find two happy books. They are about the same old, battered, "alienated" man the other poets have spoken for. But Gide's Greek city-building Theseus and Bellow's American lion-haunted Henderson emerge joyously, reverently, each with a keen, gratified sense of his own progress. From Gide's Theseus, *we have taken the hero's encounters with Dædalus and Œdipus. Only the scene in the lion's den could be detached from* Henderson the Rain King, *but it is one of the most original and inspired images of a man's metaphysical hunger we have.*

from *Theseus*

[1946]

ANDRÉ GIDE

I wanted to tell the story of my life as a lesson for my son Hippolytus; but he is no more, and I am telling it all the same. For his sake I should not have dared to include, as I shall now do, certain passages of love; he was extraordinarily prudish, and in his company I never dared to speak of my attachments. Besides, these only mattered to me during the first part of my life; but at least they taught me to know myself, as did also the various monsters whom I subdued. For "the first thing is to know exactly who one is," I used to say to Hippolytus; "later comes the time to assess and adopt one's inheritance. Whether you wish it or not, you are, as I was myself, a king's son. Nothing to be done about it; it's a fact; it pins you down." But Hippolytus never took much notice; even less than I had taken at his age; and like myself at that time, he got on very nicely without it. Oh, early years, all innocently passed! Oh, careless growth of body and mind! I was wind; I was wave. I grew with the plant; I flew with the bird. My self knew no boundaries; every contact with an outer world did not so much teach me my own limits as awaken within me some new power of enjoyment. Fruit I caressed, and the bark of young trees, and smooth stones on the shore, and the coats of horses and dogs, before ever my hands were laid on a woman. Toward all the charming things that Pan, Zeus, or Thetis could offer, I rose.

One day my father said to me that things couldn't go on as they were. "Why not?" Because, good heavens, I was his son and must show myself worthy of the throne to which I should succeed. . . . Just when I was feeling so happy, sprawled naked among cool grasses or on some scorching beach. Still, I can't say that he was wrong. Certainly he was right in teaching me to rebel against myself. To this I owe all that I have achieved since that day; no longer to live at random — agreeable as such license might have been. He taught me that nothing great, nothing of value, and nothing that will last can be got without effort.

My first effort was made at his invitation. It was to overturn boulders in the hope of finding the weapons which Poseidon (so he told me) had hidden beneath one of them. He laughed to see how quickly my strength grew through this training. With the toughening of my body there came also a toughening of the will. After I had dislodged the heaviest rocks of the neighborhood and was about to continue my unfruitful search by attacking the flagstones of the palace gateway, my father stopped me. "Weapons," said he, "count for less than the arm that wields them, and the arm in its turn for less than the thinking will that directs it. Here are the weapons. Before giving them to you, I was waiting to see you deserve them. I can sense in you now the ambition to use them, and that longing for fame which will allow you to take up arms only in defense of noble causes and for the weal of all mankind. Your childhood is over. Be a man. Show your fellow men what one of their kind can be and what he means to become. There are great things to be done. Claim yourself."

.   .   .

[Encounter with Dædalus]

Dædalus rose to welcome me. I had found him in a dim-lit room, bending over the tablets and working drawings that were spread before him, and surrounded by a great many peculiar instruments. He was very tall, and perfectly erect in spite of his great age. His beard was silvery in color, and even longer than that of Minos, which was still quite black, or the fairer one of Rhadamanthus. His vast forehead was marked by deep wrinkles across the whole of its width. When he looked downwards, his eyes were half-hidden by the overhanging brushwood of his eyebrows. He spoke slowly, ánd in a deep voice. His silences had the quality of thought.

He began by congratulating me on my prowess. The echo of this, he said, had penetrated even to him, who lived in retirement, remote from the tumult of the world. He added that I looked to him to be something of a booby; that he took little account of feats of arms, and did not consider that physical strength was the godhead of man.

"At one time I saw quite a lot of your predecessor Hercules. He was a stupid man, and I could never get anything out of him except heroics. But what I did appreciate in him, and what I appreciate in you, is a sort of absorption in the task in hand, an unrecoiling audacity, a temerity even, which thrusts you forward and destroys your opponent, after first having destroyed the coward whom each of us carries within himself. Hercules took greater pains than you do; was more anxious, also, to do well; rather melancholy, especially when he had just completed an adventure. But what I like in you is your enjoyment; that is where you differ from Hercules. I shall commend you for never letting your mind interfere. You can leave that to others who are not men of action, but are clever at inventing sound and good motives for those who are.

"Do you realize that we are cousins? I too (but don't repeat this to Minos, who knows nothing about it) — I too am Greek. I was forced regretfully to leave Attica after certain differences had arisen between myself and my nephew Talos, a sculptor like myself, and my rival. He became a popular favorite, and claimed to uphold the dignity of the gods by representing them with their lower limbs set fast in a hieratic posture, and thus incapable of movement; whereas I was for setting free their limbs and bringing the gods nearer to ourselves. Olympus, thanks to me, became once again a neighbor of the earth. By way of complement, I aspired, with the aid of science, to mold mankind in the likeness of the gods.

"At your age I longed above all to acquire knowledge. I soon decided that man's personal strength can effect little or nothing without instruments, and that the old saying 'Better a good tool than a strong forearm' was true. Assuredly you could never have subdued the bandits of Attica and the Peloponnese without the weapons your father had given you. So I thought I could not employ myself more usefully than by bringing these auxiliaries nearer to perfection, and that I could not do this without first mastering mathematics, mechanics, and geometry to the degree, at any rate, in which they were known in Egypt, where such things are put to great use; also that I must then pass from theory to practice by learning all that was known about the properties and qualities of every kind of material, even of those for which no immediate use was apparent, for in these (as happens also in the human sphere) one sometimes discovers extraordinary qualities one had never expected to find. And so I widened and entrenched my knowledge.

"To familiarize myself with other trades, other crafts and skills, other climates, and other living things, I set myself to visit distant countries, put myself to school with eminent foreigners, and remained with them until they had nothing more to teach me. But no matter where I went or how long I stayed, I remained a Greek. In the same way it is because I know and feel that you are a son of Greece that I am interested in you, my cousin.

"Once back in Crete, I told Minos all about my studies and my travels, and went on to tell him of a project I had cherished. This was to build and equip, not far from his palace (if he approved the plan and would provide the means to carry it out), a labyrinth like the one which I had admired in Egypt, on the shore of Lake Moeris; but mine would be different in plan. At the very moment Minos was in an awkward position. His queen had whelped a monster; not knowing how best to look after it, but judging it prudent to isolate it and keep it well away from the public gaze, he asked me to devise a building and a set of communicating gardens which, without precisely imprisoning the monster, would at least contain him and make it impossible for him to get loose. I lavished all my scholarship, all my best thoughts, on the task.

"But, believing that no prison can withstand a really obstinate intention to escape, and that there is no barrier, no ditch, that daring and resolution will not overcome, I thought that the best way of containing a prisoner in the labyrinth was to make it of such a kind, not that he couldn't get out (try to grasp my meaning here), but that he wouldn't want to get out. I therefore assembled in this one place the means to satisfy every kind of appetite. The Minotaur's tastes were neither many nor various; but we had to plan for everybody, whomsoever it might be, who would enter the labyrinth. Another and indeed the prime necessity was to fine down the visitor's will-power to the point of extinction. To this end I made up some electuaries and had them mixed with the wines that were served. But that was not enough; I found a better way. I had noticed that certain plants, when thrown into the fire, gave off, as they burned, semi-narcotic vapors. These seemed admirably suited to my purpose, and indeed they played exactly the part for which I needed them.

Accordingly I had them fed to the stoves, which are kept alight night and day. The heavy gases thus distributed not only act upon the will and put it to sleep; they induce a delicious intoxication, rich in flattering delusions, and provoke the mind, filled as this is with voluptuous mirages, to a certain pointless activity; 'pointless,' I say, because it has merely an imaginary outcome, in visions and speculations without order, logic, or substance. The effect of these gases is not the same for all of those who breathe them; each is led on by the complexities implicit in his own mind to lose himself, if I may so put it, in a labyrinth of his own devising. For my son Icarus, the complexities were metaphysical. For me, they take the form of enormous edifices, palatial buildings heaped upon themselves with an elaboration of corridors and staircases . . . in which (as with my son's speculations) everything leads to a blank wall, a mysterious 'keep out.' But the most surprising thing about these perfumes is that when one has inhaled them for a certain time, they are already indispensable; body and mind have formed a taste for this malicious insobriety; outside of it reality seems charmless and one no longer has any wish to return to it. And that — that above all — is what keeps one inside the labyrinth. Knowing that you want to enter it in order to fight the Minotaur, I give you fair warning; and if I have told you at length of this danger, it was to put you on your guard. You will never bring it off alone; Ariadne must go with you. But she must remain on the threshold and not so much as sniff the vapors. It is important that she should keep a clear head while you are being overcome by drunkenness. But even when drunk, you must keep control of yourself: everything depends on that. Your will alone may not suffice (for, as I told you, these emanations will weaken it), and so I have thought of this plan: to link you and Ariadne by a thread, the tangible symbol of duty. This thread will allow, indeed will compel you to rejoin her after you have been some time away. Be always determined not to break it, no matter what may be the charms of the labyrinth, the seduction of the unknown, or the headlong urging of your own courage. Go back to her, or all the rest, and the best with it, will be lost. This thread will be your link with the past. Go back to it. Go back to yourself. For nothing can begin from nothing, and it is from your past, and from what you are at this moment, that what you are going to be must spring.

"I should have spoken more briefly if I had not been so interested in you. But before you go out to meet your destiny, I want you to hear my son. You will realize more vividly, while listening to him, what danger you will presently run. Although he was able, thanks to me, to escape the witchcraft of the maze, his mind is still most pitiably a slave to its maleficence."

He walked over to a small door, lifted the arras that covered it, and said very loudly:

"Icarus, my dear son, come and tell us of your distress. Or, rather, go on thinking aloud, as if you were alone. Pay no attention to me or to my guest. Behave as if neither of us were here."

I saw coming in a young man of about my own age who seemed in the half-light to be of great beauty. His fair hair was worn very long and fell in ringlets to his shoulders. He stared fixedly, but seemed not to focus his gaze on anything in particular. Naked to the waist, he wore a tight metal belt and a loincloth, as it seemed to me, of leather and dark cloth; this swathed the top of his thighs, and was held in place by a curious and prominent knot. His white leather boots caught my eye, and seemed to suggest that he was making ready to go out; but his mind alone was on the move. Himself seemed not to see us. Proceeding no doubt with some unbroken chain of argument, he was saying:

"Who came first: man or woman? Can the Eternal One be female? From the womb of what great Mother have you come, all you myriad species? And by what engendering cause can that womb have been made great? Duality is inadmissible. In that case the god himself would be the son. My mind refuses to divide God. If once I allow division, strife begins. Where there are gods, there are wars. There are not gods, but a God. The kingdom of God is peace. All is absorbed, all is reconciled in the Unique Being."

He was silent for a moment and then went on:

"If man is to give a form to the gods, he must localize and reduce. God spreads where he will. The gods are divided. His extension is immense; theirs merely local."

He was silent again, before going on in a voice panting with anguish:

"But what is the reason for all this, O God who art lucidity itself? For so much trouble, so many struggles? And toward what? What is our purpose here? Why do we seek reasons for everything? Where are we to turn, if not toward God? How are we to direct our steps? Where are we to stop? When can we say: so be it; nothing more to be done? How can we reach God, after starting from man? And if I start from God, how can I reach across to myself? Yet if man is the creation of God, is not God the creation of man? It is at the exact crossing-place of those roads, at the very heart of that cross, that my mind would fix itself."

As he spoke, the veins swelled on his forehead, and the sweat ran down his temples. At least, so it seemed to me, for I could not see him clearly in the half-light; but I heard him gasping, like a man putting forth an immense effort.

He was quiet for a moment, then went on:

"I don't know where God begins, and still less where He ends. I shall even express myself more exactly if I say that His beginning never ends. Ah, how sick I am of 'therefore,' and 'since,' and 'because'! Sick of inference, sick of deduction. I never learn anything from the finest of syllogisms that I haven't first put into it myself. If I put God in at the beginning, He comes out at the end. I don't find Him unless I do put Him in. I have tramped all the roads of logic. On their horizontal plane I have wandered all too often. I crawl, and I would rather take wings; to lose my shadow, to lose the filth of my body, to throw off the weight of the past! The infinite calls me! I have the sensation of being drawn upwards from a great height. O mind of man, I shall climb to your topmost point. My father, with his great knowledge of mechanics, will provide me with the means to go. I shall travel alone. I'm not afraid. I can pay my way. It's my only chance to escape. O noble mind, too long entangled in the confusion of my problems, an uncharted road is waiting for you now. I cannot define what it is that summons me; but I know that my journey can have only one end: in God."

Then he backed away from us as far as the arras, which he raised and afterwards let drop behind him.

"Poor dear boy," said Dædalus. "As he thought he could never escape from the labyrinth and did not understand that the labyrinth was within himself, at his request I made him a set of wings, with which he was able to fly away. He thought that he could only escape by way of the heavens, all terrestrial routes being blocked. I knew him to be of a mystical turn, so that his longing did not surprise me. A longing that has not been fulfilled, as you will have been able to judge for yourself while listening to him. In spite of my warnings, he tried to fly too high and overtaxed his strength. He fell into the sea. He is dead."

"How can that be?" I burst out. "I saw him alive only a moment ago."

"Yes," he answered, "you did see him, and he seemed to be alive. But he is dead. At this point, Theseus, I am afraid that your intelligence, although Greek, and as such subtle and open to all aspects of the truth, cannot follow me; for I myself, I must confess, was slow to grasp and concede this fact: those of us whose souls, when weighed in the supreme scale, are not judged of too little account, do not just live an ordinary life. In time, as we mortals measure it, we grow up, accomplish our destiny, and die. But there is another, truer, eternal plane on which time does not exist; on this plane the representative gestures of our race are inscribed, each according to its particular significance. Icarus was, before his birth, and remains after his death, the image of man's disquiet, of the impulse to discovery, the soaring flight of poetry — the things of which, during his short life, he was the incarnation. He played out his hand, as he owed it to himself to do; but he didn't end there. What happens, in the case of a hero, is this: his mark endures. Poetry and the arts reanimate it, and it becomes an enduring symbol. That is how it is that Orion, the hunter, is riding still, across Elysian fields of asphodel, in search of the prey that he has already killed during his life; and meanwhile the night sky bears the eternal, constellated image of him and his baldric. That is how Tantalus' throat is parched to all eternity, and how Sisyphus still rolls upward toward an unattainable summit the heavy and ever rebounding weight of care that tormented him in the days when he was king of Corinth. For you must realize that in hell the only punishment is to begin over and over again the actions which, in life, one failed to complete.

"In the same way, in the animal kingdom, the death of each creature in no way impoverishes its species, for this retains its habitual shape and behavior; there are no individuals among the beasts. Whereas among men it is the individual alone who counts. That is why Minos is already leading at Knossos the life which will fit him for his career as a judge in hell. That is why Pasiphaë and Ariadne are yielding to their destiny in such exemplary fashion. And you yourself, Theseus, may appear carefree, and you may feel it, but you will not escape the destiny that is shaping you, any more than did Hercules, or Jason, or Perseus. But know this (because my eyes have learned the art of discerning the future through the present) — there remain great things for you to do, and in a sphere quite different from that of your previous exploits; things beside which these exploits will seem, in the future, to have been the amusements of a child. It remains for you to found the city of Athens, and there to situate the supremacy of the human mind.

"Do not linger, therefore, in the labyrinth, or in the embrace of Ariadne, after the hideous combat from which you will emerge triumphant. Keep on the move. Regard indolence as treachery. Seek no rest until, with your destiny completed, it is time to die. It is only thus that, on the farther side of what seems to be death, you will live, forever recreated by the gratitude of mankind. Keep on the move, keep well ahead, keep on your own road, O valiant gatherer of cities.

"And now listen carefully, Theseus, and remember what I say. No doubt you will have an easy victory over the Minotaur. Taken in the right way, he is not so redoubtable as people suppose. (They used to say that he lived on carrion; but since when has a bull eaten anything but grass?) Nothing is easier than to get into the labyrinth, nothing less easy than to get out. Nobody finds his way in there without first he lose it. And for your return journey (for footsteps leave no trace in the labyrinth) you must attach yourself to Ariadne by a thread. I have prepared several reels of this, and you will take them away with you. Unwind them as you make your way inside, and when the reel is exhausted, tie the end of the thread to the beginning of the next, so as never to have a break in the chain. Then on your way back you must rewind the thread until you come to the end, which Ariadne will have in her hand. I don't know why I insist so much, when all that part is as easy as good-morning. The real difficulty is to preserve unbroken, to the last inch of the thread, the will to come back; for the perfumes will make you forgetful, as will also your natural curiosity, which will conspire to make you weaken. I have told you this already and have nothing to add. Here are the reels. Good-by."

.   .   .

[*Encounter with Œdipus*]

Œdipus, when I welcomed him at Colonus, had been driven from Thebes, his fatherland; without eyes, dishonored, and wretched as he was, he at least had his two daughters with him, and in their constant tenderness he found relief from his sufferings. He had failed in every part of what he had undertaken. I have succeeded. Even the enduring blessing that his ashes are to confer upon the country where they are laid — even this will rest, not upon his ungrateful Thebes, but upon Athens.

I am surprised that so little should have been said about this meeting of our destinies at Colonus, this moment at the crossroads when our two careers confronted each other. I take it to have been the summit and the crown of my glory. Till then I had forced all life to do obeisance to me, and had seen all my fellow men bow in their turn (excepting only Dædalus, but he was my senior by many years; besides, even Dædalus gave me best in the end). In Œdipus alone did I recognize a nobility equal to my own. His misfortunes could only enhance his grandeur in my eyes. No doubt I had triumphed everywhere and always; but on a level which, in comparison with Œdipus, seemed to me merely human — inferior, I might say. He had held his own with the Sphinx; had stood man upright before the riddle of life, and dared to oppose him to the gods. How then, and why, had he accepted defeat? By putting out his eyes, had he not even contributed to it? There was something, in this dreadful act of violence against himself, that I could not contrive to under-

stand. I told him of my bewilderment. But his explanation, I must admit,
hardly satisfied me — or else I did not fully understand it.

"True," he said, "I yielded to an impulse of rage — one that could only
be directed against myself; against whom else could I have turned? In
face of the immeasurable horror of the accusations I had just discovered,
I felt an overwhelming desire to make a protest. And besides, what I
wanted to destroy was not so much my eyes themselves as the canvas they
held before me; the scenery before which I was struggling, the falsehood in
which I no longer believed; and this so as to break through to reality.

"And yet, no! I was not really thinking of anything very clearly; I
acted rather by instinct. I put out my eyes to punish them for having
failed to see the evidence that had, as people say, been staring me in the
face. But, to speak the truth — ah, how can I put it to you? . . . Nobody
understood me when I suddenly cried out: 'O darkness, my light!' And
you also, you don't understand it — I feel that distinctly. People heard
it as a cry of grief; it was a statement of fact. It meant that in my darkness I had found a source of supernatural light, illuminating the world
of the spirit. I meant: 'Darkness, thou art henceforth my light.' And
at the moment when the blue of the sky went black before me, my inward
firmament became bright with stars."

He was silent and for some moments remained deep in meditation.
Then he went on:

"As a young man, I passed for one who could see the future. I believed it myself, too. Was I not the first, the only man, to solve the riddle
of the Sphinx? Only since my eyes of flesh were torn with my own hand
from the world of appearances have I begun, it seems to me, to see truly.
Yes; at the moment when the outer world was hidden forever from the
eyes of my body, a kind of new eyesight opened out within myself upon
the infinite perspectives of an inner world, which the world of appearances (the only one which had existed for me until that time) had led me
to disdain. And this imperceptible world (inaccessible, I mean, to our
senses) is, I now know, the only true one. All the rest is an illusion, a
deception, moreover, that disturbs our contemplation of what is divine.
Tiresias, the blind sage, once said to me: 'Who wishes to see God must first
cease to see the world'; and I didn't understand him then: just as you,
yourself, O Theseus, do not understand me now."

"I shall not attempt to deny," I replied, "the importance of this world
beyond temporal things of which your blindness has made you aware;
but what I still cannot understand is why you oppose it to the outer world
in which we live and act."

"Because," said Œdipus, "for the first time, when with my inward eye I

perceived what was formerly hidden from me, I suddenly became aware
of this fact: that I had based my earthly sovereignty upon a crime, and
that everything which followed from this was in consequence tainted; not
merely all my personal decisions, but even those of the two sons to whom I
had abandoned my crown — for I at once stepped down from the slippery
eminence to which my crime had raised me. You must know already to
what new villainies my sons have allowed themselves to stoop, and what
an ignominious doom hangs over all that our sinful humanity may en-
gender; of this my unhappy sons are no more than a signal example. For,
as the fruits of an incestuous union, they are no doubt doubly branded;
but I believe that an original stain of some sort afflicts the whole human
race, in such a way that even the best bear its stripe, and are vowed to evil
and perdition; from all this man can never break free without divine aid
of some sort, for that alone can wash away his original sin and grant him
amnesty."

He was silent again for a few moments, as if preparing to plunge still
deeper, and then went on:

"You are astonished that I should have put out my eyes. I am astonished
myself. But in this gesture, inconsidered and cruel as it was, there may yet
be something else: an indefinable secret longing to follow my fortunes to
their farthest limit, to give the final turn of the screw to my anguish, and
to bring to a close the destiny of a hero. Perhaps I dimly foresaw the
grandeur of suffering and its power to redeem; that is why the true hero
is ashamed to turn away from it. I think that it is in fact the crowning
proof of his greatness, and that he is never worthier than when he falls
a victim; then does he exact the gratitude of heaven, and disarm the
vengeance of the gods. Be that as it may, and however deplorable my
mistakes may have been, the state of unearthly beatitude that I have been
able to reach is an ample reward for all the ills that I have had to suffer
— but for them, indeed, I should doubtless never have achieved it."

"Dear Œdipus," I said, when it was plain that he had finished speaking,
"I can only congratulate you on the kind of superhuman wisdom you
profess. But my thoughts can never march with yours along that road. I remain a child of this world, and I believe that man, be he what he
may, and with whatever blemishes you judge him to be stained, is in duty
bound to play out his hand to the end. No doubt you have learned to
make good use even of your misfortunes, and through them have drawn
nearer to what you call the divine world. I can well believe, too, that a
sort of benediction now attaches to your person, and that it will presently
be laid, as the oracles have said, upon the land in which you will take
your everlasting rest."

I did not add that what mattered to me was that this blessing should be laid upon Attica, and I congratulated myself that the god had made Thebes abut upon my country.

If I compare my lot with that of Œdipus, I am content: I have fulfilled my destiny. Behind me I leave the city of Athens. It has been dearer to me even than my wife and my son. My city stands. After I am gone, my thoughts will live on there forever. Lonely and consenting, I draw near to death. I have enjoyed the good things of the earth, and I am happy to think that after me, and thanks to me, men will recognize themselves as being happier, better, and more free. I have worked always for the good of those who are to come. I have lived.

Translated by John Russell

from *Henderson the Rain King*

[1963]

SAUL BELLOW

. . . The door banged, and we were in darkness. The king was running down the stairs.

Where the light came through the grating in the ceiling, that watery, stone-conditioned yellow light, I caught up with him.

He said, "Why are you blustering at me so with your face? You have a perilous expression."

I said, "King, it's the way I feel. I told you before I am mediumistic. And I feel trouble."

"No doubt, as there is trouble. But I will capture Gmilo and the trouble will entirely cease. No one will dispute or contest me then. There are scouts daily for Gmilo. As a matter of fact reports have come of him. I can assure you of a capture very soon."

I said fervently that I certainly hoped he would catch him and get the thing over with, so we could stop worrying about those two strangling characters, the Bunam and the black-leather man. Then they would stop persecuting his mother. At this second mention of his mother he looked angry. For the first time he subjected me to a long scowl. Then he resumed his way down the stairs. Shaken, I followed him. Well, I reflected, this black king happened to be a genius. Like Pascal at the age of twelve discovering the thirty-second proposition of Euclid all by himself.

But why lions?

Because, Mr. Henderson, I replied to myself, you don't know the meaning of true love if you think it can be deliberately selected. You just love, that's all. A natural force. Irresistible. He fell in love with his lioness at first sight — coup de foudre. I went crashing down the weed-grown part of the stairway engaged in this dialogue with myself. At the same time I held my breath as we approached the den. The cloud of fright about me was even more suffocating than before; it seemed to give actual resistance to my face and made my breathing clumsy. My respiration grew thick. Hearing us the beast began to roar in her inner room. Dahfu looked through the grating and said, "It is all right, we may go in."

"Now? You think she's okay? She sounds disturbed to me. Why don't I wait out here?" I said, "till you find out how the wind blows?"

"No, you must come," said the king. "Don't you understand yet, I am trying to do something for you? A benefit? I can hardly think of a person who may need this more. Really the danger of life is negligible. The animal is tame."

"Tame for you, but she doesn't really know me yet. I'm just as ready to take a reasonable chance as the next guy. But I can't help it, I am afraid of her."

He paused, and during this pause I thought I was going down greatly in his estimation, and nothing could have hurt me more than that. "Oh," he said, and he was particularly thoughtful. Silently he paused and thought. In this moment he looked and sounded, again, larger than life. "I think I recall when we were speaking of blows that there was a lack of the brave." Then he sighed and said, with his earnest mouth which even in the shadow of his hat had a very red color, "Fear is a ruler of mankind. It has the biggest dominion of all. It makes you white as candles. It splits each eye in half. More of fear than of any other thing has been created," he said. "As a molding force it comes second only to Nature itself."

"Then doesn't this apply to you, too?"

He said, with a nod of full agreement, "Oh, certainly. It applies to everyone. Though nothing may be visible, still it is heard, like radio. It is on almost all the frequencies. And all tremble, and all are wincing, in greater or lesser degree."

"And you think there is a cure?" I said.

"Why, I surely believe there is. Otherwise all the better imagining will have to be surrendered. Anyways, I will not urge you to come in with me and do as I have done. As my father Gmilo did. As we all did. No. If it is positively beyond you we may as well exchange good-by and go separate ways."

"Wait a minute now, King, don't be hasty," I said. I was mortified and frightened; nothing could have been more painful than to lose my connection with him. Something had gone off in my breast, my eyes filled, and I said, almost choking, "You wouldn't brush me off like that would you, King? You know how I feel." He realized how hard I was taking it; nevertheless he repeated that perhaps it would be better if I left, for although we were temperamentally suited as friends and he had deep affection for me, too, and was grateful for the opportunity to know me and also for my services to the Wariri in lifting up Mummah, still, unless I understood about lions, no deepening of the friendship was possible. I simply had to know what this was about. "Wait a minute, King," I said. "I feel tremendously close to you and I'm prepared to believe what you tell me."

"Sungo, thank you," he said. "I also am close to you. It is very mutual. But I require more deep relationship. I desire to be understood and communicated to. We have to develop an underlying similarity which lies within you by connection with the lion. Otherwise, how shall we maintain the truth agreement we made?"

Moved as anything, I said, "Oh, this is hard, King, to be threatened with loss of friendship."

The threat was exceedingly painful also to him. Yes, I saw that he suffered almost as hard as I did. Almost. Because who can suffer like me? I am to suffering what Gary is to smoke. One of the world's biggest operations.

"I don't understand it," I said.

He took me up to the door and made me look through the grating at Atti the lioness, and in that soft, personal tone peculiar to him which went strangely to the center of the subject, he said, "What a Christian might feel in Saint Sophia's church, which I visited in Turkey as a student, I absorb from lion. When she gives her tail a flex, it strikes against my heart. You ask, what can she do for you? Many things. First she is unavoidable. Test it, and you will find she is unavoidable. And this is what you need, as you are an avoider. Oh, you have accomplished momentous avoidances. But she will change that. She will make consciousness to shine. She will burnish you. She will force the present moment upon you. Second, lions are experiencers. But not in haste. They experience with deliberate luxury. The poet says, 'The tigers of wrath are wiser than the horses of instruction.' Let us embrace lions also in the same view. Moreover, observe Atti. Contemplate her. How does she stride, how does she saunter, how does she lie or gaze or rest or breathe? I stress the respiratory part," he said. "She do not breathe shallow. This freedom of the intercostal muscles and her abdominal flexibility" (her lower belly, which was disclosed to our view, was sheer white) "gives the vital continuity between her parts. It brings those brown jewel eyes their hotness. Then there are more subtle things, as how she leaves hints, or elicits caresses. But I cannot expect you to see this at first. She has much to teach you."

"Teach? You really mean that she might change me."

"Excellent. Precisely. Change. You fled what you were. You did not believe you had to perish. Once more, and a last time, you tried the world. With a hope of alteration. Oh, do not be surprised by such a recognition," he said, seeing how it moved me to discover that my position was understood. "You have told me much. You are frank. This makes you irresistible, as not many are. You have rudiments of high character. You could be noble. Some parts may be so long-buried as to be classed dead. Is there any resurrectibility in them? This is where the change comes in."

"You think there's a chance for me?" I said.

"Not at all impossible if you follow my directions."

The lioness stroked past the door. I heard her low, soft, continuous snarl.

Dahfu now started to go in. My nether half turned very cold. My knees felt like two rocks in a cold Alpine torrent. My mustache stabbed and stung into my lips, which made me realize that I was frowning and grimacing with terror, and I knew that my eyes must be filling with fatal blackness. As before, he took my hand as we entered and I came into the den saying inwardly, "Help me, God! Oh, help!" The odor was blinding, for here, near the door where the air was trapped, it stank radiantly. From this darkness came the face of the lioness, wrinkling, with her whiskers like the thinnest spindles scratched with a diamond on the surface of a glass. She allowed the king to fondle her, but passed by him to examine me, coming round with those clear circles of inhuman wrath, convex, brown, and pure, rings of black light within them. Between her mouth and nostrils a line divided her lip, like the waist of the hourglass, expanding into the muzzle. She sniffed my feet, working her way to the crotch once more and causing my parts to hide in my belly as best they could. She next put her head into my armpit and purred with such tremendous vibration it made my head buzz like a kettle.

Dahfu whispered, "She likes you. Oh, I am glad. I am enthusiastic. I am so proud of both of you. Are you afraid?"

I was bursting. I could only nod.

"Later you will laugh at yourself with amusement. Now it is normal."

"I can't even bring my hands together to wring them," I said.

"Feel paralysis?" he said.

The lioness went away, making a tour of the den along the walls on the thick pads of her feet.

"Can you see?" he said.

"Barely. I can barely see a single thing."

"Let us begin with the walk."

"Behind bars, I'd like that fine. It would be great."

"You are avoiding again, Henderson-Sungo." His eyes were looking at me from under the softly folded velvet brim. "Change does not lie that way. You must form a new habit."

"Oh, King, what can I do? My openings are screwed up tight, both back and front. They may go to the other extreme in a minute. My mouth is all dried out, my scalp is wrinkling up, I feel thick and heavy at the back of my head. I may be passing out."

I remember that he looked at me with keen curiosity, as if wondering about these symptoms from a medical standpoint. "All the resistances are putting forth their utmost," was his comment. It didn't seem possible that the black of his face could be exceeded, and yet his hair, visible at the borders of his hat, was blacker. "Well," he said, "we shall let them come out. I am firmly confident in you."

I said weakly, "I'm glad you think so. If I'm not torn to pieces. If I'm not left down here half-eaten."

"Take my assurance. No such eventuality is possible. Now, watch the way she walks. Beautiful? You said it! Furthermore this is uninstructed, specie-beauty. I believe when the fear has subsided you will be capable of admiring her beauty. I think that part of the beauty emotion does result from an overcoming of fear. When the fear yields, a beauty is disclosed in its place. This is also said of perfect love if I recollect, and it means that ego-emphasis is removed. Oh, Henderson, watch how she is rhythmical in behavior. Did you do the cat in Anatomy One? Watch how she gives her tail a flex. I feel it as if undergoing it personally. Now let us follow her." He began to lead me around after the lioness. I was bent over, and my legs were thick and drunken. The green silk pants no longer floated but were charged with electricity and clung to the back of my thighs. The king did not stop talking, which I was glad of, since his words were the sole support I had. His reasoning I couldn't follow in detail — I wasn't fit to — but gradually I understood that he wanted me to imitate or dramatize the behavior of lions. What is this going to be, I thought, the

Stanislavski method? The Moscow Art Theatre? My mother took a tour of Russia in 1905. On the eve of the Japanese War she saw the Czar's mistress perform in the ballet.

I said to the king, "And how does Obersteiner's allochiria and all that medical stuff you gave me to read come into this?"

He patiently said, "All the pieces fit properly. It will presently be clear. But first by means of the lion try to distinguish the states that are given and the states that are made. Observe that Atti is all lion. Does not take issue with the inherent. Is one hundred per cent within the given."

But I said in a broken voice, "If he doesn't try to be human, why should I try to act the lion? I'll never make it. If I have to copy someone, why can't it be you?"

"Oh, shush these objections, Henderson-Sungo. *I* copied her. Transfer from lion to man is possible, I know by experience." And then he shouted, "Sakta," which was a cue to the lioness to start running. She trotted, and the king began to bound after her, and I ran too, trying to keep close to him. "Sakta, sakta," he was crying, and she picked up speed. Now she was going fast along the opposite wall. In a few minutes she would come up behind me.

I started to call to him, "King, King, wait, let me go in front of you, for Christ's sake."

"Spring upward," he called back to me. But I was clumping and pounding after him trying to pass him, and sobbing. In the mind's eye I saw blood in great drops, bigger than quarters, spring from my skin as she sank her claws into me, for I was convinced that as I was in motion I was fair game and she would claw me as soon as she was within range. Or perhaps she would break my neck. I thought that might be preferable. One stroke, one dizzy moment, the mind fills with night. Ah, God! No stars in that night. There is nothing.

I could not catch up with the king, and therefore I pretended to stumble and threw myself heavily on the ground, off to the side, and gave a crazy cry. The king when he saw me prostrate on my belly held out his hand to Atti to stop her, shouting, "Tana, tana, Atti." She sprang sideward and began to walk toward the wooden shelf. From the dust I watched her. She gathered herself down upon her haunches and lightly reached the shelf on which she liked to lie. She pointed one leg outward and started to wash herself with her tongue. The king squatted beside her and said, "Are you hurt, Mr. Henderson?"

"No, I just got jolted," I said.

Then he began to explain. "I intend to loosen you up, Sungo, because you are so contracted. This is why we were running. The tendency of your conscious is to isolate self. This makes you extremely contracted and self-recoiled, so next I wish —"

"Next?" I said. "What next? I've had it. I'm humbled to the dust already. What else am I supposed to do, King, for heaven's sake? First I was stuck with a dead body, then thrown into the cattle pond, clobbered by the amazons. Okay. For the rain. Even the Sungo pants and all that. Okay! But now this?"

With much forbearance and sympathy he answered, picking up a pleated corner of his velvet headgear, the color of thick wine, "Patient, Sungo," he said. "Those aforementioned things were for us, for the Wariri. Do not think I am ever ingrate. But this latter is for you."

"That's what you keep saying. But how can this lion routine cure what I've got?"

The forward slope of the king's face suggested, as his mother's did, that it was being offered to you. "Oh," he said, "high conduct, high conduct! There will never be anything but misery without high conduct. I knew that you went out from home in America because of a privation of high conduct. You have met your first opportunities of it well, Henderson-Sungo, but you must go on. Take advantage of the studies I have made, which by chance are available to you."

I licked my hand, for I had scratched it in falling, and then I sat up, brooding. He squatted opposite me with his arms about his knees. He looked steadily at me across his large folded arms while he tried to make me meet his gaze.

"What do you want me to do?"

"As I have done. As Gmilo, Suffo, all the forefathers did. They all acted the lion. Each absorbed lion into himself. If you do as I wish, you too will act the lion."

If this body, if this flesh of mine were only a dream, then there might be some hope of awakening. That was what I thought as I lay there smarting. I lay, so to speak, at the bottom of things. Finally I sighed and started to get up, making one of the greatest efforts I have ever made. At this he said, "Why rise, Sungo, since we have you in a prone position?"

"What do you mean, prone position? Do you want me to crawl?"

"No, naturally not, crawl is for a different order of creature. But be on all fours. I wish you to assume the posture of a lion." He got on all fours himself, and I had to admit that he looked very much like a lion. Atti, with crossed paws, only occasionally looked at us.

"You see?" he said.

And I answered, "Well, you ought to be able to do it. You were brought up on it. Besides, it's your idea. But I can't." I slumped back on the ground.

"Oh," he said. "Mr. Henderson, Mr. Henderson! Is this the man who spoke of rising from a grave of solitude? Who recited me the poem of the little fly on the green leaf in the setting sun? Who wished to end Becoming? Is this the Henderson who flew half around the world because he had a voice which said *I want?* And now, because his friend Dahfu extends a remedy to him, falls down? You dismiss my relationship?"

"Now, King, that's not true. It's just not true, and you know it. I'd do anything for you."

To prove this, I rose up on my hands and feet and stood there with knees sagging, trying to look straight ahead and as much like a lion as possible.

"Oh, excellent," he said. "I am so glad. I was sure you had sufficient flexibility in you. Settle on your knees now. Oh, that is better, much better." My paunch came forward between my arms. "Your structure is far from ordinary," he said. "But I offer you sincerest congratulations on laying aside the former attitude of fixity. Now, sir, will you assume a little more limberness? You appear cast in one piece. The midriff dominates. Can you move the different portions? Minus yourself of some of your heavy reluctance of attitude. Why so sad and so earthen? Now you are a lion. Mentally, conceive of the environment. The sky, the sun, and creatures of the bush. You are related to all. The very gnats are your cousins. The sky is your thoughts. The leaves are your insurance, and you need no other. There is no interruption all night to the speech of the stars. Are you with me? I say, Mr. Henderson, have you consumed much amounts of alcohol in your life? The face suggests you have, the nose especially. It is nothing personal. Much can be changed. By no means all, but very very much. You can have a new poise, which will be your own poise. It will resemble the voice of Caruso, which I have heard on records, never tired because the function is as natural as to the birds. However," he said, "it is another animal you strongly remind me of. But of which?"

I wasn't going to tell him anything. My vocal cords, anyway, seemed stuck together like strands of overcooked spaghetti.

"Oh, truly! How very big you are," he said. He went on in this vein.

At last I found my voice and asked him, "How long do you want me to hold this?"

"I have been observing," he said. "It is very important that you feel *something* of a lion on your maiden attempt. Let us start with the roaring."

"It won't excite her, you think?"

"No, no. Now look, Mr. Henderson, I wish you to picture that you are a lion. A literal lion."

I moaned.

"No, sir. Please oblige me. A real roar. We must hear your voice. It tends to be rather choked. I told you the tendency of your conscious is to isolate self. So fancy you are with your kill. You are warning away an intruder. You may begin with a growl."

Having come so far with the guy there was no way to back out. Not one single alternative remained. I had to do it. So I began to make a rumble in my throat. I was in despair.

"More, more," he said impatiently. "Atti has taken no notice, therefore it is far from the thing."

I let the sound grow louder.

"And glare as you do so. Roar, roar, roar, Henderson-Sungo. Do not be afraid. Let go of yourself. Snarl greatly. Feel the lion. Lower on the fore-paws. Up with hindquarters. Threaten me. Open those magnificent mixed eyes. Oh, give more sound. Better, better," he said, "though still too much pathos. Give more sound. Now, with your hand — your paw — attack! Cuff! Fall back! Once more — strike, strike, strike, strike! Feel it. Be the beast! You will recover humanity later, but for the moment, be it utterly."

And so I was the beast. I gave myself to it, and all my sorrow came out in the roaring. My lungs supplied the air but the note came from my soul. The roaring scalded my throat and hurt the corners of my mouth and presently I filled the den like a bass organ pipe. This was where my heart had sent me, with its clamor. This is where I ended up. Oh, Nebuchadnezzar! How well I understand that prophecy of Daniel. For I had claws, and hair, and some teeth, and I was bursting with hot noise, but when all this had come forth, there was still a remainder. That last thing of all was my human longing.

As for the king, he was in a state of enthusiasm, praising me, rubbing his hands together, looking into my face. "Oh, good, Mr. Henderson. Good, good. You are the sort of man I took you to be," I heard him say when I stopped to draw breath. I might as well go the whole way, I thought, as I was crouching in the dust and the lion's offal, since I had come so far; therefore I gave it everything I had and roared my head off. Whenever I opened my bulging eyes I saw the king in his hat rejoicing by my side, and the lioness on the trestle staring at me, a creature entirely of gold sitting there.

When I could do no more I fell flat on my face. The king thought I might have passed out, and he felt my pulse and patted my cheeks saying,

"Come, come, dear fellow." I opened my eyes and he said, "Ah, are you okay? I worried about you. You went from crimson to black starting from the sternum and rising into the face."

"No, I'm all right. How am I doing?"

"Wonderfully, my brother Henderson. Believe me, it will prove beneficial. I will lead Atti away and let you take rest. We have done enough for the first time."

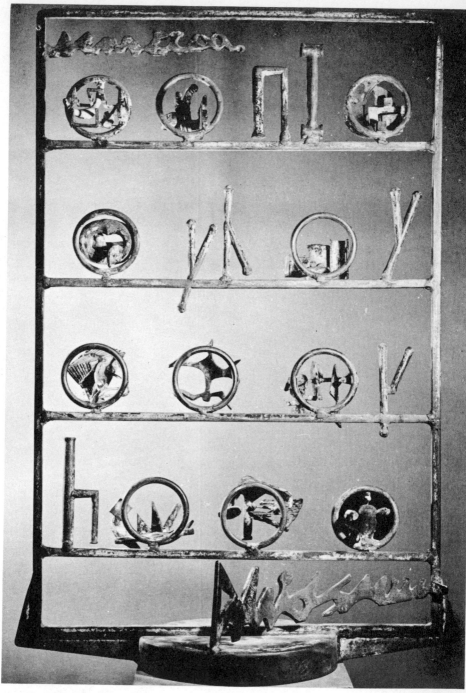

29. David Smith, *The Letter* (1950).

30. Alberto Giacometti, *Chariot* (1950).

A cage went in search of a bird.   FRANZ KAFKA

31. Pierre Bonnard,
The Breakfast Room
(c. 1930–1931).

Man is an animal with imagination.   GEORGE SANTAYANA

32. Henri Matisse, *Woman, Full Face, Beside an Aquarium* (1929).

33. Amedeo Modigliani, *Yellow Sweater* (1919?). The Solomon R. Guggenheim Museum.

Truth is not an ideal,
but a daily *way* of doing things. WILHELM REICH

34. Joan Miró, *Composition* (1933).

35. Paul Klee,
Lady Apart (1940).

The Kingdom of Heaven is within you. ST. LUKE

36. Giorgio de Chirico,
The Jewish Angel
or The Two Sisters
(1915).

37. Willem de Kooning,
Woman VI (1953).

But my God! it was my material,
and it was all I had to deal with.   F. SCOTT FITZGERALD

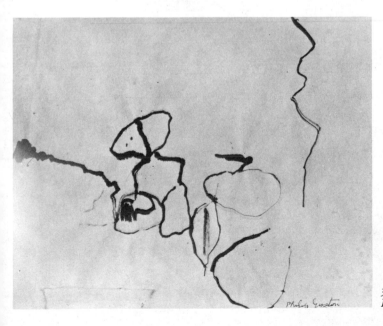

38. Philip Guston,
Drawing (1951).

39. Antonio Gaudí, *Facade of the Nativity of the Templo Expiatorio de la Sagrada Familia,* Barcelona.

40. Le Corbusier, *Notre-Dame du Haut,* Ronchamp (1950–1954).

Serve the Holy Ghost; never serve mankind.   D. H. LAWRENCE

I SA TAILLE

à Roland MANUEL

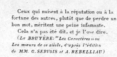

41. Erik Satie, from *Les Trois Valses Distinguées du Précieux Dégoûté.*

Ceux qui nuisent à la réputation ou à la fortune des autres, plutôt que de perdre un bon mot, méritent une peine infamante.
Cela n'a pas été dit, et je l'ose dire.
(*La BRUYÈRE*: "*Les Caractères*" ou *Les mœurs de ce siècle, d'après l'édition de MM. G. SERVOIS et A. REBELLIAU*)

It is wrong to be an "I," but it is more wrong to be a "we."

SIMONE WEIL

42. Igor Stravinsky, from *Petrouchka.*

43. George Bernard Shaw, scene from *Saint Joan* with Katharine Cornell and Maurice Evans.

Joan. O God that madest this beautiful earth,
when will it be ready to receive thy saints?
How long, O Lord, how long? G. B. SHAW

COMITATO PIRANDELLIANO
AGRIGENTO

" PRO MONUMENTO „

44. Luigi Pirandello.

. . . arrange things so that he watches himself in the act of living by placing a mirror before him . . . There will be some manifestation of pain and this is my theater. LUIGI PIRANDELLO

45. Charles Chaplin, scene from *City Lights*.

. . . gently gnashing apart the petals of his flower,
his soul, his offering, he perceives himself as he is . . .

JAMES AGEE

46. George Balanchine, rehearsal of *Agon* with Diana Adams
and Arthur Mitchell.

How hard and loving a gaze is required if we are to recognize
both God's hands at work, and press them both to our lips,
with due enthusiasm. GLENWAY WESCOTT

3

E. M. FORSTER *and* FRANZ KAFKA

"Only connect," said Forster, in the motto to one of his novels,
Howard's End. In his story "The Story of the Siren," and in
Kafka's parable "The Great Wall of China," the implicit mes-
sage is the same. God is not necessarily "dead." We are simply
not as easily, innocently, assumptively able to know him as we
once were. Despair is a presumption. We may have to discover
new resources in ourselves, and trust that the Emperor still
does want the great wall built, and that the Siren is always
there, for those who let themselves see her.

The Story of the Siren
[1928]

E. M. FORSTER

Few things have been more beautiful than my notebook on the
Deist Controversy as it fell downward through the waters of the Mediterranean. It dived, like a piece of black slate, but opened soon, disclosing
leaves of pale green, which quivered into blue. Now it had vanished, now
it was a piece of magical india-rubber stretching out to infinity, now it
was a book again, but bigger than the book of all knowledge. It grew
more fantastic as it reached the bottom, where a puff of sand welcomed
it and obscured it from view. But it reappeared, quite sane though a little
tremulous, lying decently open on its back, while unseen fingers fidgeted
among its leaves.

"It is such pity," said my aunt, "that you will not finish your work in the hotel. Then you would be free to enjoy yourself and this would never have happened."

"Nothing of it but will change into something rich and strange," warbled the chaplain, while his sister said, "Why, it's gone in the water!" As for the boatmen, one of them laughed, while the other, without a word of warning, stood up and began to take his clothes off.

"Holy Moses," cried the Colonel. "Is the fellow mad?"

"Yes, thank him, dear," said my aunt: "that is to say, tell him he is very kind, but perhaps another time."

"All the same I do want my book back," I complained. "It's for my Fellowship Dissertation. There won't be much left of it by another time."

"I have an idea," said some woman or other through her parasol. "Let us leave this child of nature to dive for the book while we go on to the other grotto. We can land him either on this rock or on the ledge inside, and he will be ready when we return."

The idea seemed good; and I improved it by saying I would be left behind too, to lighten the boat. So the two of us were deposited outside the little grotto on a great sunlit rock that guarded the harmonies within. Let us call them blue, though they suggest rather the spirit of what is clean — cleanliness passed from the domestic to the sublime, the cleanliness of all the sea gathered together and radiating light. The Blue Grotto at Capri contains only more blue water, not bluer water. That colour and that spirit are the heritage of every cave in the Mediterranean into which the sun can shine and the sea flow.

As soon as the boat left I realized how imprudent I had been to trust myself on a sloping rock with an unknown Sicilian. With a jerk he became alive, seizing my arm and saying, "Go to the end of the grotto, and I will show you something beautiful."

He made me jump off the rock on to the ledge over a dazzling crack of sea; he drew me away from the light till I was standing on the tiny beach of sand which emerged like powdered turquoise at the farther end. There he left me with his clothes, and returned swiftly to the summit of the entrance rock. For a moment he stood naked in the brilliant sun, looking down at the spot where the book lay. Then he crossed himself, raised his hands above his head, and dived.

If the book was wonderful, the man is past all description. His effect was that of a silver statue, alive beneath the sea, through whom life throbbed in blue and green. Something infinitely happy, infinitely wise — but it was impossible that it should emerge from the depths sunburned and dripping, holding the notebook on the Deist Controversy between its teeth.

A gratuity is generally expected by those who bathe. Whatever I offered, he was sure to want more, and I was disinclined for an argument in a place so beautiful and also so solitary. It was a relief that he should say in conversational tones, "In a place like this one might see the Siren."

I was delighted with him for thus falling into the key of his surroundings. We had been left together in a magic world, apart from all the commonplaces that are called reality, a world of blue whose floor was the sea and whose walls and roof of rock trembled with the sea's reflections. Here only the fantastic would be tolerable, and it was in that spirit I echoed his words, "One might easily see the Siren."

He watched me curiously while he dressed. I was parting the sticky leaves of the notebook as I sat on the sand.

"Ah," he said at last. "You may have read the little book that was printed last year. Who would have thought that our Siren would have given the foreigners pleasure!"

(I read it afterwards. Its account is, not unnaturally, incomplete, in spite of there being a woodcut of the young person, and the words of her song.)

"She comes out of this blue water, doesn't she," I suggested, "and sits on the rock at the entrance, combing her hair."

I wanted to draw him out, for I was interested in his sudden gravity, and there was a suggestion of irony in his last remark that puzzled me.

"Have you ever seen her?" he asked.

"Often and often."

"I, never."

"But you have heard her sing?"

He put on his coat and said impatiently, "How can she sing under the water? Who could? She sometimes tries, but nothing comes from her but great bubbles."

"She should climb on to the rock."

"How can she?" he cried again, quite angry. "The priests have blessed the air, so she cannot breathe it, and blessed the rocks, so that she cannot sit on them. But the sea no man can bless, because it is too big, and always changing. So she lives in the sea."

I was silent.

At this his face took a gentler expression. He looked at me as though something was on his mind, and going out to the entrance rock gazed at the external blue. Then returning into our twilight he said, "As a rule only good people see the Siren."

I made no comment. There was a pause, and he continued. "That is a very strange thing, and the priests do not know how to account for it; for she of course is wicked. Not only those who fast and go to Mass are in danger, but even those who are merely good in daily life. No one in the village had seen her for two generations. I am not surprised. We all cross ourselves before we enter the water, but it is unnecessary. Giuseppe, we thought, was safer than most. We loved him, and many of us he loved: but that is a different thing from being good."

I asked who Giuseppe was.

"That day — I was seventeen and my brother was twenty and a great deal stronger than I was, and it was the year when the visitors, who have brought such prosperity and so many alterations into the village, first began to come. One English lady in particular, of very high birth, came, and has written a book about the place, and it was through her that the Improvement Syndicate was formed, which is about to connect the hotels with the station by a funicular railway."

"Don't tell me about that lady in here," I observed.

"That day we took her and her friends to see the grottoes. As we rowed close under the cliffs I put out my hand, as one does, and caught a little crab, and having pulled off its claws offered it as a curiosity. The ladies groaned, but a gentleman was pleased, and held out money. Being inexperienced, I refused it, saying that his pleasure was sufficient reward! Giuseppe, who was rowing behind, was very angry with me and reached out with his hand and hit me on the side of the mouth, so that a tooth cut my lip, and I bled. I tried to hit him back, but he always was too quick for me, and as I stretched round he kicked me under the armpit, so that for a moment I could not even row. There was a great noise among the ladies, and I heard afterward that they were planning to take me away from my brother and train me as a waiter. That, at all events, never came to pass.

"When we reached the grotto — not here, but a larger one — the gentleman was very anxious that one of us should dive for money, and the ladies consented, as they sometimes do. Giuseppe, who had discovered how much pleasure it gives foreigners to see us in the water, refused to dive for anything but silver, and the gentleman threw in a two-lira piece.

"Just before my brother sprang off he caught sight of me holding my bruise, and crying, for I could not help it. He laughed and said, 'This time, at all events, I shall not see the Siren!' and went into the water without crossing himself. But he saw her."

He broke off and accepted a cigarette. I watched the golden entrance rock and the quivering walls and the magic water through which great bubbles constantly rose.

At last he dropped his hot ash into the ripples and turned his head away, and said, "He came up without the coin. We pulled him into the boat, and he was so large that he seemed to fill it, and so wet that we could not dress him. I have never seen a man so wet. I and the gentleman rowed back, and we covered Giuseppe with sacking and propped him up in the stern."

"He was drowned, then?" I murmured, supposing that to be the point.

"He was not," he cried angrily. "He saw the Siren. I told you."

I was silenced again.

"We put him to bed, though he was not ill. The doctor came, and took money, and the priest came and spattered him with holy water. But it was no good. He was too big — like a piece of the sea. He kissed the thumb-bones of San Biagio and they never dried till evening."

"What did he look like?" I ventured.

"Like any one who has seen the Siren. If you have seen her 'often and often' how is it you do not know? Unhappy, unhappy because he knew everything. Every living thing made him unhappy because he knew it would die. And all he cared to do was sleep."

I bent over my notebook.

"He did no work, he forgot to eat, he forgot whether he had his clothes on. All the work fell on me, and my sister had to go out to service. We tried to make him into a beggar, but he was too robust to inspire pity, and as for an idiot, he had not the right look in his eyes. He would stand in the street looking at people, and the more he looked at them the more unhappy he became. When a child was born he would cover his face with his hands. If any one was married — he was terrible then, and would frighten them as they came out of church. Who would have believed he would marry himself! I caused that, I. I was reading out of the paper how a girl at Ragusa had 'gone mad through bathing in the sea.' Giuseppe got up, and in a week he and that girl came in.

"He never told me anything, but it seems that he went straight to her house, broke into her room, and carried her off. She was the daughter of a rich mineowner, so you may imagine our peril. Her father came down, with a clever lawyer, but they could do no more than I. They argued and they threatened, but at last they had to go back and we lost nothing — that is to say, no money. We took Giuseppe and Maria to the church and had them married. Ugh! that wedding! The priest made no jokes afterward, and coming out the children threw stones. . . . I think I would have died to make her happy; but as always happens, one could do nothing."

"Were they unhappy together then?"

"They loved each other, but love is not happiness. We can all get love.

Love is nothing. I had two people to work for now, for she was like him in everything — one never knew which of them was speaking. I had to sell our own boat and work under the bad old man you have today. Worst of all, people began to hate us. The children first — everything begins with them — and then the women and last of all the men. For the cause of every misfortune was — You will not betray me?"

I promised good faith, and immediately he burst into the frantic blasphemy of one who has escaped from supervision, cursing the priests, who had ruined his life, he said. "Thus are we tricked!" was his cry, and he stood up and kicked at the azure ripples with his feet, till he had obscured them with a cloud of sand.

I too was moved. The story of Giuseppe, for all its absurdity and superstition, came nearer to reality than anything I had known before. I don't know why, but it filled me with desire to help others — the greatest of all our desires, I suppose, and the most fruitless. The desire soon passed.

"She was about to have a child. That was the end of everything. People said to me, 'When will your charming nephew be born? What a cheerful, attractive child he will be, with such a father and mother!' I kept my face steady and replied, 'I think he may be. Out of sadness shall come gladness' — it is one of our proverbs. And my answer frightened them very much, and they told the priests, who were frightened too. Then the whisper started that the child would be Antichrist. You need not be afraid: he was never born.

"An old witch began to prophesy, and no one stopped her. Giuseppe and the girl, she said, had silent devils, who could do little harm. But the child would always be speaking and laughing and perverting, and last of all he would go into the sea and fetch up the Siren into the air and all the world would see her and hear her sing. As soon as she sang, the Seven Vials would be opened and the Pope would die and Mongibello flame, and the veil of Santa Agata would be burned. Then the boy and the Siren would marry, and together they would rule the world, for ever and ever.

"The whole village was in tumult, and the hotel-keepers became alarmed, for the tourist season was just beginning. They met together and decided that Giuseppe and the girl must be sent inland until the child was born, and they subscribed the money. The night before they were to start there was a full moon and wind from the east, and all along the coast the sea shot up over the cliffs in silver clouds. It is a wonderful sight, and Maria said she must see it once more.

" 'Do not go,' I said. 'I saw the priest go by, and some one with him.

And the hotel-keepers do not like you to be seen, and if we displease them also we shall starve.'

" 'I want to go,' she replied. 'The sea is stormy, and I may never feel it again.'

" 'No, he is right,' said Giuseppe. 'Do not go — or let one of us go with you.'

" 'I want to go alone,' she said; and she went alone.

"I tied up their luggage in a piece of cloth, and then I was so unhappy at thinking I should lose them that I went and sat down by my brother and put my arm round his neck, and he put his arm round me, which he had not done for more than a year, and we remained thus I don't remember how long.

"Suddenly the door flew open and moonlight and wind came in together, and a child's voice said laughing, 'They have pushed her over the cliffs into the sea.'

"I stepped to the drawer where I keep my knives.

" 'Sit down again,' said Giuseppe — Giuseppe of all people! 'If she is dead, why should others die too?'

" 'I guess who it is,' I cried, 'and I will kill him.'

"I was almost out of the door, and he tripped me up and, kneeling upon me, took hold of both my hands and sprained my wrists; first my right one, then my left. No one but Giuseppe would have thought of such a thing. It hurt more than you would suppose, and I fainted. When I woke up, he was gone, and I never saw him again."

But Giuseppe disgusted me.

"I told you he was wicked," he said. "No one would have expected him to see the Siren."

"How do you know he did see her?"

"Because he did not see her 'often and often,' but once."

"Why do you love him if he is wicked?"

He laughed for the first time. That was his only reply.

"Is that the end?" I asked.

"I never killed her murderer, for by the time my wrists were well he was in America; and one cannot kill a priest. As for Giuseppe, he went all over the world too, looking for some one else who had seen the Siren — either a man, or, better still, a woman, for then the child might still have been born. At last he came to Liverpool — is the district probable? — and there he began to cough, and spat blood until he died.

"I do not suppose there is any one living now who has seen her. There has seldom been more than one in a generation, and never in my life will there be both a man and a woman from whom that child can be born, who will fetch up the Siren from the sea, and destroy silence, and save the world!"

"Save the world?" I cried. "Did the prophecy end like that?"

He leaned back against the rock, breathing deep. Through all the blue-green reflections I saw him colour. I heard him say: "Silence and loneliness cannot last for ever. It may be a hundred or a thousand years, but the sea lasts longer, and she shall come out of it and sing." I would have asked him more, but at that moment the whole cave darkened, and there rode in through its narrow entrance the returning boat.

The Great Wall of China
[1918]

FRANZ KAFKA

The Great Wall of China was finished off at its northernmost corner. From the south-east and the south-west it came up in two sections that finally converged there. This principle of piecemeal construction was also applied on a smaller scale by both of the two great armies of labour, the eastern and the western. It was done in this way: gangs of some twenty workers were formed who had to accomplish a length, say, of five hundred yards of wall, while a similar gang built another stretch of the same length to meet the first. But after the junction had been made the construction of the wall was not carried on from the point, let us say, where this thousand yards ended; instead the two groups of workers were transferred to begin building again in quite different neighbourhoods. Naturally in this way many great gaps were left, which were only filled in gradually and bit by bit, some, indeed, not till after the official announcement that the wall was finished. In fact it is said that there are gaps which have never been filled in at all, an assertion, however, which is probably merely one of the many legends to which the building of the wall gave rise, and which cannot be verified, at least by any single man with his own eyes and judgment, on account of the extent of the structure.

Now on first thoughts one might conceive that it would have been more advantageous in every way to build the wall continuously, or at least continuously within the two main divisions. After all the wall was intended, as was universally proclaimed and known, to be a protection against the peoples of the north. But how can a wall protect if it is not a continuous structure? Not only cannot such a wall protect, but what there is of it is in perpetual danger. These blocks of wall left standing in deserted regions could be easily pulled down again and again by the nomads, especially as these tribes, rendered apprehensive by the building operations, kept changing their encampments with incredible rapidity, like locusts, and so perhaps had a better general view of the progress of the wall than we, the builders. Nevertheless the task of construction probably could not have been carried out in any other way. To understand this we must take into account the following: The wall was to be a protection for centuries: accordingly the most scrupulous care in the building, the application of the architectural wisdom of all known ages and peoples, an unremitting sense of personal responsibility in the builders, were indispensable prerequisites for the work. True, for the more purely manual tasks ignorant day labourers from the populace, men, women and children who offered their services for good money, could be employed; but for the supervision even of every four day labourers an expert versed in the art of building was required, a man who was capable of entering into and feeling with all his heart what was involved. And the higher the task, the greater the responsibility. And such men were actually to be had, if not indeed so abundantly as the work of construction could have absorbed, yet in great numbers.

For the work had not been undertaken without thought. Fifty years before the first stone was laid the art of architecture, and especially that of masonry, had been proclaimed as the most important branch of knowledge throughout the whole area of a China that was to be walled round, and all other arts gained recognition only in so far as they had reference to it. I can still remember quite well us standing as small children, scarcely sure on our feet, in our teacher's garden, and being ordered to build a sort of wall out of pebbles; and then the teacher, girding up his robe, ran full tilt against the wall, of course knocking it down, and scolded us so terribly for the shoddiness of our work that we ran weeping in all directions to our parents. A trivial incident, but significant of the spirit of the time.

I was lucky inasmuch as the building of the wall was just beginning when, at twenty, I had passed the last examination of the lowest grade school. I say lucky, for many who before my time had achieved the highest degree of culture available to them could find nothing year after year to do with their knowledge, and drifted uselessly about with the most splendid architectural plans in their heads, and sank by thousands into hopelessness. But those who finally came to be employed in the work as supervisors, even though it might be of the lowest rank, were truly worthy of their task. They were masons who had reflected much, and did not cease to reflect, on the building of the wall, men who with the first stone which they sank in the ground felt themselves a part of the wall. Masons of that kind, of course, had not only a desire to perform their work in the most thorough manner, but were also impatient to see the wall finished in its complete perfection. Day labourers have not this impatience, for they look only to their wages, and the higher supervisors, indeed even the supervisors of middle rank, could see enough of the manifold growth of the construction to keep their spirits confident and high. But to encourage the subordinate supervisors, intellectually so vastly superior to their apparently petty tasks, other measures must be taken. One could not, for instance, expect them to lay one stone on another for months or even years on end, in an uninhabited mountainous region, hundreds of miles from their homes; the hopelessness of such hard toil, which yet could not reach completion even in the longest lifetime, would have cast them into despair and above all made them less capable for the work. It was for this reason that the system of piecemeal building was decided on. Five hundred yards could be accomplished in about five years; by that time, however, the supervisors were as a rule quite exhausted and had lost all faith in themselves, in the wall, in the world. Accordingly, while they were still exalted by the jubilant celebrations marking the completion of the thousand yards of wall, they were sent far, far away, saw on their journey finished sections of the wall rising here and there, came past the quarters of the high command and were presented with badges of honour, heard the rejoicings of new armies of labour streaming past from the depths of the land, saw forests being cut down to become supports for the wall, saw mountains being hewn into stones for the wall, heard at the holy shrines hymns rising in which the pious prayed for the completion of the wall. All this assuaged their impatience. The quiet life of their homes, where they rested some time, strengthened them; the humble credulity with which their reports were listened to, the confidence with which the simple and peaceful burgher believed in the eventual completion of the wall, all this tightened up again the cords of the soul. Like eternally hopeful children they then said farewell to their homes; the desire once more to labour on the wall of the nation became irresistible. They set off earlier than they needed; half the village accompanied them for long distances. Groups of people with banners and scarfs waving were on all the roads; never before had they seen how great and rich and beautiful and worthy of love their country was. Every fellow-countryman was a brother for whom one was building a wall of protection, and who would return lifelong thanks for it with all he had and did. Unity! Unity! Shoulder to shoulder, a ring of brothers, a current of blood no longer confined within the narrow circulation of one body, but sweetly rolling and yet ever returning throughout the endless leagues of China.

Thus, then, the system of piecemeal construction becomes comprehensible; but there were still other reasons for it as well. Nor is there anything odd in my pausing over this question for so long; it is one of the crucial problems in the whole building of the wall, unimportant as it may appear at first glance. If I am to convey and make understandable the ideas and feelings of that time I cannot go deeply enough into this very question.

First, then, it must be said that in those days things were achieved scarcely inferior to the construction of the Tower of Babel, although as regards divine approval, at least according to human reckoning, strongly at variance with that work. I say this because during the early days of building a scholar wrote a book in which he drew the comparison in the most exhaustive way. In it he tried to prove that the Tower of Babel failed to reach its goal, not because of the reasons universally advanced, or at least that among those recognised reasons the most important of all was not to be found. His proofs were drawn not merely from written documents and reports; he also claimed to have made enquiries on the spot, and to have discovered that the tower failed and was bound to fail because of the weakness of the foundation. In this respect at any rate our age was vastly superior to that ancient one. Almost every educated man of our time was a mason by profession and infallible in the matter of laying foundations. That, however, was not what our scholar was concerned to prove; for he maintained that the Great Wall alone would provide for the first time in the history of mankind a secure foundation for a new Tower of Babel. First the wall, therefore, and then the tower. His book was in everybody's hands at that time, but I admit that even to-day I cannot quite make out how he conceived this tower. How could the wall, which did not form even a circle, but only a sort of quarter or half-circle, provide the foundation for a tower? That could obviously be meant only in a spiritual sense. But in that case why build the actual wall, which after all was something concrete, the result of the lifelong labour of multitudes of people? And why were there in the book plans, somewhat nebulous plans, it must be admitted, of the tower, and pro-

posals worked out in detail for mobilising the people's energies for the
stupendous new work?

There were many wild ideas in people's heads at that time — this
scholar's book is only one example — perhaps simply because so many
were trying to join forces as far as they could for the achievement of a
single aim. Human nature, essentially changeable, unstable as the dust,
can endure no restraint; if it binds itself it soon begins to tear madly at
its bonds, until it rends everything asunder, the wall, the bonds and its
very self.

It is possible that these very considerations, which militated against
the building of the wall at all, were not left out of account by the high
command when the system of piecemeal construction was decided on.
We — and here I speak in the name of many people — did not really
know ourselves until we had carefully scrutinised the decrees of the high
command, when we discovered that without the high command neither
our book learning nor our human understanding would have sufficed
for the humble tasks which we performed in the great whole. In the
office of the command — where it was and who sat there no one whom I
have asked knew then or knows now — in that office one may be certain
that all human thoughts and desires were revolved, and counter to them
all human aims and fulfilments. And through the window the reflected
splendours of divine worlds fell on the hands of the leaders as they traced
their plans.

And for that reason the incorruptible observer must hold that the
command, if it had seriously desired it, could also have overcome those
difficulties which prevented a system of continuous construction. There
remains, therefore, nothing but the conclusion that the command deliberately chose the system of piecemeal construction. But the piecemeal
construction was only a makeshift and therefore inexpedient. Remains
the conclusion that the command willed something inexpedient. — Strange
conclusion! — True, and yet in one respect it has much to be said for it.
One can perhaps safely discuss it now. In those days many people, and
among them the best, had a secret maxim which ran: Try with all your
might to comprehend the decrees of the high command, but only up to a
certain point; then avoid further meditation. A very wise maxim, which
moreover was elaborated in a parable that was later often quoted: Avoid
further meditation, but not because it might be harmful; it is not at all
certain that it would be harmful. What is harmful or not harmful has
nothing to do with the question. Consider rather the river in spring. It
rises until it grows mightier and nourishes more richly the soil on the
long stretch of its banks, still maintaining its own course until it reaches

the sea, where it is all the more welcome because it is a worthier ally. —
Thus far may you urge your meditations on the decrees of the high command. — But after that the river overflows its banks, loses outline and
shape, slows down the speed of its current, tries to ignore its destiny by
forming little seas in the interior of the land, damages the fields, and yet
cannot maintain itself for long in its new expanse, but must run back
between its banks again, must even dry up wretchedly in the hot season
that presently follows. — Thus far may you not urge your meditations
on the decrees of the high command.

Now though this parable may have had extraordinary point and force
during the building of the wall, it has at most only a restricted relevance
for my present essay. My enquiry is purely historical; no lightning flashes
any longer from the long since vanished thunderclouds, and so I may
venture to seek for an explanation of the system of piecemeal construction which goes farther than the one that contented people then. The
limits which my capacity for thought imposes upon me are narrow
enough, but the province to be traversed here is infinite. Against whom
was the Great Wall to serve as a protection? Against the people of the
north. Now, I come from the south-east of China. No northern people can
menace us there. We read of them in the books of the ancients; the
cruelties which they commit in accordance with their nature make us
sigh beneath our peaceful trees. The faithful representations of the artist
show us these faces of the damned, their gaping mouths, their jaws furnished with great pointed teeth, their half-shut eyes that already seem to
be seeking out the victim which their jaws will rend and devour. When
our children are unruly we show them these pictures, and at once they
fly weeping into our arms. But nothing more than that do we know about
these northerners. We have not seen them, and if we remain in our villages we shall never see them, even if on their wild horses they should
ride as hard as they can straight towards us, — the land is too vast and
would not let them reach us, they would end their course in the empty air.

Why, then, since that is so, did we leave our homes, the stream with its
bridges, our mothers and fathers, our weeping wives, our children who
needed our care, and depart for the distant city to be trained there, while
our thoughts journeyed still farther away to the wall in the north? Why?
A question for the high command. Our leaders know us. They, absorbed
in gigantic anxieties, know of us, know our petty pursuits, see us sitting
together in our humble huts, and approve or disapprove the evening
prayer which the father of the house recites in the midst of his family.
And if I may be allowed to express such ideas about the high command,
then I must say that in my opinion the high command has existed from

old time, and was not assembled, say, like a gathering of mandarins sum-
moned hastily to discuss somebody's fine dream in a conference as hastily
terminated, so that that very evening the people are drummed out of
their beds to carry out what has been decided, even if it should be nothing
but an illumination in honour of a god who may have shown great favour
to their masters the day before, only to drive them into some dark corner
with cudgel blows to-morrow, almost before the illuminations have died
down. Far rather do I believe that the high command has existed from all
eternity, and the decision to build the wall likewise. Unwitting peoples
of the north, who imagined they were the cause of it! Honest, unwitting
Emperor, who imagined he decreed it! We builders of the wall know that
it was not so and hold our tongues.

   During the building of the wall and ever since to this very day I have
occupied myself almost exclusively with the comparative history of races
— there are certain questions which one can probe to the marrow, as it
were, only by this method — and I have discovered that we Chinese possess
certain folk and political institutions that are unique in their clarity,
others again unique in their obscurity. The desire to trace the causes of
these phenomena, especially the latter, has always teased me and teases
me still, and the building of the wall is itself essentially involved with these
problems.
   Now one of the most obscure of our institutions is that of the empire
itself. In Pekin, naturally, at the imperial court, there is some clarity to
be found on this subject, though even that is more illusive than real. Also
the teachers of political law and history in the high schools claim to be
exactly informed on these matters, and to be capable of passing on their
knowledge to their students. The farther one descends among the lower
schools the more, naturally enough, does one find teachers' and pupils'
doubts of their own knowledge vanishing, and superficial culture mounting sky-high round a few precepts that have been drilled into people's
minds for centuries, precepts which, though they have lost nothing of
their eternal truth, remain eternally invisible in this fog of confusion.
   But it is precisely this question of the empire which in my opinion the
common people should be asked to answer, since after all they are the
empire's final support. Here, I must confess, I can only speak once more
for my native place. Except for the nature gods and their ritual, which
fills the whole year in such beautiful and rich alternation, we think only
about the Emperor. But not about the present one; or rather we would
think about the present one if we knew who he was or knew anything
definite about him. True — and it is the sole curiosity that fills us — we

are always trying to get information on this subject, but, strange as it may sound, it is almost impossible to discover anything, either from pilgrims, though they have wandered through many lands, or from near or distant villages, or from sailors, though they have navigated not only our little stream, but also the sacred rivers. One hears a great many things, true, but can gather nothing definite.

So vast is our land that no fable could do justice to its vastness, the heavens can scarcely span it, — and Pekin is only a dot in it, and the imperial palace less than a dot. The Emperor as such, on the other hand, is mighty throughout all the hierarchies of the world: admitted. But the existent Emperor, a man like us, lies much like us on a couch which is of generous proportions, perhaps, and yet very possibly may be quite narrow and short. Like us he sometimes stretches himself and when he is very tired yawns with his delicately cut mouth. But how should we know anything about that — thousands of miles away in the South — almost on the borders of the Tibetan Highlands? And besides, any tidings, even if they did reach us, would arrive far too late, would have become obsolete long before they reached us. The Emperor is always surrounded by a brilliant and yet ambiguous throng of nobles and courtiers — malice and enmity in the guise of servants and friends — who form a counter-weight to the Imperial power and perpetually labour to unseat the ruler from his place with poisoned arrows. The Empire is immortal, but the Emperor himself totters and falls from his throne, yes, whole dynasties sink in the end and breathe their last in one death-rattle. Of these struggles and sufferings the people will never know; like tardy arrivals, like strangers in a city, they stand at the end of some densely thronged side street peacefully munching the food they have brought with them, while far away in front, in the market square at the heart of the city, the execution of their ruler is proceeding.

There is a parable that describes this situation very well: The Emperor, so it runs, has sent a message to you, the humble subject, the insignificant shadow cowering in the remotest distance before the imperial sun; the Emperor from his death-bed has sent a message to you alone. He has commanded the messenger to kneel down by the bed, and has whispered the message to him; so much store did he lay on it that he ordered the messenger to whisper it back into his ear again. Then by a nod of the head he has confirmed that it is right. Yes, before the assembled spectators of his death — all the obstructing walls have been broken down, and on the spacious and loftily-mounting open staircases stand in a ring the great princes of the Empire — before all these he has delivered his message. The messenger immediately sets out on his journey; a powerful, an indefatigable man; now pushing with his right arm, now with his left, he cleaves a way for himself through the throng; if he encounters resistance he points to his breast, where the symbol of the sun glitters; the way, too, is made easier for him than it would be for any other man. But the multitudes are so vast; their numbers have no end. If he could reach the open fields how fast he would fly, and soon doubtless you would hear the welcome hammering of his fists on your door. But instead how vainly does he wear out his strength; still he is only making his way through the chambers of the innermost palace; never will he get to the end of them; and if he succeeded in that nothing would be gained; he must fight his way next down the stair; and if he succeeded in that nothing would be gained; the courts would still have to be crossed; and after the courts the second outer palace; and once more stairs and courts; and once more another palace; and so on for thousands of years; and if at last he should burst through the outermost gate — but never, never can that happen — the imperial capital would lie before him, the centre of the world, crammed to bursting with its own refuse. Nobody could fight his way through here even with a message from a dead man. — But you sit at your window when evening falls and dream it to yourself.

Just so, as hopelessly and as hopefully, do our people regard the Emperor. They do not know what emperor is reigning, and there exist doubts regarding even the name of the dynasty. In school a great deal is taught about the dynasties with the dates of succession, but the universal uncertainty in this matter is so great that even the best scholars are drawn into it. Long-dead emperors are set on the throne in our villages, and one that only lives in song recently had a proclamation of his read out by the priest before the altar. Battles that are old history are new to us, and one's neighbour rushes in with a jubilant face to tell the news. The wives of the emperors, pampered and overweening, seduced from noble custom by wily courtiers, swelling with ambition, vehement in their greed, uncontrollable in their lust, practise their abominations ever anew. The more deeply they are buried in time the more glaring are the colours in which their deeds are painted, and with a loud cry of woe our village eventually hears how an Empress drank her husband's blood in long draughts thousands of years ago.

Thus, then, do our people deal with departed emperors, but the living ruler they confuse among the dead. If once, only once in a man's lifetime, an imperial official on his tour of the provinces should arrive by chance at our village, make certain announcements in the name of the government, scrutinise the tax lists, examine the school children, enquire of the priest regarding our doings and affairs, and then, before he steps into his litter, should sum up his impressions in verbose admonitions to the assembled commune, — then a smile flits over every face, each man throws a stolen glance at his neighbour, and bends over his children so as not to be observed by the official. Why, they think to themselves, he's speaking of a dead man as if he were alive, this Emperor of his died long ago, the dynasty is blotted out, the good official is having his joke with us, but we will behave as if we did not notice it, so as not to offend him. But we shall obey in earnest no one but our present ruler, for not to do so would be a crime. And behind the departing litter of the official there rises in might as ruler of the village some figure fortuitously exalted from an urn already crumbled to dust.

Similarly our people are but little affected by revolutions in the state or contemporary wars. I recall an incident in my youth. A revolt had broken out in a neighbouring, but yet quite distant, province. What caused it I can no longer remember, nor is it of any importance now; occasions for revolt can be found there any day, the people are an excitable people. Well, one day a leaflet published by the rebels was brought to my father's house by a beggar who had crossed that province. It happened to be a feast day, our rooms were filled with guests, the priest sat in the chief place and studied the sheet. Suddenly everybody started to laugh, in the confusion the sheet was torn, the beggar, who however had already received abundant alms, was driven out of the room with blows, the guests dispersed to enjoy the beautiful day. Why? The dialect of this neighbouring province differs in some essential respects from ours, and this difference occurs also in certain turns of the written speech, which for us have an archaic character. Hardly had the priest read out two lines before we had already come to our decision. Ancient history told long ago, old sorrows long since healed. And though — so it seems to me in recollection — the gruesomeness of the living present was irrefutably conveyed by the beggar's words, we laughed and shook our heads and refused to listen any longer. So eager are our people to obliterate the present.

If from such appearances any one should draw the conclusion that in reality we have no Emperor, he would not be far from the truth. Over and over again it must be repeated: There is perhaps no people more faithful to the Emperor than ours in the south, but the Emperor derives no advantage from our fidelity. True, the sacred dragon stands on the little column at the end of our village, and ever since the beginning of human memory it has breathed out its fiery breath in the direction of Pekin in token of homage — but Pekin itself is far stranger to the people in our village than the next world. Can there really be a village where the houses stand side by side, covering all the fields for a greater distance

than one can see from our hills, and can there be dense crowds of people
packed between these houses day and night? We find it more difficult to
picture such a city than to believe that Pekin and its Emperor are one, a
cloud, say, peacefully voyaging beneath the sun in the course of the ages.

Now the result of holding such opinions is a life on the whole free and
unconstrained. By no means immoral, however; hardly ever have I found
in my travels such pure morals as in my native village. But yet a life that
is subject to no contemporary law, and attends only to the exhortations
and warnings which come to us from olden times.

I guard against large generalisations, and do not assert that in all the
countless villages in my province it is so, far less in all the five hundred
provinces of China. Yet perhaps I may venture to assert on the basis of
the many writings on this subject which I have read, as well as from my
own observation — the building of the wall in particular, with its abundance of human material, provided a man of sensibility with the opportunity of traversing the souls of almost all the provinces — on the basis of
all this, then, perhaps I may venture to assert that the prevailing attitude
to the Emperor shows persistently and universally something fundamentally in common with that of our village. Now I have no wish whatever
to represent this attitude as a virtue; on the contrary. True, the essential
responsibility for it lies with the government, which in the most ancient
empire in the world has not yet succeeded in developing, or has neglected
to develop, the institution of the empire to such precision that its workings
extend directly and unceasingly to the farthest frontiers of the land. On
the other hand, however, there is also involved a certain feebleness of
faith and imaginative power on the part of the people, that prevents them
from raising the empire out of its stagnation in Pekin and clasping it in all
its palpable living reality to their own breasts, which yet desire nothing
better than but once to feel that touch and then to die.

This attitude then is certainly no virtue. All the more remarkable is it
that this very weakness should seem to be one of the greatest unifying
influences among our people; indeed, if one may dare to use the expression, the very ground on which we live. To set about establishing a
fundamental defect here would mean undermining not only our con-
sciences, but, what is far worse, our feet. And for that reason I shall not
proceed any further at this stage with my enquiry into these questions.

Translated by Willa and Edwin Muir

4

JEAN GENET *and* T. S. ELIOT

So man is a tightrope walker, and his existence is a pil-
grimage, and his life an Inside Job. "A cage," says one of
Kafka's shortest stories, "went in search of a bird."

The Funambulists

[1958]

JEAN GENET

 A gold spangle is a tiny gilt-metal disk with a hole in it. It is light
and thin and can float in water. At times, one or two remain clinging to
an acrobat's curls.

 The love — a love almost desperate, fraught with tenderness — that you
must show your wire will have as much strength as the wire shows in sup-
porting you. I know what objects are like, their malignity, their cruelty,
their gratitude too. The wire was dead — or, if you prefer, mute, blind.
You appear: it will live and speak.

 You will love it, with an almost carnal love. Every morning, when it
is taut and vibrating, go and kiss it before starting to practice. Ask it to
support you, ask that it accord you elegance and nervousness of limb. At
the end of the session, bow to it, thank it. At night, when it lies rolled up
in its box, go to see it, caress it. And lay your cheek against it fondly.

 There are tamers who use violence: You can try to tame your wire.
Beware. The wire, like the panther and, as it is said, the populace, likes
blood. Win it over rather.

 A blacksmith — only a broad-shouldered smith with a grizzly mustache
can dare venture such delicacies — used to greet his beloved every morning
with the words: "Well, my beauty!"

In the evening, when his day's work was done, his big paw would stroke her. The anvil was not insensitive to this treatment, and the smith knew how it thrilled her.

Charge your wire with the finest expression not of *your* self but of *its* self. You will perform your dances, your leaps and bounds — in acrobats' lingo: your heel-and-toe, kowtows, somersaults, cartwheels, etc. — not so that *you* may shine but that a steel wire which was dead and voiceless can at last sing. How grateful it will be if your bearing is perfect for the sake of its glory and not of yours!

Let the bedazzled spectators applaud it:

"What an amazing wire! The way it supports its dancer! And how it loves him!"

The wire, in turn, will make you the most marvelous dancer.

The ground will make you totter.

Who, before you, was aware of the longing that lurked in the soul of a quarter-inch steel wire? Who else was aware that it knew it was destined to make a dancer turn round in the air and click his heels? Nobody, you were the first. Know, therefore, its joy and gratitude.

I would not be surprised if, when you walk on the ground, you fall and sprain your ankle. The wire will support you better and more surely than a road.

I casually open his wallet and go through its contents. Among old photos, pay slips and lapsed bus tickets, I find a folded sheet of paper on which he has drawn curious signs: along a straight line, which represents the wire, oblique strokes to the right, strokes to the left — these are his feet, or rather the positions of his feet. They are the steps he will take. Next to each stroke is a number. Since he is trying to bring rigor, the discipline of numbers, to an art that was subject only to haphazard, empirical training, he will triumph.

So what does it matter whether he can read? He knows figures well enough to measure rhythms and numbers. Joanovici, that subtle calculator, was an illiterate Jew or Gypsy. He made a great fortune selling scrap iron during one of our wars.

. . . "a deathly solitude". . .

At a bar you can joke and have a drink with anyone you like. But the arrival of the Angel is announced. Be alone to receive him. The Angel, for us, is the evening that descends on the dazzling ring. It matters not a bit that your solitude is, paradoxically, in full light and that the darkness is composed of thousands of eyes which are judging you, and which fear and hope you will fall. You will dance in and over a desertlike solitude, blindfolded, if you can, with your eyelids buttoned. But nothing

— and above all not applause or laughter — will keep you from dancing for your image. You are an artist — alas — you can no longer reject the monstrous precipice of your eyes. Is Narcissus dancing? But it is other than a matter of coquetry, egoism and self-love. What if it were a matter of Death itself? So dance alone. Pale, livid, anxious to please or displease your image: but, it is your image that will dance for you.

If your love — and your skill and guile — are great enough to discover the secret possibilities of the wire, if the precision of your movements is perfect, it will rush to meet your foot (capped with leather): it is not you who will be dancing, but the wire. But if it is the wire that dances motionless, and if it is your image that the wire bounces, then where will you be?

Death — the Death of which I speak — is not the death that will follow your fall, but the one which precedes your appearance on the wire. It is before mounting the wire that you die. The person who will dance will be dead — intent upon and capable of all beauties. When you appear, a pallor — I am speaking not of fear but of its opposite, an invincible boldness — a pallor will spread over you. Despite your make-up and spangles, you will be ghastly, your soul will be livid. It is then that your precision will be perfect. No longer attached to the ground, you will be able to dance without falling. But see to it that you die before appearing and that it is a dead man who dances on the wire.

And what of your wound, where is it?

Where, I wonder, is the hiding place of the secret wound to which all men rush for shelter if their pride is hurt when it is wounded? It is the wound — which thus becomes the man's innermost being — that he will inflate, will fill. Every man knows how to attain it, to the point of becoming the wound itself, a kind of secret and aching heart.

If we look, with swift and avid gaze, at the passing man or woman [1] — or dog too, or bird, or pot — the very swiftness of our glance will sharply reveal to us the wound into which they will withdraw when there is danger. Indeed they are already there, attaining solitude by means of and for the wound, whose form they have assumed: their whole being is in the slouch of their shoulders which they have made their very self; their entire life empties into a mean curl of the lips against which they are — and want to remain — powerless, since it is by virtue of that sneer that they are aware of this absolute, incommunicable solitude — that castle of the soul — and that they become that solitude itself. As for our acrobat, it is visible in his sad gaze, which should reflect the images of a wretched, unforgettable childhood in which he knew he was abandoned.

It is into this wound — incurable because it is himself — and into this solitude that he must hurl himself; he will be able to discover there the strength, skill and boldness necessary to his art.

Mind what I have to say: the better to deliver yourself to Death, to make it inhabit you with the strictest exactitude, you will have to keep in perfect health. The slightest disorder would restore you to our life. The block of absence which you are going to become would be broken. A kind of dampness would spread over you and cover you with mildew. Look after your health.

If I advise him to avoid luxury in his private life, if I advise him to be a little dirty, to wear sloppy clothes, down-at-the-heel shoes, it is so that at night, in the ring, the estrangement may be the greater, so that the day's entire hope may be exalted by the approach of the fête, so that a tension may be born of the distance from an apparent poverty to the most splendid appearance, a tension such that the dance will be like a discharge or cry; it is because the reality of the Circus lies in this metamorphosis of dust into gold dust, but it is, above all, because he who is to generate this admirable image must be dead, or, if one prefers, must trudge along on earth like the lowliest, most pathetic, of human beings. I would even go so far as to advise him to limp, to cover himself with rags, with lice, and to stink. Let his person diminish more and more so that the image I speak of, in which a dead man dwells, can shine with increasing brilliance. In short, let him exist only in his appearing.

I obviously did not mean that an acrobat who operates twenty-five or thirty feet from the ground should entrust himself to God (funambulists, to the Virgin), that he should pray and cross himself before entering the ring because death is under the big tent. I was speaking to the artist alone, as to the poet. Were you to dance only a yard above the mat, my injunction would be the same. I meant, as you realize, the deathly solitude, the desperate and radiant region in which the artist operates.

I add, nevertheless, that you must risk actual, physical death. The dramaturgy of the Circus requires it. The Circus, like poetry, war and bullfighting, is one of the cruel games that remain. Danger has its function: it will oblige your muscles to achieve perfect exactitude — the slightest error will cause a fall that will cripple or kill you — and this exactitude will be the beauty of your dance.

If he dreams when he is alone, and if he dreams of himself, he probably sees himself in his glory, and he has no doubt tried a hundred, a thousand times to grasp his future image: himself on the wire one triumphant evening. Thus, he strives to represent himself as he would like to be. And it is in order to become what he wants to be, what he dreams he is, that he exerts himself. To be sure, it is a far cry from that fancied image to what he will be on the real wire. Yet that is what he is aiming at: to resemble, later, the image of himself which he is inventing today. And he does so in order that, when he has been seen on the wire, there remain in the spectator's memory only an image identical to that which he is inventing today. An odd project: to dream one's self, to make manifest a dream that will then become a dream in other heads!

The frightful death, the frightful monster lying in wait for you, is vanquished by the Death of which I have spoken.

Your make-up? Excessive. Garish. Let it extend your eyes as far as your hair. Your nails will be painted. Does anyone in his right mind walk on a wire or express himself in verse? It's sheer madness. Man or woman? Unquestionably a monster. Rather than aggravate the peculiarity of such behavior, the make-up will attenuate it, will make clear to the audience that an embellished, gilded, painted, ambiguous creature is walking, without a balancing pole, where plumbers and lawyers would never dream of going.

Therefore, let him be so sumptuously made up as to provoke nausea when he appears.

I shall try to make myself more clear.

In order to acquire the absolute silence he needs to materialize his work — which is drawn from a void that it will, at the same time, fill and make manifest — the poet can exhibit himself in whatever posture is most perilous to him. He clearly thrusts aside any curious observer, or friend or inducement that tries to orient his work toward the world. If he wishes, he can do this by emitting an odor so nauseating, so dark, that he himself is lost in it. He will be alone. His apparent malediction will enable him to be supremely audacious since he is undisturbed by any gaze. He now moves in an element akin to death: the desert. His word awakens no echo. Since what it has to utter is no longer addressed to anyone, no longer needs to be understood by what is alive, it will be ordained by a necessity that is an exigency not of life but of death.

Solitude, as I have told you, can be accorded only by the presence of the audience. You must therefore proceed otherwise and take another line of conduct. Artificially, by an effect of will, you must internalize this insensitivity to the world. As its waves rise up to you — like the coldness that started in Socrates' feet and rose to his legs, thighs and stomach — their coldness grips your heart and freezes it. — No, no, again no, you do not come to entertain the audience but to fascinate it.

Admit that it would have a curious feeling — of stupor, of panic — if it happened to see a corpse walking on the wire this evening!

— "Their coldness grips your heart and freezes it" . . . but — and this is most mysterious — there must, at the same time, escape from you a kind of vapor, a light vapor that does not blur your angles, a vapor signifying that at your center is a source which keeps feeding the icy death that entered you by your feet.

What of your costume? Both chaste and provocative. The clinging tights of the circus. Red jersey, blood-red. It displays your muscular contours to perfection, it sheathes you, it gloves you, but from the collar — open-necked, cleanly cut, as if the executioner were going to chop off your head this evening — from your collar to your hip a sash, likewise red, but with the flaps — gold-fringed — hanging loosely. The red slippers, the sash, the belt, the edge of the collar, and the ribbons below the knee are embroidered with gold spangles. No doubt so that you sparkle, but chiefly so that, while going from your dressing room to the ring, you lose in the sawdust a few loose spangles, delicate emblems of the Circus. During the day, when you go to the grocer's, they fall from your hair. One of them is stuck to your shoulder with sweat.

The bulging basket of your tights will be embroidered with a gold dragon.

I tell him about Camilla Meyer — but I would also like to talk about that splendid Mexican, Con Colleano, and how he danced! — Camilla Meyer was a German woman. When I saw her she must have been about forty. She had set up her wire a hundred feet above the cobblestones of the Cour du Vieux-Port in Marseilles. It was nighttime. The hundred-foot-high horizontal wire was lit by projectors. In order to get to it she made her way up an oblique wire — about seven hundred feet long — that started from the ground. Half-way up the slope, she rested by placing one knee on the wire and keeping the balancing pole on her thigh. Her son (he was about sixteen), who was waiting for her on a little platform, brought a chair to the middle of the wire, and Camilla Meyer, who came from the other end, reached the horizontal wire. She took the chair, only two legs of which rested on the wire, and sat down on it. Alone. She got off it, alone . . . Down below, beneath her, all the heads had lowered. Hands were covering the eyes. The audience was thus refusing the acrobat the courtesy of making an effort to keep their eyes on her as she courted death.

"What about you?" he asked. "What did you do?"

"I watched. In order to help her, to salute her. Because she had led death to the edge of darkness so that it might accompany her in her fall and death."

If you fall, you will merit the most conventional funeral oration: pool of gold and blood, pond in which the setting sun . . . You must expect nothing else. The circus is all convention.

Beware of strutting into the ring. You enter: a series of bounds, somersaults, pirouettes and cartwheels brings you to the foot of your apparatus and you dance to the top of it. From your very first bound (prepared in the wings) the audience knows it will follow you from marvel to marvel.

And dance!

But be taut. Your body will have the arrogant vigor of a tumid, excited member. That's why I advised you to dance before your image and to be in love with it. Let's face the fact: it's Narcissus who is dancing. But the dance is only your body's effort to identify itself with your image as felt by the spectator. You are now *more* than mere mechanical, harmonious perfection: heat emanates from you and warms us. Your belly burns. However, don't dance for us but for yourself. We came to the Circus not to see a whore but a solitary lover pursuing his image that flees and vanishes on a steel wire. And always in the infernal realm. Hence, it is this solitude that will fascinate us.

The Spanish crowd awaits, among other things, the moment when, with a toss of its horns, the bull slashes the toreador's breeches: through the rip, his blood and genitals. Folly of the nudity that does not strive to show and then exalt a wound! So you must wear tights, for you must be clothed. The tights will be illustrated: embroidered suns, stars, irises, birds . . . A pair of tights to protect the acrobat from the hardness of the audience's gaze, and so that an accident is possible, so that one evening the tights can give way, can tear.

Need I say it? I would not mind his assuming, during the day, the outward appearance of a toothless old female tramp with a gray wig. Seeing her, one would know an athlete was reposing beneath the tatters, and one would respect the great distance between day and night. Appearing in the evening! And he, the acrobat, not knowing which is his higher being: the verminous tramp or the sparkling solitary. Or the constant movement from her to him?

Why dance this evening? Why leap and bound in the glare of projectors eight yards from the mat, on a wire? Because you must find yourself. You are both hunter and hunted, and this evening you have driven yourself from cover, you are seeking and fleeing yourself. Where were you before entering the ring? Drearily dispersed in your everyday, commonplace gestures, you did not exist. In the light, you feel the need of martializing yourself. Every evening, for yourself alone, you will run along the wire, twisting and writhing in the quest of the harmonious being scattered and lost in the thicket of your familiar gestures: tying your shoelaces, blowing your nose, scratching yourself, buying soap . . . But you approach and attain yourself only for an instant. And always in that white, deathly solitude.

I come back to your wire: remember that you owe your grace to your wire's virtues. No doubt to yours too, but yours exist only to reveal and exhibit those of the wire. The game will enhance both of you: play with the wire. Provoke it with your toe, surprise it with your heel. Don't be afraid to be cruel to each other: though it cuts, it will make you glitter. But be careful always to observe the most exquisite politeness.

Know over whom you triumph. Over us, but . . . your dance will be charged with hatred.

One is not an artist without an element of great heartache.

Hatred of what god? And why vanquish him?

The hunt on the wire, the pursuit of your image — and the arrows with which you riddle it (without touching it), with which you wound it and make it radiant — is thus a fête. If you overtake the image, you achieve the Fête.

I feel a kind of odd thirst, I would like to drink, that is, to suffer, that is, to drink, but let the drunkenness come from the suffering that is a fête. Sickness, hunger, or prison cannot make you unhappy, since nothing forces you to be so. Be so because of your art. What do we care — you and I — about a good acrobat? You who burn will be that blazing wonder which lasts a few minutes. You burn. On your wire you are lightning. Or, if you will, a lone dancer. It is a terrible despair that makes you dance, a despair lit up by something that brightens you, consumes you. The audience? It sees only flame, and, thinking that you are performing, unaware that you are the incendiary, it applauds the fire.

Be hot. And excite the audience. The heat that issues from you and radiates is your desire for yourself — or for your image — a desire never satisfied.

Gothic legend tells of tumblers who, having nothing else, offered their stunts to the Virgin. They danced in front of the cathedrals. I don't know to what god you will address your feats of dexterity, but you need one, perhaps the one you will make exist for an hour and for your dance. Before entering the ring you were merely one of the motley crowd in the wings. Nothing distinguished you from the other acrobats, jugglers, trapezists, equestrians, ring boys and clowns. Nothing, except the sadness already in your eyes. And let it stay there. Otherwise you will be chasing all poetry from your face! — God does not yet exist for anyone . . . you arrange your dressing gown, you brush your teeth . . . Your gestures can be withheld . . .

Money? Make all you can. The dancer should rake it in till he bursts with it . . . He will have to disorganize his life in every possible way. Money can then be useful, since it entails a kind of rot that can vitiate the quietest of souls. Lots, lots of dough! Let him be filthy with it! And let it pile up in a corner of his hovel, let him never touch it. When evening approaches, he must wake up, must tear himself from this evil and at night dance on the wire.

I also tell him:

"You've got to work at becoming famous."

"Why?"

"In order to hurt."

"Is it absolutely necessary for me to earn all that dough?"

"It is. You'll appear on your wire so as to be sprayed with a shower of gold. But since your dance is all that interests you, you'll rot during the day."

So let him rot in a certain way. Let him be crushed, be sickened, by a stench that vanishes at the first clarion of evening.

. . . But you enter. If you dance for the audience, it will know you do, and that'll be the end of you. It will be on familiar terms with you. No longer fascinated, it will settle heavily into itself and you'll never pull it out again.

You enter, and you are alone. Seemingly, for God is present. I have no idea where he comes from. Perhaps you brought him with you when you entered, perhaps solitude evokes him, it makes no difference. It's for him that you hunt your image. You dance. Your face is shut. Your bearing is right, your movement precise. Impossible to withdraw, or you die for eternity. Severe and pale, dance, and, if possible, with your eyes closed.

Of what God am I speaking? I wonder. But he is absolute judgment and absence of criticism. He witnesses your quest. Either he accepts you and you sparkle, or else he turns away. If you have chosen to dance before him alone, you cannot escape from the exactitude of your bodily language, of which you become prisoner: you cannot fall.

Is God then merely the sum of all the possibilities of your will applied to your body on the steel wire? Divine possibilities!

In practice sessions your somersault sometimes escapes from you. Don't be afraid to regard your leaps as restive beasts that it's your job to dominate. The leap is inside you, untamed, dispersed — therefore unhappy. Do what you must to give it human form.

. . . "red, star-spangled tights." I want you to wear the most traditional of costumes so that you get lost more easily in your image and, if you want to carry away your wire, so that both of you finally disappear. But on that narrow path which comes from and leads nowhere — its twenty-foot length is an infinite line and a cage — you can also perform a drama.

And who knows? What if you fall from the wire? You will be carried away on a stretcher. The band will play. The tigers or the bareback rider will be brought in.

At the circus, as at the theatre, the performance takes place in the evening, at nightfall, but it can also be given in broad daylight.

We go to the theatre to enter the vestibule, the anti-chamber, of sleep, that precarious death, for the spectacle that takes place when day is done is a Fête, the gravest of fêtes and the last, something very close to our funeral. When the curtain rises, we enter a place where infernal simulacra are being prepared. The fête takes place in the evening so that it can be pure, so that it can unfold without the risk of being interrupted by a thought, by a practical demand that might mar it . . .

But the Circus! It requires full, sharp attention. It is not our fête that is being given there. It is a game of skill which requires that we remain wide awake.

The audience, which makes it possible for you to exist — without it you would never have the solitude of which I have spoken — the audience is the beast that you finally stab. Your perfection, and your boldness, will, during the time you perform, annihilate it.

Impoliteness of the audience: during your most perilous movements the spectators will shut their eyes. They shut their eyes when, in order to dazzle them, you are skirting death.

This leads me to say that you must love the Circus and scorn the world. A huge beast, risen up from diluvian times, settles heavily on cities: one enters, and the monster was full of cruel and mechanical marvels: bareback riders, clowns, lions and their tamer, a conjuror, a juggler, German trapezists, a horse that talks and counts, and you.

You are, all of you, the residue of a fabulous age. You have come down to us from ancient times. Your ancestors ate ground glass and fire, they charmed snakes and doves, they juggled with eggs, they made horses sit in council and talk.

You are not prepared for our world and its logic. You must therefore accept the hardship of living at night on the illusion of your deadly craft. During the day you stand anxiously at the circus door — not daring to enter our lives — too firmly held back by the powers of the circus which are the powers of death. Don't ever leave that huge canvas belly.

Outside is disorder, discordant noise; inside is the genealogical certainty that comes from the ages, the security of knowing you are linked in a kind of factory where your acts are shaped, the precise acts that serve the solemn display of yourselves, that prepare the Fête. You live only for the Fête. Not for the one to which good citizens treat themselves by paying. I speak of your brief illustriousness. Obscurely, in the monster's flank, you have realized that each of us must aim for that, must try to appear to himself in his apotheosis. The performance changes you, for a few minutes, into yourself. Your brief tomb illuminates us. You are locked up in it, and, at the same time, your image keeps escaping from it. It would be prodigious if you had the power to fix yourself — in both the ring and the sky — in the form of a constellation. Few heroes have this privilege.

But for ten seconds — is that little? — you scintillate.

When you practice, don't worry about having lost your skill. You start by displaying great dexterity, but before long you must despair of the wire, your stunts, the Circus, and the dance.

You will go through a bitter period — a kind of Hell — and after wandering in the dark forest you will rise up again, master of your art.

That is one of the most thrilling mysteries: after a brilliant period every artist goes through a land of despair where he is in danger of losing his reason and his mastery. If he emerges victorious . . .

Don't be afraid to regard your leaps and bounds as a herd of animals. Within you they lived in the wild state. Unsure of themselves, they tore at and mutilated each other or interbred at random. Take your flock to pasture. Let each live on good terms with the other. Crossbreed them, if you like, but carefully, not as a matter of whim. You are now the pastor of a flock of animals that were hitherto disorderly and aimless. Thanks to your charms, they are obedient and skilful. Your leaps and bounds and stunts were within you but were unaware of it. Thanks to your charms, they know that they are and that they are yourself, illustrating you.

This is all futile, inept advice. No one could possibly follow it. But I wanted only to write a poem about this art, a poem whose warmth will rise to your cheeks. My aim was not to teach you but inflame you.

Translated by Bernard Frechtman

East Coker

from *Four Quartets*

[1940]

T. S. ELIOT

I

In my beginning is my end. In succession
Houses rise and fall, crumble, are extended,
Are removed, destroyed, restored, or in their place
Is an open field, or a factory, or a by-pass.
Old stone to new building, old timber to new fires,
Old fires to ashes, and ashes to the earth
Which is already flesh, fur and faeces,
Bone of man and beast, cornstalk and leaf.
Houses live and die: there is a time for building
And a time for living and for generation
And a time for the wind to break the loosened pane
And to shake the wainscot where the field-mouse trots
And to shake the tattered arras woven with a silent motto.

In my beginning is my end. Now the light falls
Across the open field, leaving the deep lane
Shuttered with branches, dark in the afternoon,
Where you lean against a bank while a van passes,
And the deep lane insists on the direction
Into the village, in the electric heat
Hypnotised. In a warm haze the sultry light
Is absorbed, not refracted, by grey stone.
The dahlias sleep in the empty silence.
Wait for the early owl.

                    In that open field
If you do not come too close, if you do not come too close,
On a summer midnight, you can hear the music

Of the weak pipe and the little drum
And see them dancing around the bonfire
The association of man and woman
In daunsinge, signifying matrimonie —
A dignified and commodious sacrament.
Two and two, necessarye coniunction,
Holding eche other by the hand or the arm
Whiche betokeneth concorde. Round and round the fire
Leaping through the flames, or joined in circles,
Rustically solemn or in rustic laughter
Lifting heavy feet in clumsy shoes,
Earth feet, loam feet, lifted in country mirth
Mirth of those long since under earth
Nourishing the corn. Keeping time,
Keeping the rhythm in their dancing
As in their living in the living seasons
The time of the seasons and the constellations
The time of milking and the time of harvest
The time of the coupling of man and woman
And that of beasts. Feet rising and falling.
Eating and drinking. Dung and death.

   Dawn points, and another day
Prepares for heat and silence. Out at sea the dawn wind
Wrinkles and slides. I am here
Or there, or elsewhere. In my beginning.

II

What is the late November doing
With the disturbance of the spring
And creatures of the summer heat,
And snowdrops writhing under feet
And hollyhocks that aim too high
Red into grey and tumble down
Late roses filled with early snow?
Thunder rolled by the rolling stars
Simulates triumphal cars
Deployed in constellated wars
Scorpion fights against the Sun
Until the Sun and Moon go down

Comets weep and Leonids fly
Hunt the heavens and the plains
Whirled in a vortex that shall bring
The world to that destructive fire
Which burns before the ice-cap reigns.

That was a way of putting it — not very satisfactory:
A periphrastic study in a worn-out poetical fashion,
Leaving one still with the intolerable wrestle
With words and meanings. The poetry does not matter.
It was not (to start again) what one had expected.
What was to be the value of the long looked forward to,
Long hoped for calm, the autumnal serenity
And the wisdom of age? Had they deceived us,
Or deceived themselves, the quiet-voiced elders,
Bequeathing us merely a receipt for deceit?
The serenity only a deliberate hebetude,
The wisdom only the knowledge of dead secrets
Useless in the darkness into which they peered
Or from which they turned their eyes. There is, it seems to us,
At best, only a limited value
In the knowledge derived from experience.
The knowledge imposes a pattern, and falsifies,
For the pattern is new in every moment
And every moment is a new and shocking
Valuation of all we have been. We are only undeceived
Of that which, deceiving, could no longer harm.
In the middle, not only in the middle of the way
But all the way, in a dark wood, in a bramble,
On the edge of a grimpen, where is no secure foothold,
And menaced by monsters, fancy lights,
Risking enchantment. Do not let me hear
Of the wisdom of old men, but rather of their folly,
Their fear of fear and frenzy, their fear of possession,
Of belonging to another, or to others, or to God.
The only wisdom we can hope to acquire
Is the wisdom of humility: humility is endless.

The houses are all gone under the sea.

The dancers are all gone under the hill.

III

O dark dark dark. They all go into the dark,
The vacant interstellar spaces, the vacant into the vacant,
The captains, merchant bankers, eminent men of letters,
The generous patrons of art, the statesmen and the rulers,
Distinguished civil servants, chairman of many committees,
Industrial lords and petty contractors, all go into the dark,
And dark the Sun and Moon, and the Almanach de Gotha
And the Stock Exchange Gazette, the Directory of Directors,
And cold the sense and lost the motive of action.
And we all go with them, into the silent funeral,
Nobody's funeral, for there is no one to bury.
I said to my soul, be still, and let the dark come upon you
Which shall be the darkness of God. As, in a theatre,
The lights are extinguished, for the scene to be changed
With a hollow rumble of wings, with a movement of darkness
     on darkness,
And we know that the hills and the trees, the distant panorama
And the bold imposing façade are all being rolled away —
Or as, when an underground train, in the tube, stops too long
     between stations
And the conversation rises and slowly fades into silence
And you see behind every face the mental emptiness deepen
Leaving only the growing terror of nothing to think about;
Or when, under ether, the mind is conscious but conscious of
     nothing —
I said to my soul, be still, and wait without hope
For hope would be hope for the wrong thing; wait without love
For love would be love of the wrong thing; there is yet faith
But the faith and the love and the hope are all in the waiting.
Wait without thought, for you are not ready for thought:
So the darkness shall be the light, and the stillness the dancing.
Whisper of running streams, and winter lightning.
The wild thyme unseen and the wild strawberry,
The laughter in the garden, echoed ecstasy
Not lost, but requiring, pointing to the agony
Of death and birth.

                     You say I am repeating
Something I have said before. I shall say it again.
Shall I say it again? In order to arrive there,

To arrive where you are, to get from where you are not,
    You must go by a way wherein there is no ecstasy.
In order to arrive at what you do not know
    You must go by a way which is the way of ignorance.
In order to possess what you do not possess
    You must go by the way of dispossession.
In order to arrive at what you are not
    You must go through the way in which you are not.
And what you do not know is the only thing you know
And what you own is what you do not own
And where you are is where you are not.

IV

The wounded surgeon plies the steel
That questions the distempered part;
Beneath the bleeding hands we feel
The sharp compassion of the healer's art
Resolving the enigma of the fever chart.

Our only health is the disease
If we obey the dying nurse
Whose constant care is not to please
But to remind of our, and Adam's curse,
And that, to be restored, our sickness must grow worse.

The whole earth is our hospital
Endowed by the ruined millionaire,
Wherein, if we do well, we shall
Die of the absolute paternal care
That will not leave us, but prevents us everywhere.

The chill ascends from feet to knees,
The fever sings in mental wires.
If to be warmed, then I must freeze
And quake in frigid purgatorial fires
Of which the flame is roses, and the smoke is briars.

The dripping blood our only drink,
The bloody flesh our only food:
In spite of which we like to think
That we are sound, substantial flesh and blood —
Again, in spite of that, we call this Friday good.

V

So here I am, in the middle way, having had twenty years —
Twenty years largely wasted, the years of *l'entre deux guerres* —
Trying to learn to use words, and every attempt
Is a wholly new start, and a different kind of failure
Because one has only learnt to get the better of words
For the thing one no longer has to say, or the way in which
One is no longer disposed to say it. And so each venture
Is a new beginning, a raid on the inarticulate
With shabby equipment always deteriorating
In the general mess of imprecision of feeling,
Undisciplined squads of emotion. And what there is to conquer
By strength and submission, has already been discovered
Once or twice, or several times, by men whom one cannot hope
To emulate — but there is no competition —
There is only the fight to recover what has been lost
And found and lost again and again: and now, under conditions
That seem unpropitious. But perhaps neither gain nor loss.
For us, there is only the trying. The rest is not our business.

Home is where one starts from. As we grow older
The world becomes stranger, the pattern more complicated
Of dead and living. Not the intense moment
Isolated, with no before and after,
But a lifetime burning in every moment
And not the lifetime of one man only
But of old stones that cannot be deciphered.
There is a time for the evening under starlight,
A time for the evening under lamplight
(The evening with the photograph album).
Love is most nearly itself
When here and now cease to matter.
Old men ought to be explorers
Here and there does not matter
We must be still and still moving
Into another intensity
For a further union, a deeper communion
Through the dark cold and the empty desolation,
The wave cry, the wind cry, the vast waters
Of the petrel and the porpoise. In my end is my beginning.

5

SIMONE WEIL *and* RAINER MARIA RILKE

But it is hard to refuse, like Simone Weil, to join the com-
munity of the Catholic Church; or like the Christ of Rilke's
poem, to stand in the hot, dusty garden of Gethsemane, with
the inner vision suddenly withdrawn, and have only yourself,
and that infinite point at your dead center at which "the
Kingdom of Heaven" is located, to turn to.

Spiritual Autobiography
from *Waiting for God*
[1942]

SIMONE WEIL

P.S. To be read first.

This letter is fearfully long — but as there is no question of an answer —
especially as I shall doubtless have gone before it reaches you — you have
years ahead of you in which to read it if you care to. Read it all the
same, one day or another.

From Marseilles, about May 15

Father,

Before leaving I want to speak to you again, it may be the last
time perhaps, for over there I shall probably send you only my news
from time to time just so as to have yours.

I told you that I owed you an enormous debt. I want to try to tell you
exactly what it consists of. I think that if you could really understand

366

what my spiritual state is you would not be at all sorry that you did not lead me to baptism. But I do not know if it is possible for you to understand this.

You neither brought me the Christian inspiration nor did you bring me to Christ; for when I met you there was no longer any need; it had been done without the intervention of any human being. If it had been otherwise, if I had not already been won, not only implicitly but consciously, you would have given me nothing, because I should have received nothing from you. My friendship for you would have been a reason for me to refuse your message, for I should have been afraid of the possibilities of error and illusion which human influence in the divine order is likely to involve.

I may say that never at any moment in my life have I "sought for God." For this reason, which is probably too subjective, I do not like this expression and it strikes me as false. As soon as I reached adolescence, I saw the problem of God as a problem the data of which could not be obtained here below, and I decided that the only way of being sure not to reach a wrong solution, which seemed to me the greatest possible evil, was to leave it alone. So I left it alone. I neither affirmed nor denied anything. It seemed to me useless to solve the problem, for I thought that, being in this world, our business was to adopt the best attitude with regard to the problems of this world, and that such an attitude did not depend upon the solution of the problem of God.

This held good as far as I was concerned at any rate, for I never hesitated in my choice of an attitude; I always adopted the Christian attitude as the only possible one. I might say that I was born, I grew up, and I always remained within the Christian inspiration. While the very name of God had no part in my thoughts, with regard to the problems of this world and this life I shared the Christian conception in an explicit and rigorous manner, with the most specific notions it involves. Some of these notions have been part of my outlook for as far back as I can remember. With others I know the time and manner of their coming and the form under which they imposed themselves upon me.

For instance I never allowed myself to think of a future state, but I always believed that the instant of death is the center and object of life. I used to think that, for those who live as they should, it is the instant when, for an infinitesimal fraction of time, pure truth, naked, certain, and eternal enters the soul. I may say that I never desired any other good for myself. I thought that the life leading to this good is not only defined by a code of morals common to all, but that for each one it consists of a succession of acts and events strictly personal to him, and so essential that he who leaves them on one side never reaches the goal. The notion of vocation was like this for me. I saw that the carrying out of a vocation differed from the actions dictated by reason or inclination in that it was due to an impulse of an essentially and manifestly different order; and not to follow such an impulse when it made itself felt, even if it demanded impossibilities, seemed to me the greatest of all ills. Hence my conception of obedience; and I put this conception to the test when I entered the factory and stayed on there, even when I was in that state of intense and uninterrupted misery about which I recently told you. The most beautiful life possible has always seemed to me to be one where everything is determined, either by the pressure of circumstances or by impulses such as I have just mentioned and where there is never any room for choice.

At fourteen I fell into one of those fits of bottomless despair that come with adolescence, and I seriously thought of dying because of the mediocrity of my natural faculties. The exceptional gifts of my brother, who had a childhood and youth comparable to those of Pascal, brought my own inferiority home to me. I did not mind having no visible successes, but what did grieve me was the idea of being excluded from that transcendent kingdom to which only the truly great have access and wherein truth abides. I preferred to die rather than live without that truth. After months of inward darkness, I suddenly had the everlasting conviction that any human being, even though practically devoid of natural faculties, can penetrate to the kingdom of truth reserved for genius, if only he longs for truth and perpetually concentrates all his attention upon its attainment. He thus becomes a genius too, even though for lack of talent his genius cannot be visible from outside. Later on, when the strain of headaches caused the feeble faculties I possess to be invaded by a paralysis, which I was quick to imagine as probably incurable, the same conviction led me to persevere for ten years in an effort of concentrated attention that was practically unsupported by any hope of results.

Under the name of truth I also included beauty, virtue, and every kind of goodness, so that for me it was a question of a conception of the relationship between grace and desire. The conviction that had come to me was that when one hungers for bread one does not receive stones. But at that time I had not read the Gospel.

Just as I was certain that desire has in itself an efficacy in the realm of spiritual goodness whatever its form, I thought it was also possible that it might not be effective in any other realm.

As for the spirit of poverty, I do not remember any moment when it was not in me, although only to that unhappily small extent compatible with my imperfection. I fell in love with Saint Francis of Assisi as soon as I came to know about him. I always believed and hoped that one day Fate would force upon me the condition of a vagabond and a beggar which he embraced freely. Actually I felt the same way about prison.

From my earliest childhood I always had also the Christian idea of love for one's neighbor, to which I gave the name of justice — a name it bears in many passages of the Gospel and which is so beautiful. You know that on this point I have failed seriously several times.

The duty of acceptance in all that concerns the will of God, whatever it may be, was impressed upon my mind as the first and most necessary of all duties from the time when I found it set down in Marcus Aurelius under the form of the *amor fati* of the Stoics. I saw it as a duty we cannot fail in without dishonoring ourselves.

The idea of purity, with all that this word can imply for a Christian, took possession of me at the age of sixteen, after a period of several months during which I had been going through the emotional unrest natural in adolescence. This idea came to me when I was contemplating a mountain landscape and little by little it was imposed upon me in an irresistible manner.

Of course I knew quite well that my conception of life was Christian. That is why it never occurred to me that I could enter the Christian community. I had the idea that I was born inside. But to add dogma to this conception of life, without being forced to do so by indisputable evidence, would have seemed to me like a lack of honesty. I should even have thought I was lacking in honesty had I considered the question of the truth of dogma as a problem for myself or even had I simply desired to reach a conclusion on this subject. I have an extremely severe standard for intellectual honesty, so severe that I never met anyone who did not seem to fall short of it in more than one respect; and I am always afraid of failing in it myself.

Keeping away from dogma in this way, I was prevented by a sort of shame from going into churches, though all the same I like being in them. Nevertheless, I had three contacts with Catholicism that really counted.

After my year in the factory, before going back to teaching, I had been taken by my parents to Portugal, and while there I left them to go alone to a little village. I was, as it were, in pieces, soul and body. That contact with affliction had killed my youth. Until then I had not had any experience of affliction, unless we count my own, which, as it was my own, seemed to me, to have little importance, and which moreover was only a partial affliction, being biological and not social. I knew quite well that there was a great deal of affliction in the world, I was obsessed with the idea, but I had not had prolonged and first-hand experience of it. As I worked in the factory, indistinguishable to all eyes, including my own, from the anonymous mass, the affliction of others entered into my flesh and my soul. Nothing separated me from it, for I had really forgotten my past and I looked forward to no future, finding it difficult to imagine the possibility of surviving all the fatigue. What I went through there marked me in so lasting a manner that still today when any human being, whoever he may be and in whatever circumstances, speaks to me without brutality, I cannot help having the impression that there must be a mistake and that unfortunately the mistake will in all probability disappear. There I received forever the mark of a slave, like the branding of the red-hot iron the Romans put on the foreheads of their most despised slaves. Since then I have always regarded myself as a slave.

In this state of mind then, and in a wretched condition physically, I entered the little Portuguese village, which, alas, was very wretched too, on the very day of the festival of its patron saint. It was the evening and there was a full moon over the sea. The wives of the fishermen were, in procession, making a tour of all the ships, carrying candles and singing what must certainly be very ancient hymns of a heart-rending sadness. Nothing can give any idea of it. I have never heard anything so poignant unless it were the song of the boatmen on the Volga. There the conviction was suddenly borne in upon me that Christianity is pre-eminently the religion of slaves, that slaves cannot help belonging to it, and I among others.

In 1937 I had two marvelous days at Assisi. There, alone in the little twelfth-century Romanesque chapel of Santa Maria degli Angeli, an incomparable marvel of purity where Saint Francis often used to pray, something stronger than I was compelled me for the first time in my life to go down on my knees.

In 1938 I spent ten days at Solesmes, from Palm Sunday to Easter Tuesday, following all the liturgical services. I was suffering from splitting headaches; each sound hurt me like a blow; by an extreme effort of concentration I was able to rise above this wretched flesh, to leave it to suffer by itself, heaped up in a corner, and to find a pure and perfect joy in the unimaginable beauty of the chanting and the words. This experience enabled me by analogy to get a better understanding of the possibility of loving divine love in the midst of affliction. It goes without saying that in the course of these services the thought of the Passion of Christ entered into my being once and for all.

There was a young English Catholic there from whom I gained my first idea of the supernatural power of the sacraments because of the truly angelic radiance with which he seemed to be clothed after going to communion. Chance — for I always prefer saying chance rather than Providence — made of him a messenger to me. For he told me of the existence of those English poets of the seventeenth century who are named metaphysical. In reading them later on, I discovered the poem of which I read you what is unfortunately a very inadequate translation. It is called "Love." [1] I learned it by heart. Often, at the culminating point of a violent headache, I make myself say it over, concentrating all my attention upon it and clinging with all my soul to the tenderness it enshrines. I used to think I was merely reciting it as a beautiful poem, but without my knowing it the recitation had the virtue of a prayer. It was during one of these recitations that, as I told you, Christ himself came down and took possession of me.

In my arguments about the insolubility of the problem of God I had never foreseen the possibility of that, of a real contact, person to person, here below, between a human being and God. I had vaguely heard tell of things of this kind, but I had never believed in them. In the *Fioretti* the accounts of apparitions rather put me off if anything, like the miracles in the Gospel. Moreover, in this sudden possession of me by Christ, neither my senses nor my imagination had any part; I only felt in the midst of my suffering the presence of a love, like that which one can read in the smile on a beloved face.

I had never read any mystical works because I had never felt any call to read them. In reading as in other things I have always striven to practice obedience. There is nothing more favorable to intellectual progress, for as far as possible I only read what I am hungry for at the moment when I have an appetite for it, and then I do not read, I *eat*. God in his mercy had prevented me from reading the mystics, so that it should be evident to me that I had not invented this absolutely unexpected contact.

Yet I still half refused, not my love but my intelligence. For it seemed to me certain, and I still think so today, that one can never wrestle enough with God if one does so out of pure regard for the truth. Christ likes us to prefer truth to him because, before being Christ, he is truth. If one turns aside from him to go toward the truth, one will not go far before falling into his arms.

After this I came to feel that Plato was a mystic, that all the *Iliad* is bathed in Christian light, and that Dionysus and Osiris are in a certain sense Christ himself; and my love was thereby redoubled.

I never wondered whether Jesus was or was not the Incarnation of God;

but in fact I was incapable of thinking of him without thinking of him as God.

In the spring of 1940 I read the *Bhagavad-Gita*. Strange to say it was in reading those marvelous words, words with such a Christian sound, put into the mouth of an incarnation of God, that I came to feel strongly that we owe an allegiance to religious truth which is quite different from the admiration we accord to a beautiful poem; it is something far more categorical.

Yet I did not believe it to be possible for me to consider the question of baptism. I felt that I could not honestly give up my opinions concerning the non-Christian religions and concerning Israel — and as a matter of fact time and meditation have only served to strengthen them — and I thought that this constituted an absolute obstacle. I did not imagine it as possible that a priest could even dream of granting me baptism. If I had not met you, I should never have considered the problem of baptism as a practical problem.

During all this time of spiritual progress I had never prayed. I was afraid of the power of suggestion that is in prayer — the very power for which Pascal recommends it. Pascal's method seems to me one of the worst for attaining faith.

Contact with you was not able to persuade me to pray. On the contrary I thought the danger was all the greater, since I also had to beware of the power of suggestion in my friendship with you. At the same time I found it very difficult not to pray and not to tell you so. Moreover I knew I could not tell you without completely misleading you about myself. At that time I should not have been able to make you understand.

Until last September I had never once prayed in all my life, at least not in the literal sense of the word. I had never said any words to God, either out loud or mentally. I had never pronounced a liturgical prayer. I had occasionally recited the *Salve Regina,* but only as a beautiful poem.

Last summer, doing Greek with T——, I went through the Our Father word for word in Greek. We promised each other to learn it by heart. I do not think he ever did so, but some weeks later, as I was turning over the pages of the Gospel, I said to myself that since I had promised to do this thing and it was good, I ought to do it. I did it. The infinite sweetness of this Greek text so took hold of me that for several days I could not stop myself from saying it over all the time. A week afterward I began the vine harvest. I recited the Our Father in Greek every day before work, and I repeated it very often in the vineyard.

Since that time I have made a practice of saying it through once each morning with absolute attention. If during the recitation my attention wanders or goes to sleep, in the minutest degree, I begin again until I have once succeeded in going through it with absolutely pure attention. Sometimes it comes about that I say it again out of sheer pleasure, but I only do it if I really feel the impulse.

The effect of this practice is extraordinary and surprises me every time, for, although I experience it each day, it exceeds my expectation at each repetition.

At times the very first words tear my thoughts from my body and transport it to a place outside space where there is neither perspective nor point of view. The infinity of the ordinary expanses of perception is replaced by an infinity to the second or sometimes the third degree. At the same time, filling every part of this infinity of infinity, there is silence, a silence which is not an absence of sound but which is the object of a positive sensation, more positive than that of sound. Noises, if there are any, only reach me after crossing this silence.

Sometimes, also, during this recitation or at other moments, Christ is present with me in person, but his presence is infinitely more real, more moving, more clear than on that first occasion when he took possession of me.

I should never have been able to take it upon myself to tell you all this had it not been for the fact that I am going away. And as I am going more or less with the idea of probable death, I do not believe that I have the right to keep it to myself. For after all, the whole of this matter is not a question concerning me myself. It concerns God. I am really nothing in it all. If one could imagine any possibility of error in God, I should think that it had all happened to me by mistake. But perhaps God likes to use castaway objects, waste, rejects. After all, should the bread of the host be moldy, it would become the Body of Christ just the same after the priest had consecrated it. Only it cannot refuse, while we can disobey. It sometimes seems to me that when I am treated in so merciful a way, every sin on my part must be a mortal sin. And I am constantly committing them.

I have told you that you are like a father and brother at the same time to me. But these words only express an analogy. Perhaps at bottom they only correspond to a feeling of affection, of gratitude and admiration. For as to the spiritual direction of my soul, I think that God himself has taken it in hand from the start and still looks after it.

That does not prevent me from owing you the greatest debt of gratitude that I could ever have incurred toward any human being. This is exactly what it consists of.

First you once said to me at the beginning of our relationship some words that went to the bottom of my soul. You said: "Be very careful, because if you should pass over something important through your own fault it would be a pity."

That made me see intellectual honesty in a new light. Till then I had only thought of it as opposed to faith; your words made me think that perhaps, without my knowing it, there were in me obstacles to the faith, impure obstacles, such as prejudices, habits. I felt that after having said to myself for so many years simply: "Perhaps all that is not true," I ought, without ceasing to say it — I still take care to say it very often now — to join it to the opposite formula, namely: "Perhaps all that is true," and to make them alternate.

At the same time, in making the problem of baptism a practical problem for me, you have forced me to face the whole question of the faith, dogma, and the sacraments, obliging me to consider them closely and at length with the fullest possible attention, making me see them as things toward which I have obligations that I have to discern and perform. I should never have done this otherwise and it is indispensable for me to do it.

But the greatest blessing you have brought me is of another order. In gaining my friendship by your charity (which I have never met anything to equal), you have provided me with a source of the most compelling and pure inspiration that is to be found among human things. For nothing among human things has such power to keep our gaze fixed ever more intensely upon God, than friendship for the friends of God.

Nothing better enables me to measure the breadth of your charity than the fact that you bore with me for so long and with such gentleness. I may seem to be joking, but that is not the case. It is true that you have not the same motives as I have myself (those about which I wrote to you the other day), for feeling hatred and repulsion toward me. But all the same I feel that your patience with me can only spring from a supernatural generosity.

I have not been able to avoid causing you the greatest disappointment it was in my power to cause you. But up to now, although I have often asked myself the question during prayer, during Mass, or in the light of the radiancy that remains in the soul after Mass, I have never once had, even for a moment, the feeling that God wants me to be in the Church. I have never even once had a feeling of uncertainty. I think that at the present time we can finally conclude that he does not want me in the Church. Do not have any regrets about it.

He does not want it so far at least. But unless I am mistaken I should say that it is his will that I should stay outside for the future too, except perhaps at the moment of death. Yet I am always ready to obey any order, whatever it may be. I should joyfully obey the order to go to the very center of hell and to remain there eternally. I do not mean, of course, that I have a preference for orders of this nature. I am not perverse like that.

Christianity should contain all vocations without exception since it is catholic. In consequence the Church should also. But in my eyes Christianity is catholic by right but not in fact. So many things are outside it, so many things that I love and do not want to give up, so many things that God loves, otherwise they would not be in existence. All the immense stretches of past centuries, except the last twenty are among them; all the countries inhabited by colored races; all secular life in the white peoples' countries; in the history of these countries, all the traditions banned as heretical, those of the Manicheans and Albigenses for instance; all those things resulting from the Renaissance, too often degraded but not quite without value.

Christianity being catholic by right but not in fact, I regard it as legitimate on my part to be a member of the Church by right but not in fact, not only for a time, but for my whole life if need be.

But it is not merely legitimate. So long as God does not give me the certainty that he is ordering me to do anything else, I think it is my duty.

I think, and so do you, that our obligation for the next two or three years, an obligation so strict that we can scarcely fail in it without treason, is to show the public the possibility of a truly incarnated Christianity. In all the history now known there has never been a period in which souls have been in such peril as they are today in every part of the globe. The bronze serpent must be lifted up again so that whoever raises his eyes to it may be saved.

But everything is so closely bound up together that Christianity cannot be really incarnated unless it is catholic in the sense that I have just defined. How could it circulate through the flesh of all the nations of Europe if it did not contain absolutely everything in itself? Except of course falsehood. But in everything that exists there is most of the time more truth than falsehood.

Having so intense and so painful a sense of this urgency, I should betray the truth, that is to say the aspect of truth that I see, if I left the point, where I have been since my birth, at the intersection of Christianity and everything that is not Christianity.

I have always remained at this exact point, on the threshold of the Church, without moving, quite still, ἐν ὑπομένη (it is so much more beautiful a word than *patientia!*); only now my heart has been transported, forever, I hope, into the Blessed Sacrament exposed on the altar.

You see that I am very far from the thoughts that H——, with the best of intentions, attributed to me. I am far also from being worried in any way.

If I am sad, it comes primarily from the permanent sadness that destiny has imprinted forever upon my emotions, where the greatest and purest joys can only be superimposed and that at the price of a great effort of attention. It comes also from my miserable and continual sins; and from all the calamities of our time and of all those of all the past centuries.

I think that you should understand why I have always resisted you, if in spite of being a priest you can admit that a genuine vocation might prevent anyone from entering the Church.

Otherwise a barrier of incomprehension will remain between us, whether the error is on my part or on yours. This would grieve me from the point of view of my friendship for you, because in that case the result of all these efforts and desires, called forth by your charity toward me, would be a disappointment for you. Moreover, although it is not my fault, I should not be able to help feeling guilty of ingratitude. For, I repeat, my debt to you is beyond all measure.

I should like to draw your attention to one point. It is that there is an absolutely insurmountable obstacle to the Incarnation of Christianity. It is the use of the two little words *anathema sit*. It is not their existence, but the way they have been employed up till now. It is that also which prevents me from crossing the threshold of the Church. I remain beside all those things that cannot enter the Church, the universal repository, on account of those two little words. I remain beside them all the more because my own intelligence is numbered among them.

The Incarnation of Christianity implies a harmonious solution of the problem of the relations between the individual and the collective. Harmony in the Pythagorean sense; the just balance of contraries. This solution is precisely what men are thirsting for today.

The position of the intelligence is the key to this harmony, because the intelligence is a specifically and rigorously individual thing. This harmony exists wherever the intelligence, remaining in its place, can be exercised without hindrance and can reach the complete fulfillment of its function. That is what Saint Thomas says admirably of all the parts of the soul of Christ, with reference to his sensitiveness to pain during the crucifixion.

The special function of the intelligence requires total liberty, implying the right to deny everything, and allowing of no domination. Wherever it usurps control there is an excess of individualism. Wherever it is hampered or uneasy there is an oppressive collectivism, or several of them.

The Church and the State should punish it, each one in its own way, when it advocates actions of which they disapprove. When it remains in the region of purely theoretical speculation they still have the duty, should occasion arise, to put the public on their guard, by every effective means, against the danger of the practical influence certain speculations might have upon the conduct of life. But whatever these theoretical speculations may be, the Church and the State have no right either to try to stifle them or to inflict any penalty material or moral upon their authors. Notably, they should not be deprived of the sacraments if they desire them. For, whatever they may have said, even if they have publicly denied the existence of God, they may not have committed any sin. In such a case the Church should declare that they are in error, but it should not demand of them anything whatever in the way of a disavowal of what they have said, nor should it deprive them of the Bread of Life.

A collective body is the guardian of dogma; and dogma is an object of contemplation for love, faith, and intelligence, three strictly individual faculties. Hence, almost since the beginning, the individual has been ill at ease in Christianity, and this uneasiness has been notably one of the intelligence. This cannot be denied.

Christ himself who is Truth itself, when he was speaking before an assembly such as a council, did not address it in the same language as he used in an intimate conversation with his well-beloved friend, and no doubt before the Pharisees he might easily have been accused of contradiction and error. For by one of those laws of nature, which God himself respects, since he has willed them from all eternity, there are two languages that are quite distinct although made up of the same words; there is the collective language and there is the individual one. The Comforter whom Christ sends us, the Spirit of truth, speaks one or other of these languages, whichever circumstances demand, and by a necessity of their nature there is not agreement between them.

When genuine friends of God — such as was Eckhart to my way of thinking — repeat words they have heard in secret amidst the silence of the union of love, and these words are in disagreement with the teaching of the Church, it is simply that the language of the market place is not that of the nuptial chamber.

Everybody knows that really intimate conversation is only possible between two or three. As soon as there are six or seven, collective language begins to dominate. That is why it is a complete misinterpretation to apply to the Church the words "Wheresoever two or three are gathered together in my name, there am I in the midst of them." Christ did not say two hundred, or fifty, or ten. He said two or three. He said precisely that he always forms the third in the intimacy of the tête-à-tête.

Christ made promises to the Church, but none of these promises has the force of the expression "Thy Father who seeth in secret." The word of God is the secret word. He who has not heard this word, even if he adheres to all the dogmas taught by the Church, has no contact with truth.

The function of the Church as the collective keeper of dogma is indispensable. She has the right and the duty to punish those who make a clear attack upon her within the specific range of this function, by depriving them of the sacraments.

Thus, although I know practically nothing of this business, I incline to think provisionally that she was right to punish Luther.

But she is guilty of an abuse of power when she claims to force love and intelligence to model their language upon her own. This abuse of power is not of God. It comes from the natural tendency of every form of collectivism, without exception, to abuse power.

The image of the Mystical Body of Christ is very attractive. But I consider the importance given to this image today as one of the most serious signs of our degeneration. For our true dignity is not to be parts of a body, even though it be a mystical one, even though it be that of Christ. It consists in this, that in the state of perfection, which is the vocation of each one of us, we no longer live in ourselves, but Christ lives in us; so that through our perfection Christ in his integrity and in his indivisible unity, becomes in a sense each one of us, as he is completely in each host. The hosts are not a *part* of his body.

This present-day importance of the image of the Mystical Body shows how wretchedly susceptible Christians are to outside influences. Undoubtedly there is real intoxication in being a member of the Mystical Body of Christ. But today a great many other mystical bodies, which have not Christ for their head, produce an intoxication in their members that to my way of thinking is of the same order.

As long as it is through obedience, I find sweetness in my deprivation of the joy of membership in the Mystical Body of Christ. For if God is willing to help me, I may thus bear witness that without this joy one can nevertheless be faithful to Christ unto death. Social enthusiasms have such power today, they raise people so effectively to the supreme degree of heroism in suffering and death, that I think it is as well that a few sheep should remain outside the fold in order to bear witness that the love of Christ is essentially something different.

The Church today defends the cause of the indefeasible rights of the individual against collective oppression, of liberty of thought against tyranny. But these are causes readily embraced by those who find themselves momentarily to be the least strong. It is their only way of perhaps one day becoming the strongest. That is well known.

You may perhaps be offended by this idea. You are not the Church. During the periods of the most atrocious abuse of power committed by the Church, there must have been some priests like you among the others. Your good faith is not a guarantee, even were it shared by all your Order. You cannot foresee what turn things may take.

In order that the present attitude of the Church should be effective and that she should really penetrate like a wedge into social existence, she would have to say openly that she had changed or wished to change. Otherwise who could take her seriously when they remembered the Inquisition? My friendship for you, which I extend through you to all your Order, makes it very painful for me to bring this up. But it existed. After the fall of the Roman Empire, which had been totalitarian, it was the Church that was the first to establish a rough sort of totalitarianism in Europe in the thirteenth century, after the war with the Albigenses. This tree bore much fruit.

And the motive power of this totalitarianism was the use of those two little words: *anathema sit.*

It was moreover by a judicious transposition of this use that all the parties which in our own day have founded totalitarian regimes were shaped. This is a point of history I have specially studied.

I must give you the impression of a Luciferian pride in speaking thus of a great many matters that are too high for me and about which I have no right to understand anything. It is not my fault. Ideas come and settle in my mind by mistake, then, realizing their mistake, they absolutely insist on coming out. I do not know where they come from, or what they are worth, but, whatever the risk, I do not think I have the right to prevent this operation.

Good-by, I wish you all possible good things except the cross; for I do not love my neighbor as myself, you particularly, as you have noticed. But Christ granted to his well-beloved disciple, and probably to all that disciple's spiritual lineage, to come to him not through degradation, defilement, and distress, but in uninterrupted joy, purity, and sweetness. That is why I can allow myself to wish that even if one day you have the honor of dying a violent death for Our Lord, it may be with joy and without any anguish; also that only three of the beatitudes (*mites, mundo corde, pacifici*) will apply to you. All the others involve more or less of suffering.

This wish is not due only to the frailty of human friendship. For, with any human being taken individually, I always find reasons for concluding that sorrow and misfortune do not suit him, either because he seems too mediocre for anything so great or, on the contrary, too precious to be destroyed. One cannot fail more seriously in the second of the two essential commandments. And as to the first, I fail to observe that, in a still more horrible manner, for every time I think of the crucifixion of Christ I commit the sin of envy.

Believe more than ever and forever in my filial and tenderly grateful friendship.

Simone Weil

The Olive Garden
[1907]

RAINER MARIA RILKE

He went up under the gray leaves
All gray and lost in the olive lands
And laid his forehead, gray with dust,
Deep in the dustiness of his hot hands.

After everything this. And this was the end.
— Now I must go, as I am going blind,
And why is it Thy will that I must say
Thou art, when I myself no more can find thee.

I find Thee no more. Not in me, no.
Not in others. Not in this stone.
I find Thee no more. I am alone.

I am alone with all men's sorrow —
All that, through Thee, I thought to lighten,
Thou who art not. O nameless shame . . .

Men said, later: an angel came.

Why an angel? Alas, there came the night
And leafed through the trees, indifferently.
The disciples moved a little in their dreams.
Why an angel? Alas, there came the night.

The night that came was no uncommon night;
So hundreds of nights go by.
There dogs sleep; there stones lie.
Alas a sorrowful, alas any night
That waits till once more it is morning.

For men beseech: the angels do not come,
Never do nights grow great around them.
Who lose themselves, all things let go;
They are renounced by their own fathers
And shut from their own mothers' hearts.

Translated by Randall Jarrell

NOTES

T. S. Eliot

1 Without prejudice to a younger generation.

Ernest Hemingway

1 Mr. Shipman having read this informs me that Uncas after having broken down is now used as a hack by Mr. Victor Emanuel. This news does not move me one way or another.

Cyril Connolly

1 The Jewish tradition was that he was the son of a Roman Centurion, Pantheras, the Panther. Hence his aloofness to his "father" and "brethren," his ambivalent attitude to his mother and to adultery. (His definition of adultery is very sharp, and he sets "Thou shalt not commit adultery" as the only commandment beside "Thou shalt love thy neighbour as thyself." The question about the woman taken in adultery may have been put to him as a trap by those who believed this story.) I have heard a friend say that the German scholar Von Domaszewski claimed to have found on our Roman Wall the gravestone of Pantheras which showed that his legion had been in Judaea about 4 B.C. The Christians maintained that "Pantherou," son of the Panther, was a corruption of "Parthenou," of the Virgin. There is a strange poem by Hardy on this theme.

2 Taoism (pronounced Dowism) is a Monist reconciliation of the human being to the inhuman, inactive harmony of the universe. In return for such an adaption the Taoist resolves his conflict, and gains a sensation of power and tranquillity which he is loth to disturb. His quietism is akin to that of Zeno, Epicurus, Molinos and St. John of the Cross, but dangerously exposed to the corruption of *laisser-aller*.

3 "For aught we know to the contrary, 103 or 104 degrees Fahrenheit might be a much more favourable temperature for truths to germinate and sprout in, than the more ordinary blood-heat of 97 or 98 degrees. — WILLIAM JAMES.

4 Christmas Eve comes, Christmas Eve goes, and we too shall pass and nevermore return. OLD SPANISH CAROL.

5 The Middle Way. "Aristippus parlant à des jeunes gens qui rougissaient de le voir entrer chez une courtisane: 'Le vice est de n'en pas sortir, non pas d'y entrer.' " — MONTAIGNE (*Essais*, III, v).

6 Freudians consider anxiety to arise from the repression of anger or love. Kretschmer thinks there is an obscure somatic relation between anxiety and sex. Theologians associate it with the Fall, Behaviorists with undigested food in the stomach, Kierkegaard with the vertigo that precedes sin. Buddha and many philosophers regarded it as concurrent with Desire. Thus Bacon quotes Epicurus: "Use not that you may not wish, wish not that you may not fear."

7 "We are not yet ripe for growing up in the streets . . . has any good ever

come out of the foul-clustering town-proletariat, beloved of humanitarians? Nothing — never; they are only waiting for a leader, some 'inspired idiot' to rend to pieces our poor civilization." — NORMAN DOUGLAS: *Siren Land,* 1911.

8 "Spectres avaunt!" Ancient Greek spell.

9 But why was I extravagant, why couldn't I write to them? — A deeper level of anxiety becomes apparent.

Marcel Proust

1 Allusion to the author's first book, *Les Plaisirs et les Jours.*

Ezra Pound

1 One should perhaps apologize, or express a doubt as to the origin of Gongorism, or redefine it or start blaming it on some other Spaniard.

2 To be measured against the Sophoklean economy.

Jean Cocteau

1 The primary importance which people like ourselves attach to the lyrical element (although it might be supposed that we should be the first to despise it) forces us to see in it a touch of the divine. It has the power to transform the most insignificant object into an idol, and to make it seem to us to be living in a state of surprising isolation; the painter, G. de Chirico, can do this with a dry biscuit.

W. B. Yeats

1 I could not distinguish at the time between the permanent Daemon and the impermanent, who may be "an illustrious dead man," though I knew the distinction was there. I shall deal with the matter in *A Vision.*   February 1924.

2 Translated by Arthur Symons from *San Juan de la Cruz.*

Jean Genet

1 The most moving are those who withdraw into a grotesque, preposterous sign: a hair-do, a certain kind of mustache, rings, shoes . . . For a moment their entire life is concentrated in that detail, which is aglow: suddenly it goes out, because all the glory that was focused there has just withdrawn into that secret region, bringing solitude at last.

Simone Weil

1 By George Herbert.

VERMONT
MONTPELIER